A STORM OF WITCHCRAFT

Pivotal Moments in American History

SERIES EDITORS
David Hackett Fischer
James M. McPherson
David Greenberg

A Storm of Witchcraft

The Salem Trials and the American Experience

Emerson W. Baker

OXFORD
UNIVERSITY PRESS

OXFORD

UNIVERSITY PRESS

Oxford University Press is a department of the
University of Oxford. It furthers the University's objective
of excellence in research, scholarship, and education
by publishing worldwide.

Oxford   New York
Auckland   Cape Town   Dar es Salaam   Hong Kong   Karachi
Kuala Lumpur   Madrid   Melbourne   Mexico City   Nairobi
New Delhi   Shanghai   Taipei   Toronto

With offices in
Argentina   Austria   Brazil   Chile   Czech Republic   France   Greece
Guatemala   Hungary   Italy   Japan   Poland   Portugal   Singapore
South Korea   Switzerland   Thailand   Turkey   Ukraine   Vietnam

Oxford is a registered trade mark of Oxford University Press
in the UK and certain other countries.

Published in the United States of America by
Oxford University Press
198 Madison Avenue, New York, NY 10016

Library of Congress Cataloging-in-Publication Data
Baker, Emerson W., author.
A storm of witchcraft : the Salem trials and
the American experience / Emerson W. Baker.
p. cm.   (Pivotal moments in American history)
Includes bibliographical references and index.
ISBN 978-0-19-989034-7 (hardcover); 978-0-19-062780-5 (paperback)
1. Trials (Witchcraft)—Massachusetts—Salem.
2. Witchcraft—Massachusetts—Salem—History.   I. Title.
KFM2478.8.W5B35   2014
345.744'50288—dc23
2014009692

Printed in Canada

Dedicated to
the victims of the Salem witch trials
and
Peggy, Megan, and Sarah

Contents

List of Figures

List of Illustrations

Editor's Note

Few events in American history have been the subject of so much writing through so many generations, and in such a multitude of ways, as has the Salem witchcraft crisis of 1692–93. It has inspired some of the most enduring works of American literature, drama, and film, and also much of the best scholarship in American history. Interest continues to grow, and at an exponential rate. The pace of publication has doubled in the past three decades, with new fields of inquiry, and old fields renewed. Women's studies have generated much productive research. Not so productive, but highly expansive, has been the growth of popular interest in the occult. When a colleague offered a new research course on Salem witchcraft, many students registered. After the first class, a few withdrew. Some explained that they had thought it was a course *in* witchcraft.

In a crowded field, Emerson Baker's new book builds on the strength of much serious research, and it makes a major contribution. The author has an intimate knowledge of the place and time and culture in which the Salem witchcraft crisis occurred. He has published many books and essays on related subjects and has a firm command of primary sources, which survive in extraordinary abundance. On witchcraft in Salem alone, documents filled Charles Upham's two volumes in 1864, Archie Frost's WPA report in 1938, Boyer and Nissenbaum's three large tomes in 1977, and the larger project of Bernard Rosenthal and eleven associate editors in 2009. Baker knows this evidence well. He also has an unrivalled mastery of unpublished manuscripts in even greater quantity, and makes much use of material artifacts and historical archaeology.

A special strength of this book is Baker's way of working with secondary writings. Important studies of the events in Salem and of witchcraft more generally have appeared in medicine, psychology, ecology, demography, economics, law, literature, philosophy, and in many fields of social science. These materials are not merely cited here. They are to put to work, and very creatively.

This subject has always been bitterly contested, and the level of engagement today is stronger than ever. Baker has his own impassioned views, but he discusses the literature with a rare combination of balance, empathy, and maturity. He also has a willingness and even an eagerness to learn from others. Baker thinks of the "storm of witchcraft" in Salem as a perfect storm. That approach becomes a frame for integrating other scholarship in a constructive way. Every major work on the subject is discussed here, always in a large-minded, generous, and yet critical spirit.

Another strength of this book appears in its architecture, which is highly original, and very creative in another way. It may become a model for writings on other subjects. The first substantive chapter is a short narrative that spans the entire witchcraft crisis. It is a lively and fast-moving story of stories, from the first "strange events" in January 1692, through the executions of September 1692, to the last legal proceedings on May 9, 1693, when a grand jury refused to indict Tituba, the Indian slave whose confession had triggered it all. This chapter draws the reader into the book and gives a clear and coherent overview. It opens the way for five explanatory chapters, which constitute about 60 percent of the book. Each has its own narrative line and addresses an analytic question.

Chapter two is about the town of Salem and the main lines of New England's history in relation to the witchcraft crisis. It incorporates two generations of scholarship on economics, politics, religion, and war, with particular attention to its impact on Salem.

The third chapter looks more closely at Salem Village, a small outlying hamlet, now the town of Danvers. Salem Village was the throbbing heart of the witchcraft crisis. Here Baker builds on seminal studies of social and cultural tensions by Boyer and Nissenbaum, written forty years ago, but also advances far beyond that work.

The fourth, fifth, and sixth chapters examine three sets of participants: the accusers, the accused, and the judges. We get to know these people as individuals and groups, in very compelling ways. Their personal accounts awaken primal emotions in the reader and carry us to new levels of understanding.

The last three chapters are about the aftermath of the witchcraft crisis, and they invite us to reflect on the larger meaning of the event. The appendices also confront us with the appalling magnitude of this judicial tyranny: twenty people executed, at least 156 people formally accused, and 113 imprisoned in horrific prisons that killed or gravely injured many more. But at the same time, hundreds of New Englanders came to the defense of these victims. With great courage, at least two hundred people wrote individual letters or testified in support, at the height of the frenzy and at the risk of arrest and even execution themselves.

Arguably the most important and least studied fact about the Salem witchcraft persecution of 1692 is that it was brought to an end, and deliberately so. That great fact made this grievous event a pivotal moment of high importance, and not only in American history. Most societies in the early modern world judicially persecuted witches in large numbers. The first to stop was New England. No witches were executed there after 1692, because the people of this region awakened to the evil they had done. They also did something more. New Englanders of many generations have dedicated themselves to the proposition that it must never happen again. This is what Baker calls the "inextinguishable flame" of the witchcraft crisis. It is also what makes this volume a book of profound importance for years to come.

David Hackett Fischer

A STORM OF WITCHCRAFT

An Old Valuables Cabinet

If the prayers of good people may obtain this favor of God, that the mysterious assaults from hell now made upon so many of our friends may be thoroughly detected and defeated, we suppose the curious will be entertained with as rare an history as perhaps an age has had.

—Benjamin Harris, April 1692[1]

TUCKED AWAY IN A CORNER of the Peabody Essex Museum in the City of Salem sits one of the great artifacts of early American history: a small oak valuables cabinet. Its elaborate carvings, turnings and geometric shapes speak to its beauty and craftsmanship. The center panel features a sunburst that surrounds the inscription "I&BP 79." The initials refer to its owners, Joseph and Bathsheba Pope (the letter *J* was not yet utilized in the seventeenth century, so the *I* did double duty for it). The Popes were married in 1679, and the cabinet, presumably a wedding gift, was likely made by James Symonds, a master furniture maker. It was passed down in the family until it was acquired by the museum at auction in 2000. The Popes were Quakers who lived in Salem Village, members of a small but significant minority of religious dissenters who had been persecuted by the Bay Colony. In 1692 the Popes turned the tables. Like some of her neighbors, Bathsheba said she was afflicted by witches, specifically claiming that the specters of John Procter, Martha Cory, and Rebecca Nurse tormented her. Joseph Pope added his testimony against Procter. The court convicted and executed all three of the accused.

A rare early piece of locally made seventeenth-century furniture with an impeccable history of ownership and a strong tie to the Salem witch trials, the cabinet is a remarkable relic—a status reflected in the formidable $2.4 million that the museum had to pay to win it at auction in 2000.[2] Yet what makes the cabinet truly a treasure is rarely noted: the Popes' nephew was Benjamin Franklin. Specifically, Bathsheba's youngest sister, Abiah, was Franklin's mother. In one generation, one Massachusetts family would go from victims of witchcraft to producing one of the leaders of the American Enlightenment. While his aunt and uncle would join the frenzied call for witch executions, Ben Franklin would make the reasoned case for a new

Joseph and Bathsheba Pope valuables chest. Photograph courtesy of the Peabody-Essex Museum, image number 138011POPECABINET.TIF.

nation, dedicated to liberty and freedom. The Pope cabinet shows just how soon after Salem that the American colonies would turn their back on the Age of Witch Hunts and embrace the Age of Reason.

The story of the Popes and their cabinet also reveals the complexities behind witch trials in Salem and elsewhere in New England, as well as some of the inaccuracies in how these events are often portrayed. Traditional textbooks and popular tales make the trials sound like a Puritan affair, yet the Popes were Quakers. The afflicted in Salem were almost all female and are usually referred to as "girls," yet Bathsheba was forty when she made her accusations. Furthermore, men had made up the majority of accusers in New England witchcraft cases before 1692. Bathsheba and her cohorts suffered "spectral attack"—that is, they were assaulted by a spirit that was invisible to everyone except the afflicted. This, too, was rare before Salem. Typically a witch was accused of *maleficium*, or harmful witchcraft. *Maleficium* could cause injury to livestock and crops, destruction of property, or even illness or death, but a witch need not employ a specter to cause such evil. Though what happened in 1692 is often portrayed as a local affair, Bathsheba Folger Pope was born and raised on distant Nantucket Island. As the circle of accusation grew in Salem Village, the afflicted would even point the finger at people they had never seen in person. These are but a few of the contradictions behind what happened in 1692 during a witch hunt that in many ways was an aberration from earlier proceedings.[3]

The striking design motifs of the Pope cabinet provide some insights into life in 1692 as well. The decorations are an interplay of classical elements, geometry, and S-curves. Like the chest, early Salem was a rich mosaic of ideas and influences. Its settlers came from different regions and backgrounds and held a range of beliefs. Darkened with age, the cabinet now appears somber and drab—just as the Puritans are all too often depicted. Yet, constructed from different types of wood with contrasting colors and highlighted with black and red paint, in 1679 the cabinet as well as the people of Salem were far from dull. Rather they were complicated, vibrant, and bright.

Like the Pope cabinet, the story of the Salem witch trials is both a relic and a living piece of history. Little wonder that it has drawn many to it. In 1970 John Demos began an article on witchcraft in the *American Historical Review* with this statement: "It is faintly embarrassing for a historian to summon his colleagues to still another consideration of early New England witchcraft. Here, surely, is a topic that previous generations of writers have sufficiently worked."[4] Since then authors have published more than thirty books on the subject, including two outstanding ones from Demos himself. Scholars have explored the Salem story as well as many smaller episodes in early New England through a variety of perspectives. There is an equally impressive output of scholarship on witchcraft in England and Europe. In the words of Nathaniel Hawthorne, a native son of Salem who was preoccupied by the trials, it is the ultimate twice-told tale. New books comes out regularly, each with their explanations of what happened: it was a religious crisis, an outbreak of ergot poisoning (or encephalitis or Lyme disease), the result of a land squabble in Salem Village, an outbreak of frontier war hysteria, a misogynist statement of patriarchy. So it is not without considerable humility that I now offer this book. It would be impossible to do so without drawing up on this deep well of knowledge and inspiration by these historians, as much of my work builds upon and synthesizes their labors.

While each book puts forward its own theories, most historians agree that there was no single cause for the witchcraft that started in Salem and spread across the region. To borrow a phrase from another tragic chapter of Essex County history, Salem offered "a perfect storm," a unique convergence of conditions and events that produced what was by far the largest and most lethal witchcraft episode in American history. Seventeenth-century observers themselves often likened what happened to a storm. Cotton Mather described the Salem phenomenon as an "inextricable storm" as well as "inexplicable storms from the invisible world."[5] He was right on both counts, for it has seemed almost impossible either to disentangle all of its component parts or to fully explain what happened. What we can do is synthesize the many interpretations and explanations and put Salem's "storm" into its broader context as both a turning point and part of an ongoing narrative.

Were the Salem witch trials a pivotal moment in American history? The great scholar of American Puritanism Perry Miller called them a non-event. "It had no effect on the ecclesiastical or political situation, it does not figure in the institutional or ideological development." Few scholars have challenged him. Instead, most have focused more on the cause than on the long-term consequences. They stress the fact that Salem was a small part of a much larger pattern. Although England and her colonies saw fewer cases of witchcraft accusations than on the Continent, they were still common and long-standing. Between 1645 and 1647, at the height of the English

Civil Wars, more than 250 people were accused of witchcraft in East Anglia (the area to the north and east of London known for its commercial farming of wheat and other grains) and more than one hundred were executed—fifteen in one day. In Salem, a total of twenty-five people lost their lives. Nineteen were executed, one was pressed to death, and five died in prison.[6]

The great age of witch hunts in Europe and America spanned roughly the period from 1400 to 1775. From Russia to Bermuda, from Scotland to Brazil, witch hunts took place throughout the European world. During that time about a hundred thousand people were prosecuted for witchcraft and at least fifty thousand people were sentenced to death. In fact, while many Americans still feel a sense of shame about the Salem witch trials—because of their large size and particularly their late date—a European perspective eases some of the angst. By European standards Salem was not even a large witch hunt, nor was it the last. In terms of size, a series of witch hunts in the German Electorate of Cologne that started in 1626 and continued for a decade resulted in approximately two thousand people being executed.[7] And in terms of date, some persecutions continued in "enlightened" eighteenth-century Europe. In Hungary about eight hundred people were executed for witchcraft between 1710 and 1750. The Szeged trials of 1728–29 claimed twenty-one victims. Three of the accused drowned during the swimming test (people who floated were witches, while those who sank—and often drowned—were innocent). Three more of the accused died in prison, apparently during torture, and sixteen people were convicted and burned at the stake. The more scholars study witchcraft accusations, the more they realize that witchcraft accusations seem nearly universal and have occurred throughout recorded history. There were major witch hunts in fourteen nations on three continents in the second half of the twentieth century, resulting in the death of hundreds of people. Yet no place has acquired such infamy as the Witch City. Why is it that only Salem is synonymous with witchcraft, and not such places as Cologne or Szeged? Clearly some unique factors were at work to give the trials and the community such a lasting reputation.[8]

The fact that there is only one Witch City suggests that the Salem trials had significance far greater than Perry Miller recognized. Indeed, even he acknowledged that immediately after the trials, the word *witchcraft* itself "almost vanished from public discourse" and that "this silence speaks volumes."[9] There is no arguing that what happened in Salem and throughout

New England in 1692 and the following years has haunted us ever since. Most histories of Salem stop once the trials and executions end, however, and in the process they miss its lasting significance.

One reason that witchcraft disappeared from the public record was that the government of Massachusetts Bay insisted upon it. Engaging in one of the first cover-ups in American history, Governor Sir William Phips banned the publication of any account of the witch trials. Even before the trials ended, people realized that something had gone horribly wrong and that some innocent people had died. According to Puritan theology, someone who committed a sin had to confess it before God. The state failed to acknowledge publicly the sin of arresting, trying, and executing people who were innocent of any crime. Failure to do so jeopardized the Puritans' covenant with God and the very foundation of their belief.

However, Cotton Mather's *Wonders of the Invisible World*, which attempted to whitewash the whole affair, escaped censorship and gained the governor's endorsement. Mather's "spin" served to protect the fragile administration of Phips, a close political ally of the Mathers. Beset by internal division and locked in a desperate military struggle with the French and their Native allies, the new royal government could not afford a public acknowledgment that the judicial system had wrongly executed nineteen people and imprisoned more than a hundred more. Such an admission would have brought down the government and threatened the survival of the Puritan "City upon a Hill."

The suppression of the truth by Phips, Mather, and others helped to make the Salem trials a turning point in American history. Mather's book was an intellectual and moral failure, for in many ways it discredited this last great Puritan theologian and his cause. The witch trials would not end Puritanism as a dominant political and societal force, but they sealed its fate. Indeed, the witch trials contributed to the end of John Winthrop's dream of a polity that contained and embodied Puritan spiritual, legal, social, and educational ideals. For the trials and their long and disputed aftermath divided soul from soul, and brought out and magnified schism and disagreement on every level in the Bay Colony. The Congregational Church would not be disestablished as the state religion of Massachusetts until 1833. But after 1692 Puritan ministers would no longer sit at the right hand of the governor. Furthermore, the behavior of Phips and the Mathers created a lasting animosity between the governor and the Massachusetts

Bay legislature. The legislature would never again trust a royal governor, a fact that would eventually result in revolution. And despite their efforts, opposing views would surface.

The first complaint was made by Thomas Maule, a Salem Quaker who had *Truth Held Forth and Maintained* printed in New York to skirt the ban. The book was a stinging general criticism of the Massachusetts government, including a condemnation of the trials. Officials seized and burned Maule's books and imprisoned him for twelve months. Yet at his 1696 trial for seditious libel the jury acquitted Maule, a decision that is sometimes viewed as the first victory for freedom of the press in America. Few histories of Salem mention Maule, but his story is a key example of how the trials grew in importance in their aftermath, and in unexpected ways.

Efforts by accused witches and their families to restore their innocence are another significant but rarely explored aspect of the trials. There were public acts of contrition. Judge Samuel Sewall's 1697 apology and Massachusetts's 1711 Reversal of Attainder are the best known. Yet these were not sufficient. Dozens of petitions were submitted to the government asking for restoration of seized property, reimbursement for damages, and a restoration of "innocency" for victims of 1692. The last such petition was submitted in 1750, nearly six decades after the trials, and the last five witches were not officially exonerated until 2001. The recurrence of these petitions ensured that Salem's storm did not entirely blow over. Instead, as Gretchen Adams has shown in her book, *The Specter of Salem*, by the early nineteenth century Salem became a metaphor for persecution across America, one repeatedly invoked for a wide range of causes and arguments.

Rather than proposing new interpretations of the events of 1692, this book tries to make sense of the voluminous literature on the trials while also looking at the larger context, starting with the founding of Salem, the first town of Massachusetts Bay. It will explore the ongoing relationship between accusations of witchcraft and American history from 1692 until today, offering a factual summary of the events of the witch hunt from the first symptoms in January 1692 until the last of the accused were pardoned and released from prison a year and a half later. Having laid out the facts historians agree upon, the rest of the book will search for explanations, starting with an overview of Massachusetts in the seventeenth century. In many ways, the Bay Colony was a wonder—a great success story of the establishment and growth of a prosperous colony. Yet by the 1690s growing tensions were developing across Massachusetts. A range of factors, including a new charter and government, a lethal frontier war, and a decline in religious fervor, would serve as kindling for a bonfire in 1692. If Massachusetts was the tinder box, Salem was the match, and the religious and political conflict that consumed it made it ripe for a witch hunt.

I will then focus on the accused witches and the people they allegedly bewitched, exploring the many theories put forth to explain the spread of witchcraft, as well as the questions people have asked for generations. Did the afflicted fake their ailments to single out certain people for punishment as witches? Or were they innocent victims of illness or hysteria? Did people confess to being witches to try to save their lives? Or did they genuinely believe they were witches practicing black magic? Important as the afflicted and accused are, they are only part of the story.

Most studies of the trials have viewed them from the perspective of social or cultural history, yet at their heart they were legal proceedings that took part in a fragile and complicated political and imperial framework. And while in Massachusetts witchcraft was tried by secular courts, it was ultimately a religious crime. The 1692 witch hunt was closely related to religious tensions in the colony, a fact demonstrated by the fifty people named as witches—fully 30 percent of those formally accused or informally cried out upon in 1692—who were either ministers, members of minister's immediate families or their extended kin networks. I will examine the trials from the perspective of the judges who sanctioned the proceedings. They were key players in the drama, yet their roles have too often been overlooked, for it takes judges to convict people and sentence them to death. Who were these men? What was their background and beliefs that led them to send so many to their deaths? Why did Governor Phips choose them? The answers to these questions help not only explain why the Salem tragedy unfolded as it did, but also why it has become an enduring legacy. Though genealogy is sometimes snubbed by historians, it is impossible to understand the events of 1692 without considering these personal relationships. People live their lives in the context of their family, friends, and neighbors. Those connections help to explain the way some acted in 1692. The fact that six of the Salem judges were related to each other by marriages that allied their merchant families explains many of their actions.

While the actions of 1692 shook a colony and resulted in the deaths of twenty-five people, the witch hunt itself is not a signal event. Phips himself had lost many more lives and almost destroyed the economy of the Bay Colony just two years earlier while leading a failed invasion of Quebec. Nearly four hundred men died on the expedition, which cost the colony £50,000. It was a decisive event yet soon overshadowed by Salem.[10] In the last third of the book I explore how and why Salem achieved its lasting place in American consciousness, and how the community has wrestled with this heritage.

Every fall a new cohort of elementary school children learn the story of the founding of New England. It starts with the *Mayflower* and the First Thanksgiving and involves triumph over adversity, the quest for religious freedom, and the benefits of cooperation between different cultures. Yet events toward the end of the seventeenth century serve as a cautionary tale. King Philip's War ended the dream of collaboration between English settlers and Native Americans, and the Salem witch trials revealed the dark side of Puritanism.

Ironically, one reason schoolchildren still learn anything about the Salem witch trials is because of the failed effort to censor the story in its immediate aftermath. As we have seen, it would not be suppressed, and the efforts to exonerate those executed changed people's views of their government and helped bring an end to the Puritan theocracy. Salem Village underwent a long process of healing after 1692. Many people felt they could best recover from the events by leaving the community to start anew. Most notable in this Salem diaspora was the settlement of the Salem End neighborhood in present-day Framingham, Massachusetts, by the accused witch Sarah Cloyce and her extended kin, including family of her sisters, the executed witches Rebecca Nurse and Mary Esty. As people moved outward from Salem, the memory of the witch trials and their injustices spread with them. Today Salem both revels in and reviles its witch trial heritage. A memorial to the victims of 1692 was constructed on the tercentenary in 1992. It is visited by hundreds of thousands, who flock to Salem every October to celebrate Halloween in a series of events called Haunted Happenings. Witchcraft tourism is an economic engine of this postindustrial city. Salem and the trials are still very much a part of the public discourse.

We are all surrounded by the legacy of the witch trials. Pretty much anyone with even a drop of New England ancestry does not have to look all that far to find a relative involved in the witch trials, given that more than 70 people were afflicted, resulting in at least 169 accused, which led to more than 200 people signing petitions of support for the accused. Beyond this there were nine judges, two prosecuting attorneys, dozens of jurors, and a nearly endless number of people who observed the trials. There are an estimated 20 million to 30 million living descendants from the twenty-six *Mayflower* families of 1620.[11] Similar calculations suggest that there must be well over 100 million living descendants of the accused in Salem, not to mention all the other people known to have been involved in the witch trials. Descendants range from President George W. Bush and the heir to the British throne, Prince William, to actress Sarah Jessica Parker and Tom Felton, the English actor who played Draco Malfoy in the Harry Potter movies. Most Americans must either be a descendant or know someone who has such a connection. Salem's trials truly are the trials of a nation, whether we realize it or not.

Key events in history are tied to a web of contingency in which the choices people make alter the course of human events. This is no less true for the Salem witch trials. Samuel Parris chose to interpret the behavior of his daughter and his niece as witchcraft. Judges Hathorne and Corwin chose to presume that Tituba, Sarah Good, and Sarah Osburn were guilty. Tituba chose not only to confess but also to confirm the judges' fears that there were witches in Salem. Governor Phips chose a panel of judges who he knew accepted spectral evidence, even though his top advisors, Increase and Cotton Mather, were skeptical of its use.

And so it goes. No single decision guaranteed the deaths of twenty-five innocent people, but if even one of the actors in this terrible drama had made a different choice, the witch trials would not have happened, or would have ended differently. Some events turn on chance as much as on contingency. To cite one famous example, two great armies met at Gettysburg— much to their mutual surprise. Yet chance seems to have played little to no role in the events in Massachusetts in 1692. Choices led to this tragedy and its long-lasting consequences. No one understood this better than its most famous son, Nathaniel Hawthorne, who wrestled with Salem's troubled past and its relationship to the present. The narrator in his *House of Seven Gables* asks, "Shall we never never get rid of this Past? It lies upon the present like a giant's dead body." Let us therefore measure its weight.

✌

Finally, I should address a few procedural and editorial points. In 1692 witchcraft spread across Essex County and as far away as Boston and southern Maine. More people from Andover were accused than from any other town, and it is even possible that these events triggered trials in Connecticut. It might be most appropriate to refer to the subject of this book as "Essex County witchcraft" or even "the New England witchcraft crisis of 1692." For simplicity I have elected to stay with "Salem witch trials," but I acknowledge that much of New England was involved. In 1692, people would have said the trials took place in Salem, but I will follow the convention, used by many historians, of referring to it in the colonial era as Salem Town, to differentiate the urban core on the waterfront from Salem Village. Like many modern scholars, I will at times use the term *outbreak* to describe the events at Salem and other large witch hunts. It is a useful descriptor for a phenomenon that spread rapidly, like an infectious disease. However in doing so, I do not mean to endorse a biological explanation for the events of 1692.

All year dates have been modernized. England and New England used the Julian calendar until 1752, when England adopted the new Gregorian calendar. Under the Julian system, the new year officially began on March 25, though people also recognized the significance of January 1. So, for example, all dates in 1692 between January 1 and March 24 would commonly be written with both years, 1691/2, but here they will simply be referred to as 1692. By 1692, the Julian calendar had fallen ten days behind the Gregorian calendar, but dates are not adjusted for this fact in this book. Quotes have been modernized for spelling and punctuation as well, except where noted.

CHAPTER ONE

Satan's Storm

But such was the darkness of that day, the tortures and lamentations of the
afflicted, and the power of former precedents, that we walked in the clouds,
and could not see our way. And we have most cause to be humbled for error
on that hand, which cannot be retrieved.

—Reverend John Hale[1]

IN THE MIDDLE OF JANUARY 1692, strange events began to take place in the
Salem Village parsonage. Reverend Samuel Parris and his wife, Elizabeth,
began to notice that their daughter, Betty, and niece, Abigail Williams, were
behaving oddly. Betty was nine and her cousin was about eleven—vulnerable ages in a time when illness all too often proved deadly. The Parrises
must have been truly alarmed as the girls' afflictions gradually worsened, but
they initially were concerned that these were signs of sickness. Samuel later
observed that it was "several weeks before such hellish operations, as witchcraft was suspected."[2] Soon the minister called in friends and colleagues, including Reverend John Hale from neighboring Beverly, to observe the girls.
Hale noted, "These children were bitten and pinched by invisible agents;
their arms, necks, and backs turned this way and that way, and returned

back again, so as it was impossible for them to do of themselves, and beyond the power of any epileptic fits, or natural disease to effect. Sometimes they were taken dumb, their mouths stopped, their throats choked, their limbs wracked and tormented so as might move a heart of stone, to sympathize with them, with bowels of compassion for them." They also suffered "by pins invisibly stuck into their flesh, [and] pricking with irons."[3]

By the middle of February, Reverend Parris strongly suspected that his daughter and niece were bewitched.[4] On Thursday, February 25, Samuel and Elizabeth left home for a neighboring village to attend Thursday lecture—a weekly religious sermon that rotated from one town to the next. In their absence, neighbor Mary Sibley instructed the Parrises' two slaves, Tituba and her husband, John Indian, to make a witch cake, to try to detect the identity of the girls' tormentors. They baked a loaf of rye bread mixed with some urine from the afflicted girls, then fed it to the family dog. This was one of many known countermagical folk remedies, such as horseshoes placed over doorways to ward off evil. When the dog ate the witch cake, it was supposed to reveal the witch's identity. Indeed, the afflicted girls soon cried out that it was Tituba who was tormenting them.[5]

Reverend Parris traced the discovery of witchcraft in Salem Village to this incident. He would later publicly chastise Mary Sibley in front of the congregation for the "diabolical means" she used to detect witchcraft. He warned, "By this means (it seems) the devil hath been raised amongst us, and his rage is vehement and terrible, and when he shall be silenced, the Lord only knows."[6] However well intentioned her actions had been, Sibley had carried out magic. Ministers in Europe and America had long struggled with this problem. Although "white magic," such as the baking of the bread, was meant to help, it still invoked Satan. As such, Sibley was as guilty of witchcraft as the now-accused Tituba. Contrary to popular opinion, there is absolutely no evidence that Tituba and the Parris girls had engaged in fortune-telling or any other form of white magic.[7]

On the same day the witch cake was baked, two other girls, living on opposite sides of the village, suffered their initial demonic afflictions. Ann Putnam Jr. was the twelve-year-old daughter of Thomas Putnam and his wife, Ann Carr Putnam Sr. (early Massachusetts families often named the firstborn daughter after her mother, so the conventions of Sr. and Jr. are used in this book to avoid confusion). The family lived along the road to Andover, more than a mile west of the parsonage. Seventeen-year-old

Elizabeth Hubbard worked as a maid for her aunt, Rachel Griggs, and Rachel's husband, Dr. William Griggs. They lived about two miles east of the parsonage, in a part of Salem that was located just outside the bounds of Salem Village. While they lived some distance apart, both families would have known what was happening. Putnam was among Reverend Parris's inner circle of supporters, and scholars believe that Griggs was the unnamed doctor who had been attending the girls and determined that they were "under an evil hand."[8]

The afflictions of the girls in the Parris household grew worse in the days following the baking of the witch cake. Abigail and Betty blamed Tituba for their torments and claimed that her specter chased them around the house. Reverend Parris invited several area ministers as well as some Salem gentlemen to see the girls. They agreed that the children were being attacked by Satan. Meanwhile, troubles continued for Ann Putnam Jr., and Elizabeth Hubbard. Ann said the specter of Sarah Good pinched her and tried to coerce her to sign the devil's book, an act that would establish a formal covenant with Satan. Good was a poor, disaffected woman, known for her sharp tongue and outbursts hurled even at those who offered to help her. Elizabeth believed she was being stalked by a wolf sent by Sarah Good. She was also tormented by Sarah Osburn, a bedridden woman who lived on the northern edge of Salem Village, who was accompanied by "a short and hairy thing with two legs and two wings." Osburn, a widow, not only was plagued by ill health but had scandalized the community when she purchased the contract of indentured servant Alexander Osburn and married him.[9]

With four girls now afflicted, four Salem Village men traveled several miles to the coast to busy Salem Town on Monday, February 29 to begin legal proceedings against Tituba, Good, and Osburn. Ann Putnam's father, Thomas, and his brother, Edward, were accompanied by Joseph Hutchinson and Thomas Preston. The men swore out legal complaints before local magistrates Jonathan Corwin and John Hathorne, accusing the women of "suspicion of witchcraft...and thereby much injury done." Corwin and Hathorne were wealthy Salem merchants and respected politicians, though they lacked formal legal training. This had not been a concern in their work with the petty crimes and civil offenses of the local court, but both must have been taken aback by the charges of diabolical high crimes they heard that day. They issued warrants, ordering the constables to arrest the women and to have them at Ingersoll's Ordinary (or tavern) by ten the

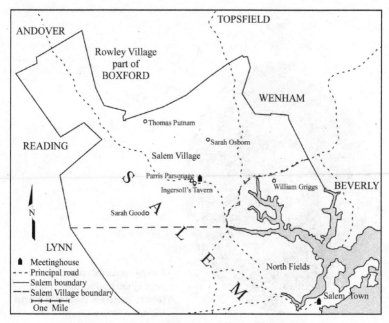

Salem and Salem Village in 1692. Drawing by the author.

next morning for questioning. The tavern was in the heart of Salem Village, a minute's walk from the parsonage and meetinghouse.[10]

The next morning so many people tried to crowd into Ingersoll's for the hearings that the proceedings had to be moved down the street to the much larger meetinghouse. All four afflicted girls were there to face their tormentors; the accused were questioned one at a time, starting with Sarah Good. Hathorne led the interrogations, more like a modern-day police detective grilling a subject for a confession than an impartial judge. From the nature of the unrelenting questions he asked, it is clear that he believed witchcraft was at work and that the three women were responsible: "What evil spirit have you familiarity with? Have you made no contact with the devil? Why do you hurt these children?" Good's denials were to no avail. When the four girls confirmed their identification of Sarah as their tormentor, she denied the charge, at which point the girls became "all dreadfully tortured and tormented for a short space of time." They claimed Good's spirit lunged out of her body at them. More denials from Sarah led to more cries and painful

Samuel Parris. Oil on cardboard miniature by unidentified artist, [1670–1680]. Courtesy of the Massachusetts Historical Society.

writhing from the girls. When pressed, Good eventually offered that Sarah Osburn was responsible for the girl's torments. Hathorne then questioned Sarah Good's husband, William Good. He had no reason to believe that she was a witch aside from her ill temperament, he said, though he concluded with the damning and punning statement, "I may say with tears that she is an enemy to all good." The judges were in no mood for humor. They determined to hold Good for trial. Although the evidence was less compelling, the court held Osburn, too, after the girls identified her as a tormentor.[11]

Tituba would prove to be the star witness, for her testimony fully confirmed fears that many witches were loose in Salem, and it unleashed a massive hunt to round up Satan's minions. A slave who was regularly described as an "Indian," Tituba most likely was born in the Caribbean or Florida and brought to New England by Samuel Parris when he migrated from Barbados in 1680. She initially denied the charges against her but under Hathorne's hounding eventually admitted she was a witch. She described how Satan had revealed himself to her. "I saw a thing like a man, and told me to serve him." She said Good and Osburn along with three strangers

The Ingersoll tavern today. Photograph by the author.

from Boston were responsible for hurting the girls. Good's familiar was a yellow bird that sucked between her fingers. The devil had threatened to kill the children and had also sent a hog, a dog, and two cats to Tituba to encourage her to attack the girls. Witches were traditionally believed to have supernatural familiar spirits—imps sent by Satan who aided them in their cruel acts. In return, the familiar, which usually took the form of an animal, sucked blood from the witch and thus gained nourishment. One of the most common forms of familiar was a cat—hence the traditional association of black cats with witches. Witches were also believed to be able to assume the shapes of animals. Thus, unusual behavior in an animal, especially a strange one, might suggest the presence of a witch.[12]

Tituba confessed that after continuous threats and pressure from the devil and his minions, she had finally relented and tormented all four girls, but then went on to apologize: "I am very sorry for it." When Tituba started her testimony, the afflicted girls had been most distressed, yet when she confessed they immediately quieted. Their sufferings recommenced when Tituba said it was the specter of Sarah Good that harmed the girls. The slave had been forced to ride "upon a stick or pole" with Osburn and Good behind her, to fly off to hurt Ann Putnam Jr. Soon Tituba herself suffered torments. She claimed that Osburn and Good had attacked her, blinded her, and prevented her from speaking freely. Salem Village's worst fears were recognized—a witch conspiracy threatened their community. Tituba would be questioned three more times over the next four days. On March 2 she provided detailed evidence of Satan's work. She had signed the devil's book with her own blood, and had also seen Good and Osburn's marks contained therein; in all, there had been marks or signatures for nine witches. She went so far as to describe how Satan and the witches' assembly had met in the Parris parsonage, remaining invisible to the minister.[13]

Tituba's testimony was noteworthy in many ways. It gave officials what they wanted: proof that a witch conspiracy was operating in their midst, along with confession of sin and sincere contrition for diabolical acts. Tituba was a compelling and genuine witness. She loved Betty and did not want to hurt her but had given way to Satan's threats, and now she threw herself on the mercy of the court. Her testimony was consistent through multiple examinations, and her details agreed perfectly with the sufferings described by the afflicted girls. Her statements were all the more believable because she described a textbook example of witchcraft: making a covenant with Satan, flying on a broomstick, attending witches' assemblies, and using witches' familiars. All had been described in detail by English authorities of the day and were in William Perkins's *A Discourse of the Damned Art of Witchcraft* (1608), a copy of which Samuel Parris was given on the first day of Tituba's testimony.[14]

Nonetheless, it is difficult to stereotype a witch, for as events in Salem would ultimately show, virtually anyone could be accused. Still, most people in the seventeenth century had a good idea of the main characteristics of the typical suspects, and the three who stood accused in Salem Village fit the bill. Witches tended to be poor and marginalized women. They often possessed a quarrelsome or troubled nature or had broken with the norms of society. To have a Native American slave, a distracted pauper, and a scandalous woman all charged with witchcraft meant they had rounded up the "usual suspects." As Salem's Reverend John Higginson later observed, initially the outbreak "was very small, and looked on at first as an ordinary case which had fallen out before at several times in other places, and would be quickly over."[15] Before 1692, more than fifty people had already been tried in New England for witchcraft, and at least fourteen had been executed. Usually no more than one or two witches were involved. Tituba said that nine witches were present in the community. The Salem witch hunt would now begin in earnest.[16]

With the alleged witches in jail, the condition of most of the afflicted girls temporarily improved—though Ann Putnam Jr. continued to be tormented by two specters. One was Sarah Good's four-year-old daughter, Dorothy, whose ghostly presence bit, pinched, and choked Ann in an attempt to get her to sign the devil's book. Ann soon identified another spectral tormentor, Martha Cory, a villager who had become a member of Parris's Church in 1690. Soon Martha's specter was also afflicting Mary Warren, a servant in the household of John Procter and his third wife, Elizabeth. The Procters rented the substantial Downing Farm, located just south of the Salem Village boundary, where they also ran a tavern. Ann was not done, however. Next she accused Rebecca Nurse, an elderly Salem Town church member of unblemished reputation. Rebecca and her husband, Francis, rented the Townsend Bishop Farm in Salem Village, which lay just to the west of Endicott Farm. Tituba had said there were nine witches. Thanks largely to Ann Putnam Jr., seven of them had been named by the middle of March.[17]

Soon their specters were haunting the other afflicted girls and also attacking new victims, including adult women and even one man: the Parrises' slave John Indian. Thomas and Ann Putnam Sr.'s teenage maid, Mercy Lewis, suffered fits so severe that several men were needed to restrain her. Mercy was in "very dreadful and solemn condition," suffering so much that people feared "she could not continue long in this world" unless the torments subsided. Soon Ann Putnam Sr. herself was also doing battle with the invisible world, and Bathsheba Pope, a middle-aged Quaker resident of Salem Village, had been temporarily struck blind by Martha Cory's specter. Sarah Bibber and another woman—probably Margaret Goodale—were tormented as well. On March 21 magistrates Hathorne and Corwin examined Cory and heard enough evidence to send her to jail to await trial. At a session two days later, they also bound over little Dorothy Good and elderly Rebecca Nurse.[18]

The Procters' twenty-year-old servant, Mary Warren, was also deeply involved in the proceedings. Early on she had shown signs of affliction, yet she recovered when John Procter, a vocal critic of the trials, "threatened to thresh her and then she had no more fits." He told Samuel Sibley that if left to the devices of the afflicted, "we should all be devils and witches quickly." He felt that a trip to the whipping post for the afflicted would end the accusations. Joseph Pope heard "Procter say that if Mr. Parris would let him have his Indian he the said Procter would soon drive the devil out of him."[19]

Elizabeth Procter and Sarah Cloyce (the sister of Rebecca Nurse) appeared before a special session of the governor and his council of assistants that met in the Salem Town meetinghouse on April 11. Under the Massachusetts Bay Charter of 1629 as well as the interim government now in place, the governor and the council of assistants acted as the colony's highest court. The elderly governor, Simon Bradstreet, stayed in Boston, but Deputy Governor Thomas Danforth and four assistants traveled to Salem, where they were joined by Assistants John Hathorne and Jonathan Corwin. The presence of these high-ranking officials indicated that events in Salem had taken on colony-wide significance. Assistant Samuel Sewall came north from Boston for the session, noting in his diary that it was "a very great assembly" and how "'twas awful to see how the afflicted persons were agitated." After listening to testimony, the court ordered Sarah Cloyce and Elizabeth Procter held over for trial, and arrested John Procter, based on accusations made against him in court. Danforth could have brought a halt to the proceedings, or at least slowed them down. Instead, his actions provided the colonial government's tacit approval of the process, causing the accusations to accelerate. Danforth and the assistants returned to their respective homes, surely helping to spread the news of witchcraft throughout the colony.[20]

As evidence of Satan's attack spread over the course of the next several days, specters of people who lived outside of Salem Village began to afflict its inhabitants. Until this point, while the afflictions and accusations had grown in number, the accused were all residents of Salem Village. There was precedent for such a large outbreak within one New England community: thirteen people had been accused of witchcraft in Hartford in 1662–63, and four had been executed. Indeed, up until this time, more witches had been executed in Connecticut than in Massachusetts. That was about to change.[21]

On April 19 the court examined four more suspects: Bridget Bishop, Giles Cory, Abigail Hobbs, and Mary Warren. The husband of Martha Cory, Giles was a member of the Salem Town Church. Having left the ranks of the afflicted, Mary Warren was soon accused of witchcraft herself. When brought before the judges, "she said that the afflicted persons did but dissemble" or feign their fits. In response to Mary's accusation, the afflicted immediately began to exhibit severe symptoms. Mary reacted with fits of her own, so she was led away to prison. The next day she confessed that she had signed the devil's book, but only because the Procters had tricked her into doing so. She suffered more fits, and accused Giles Cory and others of witchcraft.[22]

Fourteen-year-old Abigail Hobbs of Topsfield confessed as well, saying, "I have seen sights and been scared. I have been very wicked. I hope I shall be better, if God will help me." She testified that she had met the devil four years earlier in the woods "at the eastward at Casco Bay."[23] This would have been the spring of 1688, a few months before the struggle known as King William's War broke out. This conflict that would rage along the New England frontier until 1697 pitted the English settlers against the Wabanaki, the Native peoples of northern New England, and their French allies. The war brought the Hobbs family and a number of other refugees from Maine to Essex County. The afflicted girl Mercy Lewis was also a refugee, probably from the settlement of Falmouth. So the girls may have known each other in Maine and may even have been distant relatives. They were two of many war refugees who would become involved in the trials.[24]

Abigail Hobbs's confession was a turning point in the course of the witch hunt, for her description of meeting the devil in Casco Bay introduced the frontier war into the proceedings and set the stage for the arrest of Reverend George Burroughs, former minister of Salem Village as well as Falmouth, the principal settlement of Casco Bay (present-day Portland, Maine). Two days later, Ann Putnam Jr. saw his specter, as well as that of Abigail Hobbs. Ann testified that Burroughs's apparition tormented her, trying to force her to sign the devil's book. The specter boasted that he had killed his first two wives and also murdered the wife and child of another former Salem minister, Deodat Lawson. On May 4, Burroughs was arrested in Wells, Maine. The charges and his arrest caused a sensation, for here was a Puritan minister—a bastion of the faith—accused of being a witch. Five days later in Salem, Hathorne and Corwin examined Burroughs along with Sarah Churchwell, another refugee from Maine, and three women from Woburn. All five were held over for trial.[25]

The next day, the witchcraft crisis claimed its first victim. After nine weeks in prison, Sarah Osburn died in the Boston jail on May 10. The Boston prison stood on Prison Lane (present-day Court Street). John Dunton, who wrote down his observations of the Boston jail in 1686, said, "A prison is a grave of the living...'tis a house of meager looks, and ill smells: for lice, drink, and tobacco are the compound: or if you will 'tis the suburbs of Hell; and the persons much the same as there."[26] Job Tookey would describe his ten weeks in Salem jail in 1682 in a similar fashion. He was "almost poisoned with the stink of my own dung and the stink of the prison having never so much a minute's time to take the air since I came into this dolesome place."[27] It must have been far worse ten years later when it was overcrowded with accused witches, including Tookey. In that cold, dark, and damp place, the stench of unwashed bodies, chamber pots, rotting food, vomit, and dead vermin would have made conditions almost unimaginable. Inmates were infested with fleas as well as lice that often carried deadly "jail fever" or typhus. As if this was not bad enough, prisoners were manacled and chained, and had to reimburse the jailer for their room and board. Though she was only forty-nine at the time of her arrest, Osburn was bedridden. When questioned by Hathorne and Corwin, she had protested that she "was more likely bewitched than a witch." Ordering a woman in such frail health into such a prison for a prolonged period was a death sentence.[28]

Four days later, on May 14, a new Massachusetts governor, William Phips, arrived in Boston from England. The Maine native and Boston resident was ill prepared to deal with the emergency he faced. By this time, forty people had already been accused of witchcraft, and complaints would be sworn against eight more that day. Most of the accused were in jail, though two had been set free, two had fled, and Osburn had died. The new governor faced a witchcraft crisis of unprecedented proportions in the colony.[29]

The Salem witchcraft crisis could not have come at a worse time, for Massachusetts temporarily lacked the legal system to deal with it. Phips brought with him a new charter for Massachusetts Bay that invalidated all laws and courts in the colony and called for the legislature to pass a new set of laws and courts that were "not repugnant" to (that is, in agreement with) the laws of England. No trials had taken place in Massachusetts since the details of the charter had first reached the colony on February 8. The colony's elected legislature, the General Court, could establish a court, but it was not scheduled to meet until June 8. Phips could not wait until then. He needed to act immediately to rein in the crisis, which was already threatening the stability of his new government. Indeed, accusations had increased dramatically since his arrival.[30]

William Phips's response was to create a Court of Oyer and Terminer (literally meaning "to hear and determine" in the Old Northern French still used in English court terminology of the day, and to this day still heard in the United States in the phrase "oyez, oyez," traditionally used to begin court proceedings). There was plenty of precedent for such emergency courts in both England and New England. Interestingly, Phips made no mention of the witchcraft crisis when creating the court on May 27. Instead, he simply noted, "That there are many criminal offenders now in custody, some whereof have lain long & many inconveniences attending the thronging of the jails."[31] The jurisdiction was limited to just Suffolk, Essex, and Middlesex counties. Governor Phips may have deliberately left out the word *witchcraft* so that the court could deal with any pressing matters that arose aside from the witchcraft trials. However, the omission of any mention of witchcraft was probably part of an effort to keep word of the serious crisis from the English crown. Upon his arrival in the colony Phips had penned a letter to the Privy Council—the English advisors to the king who helped oversee all colonies—in which he also neglected to mention witchcraft. He would not do so until he wrote his next letter to them on October 12.

The Court of Oyer and Terminer was led by deputy governor William Stoughton, with the other judges being Bartholomew Gedney, John Richards, Nathaniel Saltonstall, Wait Winthrop, Samuel Sewall, John Hathorne, Jonathan Corwin, and Peter Sergeant. While none of the members of the court had legal training, they represented the elite of Massachusetts society. They were wealthy Puritan merchants and members of the Governor's Council, with years of experience in the General Court, as well as service as local magistrates. Most were also high-ranking militia officers, leaders of the citizen-soldier army that defended the colony in times of trouble. Indeed, in July 1692 Governor Phips would appoint Wait Winthrop to be commander in chief of the Massachusetts militia. Moreover, the judges had considerable knowledge of Salem and of the growing crisis. Corwin and Hathorne had conducted most of the preliminary court sessions; five others had participated in at least one session.[32]

Phips named Thomas Newton prosecuting attorney for the Court of Oyer and Terminer. An English lawyer practicing in Boston, Newton was no stranger to high-profile cases. The previous year he had been the prosecutor for the Special Court of Oyer and Terminer called in New York to deal with the Leisler Rebellion (in which Jacob Leisler led the seizure of the government of the colony of New York from Edmund Andros in the wake of the overthrow and imprisonment of Andros in Boston and the Glorious Revolution of 1688 in England). Those trials had culminated with the conviction for treason and execution of Leisler and his son-in-law Jacob Milborne. The crown attorney was responsible for organizing the trials, including writing the indictments, and determining the order in which people would be tried. Unlike today, the prosecutor did not question either the accused or the witnesses. That work was the responsibility of the judges. The accused had no counsel to defend them. Indeed, Massachusetts would not allow lawyers to practice for fees until 1705.[33]

The first official act of the Court of Oyer and Terminer was to order Essex County sheriff George Corwin to canvas the towns of the county for eighteen men for a grand jury to consider indictments and a pool of forty-eight "honest and lawful men" for trial juries. All freemen (voting citizens) were eligible to serve on a jury. Under the old 1629 charter, freemen had to be members of the Puritan church. However, this religious qualification was removed in the 1691 charter, allowing any adult male property owner to be a full citizen of the colony. The twenty-five-year-old who was newly appointed as sheriff had close ties to the judges, for Wait Winthrop and Jonathan Corwin were his uncles and Bartholomew Gedney was his father-in-law. Much as today, the grand jury brought together by the sheriff would read bills of indictment, examine evidence, and listen to oral testimony to determine whether the charges had enough weight to proceed to trial. If so, they would endorse the indictment with the phrase "billa vera," meaning that the charges were valid and a true bill of indictment had been issued. During the Salem witch hunt, trials would proceed very quickly after a true bill of indictment was signed—often the same day. The case would be heard before a trial jury of twelve people (called a trial jury or a petty jury) drawn from the pool of forty-eight potential jurors.[34]

How was the court to proceed given that, with the arrival of Phips and the new charter, the colony technically had no legal code in place? The laws of the old charter had been repealed, and the legislature had yet to meet to begin the long process of replacing them. No document laying out the rules of the court survives, though a close study of the court's subsequent actions suggests that it applied current English law. Indeed, its indictments often used language drawn specifically from England's Witchcraft Act of 1604, which called for the death penalty for anyone convicted of invoking evil spirits or a familiar of the devil. The judges also referred to several popular English legal treatises, including Richard Bernard's *Guide to Grand-Jury Men* (1627–30), Michael Dalton's *Country Justice* (1618), and Joseph Keble's *An Assistance to Justices of the Peace* (1683), which included a chapter on "Conjuration." These guides gave specific advice on how to examine the evidence in a witchcraft trial. Traditionally, there were only two ways to convict a witch: by the witch's confession or upon the testimony of two eye-witnesses to an act of black magic. Lacking such direct proof, Keble drew on a long English tradition of supporting evidence, particularly signs of a witch's familiars, devil's marks, and other signs of satanic presence. Keble also suggested that an accused witch's property should be searched for evidence of magic: potions, poppets, charms, spell books, or related writings were all useful supporting evidence.[35]

Such supplemental evidence was usually in short supply; hence judges in witch trials often had to resort to other means, particularly the "touch test" and spectral evidence. As regards the former, it was believed that if a bewitched person touched the witch who was afflicting her, her sufferings would immediately ease. This test would be used extensively in Salem. However, the court would rely even more heavily on spectral evidence. How much weight should be given to the claim that a person was harmed by the spirit or specter of a person when only the afflicted witnessed this manifestation of the invisible world was a hotly debated subject, though everyone in the seventeenth century believed the devil could create such harmful specters. Furthermore, he tricked witches into believing that his powers were theirs. And, of course, such powers were ultimately derived from God, for he had created Satan. The devil could make *mira*, illusions, while only God could perform *miracula*, miracles. Still, to doubt specters was to question God's existence. The controversy came not over their existence but over how to interpret them. Ministers warned that Satan was so powerful that he could create specters of even unwitting and innocent people. When these specters harmed others, these poor people would be unfairly accused of witchcraft. Satan was indeed the old trickster.[36]

Given this possibility, what were the judges of the Court of Oyer and Terminer to believe? Several days before the trials started, Judge John Richards wrote to ask his minister, Cotton Mather, for advice. Mather's reply indicates the difficulty of this problem. Among other things, Mather urged caution over the use of spectral evidence, and believed that Richards should not "lay more stress upon pure specter testimony than it will bear." Yet Mather hedged his bet, assuring Richards that God would vindicate an innocent person whom Satan tried to falsely represent.[37]

Even as the court began to organize, the afflicted girls (Abigail Williams, Mary Walcott, Mercy Lewis, and Ann Putnam) widened the circle of suspicion. On May 28 alone, complaints were made on their behalf against eleven more people. Now the accusations began to reach well beyond Salem Village. Martha Allen Carrier of Andover was accused, as was her sister, Mary Allen Toothaker, of Billerica. The girls also cried out against residents of Ipswich, Marblehead, Malden, Reading, Rumney Marsh (present-day Revere), Charlestown, and Boston. North, south, east, and west of Salem Village, the web of affliction spread. People of social rank and political importance now stood accused, including Captain John Flood and Captain John Alden—the latter the son of *Mayflower* passengers John Alden and Priscilla Mullins.[38]

Amid this growing turmoil, the Court of Oyer and Terminer started its first session on June 2, hearing the case of Bridget Bishop. Although she was not the first witch accused, crown attorney Newton put her case first, for it presented the strongest evidence for conviction. Bishop had been charged with witchcraft back in 1679 but acquitted for lack of evidence. The twice-widowed Bishop had often been before the court. Both she and her second husband, Thomas Oliver, had been convicted several times of domestic violence—in one case the brawl took place on the Sabbath. One neighbor accused her of stealing a spoon and was subsequently cursed by Bridget. A poor, quarrelsome, and suspicious woman, Bishop fit everyone's idea of a witch.[39]

The most dramatic testimony against Bishop came from the girls who had been tormented by her specter. Not only had she encouraged them to sign the devil's book, but the girls described how Bishop's specter had tortured them when they attempted to testify against her at her pretrial hearing. As was often the case at witch trials, the accusations confirmed the long-held suspicions of neighbors, who then came forward to recount a long history of Bishop's satanic acts. A total of ten witnesses testified about strange actions that surrounded her, some dating back to the 1670s. From unusual accidents and the disappearance of money to mysterious deaths and her apparent ability to summon monstrous satanic imps, Bishop was a bilious reservoir of the invisible world. The most damning evidence came from John Bly and his son William, who had been hired by Bishop in 1685 to carry out some repairs on her home. When they took down the cellar wall, they found in the holes between the stones "several poppets made up of rags with hogs' bristles with headless pins in them with the points outward."[40] Poppets with pins in them—what today people refer to as "voodoo dolls," small dolls that were clothed in part with some hair or possessions stolen from the victims and then stuck with pins or otherwise damaged to inflict pain on the victims—were all too clear evidence of image magic. The Blys did not produce the actual poppets, but this short, simple testimony would have been viewed as a tangible proof of black magic, far more damning than spectral evidence.[41]

Further physical evidence came from a panel of nine women and surgeon John Barton, who examined the body of Bridget Bishop and five other suspected witches, searching for devil's marks, the teats sucked on by Satan or a witch's familiar. After "diligent search" on Bishop, the group found a "preternatural excrescence of flesh between the pudendum and anus much like teats and not usual in women." Bridget Bishop had a witch's teat. Even more remarkable, when they reexamined Bishop several hours later, the "excrescence" had disappeared, replaced by dry skin.[42]

By the time the jury began deliberation, there was little doubt about the outcome. A long history of unexplainable acts, alleged crimes, and family violence, combined with a previous charge of witchcraft, multiple witnesses to her harmful specter's actions, evidence of image magic, and even a witch's teat, would have been enough to convict a person of witchcraft in most English courtrooms of the day. To no one's surprise, Bishop was found guilty and sentenced to be hanged. On Friday morning, June 10, Sheriff Corwin and his men led Bridget Bishop from the jail to common land at the outskirts of Salem Town, to the place that would later be known as Gallows Hill. He later reported that Bishop was "hanged by the neck until she was dead." The exact method of hanging at Salem is not known. Regardless, it would have been a slow and painful death. At the time, victims were given only a short drop, usually off a ladder or a cart. This usually resulted in death by strangulation, which could take as much as ten agonizing minutes. An observer in England in 1726 described friends and family grabbing the feet of the condemned in midair and tugging on them, to hasten their dying and end their suffering.[43]

There was a lull in supernatural activity in the two weeks following the execution of Bridget Bishop. Only three people claimed to be afflicted by specters, and no new suspects were jailed. Observers might have even believed the worst was over. The improving situation in the invisible world meant little to the accused suffering in prison, however. On June 16 Dr. Roger Toothaker died in the Boston prison while awaiting trial. It would have been little consolation to his family that the first signs of opposition to the trials had started to arise. Most significant, somewhere around the time of Bishop's execution Judge Nathaniel Saltonstall resigned from the Court of Oyer and Terminer. It became widely known that that he was "very much dissatisfied with the proceedings." There would even be claims that his specter actually afflicted people.[44]

Other members of the court and administration may not have questioned the proceedings outright, but they did want to make sure they were on the right path. On June 13 Governor Phips met with his council, with four of the judges of Oyer and Terminer (Stoughton, Sewall, Winthrop, and Sergeant) in attendance. The council asked a group of leading ministers of the colony for their opinion on the handling of the witchcraft proceedings, and in particular the use of spectral evidence. The ministers responded two days later. In the "Return of Several Ministers" penned for the group by Cotton Mather, they showed their support for the judges' difficult task. While the divines raised serious doubts about the use of spectral evidence, their deferential letter concluded by encouraging the "speedy and vigorous prosecutions of such as have rendered themselves obnoxious." Ignoring or not fully understanding the ministers' concerns about spectral evidence, the judges interpreted this statement as a green light to continue their prosecutions.[45]

A few days later, however, another minister voiced his concern. On June 25 Governor Phips and his council received two petitions complaining about the use of spectral evidence in the trials. Both were written by Boston's Baptist minister, William Milborne, who warned that "several persons of good fame and unspotted reputations" sat in jail, based solely "upon bare specter testimonies." He warned that "a woeful chain of consequences will undoubtedly follow" this overreliance on spectral evidence and would also put everyone in the colony under the cloud of a possible accusation.[46] It had been one thing for Cotton Mather and other leading Puritan ministers to point out diplomatically the potential danger of spectral evidence when the government asked their opinion. It was quite a different matter to receive unsolicited criticism of the proceedings, especially from Milborne. Not only was he the brother of recently executed New York rebel Jacob Milborne, but Puritans considered Baptists to be a radical and dangerous Protestant sect. The governor summoned Milborne before the council to explain his "scandalous and seditious paper," whereupon they required Milborne to post a hefty £200 bond to prevent a repeat of such an outburst.[47]

The Court of Oyer and Terminer reconvened on Tuesday, June 28. Five women would face the court, and all would be convicted of witchcraft. Thomas Newton had planned his prosecutions well. He built upon the success of the conviction of Bridget Bishop, choosing to try people against whom he had a strong case—particularly those who had been suspected of witchcraft before 1692. Sarah Good was the first to be tried. Several of the afflicted had affirmed that Good's specter had attacked them. Sarah Bibber said that on one occasion Good's apparition caused a great fit in Bibber's young child, and another time pinched and tortured the child so "it cried out and twisted so dreadfully." Bibber swore that in a third incident Good had "most grievously tormented me by beating and pinching me and almost choking me to death and pricking me with pins after a most dreadful manner."[48] Even worse, Tituba and several others had named Good as a witch in their confessions, saying she flew on a broomstick, had animal familiars, attended witches' gatherings, and signed the devil's book. Such evidence, combined with the fits of one of the afflicted girls, proved enough to convict her. Next, the court tried Susannah Martin, an elderly Amesbury widow, whom Cotton Mather would call "one of the most impudent, scurrilous, wicked creatures in the world." Martin was convicted as well.[49]

The magistrates then turned to Rebecca Nurse, a case that would be much more difficult for the court. Not only was seventy-year-old Rebecca a highly respected member of the Salem Town Church, but she and her family had actively prepared for her defense. The grand jury had indicted her back on June 3, the day after Bridget Bishop's indictment and trial. Presumably Rebecca's trial was delayed because of the very active work her family undertook to overturn the indictment. The Nurses solicited testimony that questioned the veracity of Rebecca's accusers, and submitted a petition signed by thirty-nine friends and neighbors in support of her innocence. As with most of the cases, the prosecution's evidence lay almost entirely upon the testimony of the afflicted, who claimed that Rebecca's specter had harmed them. The court also produced the reports of a panel of women and surgeon John Barton, who had found what they believed was a witch's teat when they inspected Rebecca. Despite the evidence, the jury returned initially with a verdict of not guilty. The decision immediately led to great turmoil in the courtroom. The afflicted girls cried out, and several of the judges seemed displeased and one went so far as to suggest Nurse should be indicted anew for the recent afflictions. Judge Stoughton asked the jury to reconsider, pointing out what he considered to be a particularly damning statement made by Nurse. The jury went back to their deliberations, but uncertainty remained, so the foreman, Thomas Fiske, returned to ask Rebecca to explain her remark. She remained silent, an action taken by the jury as a sign of her guilt, so they finally returned with a guilty verdict. Immediately afterward the Nurse family complained that Rebecca, who was nearly deaf, had not heard the question, and Fiske would acknowledge that her silence was the principal evidence of her guilt. Despite this obvious miscarriage of justice, the conviction remained, even with a reprieve from Governor Phips, who apparently rescinded it in the face of complaints by the afflicted and pressure from an unnamed Salem gentleman. Five days after Rebecca's conviction, her fellow Puritan saints formally turned their backs to her. In her presence, the Salem Town church members unanimously voted to excommunicate her.[50]

The dynamic in Salem had now changed. Previously witchcraft had been a crime common to poorer and marginal members of society. Rebecca's religious, economic, and political standing normally would have protected her from charges, or at least kept them from being taken seriously. Her conviction demonstrated that almost no one in the colony was safe.

The court session continued with cases against Elizabeth How and then Sarah Wildes. Both were Topsfield women who had long been suspected of witchcraft, and much of the testimony against them would refer back to these earlier episodes rather than to events in Salem Village, though both faced spectral evidence from the afflicted. Both women were convicted and condemned to death. On July 19, How and Wildes, along with Rebecca Nurse, Susannah Martin, and Sarah Good, were carted off from Salem prison to face execution on Gallows Hill. According to Robert Calef, before they were hanged, Salem Town's junior minister, Nicholas Noyes, gave Sarah Good one last chance to confess that she was a witch, so that she would at least not die a liar. "You are a liar," she replied. "I am no more a witch than you are a wizard, and if you take away my life God will give you blood to drink." Good drew her last words from the Bible, specifically from Revelation 16:6. During the apocalypse God punished sinners through seven final plagues, the third of which turned all the rivers and springs of water into blood: "For they shed the blood of the saints and prophets, and therefore thou has given them blood to drink." After Sarah's final words, the executions took place without further incident, though people remembered Good's curse years later, when Noyes suffered an internal hemorrhage, leaving him to die choking on his own blood.[51]

By the time of these executions, it seemed that nothing could slow the growing crisis. More people were arrested in Salem, and the accusations were rapidly spreading throughout the region. While visiting the Boston prison, Mercy Short had been cursed by Sarah Good. Soon Short began to suffer afflictions. Her minister, Cotton Mather, visited the young woman regularly throughout the summer of 1692 to try to ease her ills. Sixteen miles to the north of Salem in Gloucester, residents heard strange noises and saw phantoms of French soldiers and Native American warriors. Amazingly, two hundred miles to the southwest, Stamford, Connecticut, was also preparing for witch trials. In a case that has some eerie similarities to Salem, a teenage girl charged she was afflicted by the specters of five local women.[52]

In mid-July the focus of accusations moved west to Salem's neighbor, Andover. Two of Salem Village's afflicted girls were brought to town to find the witches responsible for the prolonged illness of Elizabeth Ballard. Soon Ann Foster, her daughter Mary Lacey Sr., and her granddaughter Mary Lacey Jr. all stood accused of witchcraft. All three Andover women quickly confessed to the crime, providing many specific details of their satanic meetings and yielding the names of neighbors who were fellow witches. When Mary Lacey Jr. confessed, she accused Martha Carrier of using black magic to kill a number of people, including two of Martha's brothers and a brother-in-law. Lacey also accused Carrier's two teenage sons, Richard and Andrew. When brought before the court for questioning, the young men refused to confess until, according to their fellow prisoner John Procter, "they tied them neck and heels till the blood was ready to come out of their noses." Procter further complained that the same treatment had been used on his son William. While such "mild" forms of judicial torture were allowed under English law to aid a confession, the General Court had legislated against their use in 1641. Of course, this law had been struck down with all the others by the new charter. The Carrier lads not only confessed but further widened the circle. They said their mother was a witch, and Richard described how he along with Mary Bradbury, Rebecca Nurse, and Elizabeth How were satanically baptized at the falls in Newbury. The accusations would soon spread throughout the town, with more than forty people accused in total. Between mid-July and September 2, most of the accused now came from Andover.[53]

When the Court of Oyer and Terminer met for its third session on August 2, it would feature a new crown attorney. Thomas Newton had resigned at the end of June to assume the position of secretary to the governor of New Hampshire. His replacement was Anthony Checkley, a Boston merchant who had served as attorney general under the Dominion of New England. Martha Carrier would be the first person to be tried during the session. So many people testified against Carrier that the court did not bother to hear the damning testimony of her sons. Cotton Mather called Martha a "rampant hag" and observed that her children and other witnesses "agreed, that the devil had promised her, she should be Queen of Hell." The court quickly convicted Carrier.[54]

Five more trials would follow that session, including four against men: John Procter, John Willard, George Jacobs, and George Burroughs. John Procter and his wife, Elizabeth, were both found guilty, largely thanks to the testimony of their servant, Mary Warren. The conviction came despite two petitions in their support with a total of fifty-one signatures. One petition attested to the good character and innocence of the Procters. The second suggested that Satan was able to impersonate the innocent. While the petitions did not impress the court, they did agree to stay the execution of Elizabeth Procter when she informed the court she was pregnant. Like the Procters, damning testimony was provided against elderly George Jacobs by his servant, Sarah Churchwell, though others, including his own granddaughter Margaret Jacobs, accused him as well. Back on May 11, Margaret had confessed to being a witch and said that George Burroughs and her grandfather were as well. Later that day at his initial examination, Jacobs had protested, "Well, burn me or hang me, I will stand in the truth of Christ!" Yet at his trial, the truth was nowhere to be found. Jacobs was found guilty and sentenced to death by hanging. John Willard did not have a servant, but his in-laws were eager to testify against him, accusing him of killing his nephew with black magic. Like everyone before him who was tried by the Court of Oyer and Terminer, Willard was convicted.[55]

The last case of the session was arguably the most important of the entire witch trials, for the accused was Reverend George Burroughs. On August 5, a large crowd gathered for the event, including the Bay Colony's most prominent divine, Increase Mather. Because Burroughs was a minister, people considered him to be the ringleader of the witches that afflicted Salem. As Increase's son Cotton Mather put it, Burroughs "had the promise of being a king in Satan's kingdom, now going to be erected." Anthony Checkley knew that in order to convict a minister he would need overwhelming evidence, so he arranged for depositions or testimony from about thirty people. The witnesses noted the evil actions of Burroughs's specter and his superhuman feats of strength, and eight confessed witches described his being "head actor at their hellish rendezvous."[56] The torments of the afflicted added to the high drama. When they tried to testify against Burroughs, they began choking on their words as if an invisible force rendered them speechless. Burroughs himself said their torments looked like the devil's work, though he had no answer when Judge Stoughton asked him why Satan was "so loathe to have any testimony born against you."[57] After this the bewitched claimed that four ghosts—visible only to them—interrupted the proceedings to confront Burroughs for murdering them. They were the ghosts of Burroughs's first two wives, as well as the wife and daughter of Reverend Deodat Lawson, another former Salem Village minister who happened to be present in the courtroom. Burroughs's denials and efforts to defend himself did not impress the court, which saw them as "tergiversations, contradictions and falsehoods."[58] The minister was found guilty. Increase Mather agreed. He would later write, "Had I been one of his judges, I could not have acquitted him."[59]

Two weeks later, Burroughs, George Jacobs, John Procter, John Willard, and Martha Carrier were carted up to Gallows Hill for execution. Margaret Jacobs had repudiated her confession and accusations, but her grandfather and George Burroughs still stood convicted. A particularly large and distinguished audience showed up for the executions of Burroughs, the king of hell; Carrier, his queen; and the members of their court. The crowd was a bit unsettled, for being executed here were four men who had previously been regarded as solid members of the community. These were far from stereotypical witches. Then there was the behavior of the condemned, who maintained their innocence and forgave their accusers as well as the judges and jury. Writing five years later, Robert Calef noted the compelling speech George Burroughs made to express his innocence, complete with a perfect recitation of the Lord's Prayer—a feat believed impossible for a witch. Burroughs's words brought tears to many eyes, and it almost seemed as if the throng would bring a halt to the proceedings. After Burroughs's execution, Cotton Mather spoke to the crowd, reminding them that the former Salem Village pastor was not an ordained minister and that "the devil has often been transformed into an Angel of Light." The reassurances of such a respected authority speaking from horseback calmed the crowd, and the executions continued.[60]

Calef claimed that the bodies were hastily thrown into a shallow common grave, leaving Burroughs's chin and hand and someone else's foot above the ground. If true, this may have been an expedient to get the bodies underground as quickly as possible, as the executions took place during a sweltering heat wave. Several evenings earlier, a friend of Samuel Sewall's had passed away and been promptly buried the next day, because his body "could not be kept" in the extreme weather.[61] Regardless of how they were buried, some of the dead did not lie long on Gallows Hill. In his will written while he was in prison, John Procter specifically bequeathed "my body unto decent burial at the discretion of my executors." This last request was apparently carried out for according to family and neighborhood traditions, the Procter and Jacobs and families removed the bodies of their loved ones under cover of darkness and secretly reburied them near their homes. A similar tradition in the Nurse family suggests that family members removed her body after her death and buried it in the family cemetery.[62]

Despite the executions, more people continued to be accused, and a growing number of them were confessing, suggesting an immense conspiracy. On July 15 Ann Foster said there were twenty-five witches at the Sabbath she attended. A week later, Mary Lacey Jr. testified she had seen seventy-seven. By the end of August three confessors agreed that there had been two hundred witches present at their black Sabbaths, and others reported hearing of more than three hundred active witches in the region. The pace of accusations quickened as well. In August and September formal charges were placed on another forty alleged witches. Only a couple of Salem residents were accused, but the afflicted of Salem Village continued to cry out on people in Andover and other surrounding towns. They were increasingly joined in their denunciations by the growing number of confessed witches. By the middle of September, forty-two confessors had named others as witches.[63]

As the accusations climbed, more opposition against the proceedings began to surface. Alarmed by the charges against his neighbor Mary Bradbury, Salisbury's leading magistrate, Major Robert Pike, wrote to express his concerns to Judge Jonathan Corwin. Pike, a fellow member of the Governor's Council, carefully laid out his concerns about spectral evidence. Although there was disagreement on the subject, he believed that the devil could assume the shape of innocent people. He worried that such controversial evidence was given too much weight in the trials. This led him ultimately to conclude that the court should rather "let a guilty person live till further discovery, than to put an innocent person to death." Cotton Mather faced similar questions about spectral evidence and growing concerns about the proceedings, spurring him to write a booklet that would serve as a defense of judges and the entire judicial process at work at Salem. He had enough written by September 2 to share a partial draft with William Stoughton.[64]

Despite the murmurs of concern, the Court of Oyer and Terminer met again in a two-week session starting September 6. The first week it heard six more cases, with everyone—Mary Bradbury, Martha Cory, Mary Esty, Alice Parker, Ann Pudeator, and Dorcas Hoar—found guilty and sentenced to hang. Esty's sister Rebecca Nurse had already been executed, and a third sister, Sarah Cloyce, had been accused and was in jail. Bradbury's case exemplifies just how out of control the proceedings had become, for seventy-year-old Mary was a well-respected woman of high social rank, the wife of Captain Thomas Bradbury, the leading citizen of Salisbury. At her trial she had presented a petition signed by 118 friends and neighbors attesting to her religious devotion and good character. Her minister, James Allen, testified that she "hath lived according to the rules of the gospel" and practiced a life "full of works of charity and mercy to the sick and poor." Furthermore, he had never "seen or heard anything of her unbecoming the profession of the gospel." Salisbury's magistrate, Major Pike, affirmed Allen's testimony, based on having known Mary for almost fifty years.[65]

Trying to keep up with the growing number of accusations, the court heard nine more cases the next week and produced nine more convictions. Abigail Faulkner, Margaret Scott, Wilmot Redd, and Mary Parker were tried, found guilty, and sentenced to hang. The other five, Ann Foster, her daughter Mary Lacey Sr., Samuel Wardwell, Rebecca Eames, and Abigail Hobbs, had pled guilty at arraignment. When Samuel Wardwell's confession was read to him, he recanted and changed his plea to not guilty. He was quickly tried, convicted, and sentenced to death. Those who held to their confessions were likewise condemned to the gallows.[66]

The Court of Oyer and Terminer adjourned on Saturday, September 17, and was not scheduled to resume its deliberations until November. However, there was still the case of Giles Cory to resolve. Indicted in early September along with his wife, Martha, Giles had pleaded not guilty. Yet he refused to answer the next customary question: would he be willing to be tried "by God and my country," that is, by a jury? In the absence of his answer, technically the trial could not proceed. So the officers of the court then undertook the traditional but very rarely used English practice called *peine forte et dure* (meaning "strong and hard punishment" in the legal Old Northern French of the day). They laid Cory down between boards and placed progressively more rocks on top of the planks to literally press an answer out of him. He still refused to reply to the question as they piled on rocks, though tradition has it that Cory's last words were, "More weight." This seems in keeping with what was known of the stubborn and quarrelsome old man who demonstrated such contempt for the court. The horrendous weight finally crushed him to death. Robert Calef noted that near the end, "in pressing his tongue being pressed out of his mouth," Sheriff George Corwin "with his cane forced it in again." Like Wardwell, Cory had seen the fate of others brought before the court, and he believed that his trial would end with his execution. So Cory "rather chose to undergo what death they would put him to." The day before his death, the Salem Town Church excommunicated Giles. A week earlier the Salem Village church had excommunicated his wife, Martha.[67]

Three days later, on September 22, Martha Cory was among the eight convicted witches who were hanged. She was joined on the gallows by Margaret Scott, Mary Esty, Alice Parker, Ann Pudeator, Wilmot Redd, Samuel Wardwell, and Mary Parker. Several of those condemned in the last court session avoided execution, including the confessed witches Rebecca Eames, Ann Foster, Mary Lacey Sr., and Abigail Hobbs. Mary Bradbury had received a reprieve, though this was a temporary measure, so her supporters eventually organized her escape from jail and put her into hiding. Abigail Faulkner was pregnant, so, like Elizabeth Procter, she received a stay of execution until after she gave birth. However, both women faced daunting odds of surviving pregnancy and childbirth under the terrible conditions in the Massachusetts prisons.[68]

The executions gave voice to a growing opposition to the trials. The quiet dignity and innocent bearing of the August victims had led many present to reconsider the guilt of the accused. Meanwhile, the September proceedings seemed even more problematic. In two weeks the court had heard fifteen cases and convicted fifteen people. It seemed like a rush to judgment, especially when the evidence in some cases was not as strong as in earlier prosecutions. Judges seemed to increasingly rely on spectral evidence, and many observers must have been taken aback by the treatment of Giles Cory. Worse, no one who confessed to being a witch had been executed, with the exception of Samuel Wardwell, who recanted his confession. Only those who refused to confess met death. Then there was the uneven treatment of the condemned. Fifteen had been condemned, but only eight had been executed.

Furthermore, there were signs of God's continued displeasure. On July 5, a large fire in Boston's North End consumed approximately fifteen houses, shops, and warehouses. Later that month Samuel Sewall complained of a "great drought." Then on August 4, news reached Boston of a horrible earthquake that had decimated Jamaica. The earthquake would cause two-thirds of the city of Port Royal to sink into the Caribbean Sea, destroying approximately two thousand buildings. Sewall reported that seventeen hundred people had perished. Another two thousand would die afterward from injuries and disease. In all, more than half of the population would succumb. One of the largest English cities in the Americas was all but gone in a disaster of biblical proportions.[69]

Meanwhile the outbreak continued to spread outward from Salem and Andover. In September people were accused in Marblehead, Reading, and Gloucester. Apparently one person was even cried out upon in Sudbury, thirty miles to the southwest of Salem. As the accusations started to decline in Andover, Gloucester threatened to become the new center of the witch hunt, with nine people accused in the seaport in the fall. There seemed to be no end in sight.[70]

Increase Mather soon took a series of actions to bring a halt to the trials. In early October he presented the manuscript of his soon-to-be-published *Cases of Conscience* to Governor Phips. The treatise contained a forceful argument against the use of spectral evidence and the "touch test." Fourteen ministers signed the book in support of Mather. And if Phips had not received the manuscript by October 9, he surely heard of it that Sunday, when the ministers read parts of the manuscript from their pulpits. The next week Mather traveled to Salem jail, where many of the Andover witches retracted not only their confessions but also their accusation of other alleged witches.[71]

Mather had been accompanied to the Salem jail by Boston merchant Thomas Brattle. On October 8 Brattle had written a lengthy letter to an unnamed minister, critiquing the trials and raising the widespread discontent about the trials among political leaders, magistrates, and ministers in the region. Among those specifically named was Samuel Willard, the influential pastor of Boston's Third Church, who had initially voiced concern about the trials and spectral evidence in several sermons back in June. Willard wrote the preface to Mather's *Cases of Conscience*, and in late October he would publish his own critique of the trials.[72]

Amid this flurry of publications, on October 12 William Phips wrote to William Blathwayt, secretary of the Privy Council. This was the first time that Phips had reported on the witch trials to his superiors in England. He told them he was forbidding any more charges of witchcraft except under extreme circumstances, for, Phips noted, "I found that the devil had taken upon him the name and shape of several persons who were doubtless innocent and to my certain knowledge of good reputation." Phips did not say so in the letter, but one of the victims recently cried out upon was his wife, Lady Mary Phips. He also banned any future publications on the subject: "I have also put a stop to the printing of any discourses one way or other, that may increase the needless disputes of people upon this occasion, because I saw a likelihood of kindling an inextinguishable flame."[73]

Phips's actions were clearly influenced not just by the accusation against his wife but also by the growing opposition among those whose opinions mattered, particularly Increase Mather, his minister, confidant, and close political ally. When questioned during the October 29 session of the legislature as to whether the Court of Oyer and Terminer would stand or fall, Governor Phips replied, "It must fall."[74] There would be no more sessions of the court.

On November 25 the legislature approved a new court system as part of its ongoing effort to re-create the legal code for the colony under its new charter. The top court in the land would be the Superior Court of Judicature, and it would take over responsibility for all capital crimes, including the witch trials. On December 7 the governor's council appointed the judges for this court. William Stoughton would continue his role as chief justice of the colony, and Samuel Sewall, Wait Winthrop, and John Richards would serve as well. These veterans of the old Court of Oyer and Terminer were joined by Thomas Danforth, the former deputy governor and critic of the witch trials. On December 12 the legislature passed a new witchcraft statute, which essentially followed the current English law against the crime. Finally, the legislature called for a special session of the Superior Court to begin on January 3 in Salem, to deal with the remaining witch trials.[75]

Phips also worked outside the formal legislative process to end the proceedings and ease the sufferings of those still accused. There were more than fifty people in jail awaiting trial. Their miserable conditions were worsening with the onset of winter in unheated cells. Phips allowed some to go free on bail. He also discussed the witch trials with the judges before their appointment to the Superior Court. In writing to English officials in February, he remarked that "some of them were convinced and acknowledged that their former proceedings were too violent and not grounded upon a right foundation but that if they might sit again, they would proceed after another method."[76] Specifically, spectral evidence and the touch test would not constitute sufficient proof for conviction. When the court first met in January, jurors asked what weight they should give spectral evidence. An unnamed judge replied, "As much as of chips in wort"—that is, no weight at all (in making beer the ingredients were boiled, creating the wort, which after straining usually contained residual chips or flakes of malt). Stoughton was furious at this change in policy. Still convinced that a witch conspiracy threatened the colony, he wanted the new court to continue the convictions and executions. Fortunately, he was part of a distinct minority of the court.[77]

Over the next two weeks the court proceeded quickly. Charges against thirty of the accused were dismissed, and the court did not even bother to hear the cases of several others. It tried twenty-two defendants and convicted only three, all of whom had confessed: Sarah Wardwell, Mary Post, and Elizabeth Johnson Jr. Stoughton signed a warrant for their execution and that of the five others who had received stays of execution under the old Court of Oyer and Terminer. Attorney General Checkley reviewed the verdicts and noted that others who had confessed had been found not guilty. Armed with this advice, Phips issued reprieves for all eight, at least until he heard the wishes of the king and queen.[78]

The Superior Court heard of Phips's decision when they met on February 1 in Charlestown to take up more witchcraft cases. Stoughton was so enraged that he walked out of the court, leaving Judge Danforth to oversee the proceedings. He fumed that "we were in a way to have cleared the land of these."[79] By hindering the execution of justice, "the kingdom of Satan was advanced and the Lord have mercy on this country."[80] Stoughton would return to preside over the last session of witch trials in late April and early May, but the results would be the same. Every one of the accused was acquitted, though none was freed until they paid their prison fees. For poor Lydia Dustin, the delay proved lethal. The Reading grandmother had been arrested back on April 30, 1692, and languished in jail for months. Lydia was finally acquitted in early February 1693, only to die in prison more than a month later, before her family could pay the jail keeper his fees. It seems fitting that Tituba, whose confessions had triggered the entire process, was one of the last to face the court. On May 9, a grand jury meeting in Ipswich refused to indict her. Fourteen months after her confession, the court reaffirmed that it now rejected confessions as well as spectral evidence. However, Reverend Parris refused to pay her prison fees, which would have amounted to a bit more than £7—perhaps half her value as a slave. Presumably he did not want her in his house, where she would serve as a constant reminder of the horrible events of the past year and a half. Tituba would be sold to another master to recover her jail fees, at which point she disappears from the historical record. Surely Samuel Parris and the residents of Salem Village would have wished the witch trials could disappear so completely and effectively.[81]

Historians are in general agreement regarding the narrative of events in Salem in 1692 and 1693, based on the surviving evidence. There is far less agreement on how to explain these events. Could the trials have been stopped sooner or even prevented from taking place? To answer that question, one must first understand the nature of Salem's and Massachusetts Bay's original establishment, and the growing tensions and problems the colony faced by the late seventeenth century.

CHAPTER TWO

The City upon a Hill

The Kingdoms of *Sweden*, *Denmark*, *Scotland*, yea, and *England* itself, as well as the Province of *New-England*, have had their storms of *witchcrafts* breaking upon them, which have made most lamentable devastations.

—Cotton Mather, *Wonders of the Invisible World* [1]

A GREAT STORM WAS BREWING in Massachusetts during the winter of 1691–92, and one cause of the dark clouds was a disastrous frontier war dragging into its fourth year. To pay for the war the government had increased taxes and been forced to issue paper money, causing rapid inflation and a downward spiral in an economy already hit hard by cold weather, drought, and crop failures. The announcement of a new charter and a new royal governor created uncertainty. Worst of all, a decline in an unwavering commitment to Puritan values—measured, for example, by Sabbath worship attendance—threatened the New England way. Massachusetts Bay had been founded as "a city upon a hill," and many feared the Puritan experiment was in danger of becoming irrelevant and perhaps even coming to an end. Such would have seemed impossible to imagine just a couple generations earlier, when the Bay Colony was established.

The founders of Massachusetts were part of what some have called the "Puritan diaspora," a substantial migration out of England between 1620 and 1640 of Puritans who fled the growing oppression of King James I and his successor, Charles I, and what they saw as the corruption of the Church of England. In his famous sermon "A Model of Christian Charity," Governor John Winthrop had proclaimed "that we shall be as a city upon a hill. The eyes of all people are upon us." Massachusetts would be a shining example of what the world should and could be, once everyone had adopted the Puritan faith. The new colony was to be a place where the Puritans could worship in peace and build their "Bible commonwealth." Winthrop noted that the people of Massachusetts Bay had entered into a covenant with God. In return for this special relationship, the Puritans would make extraordinary efforts to demonstrate their religious zeal and purity. The governor warned of the dire consequences if they let God down: "If we shall deal falsely with our God in this work we have undertaken, and so cause him to withdraw his present help from us, we shall be made a story and a by-word through the world."[2]

The Puritan movement began in England in the latter part of the sixteenth century. Its adherents believed that the creation of the Church of England (or Anglican Church) by Henry VIII had not been a strong enough reform of Catholic corruption. Indeed, they viewed the Anglican Church as far too close to the Catholicism it had supposedly replaced. The church was still tainted and full of excess. Inspired by Continental reformers such as John Calvin and Huldrych Zwingli, these "puritans"—a pejorative term used by their detractors—desired a return to what they conceived to be the simplicity and piety of the church at the time of Christ and his apostles. Unfortunately, there was far from universal agreement on what constituted that original austerity, so rather than sharing a unified faith, English Puritans had a range of views on the church and its problems. Some, such as the Pilgrims of Plymouth Colony, were separatists. They believed the church was so corrupt that they had to break with it completely and start again. The Puritans of Massachusetts Bay did not share the extreme view of the separatists. Rather, they believed that the church could be saved—but the best way to do so was to leave England and her corrupting influences and reform the church in America.

While not all Puritans would have agreed on the specific reforms for the church, all would have agreed on some points. First and foremost, Puritans

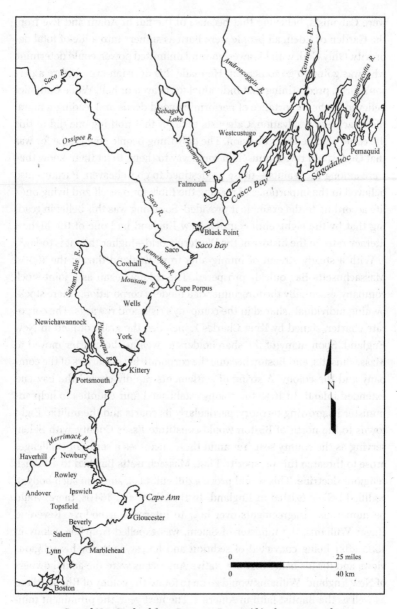

Coastal New England from Boston to Pemaquid in the seventeenth
century. Drawing by the author.

were Calvinists, believing that because of the fall of Adam and Eve from the Garden of Eden, all people were born as sinners into a life of total depravity. Only God, with his awesome and unlimited power, could determine who was going to go to heaven. He made this decision even before a person's birth, predestining that individual for heaven or hell. While Catholics believed in the importance of performing good deeds and leading a moral life in achieving salvation, Calvinists thought that nothing one did in this life could change God's decision. The only thing people could hope for was that God would reveal himself in some way to them, to let them know they were among the "saints"—those predestined to go to heaven. Puritans also believed in the importance of reading the Bible for oneself and living one's life according to the example it provided. So strong was this belief in reading that by the eighteenth century, New England had one of the highest literacy rates in the history of the Western world—higher than it is today.[3]

With a steady stream of immigrants from England during the 1630s, Massachusetts Bay quickly prospered. The colony began as a joint stock company, essentially the forerunner of a modern corporation, where stock-owning individuals shared in the company's risks and rewards. The corporate charter, signed by King Charles I, included the grant of land in New England. Soon many of the shareholders as well as the charter moved to Massachusetts, and Boston became the corporate headquarters of the company and the colony. A string of settlements rapidly circled the bay and extended inland. In 1643 the colony established four counties to help administer its growing territory, particularly its courts and the militia. Eight towns to the north of Boston would constitute Essex County, with Salem serving as the county seat. Yet amid these successes a series of challenges arose to threaten this prosperity. First, Massachusetts Bay had to establish religious doctrine. This would prove a difficult task, since no such body of codified beliefs existed in England. In the 1630s and 1640s, there would be numerous disagreements over how to interpret orthodoxy. Reverend Roger Williams, the minister of Salem, was expelled from the colony in 1635 after being convicted of sedition and heresy, both for his religious views and for his belief that the Native Americans were the actual owners of New England. Williams would go on to found the colony of Rhode Island as well as the Baptist faith in America. The next year, the prominent minister Thomas Hooker led a group of about one hundred Massachusetts Bay colonists westward to found Hartford, the first settlement in what would be the new colony of Connecticut. Hooker left in part due to his disagreement with John Cotton, a Boston minister. Shortly after, Cotton became a central figure in the Freegrace Controversy (also called the Antinomian Controversy). Cotton's followers Anne Hutchinson and Reverend John Wheelwright led a movement that threatened to split the colony over interpretations of the Bible and in particular how to achieve salvation. The controversy ended in 1638 with the banishment of Hutchinson, Wheelwright, and many of their followers.[4]

Whatever the religious differences, Massachusetts had a firm economic basis. As early as 1623, Plymouth colonist Edward Winslow had referred to New England as a place "where religion and profit jump together." A prosperous fur trade with the Native inhabitants helped to spur the economy of the region in the first decades of settlement, and the rich cod-fishing grounds of coastal New England became the backbone. Indeed, a large carved wooden replica of a codfish has hung in the Massachusetts seat of government since the early eighteenth century, a constant reminder of the fish's importance in the prosperity of the colony. Cod was a particularly important foodstuff in Catholic southern Europe, to which large quantities of the salted fish were shipped; this was ironic, as the Puritans considered Catholics to be their great spiritual enemies. The Puritans also unwittingly helped enslave Africans, as the lower-quality cod it produced fed slaves on the English sugar plantations of the Caribbean.[5] And New England's raw materials kept the sugar economy going by transporting slaves and goods.[6]

The rich stands of lumber throughout coastal New England proved beneficial to Massachusetts as well. Aside from giving the settlers a plentiful and cheap source of building materials and firewood to keep their homes warm during the long cold winters, timber served a variety of purposes. Hardwoods were used for the staves of barrels, the seventeenth-century equivalent of the cardboard box—everything was shipped in them. Lumber (particularly masts and naval stores) was also a key export to Europe. In the West Indies sugar was such a profitable crop that the islands were completely cleared of wood and all available acreage used to grow sugar cane. Hence the islands had to import the wood needed to build their homes and fuel their cooking fires. By the later seventeenth century, what may have been the first prefabricated houses were being shipped to the islands as well. Timber frames were cut and assembled in Maine and New Hampshire, then disassembled and shipped south. The English sugar colonies soon came to rely heavily upon New England for food as well. In addition to the cod that fed the islands' slaves, pork, beef, and grain also traveled south.[7]

As Boston grew into New England's economic center, its merchants and political leaders quickly realized that most of the raw materials—the furs, fish, and lumber—needed to drive this economic engine lay to the north of Massachusetts Bay, in New Hampshire and Maine. So beginning in the early 1640s, Massachusetts sought to develop and maintain either direct or indirect control over her northern neighbors, making a colony an imperial power in its own right. The ultimate victory for Parliament and the Puritans in the English Civil War and the execution of Charles I in 1649 meant that for the time being, at least, Massachusetts would be allowed to remain an expansionist power that dominated the region. The second half of the seventeenth century would be a different story.[8]

We tend to look at history through the lens of generations, be it the founding fathers, the "greatest generation," the baby boomers, or generation X. As one generation gives way to the next, there are inevitable gaps or outright conflicts. So it was with the second generation of Puritans in Massachusetts. As the children of the Great Migration came of age in the mid-seventeenth century, their society underwent growing pains. Few were rebellious and most wanted to continue the original project of building a city upon a hill. Still, many lacked the zeal of their parents and had failed to experience the personal conversion experience wherein God let them know they were among the elect, the saints destined for salvation in heaven. Lacking this, members of the second generation attended religious services but did not join the covenant and become members of the church. For this they were denied the sacraments, notably baptism of their children, thereby risking eternal damnation for the third generation.

The degree to which Puritan declension was real is a matter of scholarly debate. Although the proportion of colonists who were full church members did decrease throughout the second half of the seventeenth century, many historians note that the Puritan commitment remained strong. Indeed, the pious population's extreme concerns with a pure church and the salvation of the elect suggested the strength of piety and the continuation of the New England way. Ministers and lay leaders, however, perceived the church to be in decline, and this became their overriding concern.[9]

Faced with shrinking church membership and the threat of damnation for its youth, a religious synod developed the Halfway Covenant in 1662.

This created a partial form of church membership for the adult children of church members who had not undergone spiritual conversion. As long as they agreed to live by their church's creed, these "halfway" members were allowed to have their children baptized. The Halfway Covenant would long remain a divisive issue, and many congregations refused to adopt it. Supporters saw it as the best solution. Halfway membership would eventually lead to full membership. Opponents saw it as yet another sign of declension and refused to allow it in their churches, where membership continued to decline. Many Puritan churches were also loosening strict membership requirements. Yet, changing religious policy affected politics as well. Only property-holding male church members could be freemen, eligible to vote and hold office. So, widened suffrage allowed men whom some Puritans might consider unregenerate to weaken the saints' rule.[10]

There were other visible signs of change as well. The second generation had to face the fact that the city upon a hill, despite its success, had not influenced English religion or society. Indeed, the restoration of the monarchy with Charles II in 1660 meant an end to the Puritan revolution in England. And as New England's economy prospered, growing wealth increased the threat of worldliness and excessive pride. Ministers soon began to preach jeremiads, reminding people of their mission and their covenant with God and telling them how far they had strayed from their path. Puritans believed that everything was a sign of God's pleasure or displeasure, and they saw the difficulties they faced as individuals and as a colony as signs of God's displeasure. They needed to repent and return to their faith or face God's horrible wrath. Increase Mather was instrumental in developing the jeremiad theme as a young minister, though many Massachusetts divines contributed to the genre. One of the first was the election sermon preached to the General Court at the start of its session in 1663 by Salem's John Higginson. Five years later William Stoughton preached what would become a famous jeremiad for the election sermon.[11]

Stoughton's sermon, "New England's True Interest: Not to Lie," suggested the spiritual conflict to come when he later served as chief justice of the Court of Oyer and Terminer. The spiritually weak were assaulted by deceivers. God turned his back on them, and they became instruments of Satan. The "Brood of the Anti-Christ" were already among the Puritans of Massachusetts, though Stoughton acknowledged that they were difficult to identify. Outwardly pious, they had yielded to temptation. In this invisible world of spiritual conflict, the enemy "remain hid all the while under some fair cloak, but they shall proceed until they be known."[12] Satan and his minions had been unleashed by God to tempt Puritans into sin and degeneracy. Sermons such as Stoughton's painted a terrible picture of the horrible fate that awaited sinners and all of New England if they succumbed to temptation. In 1674, Increase Mather warned "that the Lord should seem at this day to be *numbering many of the rising generation for the sword*; as if to say, I will bring a sword to avenge the quarrel of a *neglected covenant*."[13]

The next year, Mather's warning seemed proven uncannily accurate when King Philip's War broke out. The struggle between the Native and English populations of New England was another symptom of the growing pains facing the region. Native Americans felt increasingly squeezed by the growing English population, which pushed further into their lands and threatened their traditional lifeways in the process. Fighting started in the summer of 1675 in southern New England and continued along the northern frontier until the spring of 1678.

The war was one of the bloodiest and most destructive conflicts in American history. Thousands of Native Americans and hundreds of colonists were killed, injured, or displaced, and the fighting left much of the frontier zones of New England a blackened, smoldering ruin. The war broke Native power in southern New England, with a majority of the population being killed, sold into slavery, or fleeing to northern New England or New York. The reverse held true in Maine, where the Wabanaki had destroyed most English settlements. With the Treaty of Casco (1678) the English even agreed to pay annual tribute of a peck of corn per family to the local sachems in recognition of Native sovereignty. Beyond the suffering, the war was extremely expensive. The English colonial administrator Edward Randolph estimated the English losses in houses and livestock at £150,000, and the colonies claimed it cost £100,000 to wage the war. This was at a time when the total wealth for an average English settler's estate might total £200 in real estate, livestock, and personal possessions. While these figures may be on the high side, the magnitude of the financial loss is indisputable, as is its impact on the colonies. Colonial treasuries would be depleted and colonists would face high taxes for years to come.[14]

Although most of the fighting took place far away from Essex County, the war had a powerful effect on the region. Not even people in Salem Town felt safe; they went so far as to build a half-mile-long palisade across Salem

Neck to defend against Native attack. It cost more than £250 to build that palisade and strengthen other defenses for the town. They also prayed for the safe return of the hundreds of members of the Essex County militia who had gone off to fight. Almost a third of all the Massachusetts soldiers who fought in the 1675–76 campaigns—375 men—were drawn from Essex County. Fifty-two of these men (15 percent) died. These figures do not include the fighting that continued in Maine from 1676 to 1678, largely undertaken by Essex County troops.[15]

Essex soldiers were involved in some of the deadliest fighting in the war. Forty-one were killed with Captain Lathrop at Bloody Brook in September 1675. The loss of the so-called Flower of Essex was a deep blow to the region. In June 1677, a largely Essex County contingent serving under Newbury's Captain Benjamin Swett was ambushed at Black Point, Maine; Swett and approximately fifty men were killed. Twenty-two of the dead and five of the wounded were from the county. To make matters worse, that same month the Wabanaki seized more than twenty fishing ketches and killed or captured more than a hundred local fishermen (each ketch had a crew of five or six). These were almost all Salem and Marblehead vessels. On July 15, one of these ketches sailed into Marblehead harbor. The ship had been captured by the Wabanaki, but its crew had been able to turn the tables—they reclaimed the ship and secured two of their former Native captors, both sagamores (tribal chieftains), as prisoners. Upon arriving in Marblehead the crew attempted to bring the sagamores to the constable, but a mob gathered at dockside intervened. A group of women attacked the two bound Natives; "Then with stones, billets of wood, and what else they might, they made an end of these Indians. We were kept at such distance that we could not see them till they were dead, and then we found them with their heads off and gone, and their flesh in a manner pulled from their bones." The gruesome violence demonstrates how intense were the pent-up fears and frustration the war had produced, as well as the animosity felt toward the Native Americans. The sentiments against the Wabanaki would have been particularly high in Marblehead, the temporary home to many Maine war refugees.[16]

King Philip's War left a psychological scar on the entire region that would not easily heal. In 1678 the last in a series of peace treaties were signed, finally ending the war. Yet it was at best a cautious peace, with latent fears of another war with Native Americans, particularly in northern New England, where the Natives continued to pose a substantial military threat. Cotton Mather later observed that "when the time arrived that all hands were weary of war, a sort of peace was patched up, which left a body of Indians, not only with horrible murders unavenged but also in possession of no little part of the country, with circumstances which the English might not think very honorable."[17]

In King Philip's War and its terrible losses Puritan ministers had their proof of spiritual decline and God's wrath. In 1679 the General Court called for a synod of clergy and lay leaders to look into the colony's evils and how to redress them. The greatest was "a visible decay of Godliness": profaneness, Sabbath-breaking, excessive pride, and covetousness of wealth. The synod called for a program to support moral reformation of the entire colony. This would require legislative action, as well as hard work by ministers and their parishioners. The legislature responded by tightening up laws concerning taverns, and focusing on education. There were renewed efforts to provide financial support to Harvard College, the training ground of Puritan ministers, and to require public education in communities with at least five hundred souls.[18]

The Reforming Synod of 1679 was called for after the death of Governor John Leverett, who was replaced by Simon Bradstreet. Leverett, a political realist, had exerted a moderating influence on the strict religious orthodoxy expounded by the hard-liners, including Bradstreet. The death and retirement of other leading moderates gave the upper hand to the conservatives. In the 1680s, the Massachusetts government started to take a tougher stance on moral reformation and most spiritual issues in general. The crown was paying more attention to its colony in New England and taking a hard line as well.[19]

In 1679 King Charles II issued a royal charter for New Hampshire, restoring independence to a colony that had been under the control of Massachusetts since the 1640s. This was just the beginning of the crown's efforts to curb the Bay Colony, which had been growing in territory and power for decades. New Hampshire's independence rekindled the hopes of the Mason family, which had off and on since the 1630s tried to assert their rights of the colony. Captain John Mason had been the key investor in the founding of the colony and had land claims as well. His death in 1635 came just prior to his being granted proprietorship of the colony by the king. In addition to asserting the family's claim, John's grandson, Robert

Tufton Mason, laid claim to all the land between the Merrimac River and the Naumkeag (or North) River, in Salem. He based this 1680 claim on a 1622 patent for these lands (called "Mariana" in the patent) granted by the Council for New England to his grandfather. In truth, Captain Mason had never pursued this claim, nor had he complained when this land was included in the Massachusetts Bay charter of 1629. Rather, he had focused his efforts on patents to lands north of the Merrimac. The result was a weak legal claim to the southern land, but it alarmed residents when in September 1680 King Charles II ordered Massachusetts to produce evidence of its title to the disputed lands. In February 1682 the General Court replied, documenting its title and highlighting the fact that the colony had previously settled all claims with the Mason heirs. The Mason family would eventually drop their claims to land south of New Hampshire in Essex County, but this possibility would hang over landowners' heads for some years. Soon they would have far more to worry about, however.[20]

In 1684 Charles II continued his campaign against the colony by formally revoking Massachusetts Bay's charter. It would be hard to overstate the importance of the 1629 charter to the colony, or the sense of loss this action brought. The original charter was the source of the colony's freedom and autonomy. Unlike with other joint stock colonies such as the Virginia Company, the charter was held in Massachusetts, meaning that decisions affecting the colony were made on this side of the Atlantic. The government that ran the colony was known as the General Court and consisted of an annually elected governor and a bicameral legislature. Each town elected its representatives to lower body, the House of Deputies (corresponding to today's House of Representatives), and the freemen of the entire colony elected the eighteen members of the upper body, the House of Assistants (the forerunner of today's State Senate). The members of the General Court in turn elected the governor. Assistants served not only as the upper body of the legislature but also as magistrates, for they were the judges in their county courts, and the governor and the assistants served as the supreme court of the colony, hearing civil cases as well as high crimes. Under the charter, Massachusetts had established a legal code that was similar to England, but had its own unique ways of doing things. Perhaps most significant were the religious policies of the colony in which Puritanism was the established religion. No other faith—not even the Church of England—was allowed freedom of worship. Everyone had to attend Puritan religious services, and financial support of the minister was mandated by law. In many ways, the charter was the very foundation of the city upon a hill. Without the charter and its protections, Massachusetts was in danger of becoming merely another crown colony, like New York or Jamaica.[21]

The death of Charles II in 1685 delayed the formation of a new government, but in the fall of 1685 Joseph Dudley was given a commission as president of the Council for New England, a provisional government in which the Massachusetts native headed a council appointed by the new king, James II. Dudley, the son of the late Governor Thomas Dudley and brother of poet Ann Dudley Bradstreet, was the leader of the Massachusetts royalists. In December 1686 Sir Edmund Andros arrived in Boston and assumed authority as the governor of the Dominion of New England. The Dominion brought together in one supercolony Massachusetts Bay (including Maine), Plymouth, Rhode Island, and Connecticut. In 1688 New York and East and West Jersey (the Jerseys would later be combined into New Jersey) were added as well.[22]

The establishment of the Dominion triggered a serious spiritual and political crisis in Massachusetts. The Andros regime brought with it toleration for all Protestants. While the modern observer might see this as a good thing, Puritans believed it was a disaster for Massachusetts. The Puritan church lost its special place in the colony. Governor Andros went so far as to take over Boston's South Church as a place of worship for Anglicans—a move Puritans believed defiled the church. Even Quakers and Baptists, once persecuted, were allowed to worship freely. In the minds of the Puritans, the revocation of the charter and the rule of Andros were yet more ominous signs of God's displeasure with New England. The Puritans' covenant with God was under dire threat.[23]

The establishment of the Dominion posed a political threat as well. Massachusetts lost its representative government, for the governor and his council were now appointed by the king. Gone was the elected General Court. Leaders in Essex County would challenge these new restrictions, which struck at what they considered to be the rights of Englishmen. The first resistance arose soon after Dudley's provisional government assumed power. In the summer of 1686, a number of citizens in the towns of Ipswich and Rowley refused to observe the public fast called for by Dudley and his council as a blessing for the new government. Dudley dispatched Salem magistrate Bartholomew Gedney to bring the offenders to justice. Lieutenant

John Gould of neighboring Topsfield was arrested after he made treasonous comments to his company at a militia muster. Gould refused to accept the new government and pledged his company to support its overthrow. He managed to get off with a substantial fine and a bond guaranteeing his good behavior. This was just a sign of things to come the next year—and of course much later, in the years leading up to 1775.[24]

In 1687 Andros passed a new tax act. He thought it a prudent action, as he inherited an empty treasury and a substantial colonial debt. However, it faced considerable opposition in his council, and in several Essex County towns, citizens formally opposed the tax, which they viewed as unfair and levied by an unrepresentative government. Again opposition started in Ipswich, which refused to appoint a tax collector. Topsfield and Rowley soon followed suit. They claimed they could be taxed only through an elected assembly, and to try to do so otherwise infringed on their rights as Englishmen. Andros acted swiftly and decisively to crush the Essex tax revolt before it could spread, arresting more than thirty men. On September 19, three prominent magistrates from the late charter government—Major Nathaniel Saltonstall, Major Samuel Appleton, and Dudley Bradstreet— also were placed under house arrest for sedition. Two days later, a dozen of the would-be rebels were brought before Andros and his council to explain their actions. The arrested were officials from Ipswich, Topsfield, and Rowley, along with men from Andover and Bradford. Their leader, outspoken Ipswich minister John Wise, invoked the liberty of the Magna Carta and the rights of Englishmen. The council was not impressed and verbally berated the "factious" men. Councilor Robert Mason, the would-be proprietor of New Hampshire, said the only privilege they had was the right to not be sold as slaves. Another councilor threatened that their liberties would follow them to the end of the world. Andros himself held them up to ridicule, asking whether they thought "Jack and Tom should tell the king what moneys he should have for the use of his government."[25]

The dozen men were jailed to await trial before a Court of Oyer and Terminer. Andros chose four of his councilors, Joseph Dudley, William Stoughton, John Usher, and Edward Randolph, as its judges. In what was a mockery of a fair trial, all twelve were quickly found guilty on October 21. They were then returned to jail for another three weeks before sentencing. All were fined heavily and placed under bond of good behavior, and they agreed on behalf of their communities to promptly elect a tax collector.

Wise was banned from preaching, though he appealed to Andros, who granted him clemency and allowed him to return to the pulpit. These civic leaders were unaccustomed to such rough treatment. In all they spent close to three months in jail. Saltonstall and Bradstreet fared considerably better. Both issued extensive apologies and acknowledged their errors. They were detained for fifteen days but were released when they agreed to post £1,000 bond for good behavior. Samuel Appleton refused to post bond, so Andros made an example of him. The aged major, in fragile health, spent the winter of 1687–88 in Boston's dank stone jail. Imprisoned without facing any formal charges, Appleton made repeated demands for a writ of habeas corpus, and finally was set free after three months. The treatment of Saltonstall, Bradstreet, and Appleton shocked the Puritan establishment. All three were leaders of the colony, men who held high office under the old charter. The presentment and humiliation of town selectmen, magistrates, militia officers, and other prominent citizens were new experiences for the Bay Colony. The seemingly absolute but arbitrary power of the Court of Oyer and Terminer seemed to presage what would happen in Salem five years later.[26]

The rough handling of the principals in the tax revolt was indicative of the sweeping changes Andros made to the legal and judicial system of the Bay Colony. The governor found the laws of Massachusetts Bay to be at odds with English law, so he began efforts to bring the former into line. Some of the changes must have seemed minor to Andros, but they had major repercussions. Notably, he instituted the English practice of witnesses swearing an oath on the Bible. Massachusetts Puritans had never done so, for it suggested idolatry and Anglicanism. Now when they refused they were fined. Under the 1629 charter, juries had been chosen from the freemen of the colony. Under the Dominion, Andros appointed the sheriffs, who were responsible for choosing members of the jury. They no longer had to be freemen of the colony—so they need not be members of the Puritan church. Soon complaints arose of "packed and picked juries" that did the bidding of Andros and his sheriff. Under the old charter it had been the local members of the House of Assistants who constituted the bench for county courts. Andros replaced these men with his appointees. In Essex County they were William Stoughton, Joseph Dudley, and John Usher—all wealthy Bostonians with no local knowledge. Furthermore, as Andros centralized the government, he required that more cases be tried in Boston. This meant that defendants often faced jurymen who were strangers, and they had to pay additional travel expenses to court. In another assault on the purse, the government substantially increased court fees and raised many fines to excessive levels. The residents of the Bay Colony had traditionally been extremely litigious, frequently engaging in lawsuits. The huge volume, broad scope, and often petty nature of civil lawsuits sometimes suggest to the modern observer that early New Englanders were a fractious and quarrelsome lot. The truth is just the opposite, for while they had their differences and Puritan leaders encouraged informal local arbitration to resolve disputes, the legal system acted as a safety valve, mediating differences and resolving conflicts between individuals and within communities. The changes instituted by Andros made people reluctant to file charges and go to court, so there was a precipitous drop in civil cases. This meant that a significant number of disputes and conflicts continued to fester and grow without resolution.[27]

Land ownership proved to be another divisive issue. While the Mason family's threat had faded, residents were shocked to learn that the revocation of their charter had voided all title to their lands. Under the 1629 charter, the General Court had created townships and given the proprietors of the towns the right to divide the land as they saw fit. This was in contrast to England, where all land was granted by the crown. James II instructed Andros to make landowners apply for a royal patent, which would mean that they held their land directly from the crown. This could be costly, as the settlers had to pay a fee for this process and agree to pay an annual quitrent on the land (essentially a property tax). Andros filed suit against some of the large landowners, including Samuel Sewall, to make an example of them and force them to comply. Furthermore, lands that were still held in common by the towns of the colony now reverted back to the crown, for Andros to distribute as he saw fit. Many towns, particularly those in Essex County, scrambled to bolster their title claims to their common lands. In the 1630s, settlers had denied Roger Williams's claim that the Natives owned the land. Now they sought out the descendants of Native American sachems and purchased titles to their land from them. In 1686, representatives of Salem, Lynn, and Reading bought the Native claim of title to their townships from the descendants of Sagamore George, and Beverly purchased title from the heirs of Sagamore Masconomet. Andros completely discounted the Native deeds, saying they were of "no more value than a scratch with a bear's paw."[28] Salem's Captain Stephen Sewall and

Reverend John Higginson took issue with Andros's view. They said that Massachusetts had received the land from God, "with the consent of the Native inhabitants." Andros's reply drew a line in the sand: "Either you are subjects or you are rebels."[29]

Several of his supporters benefited from Andros's actions, receiving lands previously granted to towns or individuals. Overall, Andros's land policy created a great deal of outrage and considerable uncertainty among the colonists. They had worked hard to establish settlements, build homes, and defend them from attack in King Philip's War. Now they had to pay for that privilege or lose everything. What would be next?[30]

Colonists faced more bad economic news as Andros began to enforce the Navigation Acts in order to pull Massachusetts into the evolving imperial system. Bay Colony sailors and merchants had conveniently ignored the acts since their establishment in the 1650s and 1660s, but Andros's henchman Edward Randolph, a royal customs officer, began seizing ships that were in violation of the laws, and established a maritime court to try the offenders. This enforcement damaged New England's Atlantic trade, slowing the economy and increasing opposition to Andros, particularly among the powerful merchant class. Even Randolph noted the strain. In 1689 he wrote, "This country is poor, the exact executions of the acts of trade hath much impoverished them." There were other contributing factors to the depression that had hit Massachusetts. The New England fishing industry faced setbacks, as it was now prohibited from fishing off French-held Nova Scotia, and it suffered from a shortage of salt for the cod it did catch. Meanwhile, New England lumber exports dropped due to factors beyond local control. A severe drought in the West Indies had damaged the sugar crop and left planters with less molasses and silver with which to purchase wood.[31]

Even the climate seemed to be part of the conspiracy against New England. The 1680s and 1690s were part of the Maunder Minimum, the most extreme weather of the Little Ice Age, a period of colder temperatures occurring roughly from 1400 to 1800. Strikingly cold winters and dry summers were common in these decades. The result was not just personal discomfort but increasing crop failures. Starting in the 1680s, many towns that had once produced an agricultural surplus no longer did so. Mixed farming began to give way to pastures and orchards. Once Massachusetts had exported foodstuffs; by the 1690s it was an importer of corn, wheat, and other cereal crops. Several scholars have noted the high correlation between eras of extreme weather earlier in the Little Ice Age and outbreaks of witchcraft in Europe; Salem continues this pattern.[32]

On top of the economic difficulty and political and spiritual crisis the Bay Colony was facing, there was a looming military calamity. As a career army officer, Colonel Andros recognized the substantial threat posed by the Native Americans of northern New England and their French allies. When war broke out in Maine with the Wabanaki in the summer of 1688, Andros was ready. He led soldiers to Maine and restored a tenuous peace, backed up by his establishment of a string of forts and garrison houses, manned by more than seven hundred soldiers. Meanwhile, two royal ships and two provincial ships patrolled the northern coast. Many colonists complained that Andros's actions were excessive. Massachusetts men had to staff the Maine defenses, and doing so drained the colony's treasury. Traditionally the men had served in town-based militia units, under local officers. Andros's reorganization of the military meant these militiamen now served under Andros's officers—regulars in the king's army. These officers considered their soldiers to be undisciplined and ill-mannered, while the militiamen saw their commanders as overly strict and cruel.[33]

As it turned out, the situation on the frontier helped precipitate Andros's downfall. Some conspiracy-minded colonists thought that the royal governor had actually launched his military expedition to gain the French and Natives as allies so that he could quell Puritan New England. Traditional Puritan paranoia toward Catholics fueled this fear, which combined with the long list of grievances against Andros and his henchmen. When word reached Massachusetts that William and Mary had invaded England, that was signal enough. So desperate was the situation that people did not even wait to hear whether the Glorious Revolution was successful. The Dominion was overthrown by an uprising in Boston on April 18, 1689, in which hundreds of armed men seized Andros, Randolph, and their associates and threw them in prison (Andros would eventually be allowed to return to England). To fill the void in government, the venerable Governor Bradstreet and his old charter government resumed authority as a provisional government, complete with new elections to the General Court.[34]

While the 1629 charter had been temporarily restored, everything else began to unravel. Now trouble truly began on the frontier. Most of Andros's officers were arrested, and the militiamen quickly abandoned

their posts and came home, leaving the Maine frontier almost defense-
less. The Wabanaki took immediate advantage, renewing their attacks in
the summer of 1689 with devastating effect. For example, at Pemaquid, the
northeasternmost English settlement, Lieutenant James Weems commanded two hundred men at Fort James. When word of Andros's overthrow
reached the area, local residents took Weems and his officers into custody.
After due consideration, the local Council of Safety reinstated Weems.
However, by then most of the garrison had abandoned their posts and
returned to Massachusetts. Weems was left with just thirty men, and these
troops seemed reluctant to accept his authority. Considering him more an
advisor than a commander, the troops often did as they pleased. To make
matters worse, the provisional government failed to support the fort. Weems
lacked proper supplies and had to pay the troops out of his own pocket. Not
surprisingly, the town and the fort easily fell to a Wabanaki war party. By the
end of 1689, all English settlements north of Falmouth had been abandoned.
More than three hundred residents had been killed or taken captive, and
property losses were estimated at £40,000—an immense sum.[35]

The widespread problems faced by the colony increasingly came to be
viewed through the lens of the jeremiads the ministers continued to preach.
Massachusetts's sufferings were a challenge from an unhappy God. Only
a colony-wide effort at moral reformation could improve matters. So on
March 13, 1690, the General Court issued a public order for Universal
Reformation. "That this poor land has labored under, a long series, of
afflictions, and calamities, whereby we have suffered successively in our
precious, and pleasant things, and have seen the anger of righteous God
against us...That a corruption of manners attended with inexcusable
degeneracies, and apostasies found in too many among this people, is the
cause of that controversy, which the God of our fathers has for many
years been maintaining with us." The situation "arriving to such an ex-
tremity, that an axe is laid to the roots of the trees, and we are in eminent
danger of perishing, if a speedy reformation of our provoking evils prevent
it not." They gave a "very solemn admonition" to the public to "give
demonstrations of thorough repentance." They complained that the laws of
the colony "against vice, and all sorts of debauchery and profanity...too
much lost their edge by the late interruption of the government," and they
ordered that officials now vigorously enforce them, "particularly the laws
against blasphemy, cursing, profane swearing, lying, unlawful gaming, Sabbath

breaking, idleness, drunkenness, uncleanness, and all the enticement and nurseries of such impieties." The General Court had the order published and posted, and instructed ministers to read it at Sunday meeting. Nine assistants attended the session that approved the order, and a majority would serve as judges of the Court of Oyer and Terminer in 1692: John Richards, Samuel Sewall, Jonathan Corwin, Wait Winthrop, and John Hathorne. Presumably many ministers were encouraged by the General Court's instruction to continue to preach jeremiads.[36]

The campaign for moral reformation did nothing to stop the Wabanaki, however, who continued to press their advantage in the spring of 1690. On May 20, Fort Loyal in Falmouth fell, with more than two hundred dead or captured, many of them killed after the fort surrendered. The French had guaranteed safe passage of the garrison to the English settlements to the south, but they could not contain their Native allies, who fell upon the English after they surrendered. Almost a hundred miles of coastline had been abandoned since the overthrow of Andros. The once prosperous Maine settlements were reduced to smoldering ruin, and only three towns north of the Piscataqua—Wells, York, and Kittery—remained in English hands. Close to four hundred refugees fled to Essex County, while others headed to Boston. The colony's already shaky finances were further strained by the mounting war costs.[37]

Massachusetts tried to seize the initiative by launching two expeditions against the French. The week before Fort Loyal fell, a small naval expedition led by Sir William Phips took Port Royal in Acadia. The ease of the victory and the profits from plundering the settlement soon convinced the provisional government to take bolder steps, despite warnings from some. Thomas Newton (the future prosecuting attorney at the witch trials) complained that "we have suffer'd greater loss by far at Casco than we have gained at Port Royal."[38]

In August Sir William Phips led a flotilla of thirty-four vessels carrying twenty-three hundred New England troops to attack Quebec. The expedition worked in concert with New York and Connecticut militia under Wait Winthrop's brother, Fitz-John. They would march north through New York, thus drawing Governor Frontenac out of Quebec to defend Montreal. However, the thrust against Montreal quickly dissolved, and the expedition against Quebec was a complete disaster. Adverse weather meant the fleet took two months to reach Quebec, completely losing any element of surprise. Frontenac was safely ensconced in the well-fortified city, with more men than Phips. After some brief skirmishing and a largely fruitless naval bombardment of the city the expedition headed home. The return voyage would prove disastrous. Food ran low as the unexpected length of the expedition strained ships that had been poorly supplied from the start. A major smallpox epidemic ravaged the fleet, and stormy seas led to the loss of four ships. Probably close to four hundred perished on the expedition, while the survivors managed to spread smallpox throughout the colony, causing many more deaths. The huge financial losses from the expedition would seriously hinder the colony's efforts to wage a war that would last until 1697. The government called for a massive increase in taxes, but it was not enough to cover the huge debt incurred from the failed expedition. In December 1690, Massachusetts was forced to issue paper currency to pay its creditors—principally the unpaid soldiers of the Canada expedition. There was little in the way of specie to back up the paper, however, and inflation soon overwhelmed the colony.[39]

The conflict was quickly approaching Essex County, escalating fear of attack. When Captain John Alden (the future accused witch) came to Marblehead in July 1690 to remove several cannon that defended the harbor, so that they could be used in the invasion of Quebec, he was met with what the General Court called "an insurrection of the people." The Marblehead militia captains ordered the beating of the drums, which soon gathered sixty to seventy men who angrily refused to let Alden strip the town of its defenses. The irate mob on the waterfront of Marblehead may have reminded Alden of the fate of the two Wabanaki captives brought into port in 1677. He wisely did not press the issue and returned to Boston empty-handed.[40]

Many Salem residents had suffered firsthand in King William's War. In the early 1680s numerous Essex County men had bought land in Maine, which was being resettled after the destruction of King Philip's War. Some of these men merely joined the widespread speculation in frontier lands that took place during that decade, but a good number of families moved up to Maine and settled there. For example, in 1680 the General Court granted the township of Westcustugo (present-day Yarmouth, Maine) to thirteen men, almost all from Essex County. The proprietors included George and John Ingersoll and Captain John Putnam's son Jonathan. George, John, and three other Ingersolls are included on a 1688 list of the owners of house lots in Falmouth, a few miles south of Westcustugo. Two more of the Ingersolls' kinsmen, brothers Robert and John Nicholson, are on the list, as is Thomas Cloyce, the uncle of the afflicted girl Mercy Lewis. Robert Nicholson was married to Winifred Bonython, whose family were the proprietors of Saco. Her niece was the afflicted Sarah Churchwell. These and many other former residents of Salem and Essex County sought refuge down south when they had to abandon their Maine homes—those who survived, that is. Thomas Cloyce was killed when Falmouth was attacked in 1690. His sister-in-law Sarah Cloyce would be charged with witchcraft two years later.[41]

More than forty participants in the Salem witch trials—from afflicted girls and accused witches to Governor Phips—had lived in Maine, owned land there, or had a close family member from the frontier. In the exodus, people had lost their lives and their homes, and real estate speculations were now worthless. Residents of Salem and surrounding towns had to take in evacuees while also sending loved ones north to fight. Everyone contributed higher taxes to pay for the war and to care for the refugees. And many waited in fear for the Wabanaki and their French allies to attack Essex County.[42]

The war had an impact on the witch trials in 1692. New Englanders had long considered the Native population to be heathens in league with the devil. In the course of the seventeenth century, French fur traders and Jesuit missionaries in northern New England and the borderlands of Quebec and Acadia had cemented an alliance with the Wabanaki and converted many of them to Catholicism. In the minds of the Puritans, the only thing that could possibly be worse than being a heathen was being a Catholic. English fears of Catholics had been confirmed by the Gunpowder Plot of 1605, when a cabal had threatened to blow up Parliament. Those qualms had been nurtured by the Stuarts, who earnestly desired to rule as Catholic absolute monarchs. And the fears came into full bloom in the Popish Plot (1679–81), a fictitious conspiracy to take over England and Scotland that resulted in widespread anti-Catholic hysteria. Now the plot had come to America: the Pope and his minions, along with their heathen associates, had allied with Satan to destroy New England.[43]

Soon the discovery of the plan for a slave insurrection suggested that slaves had joined Satan's unholy alliance. In 1690 an escaped black slave revealed the plot when he was captured. He claimed he had run away to join Isaac Morrill, a French-speaker from the Isle of Jersey who had recently arrived in Newbury. The slave claimed that Morrill had been spying in the region in preparation for an invasion of northern Essex County by five hundred Native Americans and three hundred French troops. The freed black and Indian slaves would add to this onslaught. A second slave confirmed that Morrill, aided by a French fleet, planned to destroy the English and their settlements. Morrill was soon arrested and put in jail, thus foiling the plan.[44]

The growing war panic combined with losses in Maine and the failure of the Quebec expedition did nothing to ease the growing partisanship in provincial politics, providing more evidence for Satan's presence. There had been some political disagreements under the old charter, but nothing like the factionalism that began to emerge after the Glorious Revolution. Andros had been a lightning rod—removing him was something almost all people could agree upon. Once he was gone from office, the provisional government of Bradstreet and most of his old deputies, now without a charter, reported to England and awaited word of the formation of an official government. Unfortunately, William and Mary were busy with more pressing matters of state, and it would be two years before Governor Phips would arrive with a new charter. In the meantime, factions began to reemerge. Puritan conservatives pressed for a return of the 1629 charter, and die-hard royalists wanted a continuation of the Dominion of New England. In between there were a range of opinions, though the common denominator was a desire for a competent and honest administration that could effectively defend the colony. With the provisional government seemingly powerless to stop the reverses in the war, the complaints against it grew.[45]

There was a major shift in politics and political leadership in the 1680s in towns throughout Massachusetts. The politics of deference gave way to a new order, as more men became actively involved in local politics. In large part, this was a response to two related factors: war and taxes. King Philip's War had placed a substantial new burden on each town to provide money and soldiers for the colony. Taxes skyrocketed during the war. For example, from June 1675 to August 1676, Woburn paid £530 in rates (taxes), a far cry from the £30 it had paid the previous year. The colony's rates consisted in part of a poll tax, a regressive tax on individuals which made a much heavier proportional burden on the poor. Although fewer rates were called for after the war ended, taxes remained several times above their prewar levels. High taxes and a postwar economic slump meant the 1680s were a decade of hardship. In 1684, no less an authority than Governor Bradstreet warned Edward Randolph, "The people here as you know are generally very poor." That same year, the small central Massachusetts town of Mendon complained to the General Court that the colony's taxes were so high, they could no longer afford to hire a minister.[46]

Growing taxes led to increased attention to and participation in town meetings, rising acrimony, and heated debates over budgets and other matters. Massachusetts towns had always had their internal divisions and disputes, but deference had been shown to traditional leaders; after the parties were asked to pray and reflect over the matter, they usually reached a peaceful compromise. In the 1680s, however, those long-standing community leaders and political brokers were being turned out of office by an angry electorate. It was a generational change, as younger men assumed a growing role in governing the colony. The change was also felt in the town militias. As war began in 1688 and men were called to duty on the frontier, they demanded to be led by officers they trusted. Commanders with decades of experience frequently were seen as old and out of touch, and younger men were voted in—often those who had actively campaigned for the post. Such self-serving efforts were also new to Massachusetts politics. In February 1690 the General Court added to this explosive mix by expanding suffrage. Now any adult male of good character who owned a modest amount of property and paid taxes could become a freeman of the colony. Some estimate that the approximately ten percent of the adult males of the colony eagerly took up the opportunity to become freemen in the sixty days following the legislation.[47]

Regardless of who was elected, the interim government seemed completely unable to run the war against the French and their Native allies. Since most of the fighting occurred in New Hampshire and Maine, much of the responsibility fell to the men of nearby Essex County. Salem's Bartholomew Gedney, colonel of the Essex County militia, was particularly busy. In May 1690, when residents of Wells threatened to abandon their town unless they received support from the militia, Gedney scrambled to find troops. Sergeant John Walcott of Salem Village offered to serve, but his father, Captain Jonathan Walcott, had difficulty finding men to accompany his son, especially on such short notice. Several months later Gedney was trying to raise more troops, this time targeting the Maine men who were living a tentative existence as refugees in Salem. Most lacked proper homes and jobs and were probably desperate for work and eager for revenge against the Wabanaki. Gedney optimistically declared them "prompt and ready for service."[48]

As recruiting became more difficult and resources drained away, it became increasingly clear that the colony needed aid. On November 29, 1690, Gedney, Stephen Sewall, and John Higginson Jr. were among ten Salem men who wrote the governor and assistants urging them to ask the crown for help in the war, "being under a deep sense of the deplorable condition of this poor country, by reason of our French and Indian enemies."[49] The following April, Gedney and William Stoughton were among the seven commissioners appointed to go to Wells to negotiate an extension of a truce. Gedney did not actually make the trip but four other commissioners did, and the Natives agreed to a temporary extension. By this time, Wells was the northernmost settlement left in Maine. All the English townships north of it had been abandoned by the settlers and destroyed by the Wabanaki and their French allies.[50]

The colony seemed poised to fall into anarchy. The growing military and financial disaster highlighted the interim government's ineffectiveness. People began to publicly call the government into question, and soldiers' resentment grew as their paper money continued to lose value. An increasingly partisan General Court wrestled with these problems without solution. The optimism of the Glorious Revolution was gone, and people yearned for a government that could stabilize the colony. As one pessimistic writer succinctly put it, "I question whether we shall live to see any more happy days."[51] Cotton Mather believed the terrible events were a sign of the pending second coming of Christ: "I am verily persuaded, the judge is at the door; I do without any hesitation venture to say, the great day of the Lord is near, it is near and it hastens greatly."[52]

Finally in late 1691 there was some hope that steady and secure government was coming. After many months of careful negotiations between the Massachusetts agents and the crown, a new charter was issued for Massachusetts Bay on October 7, 1691. The charter gave unprecedented privileges for a royal colony, confirmed ownership of Maine, and incorporated Plymouth Colony into an expanded Massachusetts Bay Colony. Although the deputies to the assembly would be elected by the freemen of the colony, and the assembly would elect the governor's council, the governor, who was appointed by the king, would have far-reaching power.

He would be able to veto the choice of a councilor as well as the assembly's bills. The governor and council would have full control of the appointment of sheriffs, judges, and other officials. This was a vast improvement on the Dominion of New England, but it would be far from enough for the Puritan old guard. While Increase Mather grudgingly accepted the new charter as the best they could get, his fellow agents Elisha Cooke and Thomas Oakes instead looked for a legal challenge or other ways to block the new charter. They were particularly angered over the liberty of conscience granted to all Protestants, which meant that Massachusetts was no longer a Puritan colony. Indeed, the charter confirmed the change already made by the provisional government—freemen of the colony no longer needed to be members of the Puritan church.[53]

Unfortunately, the new charter left many things still up in the air. It essentially voided all of the laws of Massachusetts Bay, leaving the substantial task of rewriting them to the new government. The irregularities noted by Andros now had to be addressed. All laws had to be in harmony with English law, and any laws passed had to be approved by the crown. This presented the legislature with a huge and pressing task, for the colony functioned in something of a legal no-man's-land until a new law code was passed and approved by parliament. Until that time, no legal decision was truly on firm ground, extending the uncertainty that had begun under the Dominion and continued under Bradstreet's interim government. The problem was particularly acute for the judicial system, which had to be re-created by the General Court. Many people had been unwilling to bring their civil cases before the Andros court, which they saw as biased, and the uncertainties (critics would go so far as to label it anarchy) of the inter-charter years did nothing to encourage people to come forward. So by 1692 there was a reservoir of pent-up local complaints and differences between neighbors. Unfortunately, the new charter provided no immediate solution. The county courts could not meet until they were re-created by the legislature. This meant that unresolved conflicts would continue to grow and even boil over, with some disputes even helping to fuel witchcraft accusations.[54]

The competence of the new governor, Sir William Phips, was also a concern. Although he was a political ally of the Mathers, he was a rustic character from Maine, only recently accepted for membership in the Mathers' church. He had little political experience, and the colony was still recovering from his failed Quebec expedition. Even worse, it would be months before Phips arrived in Massachusetts to assume authority under the new charter. Although rumors of the new charter and Phips's appointment had been swirling for months, news of his appointment reached Massachusetts only in late January 1692, about the time that witchcraft accusations were beginning in Salem Village. The new governor would not arrive in the colony until May 14. In the meantime, uncertainty and instability would build like a storm over the city upon a hill.[55]

CHAPTER THREE

Drawing Battle Lines in Salem Village

The Lord said unto my Lord, sit thou at my right hand,
until I make thine enemies thy footstool.

—Beginning of Samuel Parris's sermon, November 22, 1691[1]

SALEM VILLAGE WAS IN MANY ways a typical settlement in Massachusetts Bay, and yet history has made it stand out—as the location of what was by far the largest and most lethal witch hunt in American history and the last major episode in the English-speaking world. What was so special about Salem? As we have seen, the same conditions made the entire Massachusetts Bay Colony in the early 1690s vulnerable to a witchcraft crisis. Clearly, other factors had to be at work in Salem.

The initial English settlement of Salem dates to 1626, when Roger Conant led a group of about twenty families to the place the Pawtucket Indians called Naumkeag, "fishing place." It was an apt description for the sizable, plentiful, and well-protected harbor. The location had been a thriving Native village until 1616, when a great plague began. The Pawtucket had no resistance to newly introduced European diseases, and in a three-year

period much of the Native population of coastal eastern New England succumbed. When Conant and his group arrived, there were only a handful of
Native Americans left, and Naumkeag was largely a widowed landscape of
deserted cornfields and desolate wigwams. The Englishmen moved south
from Cape Ann, when they abandoned the Dorchester Company's fishing
station there. The subsequent bankruptcy of the Dorchester Company meant
that the settlement at Naumkeag would become a part of a new venture,
eventually named and chartered as the Massachusetts Bay Company. In
1628 the company sent John Endicott, the new governor, along with about
one hundred settlers to pave the way for a major migration. Although there
were some disagreements between Conant and Endicott and their respective followers, the two groups peacefully worked out their differences.
As a symbol of that harmony, they renamed their settlement Salem, from
shalom, the Hebrew word for "peace" (as in Jerusalem, which means "city
of peace"). In the summer of 1630 a fleet of eleven ships and seven hundred
settlers arrived in Salem, led by yet another new governor, John Winthrop.
He and the majority of the new arrivals decided to push farther south down
the coast, where they established Boston, making it the seat of the new colony. Thus, Salem was the first settlement of Massachusetts Bay, and though
it was quickly eclipsed in size and authority by Boston, it would remain the
second most important settlement in Massachusetts Bay throughout the
colonial era, a populous and prosperous port town that provided political,
religious, and economic leadership to the colony.[2]

The early settlers of Massachusetts Bay have traditionally been depicted
as a somewhat homogeneous group of English Puritans who largely hailed
from East Anglia. While the population was overwhelmingly English and
most believed in some version of Puritanism, there was still considerable diversity in Salem and other Massachusetts towns. The early settlers of Salem
came not just from East Anglia but from different parts of England. Conant
and Endicott and most of their followers, for example, hailed from the
southwest of England, the region known as the West Country. At the time
each part of England had its own unique practices, customs, and religious
beliefs, and settlers brought these traditions with them to Massachusetts.
For example, West Country inhabitants were less likely to be adherents
to Puritanism than East Anglians. In its initial English settlement, then,
America was a place in which various English traditions collided and inter-
acted while maintaining their own distinct identities.[3]

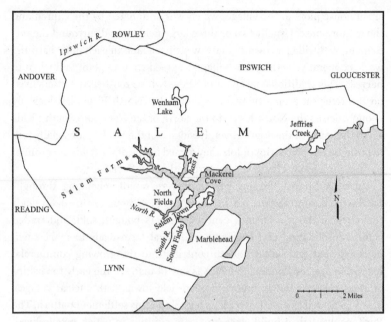

Map of Salem in the early 1640s. Drawing by the author.

Salem Village from the 1630s through the 1650s was similar to settlements elsewhere in the region. As the growing population needed new land, people gradually began to move away from the initial coastal townships, into the interior. Settlers received grants of land in the area first known as Salem Farms (and later known as Salem Village), and moved into other parts of Salem's expansive hinterlands. Like most of the founding towns of Massachusetts Bay, Salem covered a huge geographic area. The initial town boundaries include not only what is now the City of Salem but also all or parts of present-day Peabody, Danvers, Marblehead, Middleton, Beverly, Manchester, Wenham, Topsfield, and Swampscott.[4]

The original settlement took root on the harbor front at Salem Neck, bounded by the North and South Rivers. This area soon grew to be the waterfront sometimes known as Salem Town. The Neck tended to be settled by families that had migrated from East Anglia. Settlement on the Neck and adjacent acreage reflected English medieval traditions of small, nuclear villages in which people lived in close proximity to each other and the church and practiced open-field farming. In such a community everyone lived on small house plots in the village, which was dominated by the church and the manor house. Usually two or three large fields would surround the settlement, with villagers owning narrow strips of land in each field. Farming was a cooperative activity; the villagers agreed what to plant and when to harvest. This tradition continued in Salem, where most early settlers lived on the Neck on a one- or two-acre house lot. North Fields lay, logically enough, across the North River, to the north of the Neck, and South Fields sat to the south of the South River. Residents of the Neck made a daily trek to farm the ten-acre strips or lots they owned in one of the fields. A common pasture for livestock lay at the western end of the Neck.[5]

These traditional farming practices were rapidly changing throughout England, and particularly in East Anglia. Although some open fields remained in the seventeenth century, farmers bought, sold, and traded acres, consolidating and enclosing individual farmsteads to make them more efficient and better able to contribute to the growing commercial market in greater London. Salem was one of many of the early townships of Massachusetts Bay to maintain open-field towns with nuclear villages. Spiritual as well as practical reasons lay behind this settlement pattern. The Puritans wanted to build close-knit communities in which people lived, worked, and prayed together. At the same time, a nuclear settlement was more easily defended in case of attack. And with the meetinghouse in the middle of the village, all residents would have only a short walk to attend worship services. In most Massachusetts towns the outlying fields were turned into enclosed farms within a few years or at most several decades after settlement, just as was happening in England. Historians have put forward many explanations for the shift. Some see it as East Anglians demonstrating their regional preference. Others see the convenience of living on one's farmland as outweighing spiritual needs. Still others point to the arrival of new immigrants and the concomitant need for more land. Yet in Salem throughout the seventeenth century both the North and South Fields continued to consist of relatively small lots of farmland owned and worked by individual inhabitants of the Neck.[6]

Meanwhile, the Old Planters, largely immigrants from the West Country, lived on larger tracts, roughly one hundred to two hundred acres, lying to the north and west of Salem Neck. While it was only fitting that these first comers be granted more land, it was also fortuitous, for those from the West Country practiced a very different kind of agriculture than did East

Anglians. The rocky lands of Cornwall, Devon, Somerset, and Dorset in the southwest of England were better suited for livestock than for cereal crops. Farmers tended to live on their own enclosed farmsteads, apart from their neighbors, and did not need to work in concert with them. Roger Conant and most of the Old Planters lived on the north side of Salem Harbor on their large tracts, near the Bass River. In 1668 this region would split off from Salem and form the town of Beverly (named after a town in England).[7]

Still other parts of Salem drew different sorts of settlers. Aside from Salem Harbor, there were smaller anchorages to the south at Marblehead and to the north at Jeffries Creek. Both appealed to those who combined fishing with farming for a living. Marblehead in particular attracted those who seemed much more interested in pursuing cod than Puritan worship. Few church members lived here, and the area quickly gathered a profane reputation. Salem did not complain when Marblehead became a separate township in 1648. Yet the towns have always been somewhat tied to each other. Marbleheaders attended worship in Salem—or at least in theory were supposed to attend—until their own meetinghouse was constructed and a church formed in 1684. Furthermore, Marblehead provided many of the hands who manned the fleets of Salem's merchants. To the north, the settlement at Jeffries Creek incorporated as the town of Manchester in 1643. West of Manchester, settlement began at Great Pond (present-day Wenham Lake) in late 1638 with lands granted to a group of East Anglians, many of whom had migrated together from Suffolk, England. An isolated pocket of settlement far removed from Salem Town, Wenham was incorporated as a town in 1643.[8]

To the west of Salem Town and Beverly lay the large interior section known as Salem Farms. Here were the largest individual tracts of land granted by the town, as well as a few granted by the Bay Colony. In a society in which land equaled status and civic leaders were drawn from the upper ranks, Salem and other Massachusetts towns granted the largest holdings to these pacesetters as a reaffirmation of their place in society and to give them the means to devote more time to running the town's affairs. It should come as no surprise that the largest landholder in Salem Farms was John Endicott. The former governor of Naumkeag continued to lead the community after the arrival of Governor Winthrop and would become governor of Massachusetts Bay in the 1650s, after John Winthrop's death in 1649. Endicott's neighbor to the south was Emmanuel Downing, Winthrop's brother-in-law. When he arrived in Salem in 1638, Downing purchased a three-hundred-acre parcel, and soon was granted an adjoining five hundred acres of upland and eighty of meadow. Other prominent citizens were given large tracts in Salem Farms, including William Hathorne, who would receive two hundred acres in the western part of the farms, around Hathorne Hill. West of Hathorne (in present-day Middleton) lay seven hundred acres that the General Court granted in 1638 to Richard Bellingham, a future governor. The colony often granted such large interior parcels to colonial leaders, essentially to reimburse them for their time and expense in their otherwise unpaid service to the colony.[9]

The elite leadership of the colony developed large estates that mimicked those of England's gentry. Downing is a good case in point. He named his 880-acre estate Groton, after his wife's home in England, and he surely intended to live there as the lord of the manor. He even went to great expense to bring a "duck coy" (decoy) with him from England—an elaborate series of nets and hoops employed on a pond to catch ducks, so that he and his guests would be provided with fresh game. Soon after his arrival in Massachusetts in 1638, the General Court granted Downing the right to establish a coy in Salem, prohibiting anyone else from discharging a gun within a half mile of the pond without Downing's permission. Downing promptly purchased another fifty-acre parcel with two ponds, long known as the Coy Ponds, in present-day Marblehead.[10]

Not all the settlers of Salem Farms were granted such lofty holdings, and many of the vast tracts were soon divided or occupied by renters. Hathorne's growing civic responsibilities and merchant interests drew him to Salem Town. Although all his children, including John, the future judge, were born at Hathorne Hill, in 1647 he sold his lands in Salem Village to John Putnam, Daniel Rea, and Richard Hutchinson. Governor Richard Bellingham sold his seven hundred acres to Bray Wilkins and two other men in 1660. Two years later, when the General Court granted three hundred adjoining acres to Major-General Dennison, he immediately sold the tract to Wilkins. Emmanuel Downing returned to England in 1652 and leased his lands to a series of men, culminating with John Procter in 1666. After the death of Governor Endicott and his son, some of the Endicott property was rented. Notably, in 1678 Francis and Rebecca Nurse entered into a twenty-year rental agreement with an option to purchase a substantial tract to the west of the Endicott home farm and orchard.[11]

In the 1650s and 1660s Salem underwent a transformation, with the basis of the community's economy shifting from farming to commerce. This would have a particular impact on Salem Farms. Originally, lands here were granted to a wide range of individuals, including merchants, craftsmen, and artisans who practiced their trades and carried out subsistence farming. In the 1650s these men were increasingly drawn to the growing mercantile activity of Salem peninsula, an emerging urban waterfront core. As William Hathorne and others sold their lands in Salem Farms for smaller holdings on the peninsula, property in the Farms was sold to men interested in commercial farming—crops that could feed the growing populations of Salem and Boston, or be shipped to other English colonies in North America or the Caribbean. Some men amassed substantial agricultural holdings. John Porter Sr., for example, became Salem's largest landowner, holding more than fifteen hundred acres by 1650. Much of this land was farmed by Porter and his sons, though at least a dozen families were their tenants. Porter even owned a warehouse in Salem Town for his agricultural exports. While Porter concentrated his holdings, other grants were dispersed. Two hundred acres originally granted to two prominent early settlers (Francis Weston and Elias Stileman) were sold and divided into smaller farms. By 1660 this parcel had been divided among ten families, forming the core of Salem Village.[12]

The growing specialization of Salem Farms and Salem Village would lead to other problems. As the value of land grew in the 1650s and 1660s disputes arose over the boundaries between Salem and the adjoining towns of Topsfield and Lynn. Moreover, as civic leaders such as Hathorne and Endicott moved away from Salem Farms, they lost touch with their former neighbors, and the residents of the Farms began to feel isolated and alienated from town politics. Their departure left a leadership vacuum, leading to the rise in prominence of the Putnam family. In 1647, John Putnam Sr. purchased Hathorne Hill and received a grant from the town of a hundred acres. His three sons, Thomas, John junior, and Nathaniel, would serve as selectmen, in which role they defended the interests of the small farmers and tenants of Salem Farms. As Salem Town grew as a maritime commercial center virtually all residents prospered. Yet the merchants accumulated far more wealth than their farming neighbors. After 1660, the merchants of Salem controlled a substantial amount of the town's wealth. Soon this economic fact would be reflected in the political and social leadership of the community, leading to disquiet among the residents of Salem Farms.[13]

In one part of Salem Farms, this disquiet manifested itself in the widespread acceptance of Quakerism. The southernmost section of Salem Farms, The Woods, was located along the Lynn line. Virtually all of Salem's Quakers were mariners, artisans, or owners of small farms who came from The Woods, constituting the most substantial Quaker community in early Massachusetts. However, this was a colony where authorities dealt harshly with Friends, whom they viewed as apostates. And while it reserved the most severe penalties—whippings and several times even death—for those Quakers who dared to proselytize in Massachusetts, the Quaker residents of Salem had no easy time of it. By the mid-1660s there were sixty-three Friends (thirty-seven men and twenty-six women) in Salem, about 9 percent of the adult population.[14]

The distance of Salem Farms to Salem's core settlement and its meetinghouse along the harbor would soon lead to efforts by those in the Farms to separate from the mother town. Some homes were as far as seven miles away, making it extremely inconvenient for Farms residents, who had to go to the town regularly to perform their civic duties and, most important, to worship on the Sabbath. Often when newer outlying settlements reached a critical mass of population, they applied to their parent town and the General Court to be granted a separate township. Indeed, Wenham (1643), Manchester (1645), Marblehead (1649), and Beverly (1668) all won independence. Sometimes this could be a lengthy and contentious process, as turned out to be the case in Salem. It took thirteen years for the settlers of Wrentham to receive independence from Dedham, even though all residents of Wrentham lived more than fifteen miles away from the Dedham meetinghouse. Near the culmination of the struggle in 1673, Wrentham settlers accused Dedham of keeping them in a state of colonial dependency.[15]

Salem Town dragged its feet even longer than Dedham did when Beverly attempted to split off. The initial step came in 1647 when the residents of Mackerel Cove on the east side of the Bass River successfully petitioned to be released from night watch duty, due to their distance from Salem Town. Three years later it took three petitions from these men and their neighbors before Salem agreed to let them hire their own minister. In 1659 these residents petitioned to complete the separation process and become an independent town, but to no avail. Seven years later, Salem finally allowed a quasi-independence by which the Mackerel Cove men could elect selectmen and other officers but still acted in concert with Salem. In 1668 the split was formalized and the General Court incorporated Beverly as a town—twenty-one years after the effort began with the Mackerel Cove petition.[16]

Salem Village stated making noises for independence from Salem Town just as Beverly's separation was being finalized. It appears that Beverly's independence was a tipping point, and Salem Town decided it had allowed too much of its township to be carved off. While it was not uncommon for new towns to be partitioned out of old ones, this happened only nine times prior to 1670 in Massachusetts, with four of the nine cases involving a town being created by separation from Salem. Salem Town was therefore not enthusiastic to see it happen again. Given Beverly's example, Salem Village should have anticipated a prolonged struggle but did not.[17]

The battle lines between Salem Town and the Salem Farms/Salem Village region were quickly drawn. A 1666 petition from several residents of Salem Farms to hire their own minister fell on deaf ears at town meeting. The next year the town took issue with the men from Salem Farms being exempted from night watch duty due to their distance from town, even after a petition to this effect from thirty-one Salem Farmers received approval from the General Court. The issue came to a head again in 1669, when Salem Town raised a tax to build a new meetinghouse. Twenty-eight residents of Salem Farms refused to pay unless the rest of the town agreed to contribute when the Farmers built their own meetinghouse. Their concern was ignored by the church, and the next year the Salem Farmers petitioned the General Court for permission to build a meetinghouse and hire a minister.[18]

Because of continued opposition from Salem Town, it took two years, but on October 8, 1672, the General Court granted Salem Village the right to organize itself as a parish and hire its own minister. Finally, people would not have to make the long trek to the harbor for Sabbath. Yet it was only a partial victory. The village still remained a part of Salem. Furthermore, while the Salem Village committee could collect taxes to build a meetinghouse and pay a minister, the General Court had not allowed them to form a church. In seventeenth-century New England, everyone went to the meetinghouse to attend worship. A church was not a building; rather, the term referred to a core group of congregants who were "saints," that is, had been accepted into full church membership, with eligibility to receive the sacraments of communion and baptism for their children. Villagers who wished to receive these sacraments had to be accepted as church members in Salem Town or in neighboring towns.[19]

Salem Village's parish status would help lead to the largest witchcraft outbreak in American history. Paul Boyer and Stephen Nissenbaum's 1974 book, *Salem Possessed: The Social Origins of Witchcraft*, remains one of the most important works written on the trials, in large part because of the pioneering way it details how parish status combined with other factors to exacerbate tensions and give rise to factionalism. Lacking a formal town government and a church membership, Salem Village experienced a power vacuum. The only elected body was the village committee, which oversaw the hiring and paying of a minister and the construction and upkeep of the meetinghouse. The committee would become a center of dissension in a community where factionalism became increasingly acrimonious.[20]

Surely no one in Salem Village foresaw such difficulties in December 1672, when the residents voted to spend £40 to build a meetinghouse on an acre of land donated by Joseph Hutchinson. The following spring, the village men raised the 34-by-28-foot building. The open and simple structure was typical of neighboring meetinghouses. It was two stories tall, with the second floor consisting of a balcony. As a gesture of communion, the Salem Town church donated its old pulpit and bench for the deacons to sit on. All benches would have faced the pulpit, where the minister delivered his sermons and read from the Bible. The building initially lacked any glass windows, relying on shutters to keep out animals and foul weather. There was neither fireplace nor chimney, so the meetinghouse would have been particularly cold during the winter, especially since Puritan services lasted much of the Sabbath. The seating pattern reflected social rank, with the wealthy and prominent at the front. Women sat on one side and men on the other. The balcony was reserved for children, servants, and slaves.[21]

Clearly, Salem Village's indeterminate status was not the only cause of the trials. No witch trials took place in Beverly or Wrentham, nor in other towns that went through similarly difficult foundational processes. Though Newton was a parish of Cambridge for more than thirty years before achieving independence, it appears never to have developed serious factions. Other towns had courted controversies over creating parishes and choosing a minister, as exemplified by the early career of Jeremiah Shepard, a 1669 Harvard graduate who was invited to Rowley as a successor to his deceased brother Samuel in late 1672. Jeremiah was initially given a one-year contract (it would be renewed twice), but from the start he was a polarizing figure who had his detractors. Some worried that Rowley could not afford

Replica of the Salem Village meetinghouse. This replica, depicting the meetinghouse as
it was in 1692, was built on the grounds of the Rebecca Nurse homestead in 1984. It was
constructed as a set for the movie *Three Sovereigns for Sarah*, the story of Sarah Cloyce
and her sisters, Rebecca Nurse and Mary Esty. Photograph by the author.

two ministers (Samuel Phillips served as teacher, or assistant pastor). Some
complained of Shepard's "loose tongue," while others were "not satisfied to
his piety, nor spirit," nor the company the young minister kept. When his
contract was not renewed for a fourth year, Shepard took his case to the
entire town. Reverend Phillips, who by now opposed Shepard, noted his
"evil speech" made before town meeting in February 1675. Phillips further
observed that one church member hated Shepard so much that "if she had
an opportunity he doubted not that she would cut his throat." When his
contract expired several months later, Shepard refused to leave town or
the pulpit. One Sunday morning the two ministers had a nasty confrontation before the entire congregation over who was going to give the sermon,
Shepard or Phillips.[22]

Shepard was forced to sue for his salary for the third year of his contract,
which the selectmen had refused to pay. After a long, bitter, and very public
dispute that created a lasting division within Rowley, the parties eventually reached a financial settlement. Shepard soon was invited to preach
in nearby Chebacco, a district of Ipswich, which is now the town of Essex.

Settlers of the district lived up to seven miles away from Ipswich church, so they were attempting to gain permission from Ipswich and the General Court to establish a parish, build a meetinghouse, and hire a minister. However, objections were raised by people living in the center of Ipswich, and the General Court had to appoint a commission to sort things out. In the meantime, Shepard moved on to a position in Lynn, and Reverend John Wise soon began his long and successful career in Chebacco Parish. While the religious discord in Rowley and Chebacco was substantial, it never led directly or indirectly to witch trials. Both communities would see only a handful of accusations in 1692.[23]

Two Essex County communities that did suffer from serious factional conflict in the 1670s and 1680s would be at the center of the witchcraft outbreak: Salem and Andover. Andover was established in 1642, but by the 1680s it was undergoing growing pains. The construction of a new meetinghouse in 1680 necessitated the establishment of a new seating plan, which caused considerable consternation. This was followed by a division concerning the successor to Francis Dane. The old and infirm minister had served Andover for more than thirty years and now needed help. In 1682 Thomas Barnard was hired to assist Dane, but the town did not feel it could afford to pay two ministers. Factions developed around the two men, with Barnard's supporters concentrated in the older, northern part of town and Dane's followers tending to reside in the more recently settled southern part of Andover. The differences in Andover seem to have followed English regional lines as well, as Dane had strong support among his fellow Hertfordshire men, as well as Scots and other settlers from the north and west of England, while Barnard's followers came from the West Country. Remarkably, groups from these different regions would retain close bonds through marriage alliances until the early eighteenth century. Tensions would build between the factions in 1689 when men from the north of Andover tried to close a tavern opened in the southern end of town by Dane's kinsman William Chandler.[24]

Salem Village would develop similar factional problems, largely forming around control of the ministry. It was unclear who had the right to hire and fire the minister, and this ambiguity would prove the ideal breeding ground for factionalism. As previously noted, the General Court only permitted the village to build a meetinghouse and hire a minister to preach in it, not to create a church; the "saints"—church elders—who lived in Salem

Village were actually members of the Salem Town church or other neighboring churches. The details of the hiring of the village's first minister, James Bayley, are not recorded, but it appears that the freemen of the village assumed this responsibility, for it was all the families of the village, not just the saints, who attended worship services. Indeed, in 1673 the villagers as a group voted to retain Bayley as their minister.[25]

The congregation's assumption of religious decision making clearly did not sit well with those Salem Town saints who lived within the boundaries of the village. They believed that they alone held the power to hire a minister. Signs of trouble quickly emerged. In 1673, even as the villagers agreed to keep on Bayley, fourteen residents did not pay their taxes to support his ministry. By 1679, a powerful minority of villagers, led by Nathaniel Putnam and Bray Wilkins, called for Bayley's removal. Unfortunately, given the village's political ambiguity, there was no simple way to resolve such conflicts, and animosity boiled over. Bayley's opponents petitioned the General Court, which, after considerable wrangling, approved the current system of letting the entire village agree on the appointment of ministers—at least until Salem Village established a covenanted church. Even this did not resolve the conflict. In 1680 the anti-Bayley faction gained the majority of seats on the Salem Village committee and forced Bayley to step down. In 1682 he accepted a call to be minister in Killingworth, Connecticut, and left Salem Village and its bitter factionalism behind.[26]

It soon became clear that the problem lay with the villagers and not with Bayley, for they would quickly have similar problems with their next minister. In April 1680 Nathaniel Putnam led a committee dominated by opponents of Bayley who were chosen to search for his replacement. In November 1680 the inhabitants voted to hire Reverend George Burroughs. Born in England and raised in Roxbury, Burroughs graduated from Harvard in 1670, a year after James Bayley. At the time, Harvard was a small institution. There were ten graduates in Bayley's class and only four in Burroughs's, so the men would have known each other fairly well, and they may have corresponded or even discussed Salem Village. Even had Bayley warned him against accepting the position, Burroughs was probably desperate for a job. He had served as minister in Falmouth, Maine, until the community was abandoned in August 1676, during King Philip's War. Like most of his Maine neighbors, Burroughs sought refuge in Massachusetts, living in Salisbury. He served for a time as the assistant to the elderly Reverend John Wheelwright, and then performed briefly as interim pastor after Wheelwright's death in 1679. Perhaps, too, Burroughs saw the Salem Village position as temporary. He never purchased land in Essex County and never sold his abandoned homestead in Maine, so it is possible he was simply biding his time, waiting for the resettlement of Falmouth. He would not need to buy a home in Salem Village, as it turned out: soon after he was hired, the town agreed to build a parsonage for him.[27]

Burroughs's tenure was shorter and more turbulent than Bayley's. In April 1682, merely a year and a half after coming to Salem, one of Burroughs's parishioners wrote to him complaining that "brother is against brother and neighbors against neighbors, all quarreling and smiting one another." By the spring of the following year the village committee stopped paying Burroughs, so he left town. The resettlement of Falmouth was under way, and Burroughs was preparing to resume his old post there. When he returned to Salem on May 3, 1683, to meet with the village committee to square his accounts, Captain John Putnam had Burroughs arrested for debt. Putnam had regularly advanced the minister money, in anticipation of receiving his salary. So when the village cut off the salary, Putnam sued Burroughs to ensure his repayment. The issue was eventually settled out of court, but it demonstrated just how acrimonious village politics had become. Furthermore, the image of the minister being arrested by the Essex County marshal must have made a lasting impression on many villagers.[28]

Even as the village began to suffer internal conflicts, it also endured a series of boundary disputes with the neighboring towns of Topsfield, Andover, and Wenham. In a time when town grants sometimes overlapped and boundary surveys were often imprecise, such disputes were common. These disagreements were serious matters, for they determined which community collected taxes on which properties. In 1679 Salem Village complained to the General Court that Wenham was attempting to claim lands that would deprive the village of many acres of lands and several families, as well as the taxes these people paid to support the ministry. The wife of John Dodge of Salem Village voiced concern over the rates and threatened that "if the Wenham men came there for rates she would make the blood run about their ears."[29] On another occasion Goody Dodge exchanged blows with a party of Wenham officials, only to have her elderly neighbor Goodman Edwards save her from further abuse when he entered the fray wielding a hoe. Tensions over disputed lands were even higher with neighboring Topsfield. In this case, both Salem and

Topsfield's parent town, Ipswich, had made some overlapping grants, so there were two claimants to some parcels. John Putnam Sr. of Salem Village owned much of the contested acreage. In 1682 Jacob Towne, John How, and Thomas Baker met with Putnam, asserting that they had liberty from the town of Topsfield to clear trees from lands Putnam claimed on the Topsfield side of the town line. The dispute between Putnam and the Topsfield men would not be resolved until long after the witch trials.[30]

Meanwhile, ministerial troubles continued in the village. Following Burroughs's departure, almost a year passed before the village found a replacement. In February 1684 Deodat Lawson was hired. Lawson, the son of an English Puritan minister, was educated at Cambridge and had immigrated to New England in the 1670s. He served for at most two years as pastor at Edgartown on Martha's Vineyard. By 1682 he had moved to Boston, where he worked in some secular pursuit until moving to Salem Village. Inevitably there was conflict. A group of villagers pressed Salem Town to gain permission to establish a covenanted church and to have Lawson fully ordained as their minister. In 1686 the village committee, including Captain John Putnam and his nephew Thomas Putnam, supported this effort.[31]

Others were opposed. In January 1687 Job Swinnerton, Joseph Hutchinson, Daniel Andrew, and Andrew's brother-in-law Joseph Porter filed a petition expressing grievances over the possible ordination of Lawson. Hutchinson seems to have been particularly troubled. He had donated the land for the meetinghouse; now he began to fence in the property and actively farm part of it, reducing access to the meetinghouse to a solitary gate. Factions formed around Lawson. The next month arbitrators from Salem Town sided with the opponents of ordination and encouraged the villagers to "desist at present the ordination of the Reverend Mr. Lawson till your spirits are better quieted and composed."[32] Within a year Lawson had moved on.

In a span of sixteen years three ministers had departed Salem Village due to factionalism. This was far from the norm. During the 1680s, a total of sixty-three men were hired as ministers by New England towns. They would serve an average of twenty-two years in those positions. As the Salem villagers admitted in a 1695 petition to Increase Mather and other divines, "We have had three ministers removed already, and by every removal our differences have been rather aggravated."[33] The community would endure yet more conflict as it sought and hired a fourth minister. In the spring of 1689 Salem Village entered negotiations with Reverend Samuel Parris,

Harvard-educated and apparently desperate enough to consider taking the vacancy in the contentious village.

Parris was born into a Puritan merchant family in London in 1653. In the late 1650s his family migrated to Barbados, where his father, Thomas, was a merchant and sugar plantation owner. When Samuel was approximately seventeen, Thomas sent him to Massachusetts to attend Harvard College. He probably came to Massachusetts in the company of his uncle, Thomas Oxenbridge, who migrated from Barbados in 1670 to become minister at Boston's First Church. Samuel's path had been laid out. Yet in 1673 the path took a turn. Samuel's father died, so he returned to Barbados after completing perhaps three years of Harvard's seven-year course of study, which culminated with the master of divinity degree. Some historians have suggested that he might have left Harvard because his father's death meant that he could no longer afford the substantial cost. However, Thomas had left Samuel all of his Barbados estate, worth perhaps about £7,000—an immense sum, especially for a twenty-year-old bachelor—and he should have been more than set for life. Had he remained in Massachusetts, he would have been among the wealthiest men in the colony. Clearly he left Harvard because he no longer wanted to pursue a career in the ministry. Instead, he would be a merchant, like his late father.[34]

Back in Barbados, Parris worked as a sugar merchant and broker. His income was enhanced by leasing the family sugar plantation. Yet within a few years his inheritance had dwindled. Exactly how and to what degree is unclear, but it seems to have been close to a total financial meltdown. This is rather surprising, since under most circumstances about the only thing that kept a Barbados sugar plantation owner from amassing substantial wealth was death from tropical disease. Some historians have suggested that the Parris plantation was among the many destroyed in the huge hurricane that devastated the island in 1675, yet it appeared to be functioning in 1679. A decline in the price of sugar in may have also been a factor. Regardless, Parris sold his properties in Barbados and moved to Boston in 1680 or early 1681. Here he married Elizabeth Eldridge (or Eldred) and continued to work as a merchant, but his reduced circumstances were soon apparent. In March 1682 he bought his first property in Boston, purchasing a shop and wharf from merchant Richard Harris for £270. Yet he had to borrow an additional £420 from Harris to purchase goods and begin operating as a merchant. A year later, Harris sued Parris to recover the loan.[35]

His biographer suggests Parris was a man driven to succeed—to provide the financial security for himself and his family that he had known as a youth. His studies at Harvard, his sugar plantation, and his work as a Boston merchant should have almost guaranteed considerable wealth and status, but Parris had failed at all of these undertakings. By 1689 his Harvard schoolmates were by and large accomplished ministers and respected members of their community. Meanwhile, the Boston waterfront was filled with the mansions and warehouses of prosperous merchants. Parris must have been particularly troubled by the rags-to-riches career of William Phips, whose warehouse sat next to Parris's in Boston. In the aftermath of the Salem witch trials, quoting from the Book of Numbers, Parris averred that "*God* has been righteously *spitting in my face.*"[36]

In any event, in the spring and summer of 1685 Parris served as temporary minister in the central Massachusetts frontier town of Stow. He continued to work as a merchant in Boston but enjoyed his work in Stow enough to seek a permanent ministerial appointment. On November 15, 1688, a committee from Salem Village began discussions with Parris, and soon invited him to give a sermon in the village on November 25. After the sermon, the congregation voted to offer the position to Parris. On December 10 they made him a formal offer, beginning what would turn into months of hard bargaining over the position.[37]

The village committee offered Parris the same salary paid to Deodat Lawson—£60 a year, with no expectation of an increase in the future. Although the money was below average, Salem Town would finally allow the new minister to be ordained, so, unlike his predecessors, he would enjoy the full rights and authority of his office. Another benefit was that he could live in the village-owned parsonage. Parris told the committee he would consider the offer and that "they should know in good time." Yet he never got back to the men. Instead, he waited for the villagers to invite him to Salem again to discuss the offer. This time he conditionally accepted a salary of £60, with a third to be in currency rather than provisions—hard currency was scarce in early Massachusetts and hence worth more than its face value. Parris provided the villagers a long list of other terms, and also asked that he be considered for a pay increase in the future should the community prosper (though he was willing to receive a reduction should it not). He asked to have control over what he was given for provisions, and that he receive them "at the price now stated," or lower, should prices drop. As the colony had recently entered into a war, foodstuffs were sometimes in short supply and prices were increasing. Parris was effectively seeking a hedge against inflation. Further, he asked for free firewood, as well as that contributions from people outside the congregation be considered a bonus over and above his salary. This concession, he noted, had been made to Reverend Lawson.[38]

In more affluent Salem Town, Reverend John Higginson's annual salary was £100 plus forty cords of firewood. When John Hale first came to Beverly in 1664, his salary was £70, and upon his marriage it was raised to £74. When Joseph Capen was hired in Topsfield in 1681, he was offered £75. Salem Village, by contrast, struggled to pay its minister. James Bayley was first paid £40 plus £7 for firewood. That salary was eventually increased to £55. In 1679–80, when the Bayley dispute reached Boston, the General Court ordered the village to increase his salary from £55 to £60. Bayley would receive a much more comfortable salary of £70 in Killingsworth, Connecticut.[39]

In the end, after considerable haggling and debating, the villagers ironed out a contract with Parris that met most of his demands. He began to preach in the village in July 1689, fully eight months after discussions began. Yet it soon became clear that the negotiations were not over. At Parris's encouragement, at an October 10 meeting a group of the villagers voted with only one objection to give Parris ownership of the parsonage and surrounding two acres of land. At the same time, this group voted to nullify a 1682 vote whereby the village had made it illegal to give or sell the parsonage to anyone. It was most unusual for a minister to be given—as opposed to leased—a parsonage, especially under such questionable circumstances. Unfortunately, a list of the names of the villagers present at the meeting does not survive. We do know that the men appointed to carry out the property transfer consisted entirely of members of the prominent Putnam family and their allies, so it seems likely that they dominated the meeting. Giving the property to Parris was a decision that would be questioned and debated by the villagers for years.[40]

From the time Salem villagers first approached Parris to the time they voted to deed him their parsonage, almost a year had passed. These negotiations were unusually lengthy and complex, suggesting several things. First, Parris appears to have studied Salem Village well and fully understood what was waiting for him. He knew about past problems with the ministers, and the details of their contracts. Considering that he insisted on a specific benefit given to Deodat Lawson, it is likely that he discussed the situation with the former minister, who lived in Boston at the time. Second, Parris wanted no more of the insecurity that he had faced on Barbados and in Boston. He drove a hard bargain, one that secured respectability and a modest level of economic security. Third, years of disputes not only had made villagers desperate for a minister who could bring peace but also meant that few were interested in the job. In fact, so notorious was the village's reputation that no one with a Harvard degree would be tempted to consider the position. Parris apparently had no competition, despite the months of negotiation, presumably because no one else was interested. He must have realized this and sensed the desperation; he knew he could push hard in the negotiations. In the end, Parris won his demands but also sowed the seeds of further strife in the community. Surely even before Parris was ordained, some villagers must have realized that they had settled for far less than they needed, and gotten a hard-nosed merchant rather than a man of God capable of uniting the village.[41]

The Salem Village parsonage that Parris had won was a substantial house for the day, befitting the prominence of the minister in the community. Built with a massive timber frame, the core of the house measured forty-two feet long and twenty feet wide. The two-story home consisted of two rooms on each floor, with one room on each side of the massive central chimney, in what is known as a hall-and-parlor plan. The principal room downstairs was the hall, where most daily activities took place, from cooking around the large fireplace to eating meals and reading the scriptures. The other first-floor room was the parlor, which served as a more formal living space. It housed the family's best possessions and also doubled as a master bedroom. Upstairs, the hall chamber and parlor chambers normally served as bedrooms, though Reverend Parris used one for his study. A lean-to had been added onto the back of the Salem Village parsonage by 1692, for Tituba described the devil approaching her once when she was in the "lean-to chamber." In 1692 the lean-to of the Parris parsonage probably consisted of just one service room—possibly the dairy—which measured approximately ten feet by ten feet. A lean-to running along the full length of the back side of a home creates a house form known as a saltbox, a form often considered to be the typical home of early New England because so many survive to this day. However, the average family in the 1690s occupied a much more humble residence, perhaps consisting of just one room, with lofts above for sleeping. Some of these houses had dirt floors. None of these small, simple homes survive, as they were either expanded into larger dwellings or torn down to make way for more substantial houses.[42]

Despite its impressive size, the Salem Village parsonage had its modest features as well, another sign of the limited financial resources of the community. The house had only a fifteen-by-fifteen-foot cellar, under just one room. This cut building costs considerably, as digging and stoning a cellar required a substantial amount of work, most of it done by a skilled stonemason. This cellar was inside the footprint of the building and did not serve as its foundation. Instead, the house sat on substantial timber beams that were laid directly on the ground. The only stonework was a small pile of rocks placed under the beams at the corners, to level the ground and add a bit of stability.[43] Such earthfast buildings were relatively common in New England in the seventeenth century and were even lived in by some wealthy colonists. However, with wooden sills sitting directly on the earth, such dwellings have relatively short life expectancies. The Salem Village parsonage lasted barely a hundred years. In 1784 Reverend Benjamin Wadsworth built at his own cost a substantial Georgian home close to the decaying old parsonage. While the Salem Village parsonage is long gone, the 1683 residence of the Topsfield minister still stands. The Parson Capen house (named for its first occupant) was a two-story hall-and-parlor house of dimensions almost identical to those of its Salem Village counterpart. The main difference between the two was that the Topsfield parsonage featured a substantial stone foundation under the entire home. Like its old parsonage, the community of Salem Village lacked a solid foundation, and decay would quickly commence.[44]

Regardless of whether people lived in a saltbox or a cape, there was no escaping the fact that these houses were small, crowded, and dark, with very little privacy, a far cry from the quaint homes depicted in New England lore and legend. Windows were expensive imports from England, so they tended to be small, and their greenish glass further reduced the light. Candles and simple oil lamps did not help the situation, nor did the unpainted interior woodwork. The home would have been full of smoke from the fireplaces and other smells of daily living, ranging from the unemptied chamber pot to the stew bones from last night's dinner, thrown just outside the front door. Nonetheless, they were more than adequate for early New

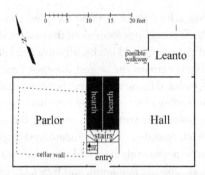

Plan of the Salem Village parsonage in 1692. This conjectural reconstruction
of the first floor (and the cellar underneath it) is based the documentary record as well
as the 1970 excavation of the site. Drawing by the author.[45]

Englanders, who spent long hours outside, tending to their livestock, crops,
and other chores.[46]

While New England Puritans worked hard and lived in a hierarchical
and patriarchal society, they are often wrongly stereotyped as dull, prudish
people who work dark clothes and constantly frowned. The Puritans had
a rich, vibrant culture. They believed in sober mirth—they had fun and
enjoyed a good joke. They drank in moderation and partook of companion-
able meals at the tavern. They enjoyed fine possessions. Puritan furniture
was often painted in gaudy colors, or richly carved out of woods of differing
hues. Fancy chair seats were embroidered in "turkey work," resembling the
bright and ornate Turkish carpets that graced some homes. Puritans dressed
to their station. The wealthy often wore brightly colored clothes decorated
with fancy lace and with gold and silver buttons. Only those of more modest
wealth and status who tried to dress like their betters found themselves before the court for violating the sumptuary laws.[47]

Most fancily dressed people in Salem Village would have been members
of the Putnam and Porter families, the elite of the community, who were
also the leaders of the growing factional conflict within it. John Putnam
Sr. and John Porter Sr. were early and successful settlers of Salem Farms.
Respected members of the Salem Town church, both men would serve as
selectmen and hold other local offices. By John Putnam's death in 1662
he had amassed eight hundred acres of land in the western part of Salem
Village to pass on to his sons. John Porter Sr. was the largest property owner
in Salem and one of the wealthiest men in the region. When Porter died in

1676, his estate was valued at £2,753 and included almost two thousand acres of land, with most holdings focused on the eastern side of the village. His farm included sixty sheep and lambs, fifty-five head of cattle, and thirteen horses, making it perhaps the largest livestock farm in the region. A guest to his well-appointed home would have been impressed with his many fine possessions, including silver spoons—a rare mark of wealth, status, and refinement at the time. Noteworthy, too, was that the probate inventory drawn up at his death recorded his three indentured English servants and two "Negro servants," presumably slaves. Most of this estate was passed on to Porter's three sons, Joseph, Benjamin, and Israel. On his death, they became the wealthiest men and largest taxpayers in Salem Village.[48]

Having settled on the eastern side of Salem Village, the Porters tended to associate more with Salem Town than with the village. Israel and Joseph Porter each served but one year each on the Salem Village committee, but Israel served twelve terms as a Salem Town selectman. Furthermore, none of the Porters joined the Salem Village church. Meanwhile, the Putnams became leaders of a sizable faction of Salem villagers made up mostly of residents of modest wealth. Though they were opponents on a number of issues, the Putnams and Porters were not always at odds with each other. Both families had supported Reverend James Bayley, for example. As late as 1690, members of both families would sign yet another petition by villagers to Salem Town, requesting separate township status. However, Samuel Parris and his role in the witchcraft crisis seem to have divided the families and their supporters into fiercely opposing political factions.[49]

On Tuesday, November 16, 1689, the Salem Village church was officially gathered, and Samuel Parris was ordained as its minister. Reverend Nicholas Noyes, Salem Town's junior minister, presided, and he was assisted by neighboring ministers Samuel Phillips of Rowley and John Hale of Beverly. Following the ordination ceremony, Parris gave his sermon, which stressed the importance of the sacraments. For decades, the Israelites, wandering out of Egypt and into the desert, had lacked sacraments. Then, led by Joshua, they crossed the Jordan River and God admitted them into a covenant with him. Similarly, the residents of Salem Village had lacked access to the sacraments. Some had sought them out occasionally in neighboring churches, but now they were available to all on a regular basis. Just as God had removed dishonor and the foul "Egyptian-like disgrace and reproach" for the Israelites, He would forgive Salem Villagers who now accepted the covenant and lived by it. It was the start of a new day in the village, a day for "rolling away your reproach from off you, by getting into the covenant of grace, and so coming under the seals of the covenant."[50]

Parris laid out their mutual responsibilities. As a servant of God, he noted, his duty was to be not only a role model but a judge of men—to "make difference between the clean, and unclean: so as to labor to cleanse and purge the one, and confirm and strengthen the other." Parris asked the villagers to love, respect, and obey him, to pray for him, and "to endeavor by all lawful means to make my heavy work as much as in you lies light and cheerful." Furthermore, their quarreling and "unchristian like behavior" must come to an end, otherwise Parris's life among them would be "grievous" and the former merchant noted his labor would be "unprofitable." They now had an ordained minister and a church that would help to heal their wounds and bring the community together. Furthermore, parishioners were on notice that Parris was beginning a campaign to expand the membership in that newly created church, as well as a crusade for moral reformation. Using the example of the Canaanites that Joshua had defeated, Parris warned, "When wicked men think themselves most secure many times they are most in danger."[51]

Following the sermon, Parris and his wife were among the twenty-seven villagers who signed the covenant, officially creating the Salem Village church. All were saints in other congregations who had transferred their membership to start the new church. The covenant itself is unremarkable and quite similar to those from neighboring churches. Nowhere does it suggest the turmoil that had enveloped the village, or the greater tragedy that lurked in the future. The only hint of trouble lies in the identities of the signers of the document. Twelve Putnams had joined the covenant, including Thomas Putnam Jr.'s sister, Deliverance Putnam Walcott. They were joined by Bray Wilkins and three members of his clan, who were neighbors and close political allies of the Putnams. So aside from Reverend Parris and his wife, sixteen of the twenty-five signers of the covenant (and ten of the sixteen men) were from just two families who, collectively, owned much of the land in the western end of Salem Village. None of the Porters signed the covenant, though many of them were members of the Salem Town church and thus qualified.[52]

Almost immediately, opposition began to form against Parris, as it had against the three previous ministers. When the villagers next met on December

17, they ordered Constable Edward Bishop to collect the ministerial rates from the thirty-eight families who were delinquent in their payments. It was an ominous sign to have more families withhold their taxes than had signed the covenant, and noticeable that not a single covenant signer owed any taxes. The tough financial times may explain why some parishioners were delinquent in their taxes. By the fall of 1691, the colony's unstable finances and the growing expenses of war had forced the General Court to raise taxes on local property owners to unprecedented levels. And as rumors circulated of enemy troops operating in Essex County, people must have truly wondered what, if anything, they were receiving in return for their taxes. Some residents may have shown their displeasure with the choice of minister and his financial settlement in a time-honored way in Salem Village—by withholding their taxes.[53]

Soon some became opposed to Parris for religious reasons. He had acted quickly to grow the church, and in his first year in office the number of members doubled. This increase was all the more remarkable considering that Parris established a rigorous test for membership when neighboring towns were loosening requirements in the face of declining membership. Under the leadership of Reverend John Higginson, for example, Salem Town's church had adopted the Halfway Covenant in 1665 (though the church accepted it only after Higginson threatened to resign). Salem Town also changed the requirements for church membership. Public confession of faith was replaced by private confession to the minister, along with the candidate's good behavior for one month. Easing membership and the Halfway Covenant made it easier to baptize the next generation of worshipers and allowed many leaders of the community to finally join the church. Rowley, Beverly, Lynn, and Marblehead all adopted the Halfway Covenant as well. Topsfield was the only holdout. So most of the saints who signed the Salem Village covenant had initially become church members in neighboring towns under looser rules than Parris now enforced for new members.[54]

Parris refused to compromise. Soon after his ordination, he met with the church members, and they agreed to an oral confession, supported by testimony from church members. The village church also rejected the Halfway Covenant, allowing baptism only to children whose parents were full members of the church. These policies would have a disastrous effect on church membership and created a rift in the community. Parris's campaign to increase membership soon reached a plateau. During his second year in

Salem, the church attracted but seven new members. Perhaps even more troubling was a growing absenteeism at weekly services and the failure of church members to show up regularly for communion.[55]

After the evening service on December 7, 1690, Parris complained about the waning attendance by church members. He also aired other concerns. He criticized the Lord's Table, equipped with just two pewter tankards for communion, and asked the congregation to make generous contributions to better furnish it. Finally, he raised the issue of electing church deacons— a seemingly straightforward process that would nonetheless drag on for months in the quarrelsome congregation. The two lonely pewter tankards on the communion table must have made Parris wistful about life in Boston, where wealthy congregations provided silver for the communion ware. He was pastor in a rural backwater, arguably the poorest and most contentious parish in the colony.[56]

Clearly, by 1691 Salem Village was divided on a range of issues, not the least of which was the Halfway Covenant. James Bayley had favored adopting the Halfway Covenant, while his successor, George Burroughs, had not. Perhaps this explains at least in part the Bayley supporters' opposition to Burroughs. Though the evidence is admittedly thin, Deodat Lawson appears to have supported the covenant. Parris, of course, opposed it. The village seemed unable to resolve the matter.[57]

Parris had based his stance on church membership and all other religious matters in Salem Village on a call for moral reformation. Some historians have suggested that his actions were the result of incompetence or ignorance. To the contrary—he was very knowledgeable about contemporary religious practices and firmly supported the efforts at moral reform that were under discussion at the time. Rather, it was his rigid commitment to orthodoxy and his evangelical piety that led him to fervently struggle to purify Salem Village.[58]

Parris's campaign for moral reformation and his effort to build his congregation initially stressed the benefits of being a member of the elect. He emphasized above all the sacrament of communion (or the Lord's Supper), which the church agreed to celebrate every six weeks at the end of the Sabbath worship service. Saints were required to attend, and the non-elect were not allowed to participate. In the summer of 1691, as Parris's recruitment efforts increasingly fell on deaf ears, his sermons began to take on a more strident, even warlike tone. In his sermon of July 19, 1691, for example, he noted that in giving his life "Christ Jesus hath purchased victory and conquest for believers.... Christ puts believers into a conquering capacity.... Christ furnisheth ye believer with skill, strength, courage, weapons, & all military accomplishments for victory. They are well appointed for war."[59] Parris's allusion to Christ's war against sinners may have been a reference to the growing hostilities on the northern frontier. A truce had been agreed to in November 1690, with formal treaty negotiations and an exchange of prisoners to start May 1, 1691, in Wells. However, the Wabanaki chiefs failed to meet the Massachusetts delegation, which included William Stoughton and Bartholomew Gedney. Fighting soon resumed, involving troops from Essex County.[60]

On October 11, 1691, continuing on the theme of Jesus's suffering, resurrection, and ascension into heaven, Parris noted that "Christ ascended with the sound of a trumpet.... Christ ascended in triumph." Like a conquering Roman, "this great champion" ascended in a chariot, followed on foot by his captives: "all our enemies, death, hell, the law and the devil."[61] So Christ, the "most glorious redeemer," offered salvation, but sinners who did not "embrace his offer" should know that "he is able to open the earth under thy feet to swallow thee; and to break the clouds over thy head to consume thee." Parris increasingly inserted martial imagery into his sermons, a direct challenge to those sinners who would reject Christ's offer and refuse to join the covenant. It would not be long before his opponents took up the gauntlet.[62]

A few days later, Parris's campaign against sinners broke out into open warfare in Salem Village. On October 16, 1691, elections were held for the village committee. The five men elected—Joseph Porter, Joseph Hutchinson, Daniel Andrew, Joseph Putnam, and Francis Nurse—were all opposed to Parris. A majority present at the village meeting voted not to collect Parris's salary for the year, though in theory the committee existed solely for that purpose. In truth, some villagers had been unhappy with Parris and the conditions of his hire since his arrival in Salem. The thirty-eight households that had refused to pay the rates to support the minister's salary in the fall of 1689 accounted for 20 percent of his pay. It still had not been paid a year later. The next year even fewer villagers paid their rates. In April 1691, the Village Committee determined that 29 percent of the 1690–91 rates remained unpaid. Many also refused to maintain the meetinghouse. In October 1690 the village had voted to make much-needed repairs to the eighteen-year-old building. Again, many were reluctant to contribute. In

April 1691, the village meeting wrote a petition to the General Court, asking it to order those who had not paid their assessment to do so.[63]

Parris's situation soon became dire. During November he called several meetings of the male members of the church. Seventeen men gathered at his parsonage on November 1. They agreed to send three representatives to the village committee, urging that they collect the rates and provide for the minister's other needs—particularly his firewood, which was all but gone. Firewood had been included in the long list of items that Parris had negotiated for when he first agreed to take the position in Salem Village, but somehow it had never made it into the written version of that agreement. When the church representatives attended the village meeting on November 10, the committee refused to listen. Rather, the committee insisted that the church members and the pastor send them a signed letter making the request for his salary and firewood. A subsequent meeting of Parris and the church men resulted in a decision to file suit against the village committee in the Essex County Court, which was meeting the next week. Parris also put out another plea to the church members for firewood.[64]

Cut off from his salary and firewood, a desperate Parris raised his warlike tone in his sermon on November 22. His text was from Psalm 110: "The Lord said unto my Lord, sit thou at my right hand until I make thine enemies thy footstool." God's word was "quick & powerful sharper than any two edged sword." The message was clear: the enemies of Parris and Salem Village church faced the wrathful vengeance of a righteous God.[65]

The village committee, however, paid no attention to Parris. They responded by calling a village meeting for December 1, to discuss their concerns with the minister. First, they questioned the legality of Parris's original contract with the town, approved by the village back on June 18, 1689. Second, they questioned the irregular manner in which the parsonage had been deeded to Parris back on October 10, 1689. Finally, they would discuss Parris's salary for the coming year and determine whether it would be paid by raising rates or by voluntary subscription. Essentially they were maneuvering to remove Parris from office. Unable to fire him, they planned to cut off his salary and his firewood and remove him from the parsonage.[66]

It is unclear whether the December 1 meeting ever took place. Parris himself recorded nothing that day in the Salem Village record book (though he also failed to write down any of his sermons for December). A deposition made by three of Parris's opponents in 1697, however, describes a contentious village meeting to which Parris was summoned to speak to his understanding of the initial agreement made between the village and him back on June 18, 1689. Parris violently objected to the terms listed in the record book, saying that "he never heard or knew anything of it, neither could or would he take up with it, or any part of it; and further he said they were knaves and cheaters who entered it."[67]

Salem Village's factional politics were not unique. Nostalgic views to the contrary, early New England towns were often rife with conflict, and religious issues were often at their heart. People regularly argued over the location of the meetinghouse and the seating plan for the congregation. Puritans also argued over the minister's doctrine. Boyer and Nissenbaum suggested that these factions, and ultimately the accusations of witchcraft, were grounded in the "dramatic commercial changes transforming Salem Town and their impact on Salem Village."[68] Economic anxieties preoccupied all villagers, and they seem to have been particularly frightening for the Putnams and their allies. This group included many of the less well-off families who tended to live in the western end of Salem Village, further from the lure of commercial opportunities in Salem Town. As a result, Boyer and Nissenbaum suggest, these people were seeing an erosion of their economic, social, and political standing in the community. Recently, historians have argued that religion, not social or economic forces, was of primary importance. In reality, while scholars might argue over which factor was the most important, economic well-being, social standing, and religious orthodoxy all were significant factors not just in Salem but in virtually every outbreak of witchcraft during the great age of witch hunts.[69]

Regardless of which factor ultimately was most important, the witchcraft accusations resulted from a long-standing failure of leadership. Not only did Salem Village's ministers fail to help resolve the divisions, but something about the ministry there brought out the worst in them. Overall, this was not a group to inspire confidence, let alone build a community of Christian believers in the face of adversity. Given its small size, poor pay, and frontier location, Salem Village was not able to attract the gifted divines who could have healed its wounds. None of those who served there had a particularly long or impressive career in the pulpit. James Bayley waited three years after graduating from Harvard in 1669 before getting his first job—in Salem Village. It would take him two years after leaving Salem before finding another position, in Killingworth, Connecticut—another frontier town. He lasted only nine years in Killingworth before moving back to Roxbury and spending the rest of his life as a doctor.[70] George Burroughs's career was of course cut short by his execution for witchcraft, but there is little in it to suggest he would have gone on to have an impressive career, given he was only able to gain positions in the frontier town of Salem Village, in Falmouth, and briefly in Wells, Maine. Indeed, his return to the dangerous edges of the frontier in Casco Bay in 1683 hints at his desperation. Falmouth had been entirely destroyed by King Philip's War and remained under constant threat during the uneasy peace of the postwar years. It appears that it took Burroughs four years to achieve his first position in Falmouth. Having fled from there in 1676, it took him five more years before his hire in Salem Village. These gaps in his resume suggest he was not considered a strong candidate for vacancies.[71] Deodat Lawson had a peripatetic career in England and New England, sometimes leaving the ministry for other pursuits. After departing Salem, he would need six years to land his next posting, in the Second Church of Scituate, Massachusetts. After less than four years there he returned to England, apparently intending to visit, but he never returned. In September 1698, his flock lamented about what to do, given "the long and still continued absence of their pastor."[72]

However, most historians of Salem witchcraft agree that Samuel Parris was the person who hardened the factions and ultimately galvanized them into action. His business failures and personal insecurities, combined with a combative personality and rigid orthodoxy, all but guaranteed his failure as a minister. Under his leadership, the tensions and divisions in Salem Village heightened. Parris's church stopped growing. Not only was absenteeism increasing, but the number of new members and baptisms declined in 1691. There would be no new members of the church and only seven baptisms between December 1691 and November 1692, a remarkably low figure given that there were approximately four hundred villagers who were neither baptized nor church members. The battle lines were drawn for a new kind of war—against sinners and worse.[73]

CHAPTER FOUR

The Afflicted

Talk of the devil and he is bound to appear.

—Proverb[1]

LOCAL CONFLICT AS WELL AS colony-wide problems led to the witchcraft crisis of 1692. Massachusetts Bay's military failures, religious tensions, and political and legal uncertainties were magnified in Salem Village, a place of endless strife and ministerial troubles. Yet in the end what happened at Salem in 1692 hinges largely on two groups—the alleged witches and their accusers. We start with the latter, those who declared themselves afflicted by the former, as well as the family members and friends who supported them. Indeed, as the key accusers were girls and young women who lacked legal status, there would have been no trials unless charges had been pressed by the male heads of the families of the afflicted.

What caused people to become afflicted? The explanations put forward seem nearly endless, but they can be placed in several basic categories: physical ailment, mental illness, group hysteria, and outright fakery. Some of the afflicted, though not all, would join the ranks of the accusers. Traditionally, the victims of Salem witchcraft have been referred to as "the afflicted girls," yet the group included some adult women, notably Ann Putnam Sr., and a couple of men, including the Native American John Indian as well as Judge Corwin's son. These people temporarily turned the legal system on its head, with marginalized elements of society dominating the courtroom as testimony givers and accusers in the most famous trials in early American history.[2]

During the fall and winter, a group of adolescent girls in a small northern community began to act strangely. Their symptoms ranged from subtle twitches to violent jerking of body parts and verbal outbursts. One girl woke up from a nap to find her "chin was jutting forward uncontrollably and her face was contracting into spasms." She was still twitching several weeks later when her friend "awoke from a nap stuttering and then later started twitching, her arms flailing and head jerking." Though beginning with one group of friends, the numbers of the afflicted rapidly grew outward. Soon there were twelve, next sixteen, and then eighteen suffering, in a community of just six hundred people. Even one teenage boy and a thirty-six-year-old woman would show symptoms of distress. In public gatherings, which traditionally called for quiet obedience from the youths, one cry would trigger another, leading to a din of outbursts and erratic behavior. Worried mothers and fathers were astonished as their children acted uncontrollably. Experts were summoned to try to determine the cause of their afflictions. The specialists took their time and explored all the possibilities. They checked the girls' physical and mental health and their activities. They studied their surroundings, carried out tests, and conscientiously considered all plausible explanations for what was happening. In the end, they could not all agree on a single cause. However, most agreed that the afflicted girls suffered from "conversion disorder," and that collectively they suffered from a mass psychogenic illness—what is often called mass hysteria. The outbreak in question occurred in Le Roy, New York, in 2011–12.[3]

Le Roy is a small working-class town of just under eight thousand in upstate New York. Like Salem did in 1692, Le Roy faces tough economic times. Once a prosperous manufacturing town, most of the factories closed in the 1960s, and the town has been looking for a return to prosperity ever since. In October 2011, a small group of the six hundred students at the local junior/senior high school began to exhibit these strange neurological symptoms. "Conversion disorder" was first identified by Freud, who suggested that a person's anxieties could be "converted" into physical afflictions. These symptoms can include not only the tics, fits, and strange behaviors witnessed at Le Roy but also numbness, blindness, paralysis, and an inability to speak. Although a psychological ailment, conversion disorder causes physical symptoms that are completely real—they are not in any way faked or controllable by the sufferer. Conversion disorder usually comes as a result of stress or trauma. In LeRoy, many of the girls faced difficult family circumstances. Several had recently suffered serious family illness or trauma, and many lacked a stable relationship with their biological fathers. One was in a foster home, another was in the custody of an older sibling, one was a single mother estranged from her parents, and one "was close to homeless after she and her mother left her father's trailer." Others believed that environmental toxins left by the factories were to blame, but extensive testing ruled out this possibility. One doctor treated a few of the girls for PANDAS (pediatric autoimmune neuropsychiatric disorders associated with streptococcus), a disease in which the neurochemistry of young people is altered by a strep infection. Only slowly did the girls come around to accepting the diagnosis of conversion disorder and the stigma that came with even a temporary mental illness.[4]

On rare occasions, conversion disorder can become an epidemic. Mass psychogenic illness remains controversial and poorly understood. Half of the known recent cases have occurred in schools, principally among young women. Outbreaks tend to begin among high-status groups and spread downward. At Le Roy the first victims were cheerleaders, a close-knit group that sits near the top of the pecking order in most high schools.[5]

In Salem more than three centuries earlier, the first ones afflicted were the daughter and niece of the minister, the man with arguably the highest social status in Salem Village. They were also perhaps the children in the village under the greatest stress. For months Samuel Parris had been preaching on the approaching war with Satan. Recently there had even been evidence that he was right. In late October 1691, Martha Sparks of Chelmsford in Middlesex County had been charged with witchcraft and sent to prison. Then in late December or early October eleven-year-old Mary Knowlton of Ipswich began to show signs of bewitchment. News of these cases must have spread quickly across the colony.[6] Parris continued to demonize his enemies, and his sermons were calculated to scare his opponents into repenting and ending their opposition to his ministry. It must have been almost unbearable for his daughter Betty and her cousin Abigail to reside in the parsonage while an agitated Reverend Parris prepared to battle Satan and his allies. Since his enemies had cut off Parris's supply of firewood, the home may have been rather cold. Parris looked for explanations for the villagers' enmity toward him and for what was happening to the girls in his household, though he was initially hesitant about accepting the diagnosis of witchcraft. It must have been acutely embarrassing for a minister to publicly acknowledge that Satan had invaded his parsonage and attacked the souls of his children. Though he would publicly chastise her, Parris was fortunate that Mary Sibley baked the witch cake, for the minister could now blame the arrival of Satan on this white magic rather than on the actions of his daughter and niece.

The first victim outside of the Salem Village parsonage was Ann Putnam Jr., a daughter of Thomas Putnam Jr. and his wife, Ann senior, members of one of the leading families of the village. The family circumstances of Thomas and Ann were difficult. Both of their late fathers had been rich and powerful men, yet the couple had received only a small portion of what they believed to be their rightful inheritances. These difficulties and somewhat reduced circumstances may have been felt by Ann junior, the oldest of their ten children. Another afflicted girl was Mary Walcott, the daughter of Captain Jonathan Walcott, the leader of the Salem Village militia, and stepcousin of Ann Putnam Jr. As next-door neighbors of the Parris family, the Walcotts would have been among the first to learn of the strange illness that beset Betty and Abigail.[7]

Soon these children of prominent citizens would be joined by young women from other ranks—notably servant girls. Elizabeth Hubbard, Mary Warren, and Mercy Lewis were orphans who worked as servants. Sarah Churchwell was a domestic as well. They were all at the bottom rung of society, with dim future prospects. They led difficult, stressful lives punctuated with trauma. John Procter threatened to beat Mary Warren if she did not stop her fits. According to Sarah Churchwell's testimony, the specter of her master, the elderly George Jacobs, "called her bitch witch & ill names" and also beat her with one of his two canes—suggesting the real George may have verbally abused her and struck her on occasion. Some have gone so far as to suggest that some of the girls showed behavior that was consistent with being victims of sexual abuse. Although it is an interesting possibility, solid evidence for such abuse is lacking.[8]

Mass psychogenic illness, if not recognized and treated, can worsen and spread. This is not surprising, as an unresolved emergency naturally leads to more anxiety, which is the very source of the illness. In Le Roy the initial circle of afflicted grew as families were initially unwilling to accept a diagnosis of mass hysteria and looked for other possible answers, though of course no one suggested demonic possession and sorcery. Only when the girls started treatment for psychogenic illness did their symptoms gradually improve. In Salem there was no such treatment available to the afflicted. The deepening crisis increased anxiety, which in turn fueled the growth of symptoms and their spread to more people.[9]

According to current thinking, the symptoms of mass psychogenic illness are interpreted in different ways, depending upon what the society of the time sees as an external threat. The Le Roy community immediately became convinced that environmental toxins could be the cause. There were natural gas wells on school property and toxic waste cleanup sites only a few miles away. An incident similar to Le Roy occurred in a Tennessee school in 1998, and again toxic exposure was assumed to be the source.[10] In 2004 a driver of a public bus in Vancouver became ill after an encounter with a person allegedly of Middle Eastern heritage. When the man was getting off the bus, he asked the driver how his day was going. The driver replied that it was going well, and the passenger cryptically responded, "It won't be for long."[11] Soon the driver became nauseated and started vomiting. A passenger, trained paramedics, and others who came to his aid and heard his explanation started suffering similar symptoms. Occurring in the long shadow of 9/11, the "toxic bus" episode was first believed to be a case of bioterrorism, though eventually it was diagnosed as mass psychogenic illness.[12]

While the symptoms of mass psychogenic illness seem to match those of the young girls who were first afflicted, it is but one of many possible explanations for what happened in 1692. Even today this illness is controversial, though clinicians can rely upon sophisticated scientific tests to rule out other possibilities. Thus we begin to see the difficulty of explaining what happened in Salem. Science cannot solve all the mysteries of the present, let alone the past. What happened in Salem likely had many causes, and as many responses to those causes. Mary Beth Norton, for one, has paid close attention to the nineteen afflicted people who were named in legal complaints, formally listed in indictments, or active in the legal proceedings and has divided them into three groups. One was a small group of five young girls age thirteen and under (including two who became involved much later when accusations spread to Andover). Another consisted of young people in their teens and early twenties. This group included several servants and at least one man. Finally there were two women in their thirties. There were others who made a deposition, complaining that they suffered some sort of affliction. All told, more than seventy people claimed they or their property had been injured in one way or another. It seems unlikely one explanation could fit all these experiences.[13]

The step from affliction to accusation was a short one. Today we attribute mass psychogenic illness to global concerns about toxic waste and terrorism, but in 1692 the omnipresent threat was witchcraft. Historians disagree as to what provoked the accusations, and they draw from a variety of sociological, psychological, medical, and theological possibilities. Ultimately, the question is whether the afflictions, and therefore the accusations, were genuine or deliberate acts of fraud. Not surprisingly, there is no agreement on the answer. Most historians acknowledge that some fakery took place at Salem. A close reading of the surviving court records and related documents suggests that more fraud took place than many cared to admit after the trials had ended. Given the nature of society in seventeenth-century Puritan Massachusetts, that reluctance is understandable, for anyone who made a false accusation of witchcraft immediately damned himself or herself to an eternity of suffering in hell. All but the youngest children would have been aware of this. Even if the sin was not uncovered on earth, it would be known to God. Yet this caution should be balanced against the actions of someone such as Abigail Hobbs, the teenager who openly bragged that she had disobeyed her parents because she had sold her soul to Satan and feared nothing. She went so far as to mock the Puritan faith, at one gathering making a show of sprinkling water in her stepmother's face and saying "she baptized her in the name of the Father, Son and Holy Ghost."[14] Whether Hobbs was "acting out," suffering from mental illness, or simply enjoying being at center stage in a world where youths were truly meant to be seen and not heard seems unclear.

While some scholars have characterized Hobbs and her companions as girls rebelling against the repressive patriarchal nature of Puritan society, the reverse could also be true: that through their accusations they were upholding it. Most observers acknowledged the existence of a major witchcraft outbreak in Salem. A girl or young woman suffering from an undiagnosed affliction must have felt a great obligation to protect her community and to do what her elders and superiors clearly thought was right: help convict people of witchcraft. A devout young Puritan girl would be unlikely to challenge the wisdom of the spiritual and secular leaders of her community.

Conversion disorder, one of several psychological conditions that Abigail Hobbs and other afflicted people might have suffered from in 1692, shows heightened awareness of one's surroundings. Scholars have long noted the connections between the witchcraft outbreak and King William's War, which raged on Massachusetts's northern frontier and was responsible for the war hysteria that seems to have been present in Salem Village and throughout Essex County. Abigail Hobbs, Mercy Lewis, Susannah Sheldon, and Sarah Churchwell were all war refugees who had previously lived in Maine. They had been uprooted by the war, had lost family members to the conflict, and had had their homes destroyed. Some of them may have been suffering from what we now recognize as post-traumatic stress syndrome. This certainly seems to be the case for the afflicted girl Mercy Short. Her parents had been killed, her home destroyed, and she herself taken captive during the combined French and Native raid on Salmon Falls (or Newichawannock) in the spring of 1690. Marched to Quebec, she was forced to convert to Catholicism. Redeemed in the fall of 1690, she became a maid in a Boston household and grew afflicted after an encounter with an accused witch in the Boston prison in May 1692.[15]

Mercy's symptoms, well recorded by her pastor, Cotton Mather, strongly suggest a case of post-traumatic stress as well as a state of panic or hysteria over the ongoing war. "There exhibited himself unto her a devil having the figure of a short and black man," noted Mather in his notes of her testimony, and "he was not of a negro, but of a tawny, or Indian color." The devil showed her his book, which was "somewhat long and thick (like the waste-books of many traders)...and filled not only with the names or marks, but also with the explicit...covenants." Satan and his company tempted her to sign and receive great wealth, showing her, again in the words of Cotton Mather, "very splendid garments...and many more conveniences...When all these persuasives were ineffectual, they terrified her with horrible threatenings of miseries which they would inflict upon her." Satan, appearing to her as a Native American, tried to force her to sign his book and join his covenant, just as she had been forced to become a Catholic. When she refused, he tortured her.[16]

This encounter also sounds uncannily similar to the Native American land sales that had been so common in the 1680s, as merchants speculated in frontier lands. The process would have been familiar even in Essex County, where officials had sought out the heirs of long-dead Native sachems to purchase title to their townships. All this was part of an effort to bolster claims of ownership when Governor Andros threatened to vacate titles to individual holdings as well as town common lands. To gain title, a merchant entered into a covenant, written in his ledger, with an Indian. In 1692 it became all too easy for people to equate signing a Native American deed with signing Satan's book. Many admitted that they had written agreements with heathen agents of the devil. William Barker Sr., for one, confessed he agreed after "the devil told him he would pay all his debts and he should live comfortably." Others signed the covenant because they thought it would bring them great wealth, but Satan had tricked them. The lands purchased in an unholy covenant were now worthless, for as Mercy knew all too well, the residents of the once promising frontier were now dead, captives, or refugees. Thus, Indian land speculation had tainted society and helped fuel the witchcraft outbreak.[17]

The devil's book plays a prominent role in the Salem trials. Its presence reflects a growing reliance on written and signed contracts in an increasingly commercial New England, plus a recent emphasis on signatures as a legal requirement as well as an emblem of loyalty and allegiance—be it signing a church covenant, an oath of loyalty to the government, or even a confession of witchcraft. In England, signed confessions had become particularly popular during the East Anglia witch hunt of 1645–47. There was also a tremendous growth in the number of books published in Massachusetts in the 1680s, and an appreciation for them among the highly literate Puritan population.[18]

Given that she had watched her home and entire village burn down, Mercy Short not surprisingly found flames of fire and burning to be the cruelest of all torments. When Satan gathered with his followers, they included French Canadians as well as Indian sagamores, "diverse of whom she knew, and particularly named them." Mercy also named some English accomplices of Satan, though these Cotton Mather kept to himself, for he considered the named to be innocent. If not for what turned out to be Mather's good judgment, the accusations might have spread out from Boston as well as Salem. Mather professed himself amazed by Mercy's ability to provide textbook-perfect descriptions of the devil and his temptations as well as his torments. He would have been less surprised had he realized that Mercy's neighbors in Salmon Falls had been the Hortados, whose home suffered "lithobolia" (a term for a stone-throwing demon) attacks for months on end in 1682. Mercy, then an impressionable seven-year-old, had probably sat through months of lectures from Reverend John Emerson (the nephew of the Gloucester minister of the same name), who would have warned his congregation how to spot Satan, and how he would try to tempt them. In 1692 the younger Emerson was a war refugee living in Charlestown, but he traveled several times to Salem to help out with the trials. He heard the confession of Dorcas Hoar and tried to convince Martha Tyler to confess as well.[19]

The war itself was just part of the concern. Increase Mather observed that demons were "not so frequent in places where the Gospel prevaileth as in the dark corners of the earth," and northern New England was just that, a "dark corner" of piety—inhabited by "heathen" Native Americans, "Papist" French, and non-Puritan Englishmen, including Quakers, Baptists, Antinomians, Royalists, and supposedly godless fishermen. Satan and his minions particularly infested the "East and West Indians" as well as the "popish countries."[20]

Cotton Mather compared King William's War to the struggle against Satan being waged in Salem and blamed the Indians for both conflicts in *Decennium Luctuosum*, his 1699 "history of remarkable occurrences, in the long war, which New-England hath had with the Indian savages."

The story of the prodigious war, made by the *spirits* of the *invisible world* upon the people of New-England, in the year 1692, hath entertain'd a great part of the English world with a just astonishment. And I have met with some strange things, not here to me mentioned, which have made me often think that this inexplicable war might have some of its original among the Indians, whose chief sagamores are well known unto some of our captives to have been horrid *sorcerers*, and hellish *conjurers*, and such as conversed with *demons*.[21]

Englishmen had long considered Native Americans to be minions of Satan, a fact reflected in what they called them. Unable to pronounce Native names, English settlers of New England often gave them nicknames, the most famous being "King Philip" for Metacomet. English settlers on the banks of the Damariscotta River in Maine chose to call the local sachem "John Cotta," a play on Damariscotta as well as an allusion to witchcraft, for John Cotta was the leading English witchcraft authority of the day, the author of *Triall of Witch-Craft Shewing the True Method of the Discovery* (1616). No one but a Maine Indian sachem would know as much about the dark arts as the leading English expert. The sachem lived not far from Merrymeeting Bay, and Englishmen often referred to witches' gatherings as "merry meetings." At least one Native American place name shows up as the name of a witch's familiar in England. Pyewacket was a name of one of the imps—familiars of witches—that Matthew Hopkins detected in his witch hunt in East Anglia in 1645–47. Interestingly, Pigwacket or Piwacket was the name of a group of Native Americans living in the White Mountains around the headwaters of the Saco River in the far interior of New Hampshire and Maine. Only a few years before Hopkins's discovery of an imp, which, Hopkins said, "no mortall could invent," Darby Field became the first Englishman to climb the White Mountains and to report the existence of the Pigwacket. This unique and exotic name for a people he believed to be in league with the devil obviously had made an impression on Hopkins.[22]

The Maine frontier was a dark enough place because of the Natives and the French, but Cotton Mather warned that even in the outskirts of Puritan New England one had to be on guard, for "Satan *terribly* makes a *prey* of you, and *leads you captive to do his will*."[23] No one was safe. Take the example of Benjamin Blackman, a young Harvard-trained minister who moved to Saco, Maine, in the early 1680s. Rather than practice his profession, Blackman became a land speculator. Some of his purchases were on behalf of men from Andover who hoped to settle in the region. Meanwhile, Saco, desperate for a minister, hired William Milborne, a Baptist—the same William Milborne who would move to Boston during King William's War and be one of the first to speak out against the witch trials. The Province of Maine had been established in the 1630s as an Anglican colony, but a shortage of settlers and ministers meant that nearly everyone was welcome, including Reverend John Wheelwright and his Antinomian followers, who established Wells. Although Massachusetts extended authority into New Hampshire in the 1640s and Maine in the 1650s, officials in Maine maintained toleration for a wide range of Protestant beliefs.[24]

While trauma linked to the war in a dark corner of New England seems likely to have been a source for some of the afflicted, scholars have also recently raised the possibility that a few accusers suffered from sleep paralysis. This very real condition was diagnosed only in the twentieth century, but it seems to explain at least the occasional alleged supernatural affliction. Sleep paralysis usually occurs as one is falling asleep or awakening. In this state, people are able to see and hear, but they have very limited capacity to move or speak, because muscle activity is suppressed during REM sleep. Somewhere between 5 and 20 percent of the population have experienced sleep paralysis at least once as a nightmare. It is accompanied by a feeling of weight on the chest, possibly a choking sensation, and the conviction that the individual is in some way under attack. Indeed, the term *mare* (as in *nightmare*) is related to the Germanic *mahr* and the Old Norse *mara*, both of which refer to a supernatural being that suffocates people by lying on their chest during sleep. Consider, then, Richard Coman's testimony that Bridget Bishop entered his home while he was sleeping, lay on his breast, "and so oppressed him that he could not speak nor stir no not so much as to awake his wife although he endeavored much so to do it." The next night Bishop returned and "took hold of him by [the] throat."[25] John Louder attested that he had had a dispute with Bishop over her chickens getting loose in his yard. Not long afterward, he went to bed and then felt a great weight upon his chest. Looking into the bright moon, he realized it was Bridget Bishop sitting on his chest. She grabbed his throat and almost choked him. Louder "had no strength or power in my hands to resist or help myself." Two men made similar complaints against Susannah Martin.[26]

Sleep paralysis can explain only a part of Louder's complaints against Bishop. He also accused her of attacking him with a "black thing" that had a body like a monkey's, claws like a rooster's, and a face "more like mans than a monkey's." The beast flew at him and flung dust that hit him in the chest, striking him dumb for three days. Louder's spectacular testimony suggests he had had a nightmare as a part of his sleep paralysis. It is also possible Louder suffered from the mass hysteria that gripped his community. Or, possibly, Louder deliberately lied. His deposition demonstrates the limits to efforts to make rational explanations of the supernatural acts described in 1692. It also serves as a reminder that there were dozens of people beyond the small circle of afflicted girls who believed they had suffered supernatural attacks and were willing to sign depositions to that effect.[27]

There is no evidence to support the tradition that the Parris girls were involved in fortune-telling and that guilt from this practice manifested itself in their bewitchment. Anyone who has seen Arthur Miller's *The Crucible* knows the powerful but ultimately misleading image of Tituba directing the neighborhood girls in this adventure. Certainly fortune-telling was all the rage at the time, despite the concerns it raised in ministers and other leaders of society. For, as Increase Mather wrote just a couple years after Salem, "ungodly fortune-tellers" revealed things that could only be known "by the help of evil angels"—that is, agents of the devil.[28] And while Deodat Lawson complained of the use of fortune-telling when he preached in Salem Village amid the witch trials, such practices had little if anything to do with the witchcraft crisis in 1692. Absolutely no contemporary record links Tituba to such activity, and there is only one oblique mention of fortune-telling among the afflicted girls. John Hale, in his *Modest Inquiry into the Nature of Witchcraft*, described one girl as trying to learn a bit about her future husband: "I knew one of the afflicted persons, who (as I was credibly informed) did try with an egg and a glass to find her husband's calling; till there came up a coffin, that is, a specter in likeness of a coffin. And she was afterwards followed with diabolical molestation to her death; and so died a single person."[29] Egg white suspended in a glass of water formed shapes that foretold future events. In this case this device, called a Venus glass, made an uncannily accurate prediction, for the coffin shape presaged the girl's death before she could marry. Although the girl is not named, the circumstances suggest that she was either Susannah Sheldon or Mary Warren, both of whom disappear from the records and had quite possibly died by 1697, when Hale completed his manuscript. Susannah Sheldon particularly fits the bill as a girl with "diabolical molestation," for by 1694 she had moved to Rhode Island, where she was ordered to appear before the court as a "person of evil fame."[30]

Almost as persistent a myth as fortune-telling are a range of possible medical explanations. By far the most popular is that the afflicted girls were suffering from convulsive ergotism, a diagnosis first suggested in 1976. Ergot is a fungus that grows on damp cereal grains, and particularly the rye New Englanders used to make their bread. Ingesting it can produce not only strange tics and behavior but also LSD-like trips, which could explain the afflicted in Salem seeing specters. While this sounds like a neat solution to the problem, scholars soon after quickly demonstrated that the descriptions of the afflicted girls did not match the symptoms. Surviving accounts mention no vomiting or diarrhea, not to mention the gangrene or neurological damage that ergot poisoning inflicts upon the limbs. Nor do the symptoms of ergotism come and go, as apparently did the afflictions in 1692. Furthermore, prolonged exposure to ergot for the months of affliction witnessed at Salem would have led to permanent dementia and in extreme cases death. Most of the girls led fairly normal and obscure lives after their involvement in the trials, with no sign of mental or physical illness. Indeed, most of them lived to a healthy old age. An even bigger problem for the ergot theory is every member of the family would have eaten infected bread and thus shown symptoms, but they did not. Moreover, the theory rests on there being one communal supply of rye that was infected. Yet those complaining of witchcraft came not only from across Salem Village but from neighboring towns as well. It is simply impossible that all of them could have gotten their rye from a common source. Intriguing as it is, the ergot theory does not hold up under close inspection.[31]

Several other diseases have been put forward as possible culprits, ranging from encephalitis and Lyme disease to what is known as "Arctic hysteria," yet none of these seem to fit, either. Many experts question the very existence of Artic hysteria, which results in such behavior as people stripping off their clothes and running naked across the wild tundra. The accounts mention no such streaking in Salem, and while the supposed symptoms of witchcraft began in January, more people showed symptoms in the spring and summer. And even if Arctic hysteria is a medical condition, only Inuit societies of the Arctic seem to have suffered from it. Encephalitis, the result of an infection transmitted by mosquito bite, does not really seem plausible, given that the first symptoms of bewitchment appeared during winter. And while the bull's-eye rash often produced on the skin by Lyme disease might explain the devil's mark or witch's teat, it falls short of accounting for the behavior of the afflicted.[32] None of the suggested diseases fit because a close reading of the testimony suggests that the symptoms were intermittent. The afflicted had stretches when they acted perfectly normally, interspersed with acute fits.

Those who would search for modern medical explanation try to view a seventeenth-century phenomenon through twenty-first-century glasses. There was a perfectly good seventeenth-century medical condition that explained the behavior of the sufferers: they were bewitched. In 1692 everyone believed in the existence of witches in league with the devil, who had been created by God as a challenge to man. During the Salem witch trials, there was no dispute over the existence of witches. All ministers and learned people knew that witches were real and that they had the power to harm. The debate was over how one detected witchcraft and whether the victims were truly victims or were just faking their ailments.

Historians Bernard Rosenthal and Peter Hoffer have done the most thorough job of laying out the case for deliberate fraud in Salem. They believe it was widespread, and they cite a number of examples to support their claim. For example, on March 24, 1692, Deodat Lawson observed in a sermon he preached in Salem Village that "some of the afflicted, as they were striving in their fits, in open court, have (by invisible means) had their wrists bound fast together with a real cord, so as it could hardly be taken off without cutting. Some afflicted have been found with their arms tied, and hanged upon a hook, from whence others have been forced to take them down that they might not expire in that posture." How could the afflicted have their wrists bound so tight with a rope that it had to be cut off, or have their arms tied and placed on a hook, unless there was a conspiracy of fraud among the accusers?[33]

Many of the sufferers alleged they were pinched or had pins allegedly stuck in them by specters. In the seventeenth century pinching was a common punishment for a youth who misbehaved. So this sort of spectral attack might indeed be related to hysteria, triggered by guilt over wrongdoing. However, the misbehavior would include acting out as well as fraudulent accusations and actions, including sticking pins in oneself and blaming someone's specter for it. In the seventeenth century, as today, there were troubled youths who harmed themselves. It is possible that because of their mental state they might not always be willing to admit they did this. The practice of sticking pins in the flesh was common among youths making fraudulent claims about demonic possession or spectral affliction. Pins were common household items that could not be individually traced. Their role in sewing and other domestic activities was a reminder of the servile place in society of those making the accusations. Furthermore, while being stuck with a pin was painful, certainly it was bearable, particularly if it could be stuck through dead skin or calluses. Indeed, adolescents today regularly undergo body piercings that would appear far more painful than a small straight pin. Then as now, a pin or a piercing brings dramatic attention and, as one might say, helps to make a point.[34]

In one of the most famous cases of witchcraft fraud in English history, Anne Gunter went beyond sticking pins in herself and dramatically vomited up pins, expelled them through her nose when sneezing, had them "wrung out of her breast," and even "voided some pins downward as well by her water." They seemed to miraculously come out of every opening, making her a human "pinpillow." In 1605 Anne's case was heard before King James I, himself a noted witch hunter, who got her to admit to her fraud. Gunter's case was so famous that it was not only noted by historians but also preserved by playwrights. A scene in Ben Jonson's *Volpone* (1606) in which a demoniac fraudulently vomits pins is considered by many to be borrowed from the Gunter case. Much better known, Shakespeare's *Macbeth* was first performed the year after the Gunter case, so its witches may owe their inspiration in part to Anne as well.[35]

The afflicted girls of Salem had a wide body of knowledge of cases of witchcraft that went well beyond Anne Gunter. Many accounts of recent cases were circulating in print in 1692. The importance placed by Puritans on individuals reading the Bible for themselves meant that at the time of the Salem trials literacy rates were rapidly climbing. Although female literacy rates trailed men's, a minister's daughter and niece would have been able to read. Marginalized members of society such as young servant girls might not have been able to study these accounts. But even if they could not read, knowledge of witchcraft, particularly published cases, seems to have spread rapidly in the vigorous oral culture of the seventeenth century.[36] Indeed, the symptoms of the afflicted in Salem seem to suggest direct knowledge of several recent outbreaks, including the Lowestoft case in England and the recent affliction of the Goodwin children of Boston. Accounts had been published of both of these cases. Deodat Lawson observed a "grievous fit" by Abigail Williams, who ran dangerously about the house, going near the fire, gathering firebrands, and throwing them, "sometimes making as if she would fly, stretching up her arms as high as she could, and crying 'Whish, Whish, Whish!' several times." Lawson was told that on other occasions Abigail would appear to try to run up the chimney and "had attempted to go into the fire."[37] Martha Goodwin would have to be restrained as well, to keep her out of the fire. In the Lowestoft case, a bewitched girl "ran round about the house holding her apron, crying hush, hush." Like Abigail, she showed a strange fascination with fire. Abigail was not known to vomit pins, but she was stuck by them on multiple occasions. The Lowestoft outbreak occurred in 1662, but the account that included these details was not published until 1682, and then it rapidly became widely available.[38] In

1688 Cotton Mather observed the Goodwin children in Boston, and the next year he published *Memorable Providences, Relating to Witchcrafts and Possessions*, an account of their case. Here, too, the account suggests that the tormented pretended to fly: "Yea, they would fly like geese; and be carried with an incredible swiftness through the air, having but just their toes now and then upon the ground, and their arms waved like the wings of a bird."[39] The Lowestoft case was published in 1682, and Mather's account of the Goodwins was printed in 1689. So these would have been the latest and best-known cases of witchcraft—presumably known not only to ministers and doctors but also to young girls, especially those who lived in a parsonage.

Memorable Providences even included a description of witchcraft in Mora, Sweden. In the spring and summer of 1679 Mora had witnessed a huge witch hunt. Based largely on spectral evidence recounted by numerous children, sixty suspects were interrogated and twenty-three were burned at the stake. Such widespread participation of children, the quick spread of charges, and the use of spectral evidence all made the case seem quite unusual and extreme, though it bears uncanny similarities to the situation in Salem. As Norton has noted, "Consciously or unconsciously, the Salem Village afflicted had incorporated the previously recorded behaviors into their own repertoires."[40]

Even in 1692 some observers believed fraud was at work. Reverend Samuel Willard questioned the credibility of the afflicted, noting "the common vogue, that they are scandalous persons, liars, and loose in their conversation and therefore not to be believed."[41] There was some courtroom evidence to support such a charge. A supporter of Elizabeth Procter testified that he had heard one of the girls admit "that she did it [for] sport they must have some sport."[42] The Nurse family made a well-organized campaign to discredit Rebecca's accusers. They produced depositions that questioned the veracity of both Mercy Lewis and Betty Hubbard. They pointed out that Susannah Sheldon contradicted herself in her testimony. And they gave repeated examples of the unruliness and dishonesty of Sarah Bibber, as well as the fact that she "could fall into fits as often as she pleased."[43] Historian Peter Hoffer has taken it further, calling the pack of girls "a gang of juvenile delinquents."[44]

While it is possible that the erratic behavior of the girls sparked a mass psychological phenomenon, a considerable amount of deliberate fraud eventually took place, carried out for a range of reasons. Scholars have speculated that Abigail Williams might have accused people because of the attention she received.[45] A good example came on March 20 when Reverend Deodat Lawson gave a guest sermon in Salem Village, a chance for him to address the witchcraft outbreak directly. Lawson noted that several of the bewitched girls in attendance "had several sore fits, in the time of public worship, which did something interrupt me in my first prayer; being so unusual." It was indeed extremely unusual for anyone to interrupt a minister, and unheard of for children to do so. It did not stop there, for soon the girls were complaining and actually telling the minister how to run the service. "After psalm was sung, Abigail Williams said to me, 'Now stand up, and name your text': And after it was read, she said, 'It is a long text.' In the beginning of sermon, Mrs. Pope, a woman afflicted, said to me, 'Now there is enough of that.' And in the afternoon, Abigail Williams upon my referring to my doctrine said to me, 'I know no doctrine you had, If you did name one, I have forgot it.'" Only when these girls and women were suffering from the effects of witchcraft could they break the bounds of Puritan society, even questioning the minister's doctrine. Ann Putnam Jr. went so far as to hint that Lawson might be a witch by associating him with a familiar. The minister noted that during his sermon, Ann "said there was a yellow bird sat on my hat as it hung on the pin in the pulpit; but those that were by, restrained her from speaking loud about it."[46]

As John Demos has demonstrated, Elizabeth Knapp exhibited similar behavior when she was afflicted in Groton in 1671. This case was well known in 1692 because Elizabeth's minister, a young Samuel Willard, had published a detailed account of his efforts to ease her suffering. Willard described the performances Knapp gave to the gathered household audience. She was "seized in such ways that six persons could hardly hold her; but she leaped and skipped about the house perforce, roaring and yelling deadly sighs." She would strike those who tried to hold her and spit in their faces, "barked like a dog and bleated like a calf," and would verbally assault Willard with a deep "grum" voice that seemed to come from deep within her. Demos convincingly argued that Knapp was suffering from conversion disorder.[47]

Still, questions remain as to the degree to which the actions of such young girls were voluntary and deliberate. It is quite possible that the involvement of Betty Parris and Abigail Williams in the witch hunt can be explained entirely as a case of mass hysteria. Both Betty and Abigail disappear from the proceedings relatively early on. In late March her parents sent Betty away from the village, to the Salem Town home of Stephen Sewall. Sewall was a distant kinsman, as his brother Samuel was married to Parris's cousin. Sending Betty out of town removed her from the spotlight and the interaction with other girls, and apparently it led to her recovery, for she is not mentioned in the proceedings after this time. Abigail Williams, too, would soon vanish from the proceedings, making her last appearance before the court on June 30. Their exit marks the end of one stage of the witch hunt and the beginning of a second phase, during which deceptive if not fraudulent behavior was a much more real possibility.[48]

With the departure of Betty and Abigail, the majority of the witchcraft accusations came from a group of six girls: Ann Putnam Jr., Betty Hubbard, Mary Walcott, Mercy Lewis, Susannah Sheldon, and Mary Warren. All were between seventeen and twenty, except for twelve-year-old Ann. Most of the contemporary critics of the trials who observed them firsthand believed that some degree of deliberate fakery was involved with these older girls who claimed to be afflicted. Their behavior in the court often appears to have a stage-managed quality to it. Consider the case of Mary Warren, the twenty-year-old servant of John and Elizabeth Procter. She was initially one of the sufferers. Yet she soon switched sides, claiming that the girls "did but dissemble." This change of heart apparently took place after John Procter either beat her or threatened to do so for her accusations. Conveniently, soon Mary Warren's specter was hurting the girls, so a complaint was filed against her. When she was brought before the court, the girls suffered convulsions. Warren immediately fell into a fit as well, and appeared to be struck dumb. Only days later, in jail, would she be able to speak, saying the Procters were witches. She claimed the couple had tortured her and tricked her into touching a book that she only now realized had to be the devil's book. Still in prison three weeks later, Warren had severe fits and accused several more women of witchcraft. There was no further word of charges of witchcraft against Warren, and she returned to the court as one of the most active accusers.[49]

What exactly did Warren mean when she said the girls "did but dissemble"? Edward and Sarah Bishop and Mary Esty testified that when they were jailed with Warren, she said that the judges should take no notice of what the girls said. She warned that when "I was afflicted I thought I saw the apparition of a hundred persons," but "her head was distempered" at the time and "she could not tell what she said." Yet "when she was well again she could not say that she saw any of apparitions at the time aforesaid."[50] While *dissemble* could mean "to deceive," it could also mean "to disguise" or "to pretend." Warren believed she had been "distracted," that is, suffering some sort of mental illness, when she experienced the symptoms. She assumed the other bewitched suffered similarly—perhaps a case of mass hysteria? Now that she was well, she tried to set the record straight, but in doing so, she questioned the legitimacy of the testimony of them all.

Of course, one can choose not to believe Warren, to view her supposed distractions simply as a way to avoid being beaten by John Procter and also to get the court to overlook the damning false testimony she had already given. Regardless of whether the torments were real or an act, the actions of the girls toward Mary Warren and her response seem quite calculated. The girls convulsed almost on cue. Faced with no alternative, she replied in kind. Uncertain of what to say, she pretended to be mute. Several un-pleasant weeks in the Salem jail would provide her with time to think and to realize that, given the alternatives, she was better off casting her lot with the accusers. After all, both the Procters were in jail, so she was safe from the threat of further beatings. By the middle of May, Warren was again suf-fering fits and accusing more people of witchcraft.

Warren's charges and testimony against Abigail Soames would mark the first use of the touch test in the Salem court. As can be seen in the questioning of Soames, the judges began to standardize these procedures even before the Court of Oyer and Terminer first met. It would be an im-portant turning point in the trials, for under Warren's leadership, it was a process used to convict a good number of witches, usually in combination with the evil eye. Both would appear to be carefully managed courtroom procedures. Justices Hathorne and Corwin experimented with the touch test on May 13, during Abigail Soames's examination, witnessed by Mary Warren. "Soames casting her eye on Warren struck her into a dreadful fit, and bit her so dreadfully that the like was never seen on any of the afflicted, which the said Warren charged the said Soames with doing of, saying that the said Soames told her this day she would be the death of her." The judges commanded Soames to "take Warren by the hand, and she immediately recovered." The court recorder noted that "this experiment was tried three times over and the issue the same." The judges then tried to reverse the experiment by asking Warren to take Soames's hand, but Warren would go into a fit when she tried to do so. Mary claimed that Abigail's specter would not allow her to touch the accused. The fact that this pattern—of evil being healed by the accused's touch—was repeated three times indicates that it was indeed an experiment. Once perfected at Soames's examination, it would be regularly used by Court of Oyer and Terminer, providing key evidence to convict Bridget Bishop and many others. Almost invariably Mary Warren would be among the bewitched to participate in these tests.[51]

Thomas Brattle described the science the judges said was behind the touch test: "The Salem justices, at least some of them, do assert, that the cure of the afflicted persons is a natural effect of this touch; and they are so well instructed in the Cartesian philosophy, and in the doctrine of effluvia, that they undertake to give a demonstration how this touch does cure the afflicted persons; and the account they give of it is this; that by this touch, the venomous and malignant particles, that were ejected from the eye, do, by this means, return to the body whence they came, and so leave the afflicted persons pure and whole." Brattle's disagreement with the judges was not that they believed in witches or that they were not scientific in their approach to the evidence. Rather, he felt they were misusing Cartesian philosophy, which led to wrongful verdicts.[52]

Some have pointed to the actions of the court as evidence of how backward and superstitious people were in the seventeenth century. Nothing could be further from the truth. The judges were highly educated for their time. Their use of spectral evidence was part of a broader scientific effort to gain knowledge of the soul and the invisible world.[53] Given there were no set trial procedures or certain ways to detect a witch, they even carried out what they called "experiments" in the use of the evil eye and the witch's touch. These tests seem laughably simple on the surface, but in carrying them out the judges drew upon some of the latest scientific advances and were supported by some of the leading English religious, legal, and philosophical minds of the day. No less a scientist than Robert Boyle had been studying both curing touches and the evil eye. In 1666 Boyle noted in *The Origine of Formes and Qualities according to the Corpuscular Philosophy* (1666) that spirits and souls had some ability to interact with the physical world. The same year Boyle had been among a group of natural philosophers in London who had witnessed Valentine Greatrakes, the so-called Irish Stroker, perform several miraculous cures simply by touch. Boyle, the president of the Royal Society, was so impressed that he endorsed the efficacy of Greatrakes's cures. He was also among a group of early scientists and theologians trying to prove the existence of Satan and the supernatural world, for if Satan did not exist, how long would it be before people doubted the existence of God, who had created Satan?[54]

The touch test had been used to convict the Lowestoft witches, who were tried before no less an authority than Chief Justice Sir Matthew Hale at Bury St. Edmunds. He accepted that test, even when it seemingly proved to be unreliable. When one of the Lowestoft sufferers was blindfolded, her torments were ended with equal success by the touch of a random observer and by the touch of the accused. Remarkably, supporters argued successfully that the afflicted had been bewitched into believing that they were touched by one of the witches. Clearly, many considered the touch test to be of dubious use. When it was employed in Andover in 1692, observers took the precaution of similarly blindfolding the troubled girls, though in this case they seem to have successfully identified the accused. Thomas Brattle and others remained skeptical. He mused, "I know a man that will venture two to one with any Salemite whatever, that let the matter be duly managed, and the afflicted person shall come out of her fit upon the touch of the most religious hand in Salem."[55] He also noted that according to some Salem courtroom observers, sometimes the touch of the accused did not always immediately relieve the torments; if the judges ordered the sufferer to grab harder and harder, eventually the suffering would end. Brattle had similar concerns with the evil eye, wondering why only the supposedly bewitched afflicted were sent into fits by the poisoned look of the accused. Brattle concluded, "This Salem philosophy, some men may call the new philosophy; but I think it rather deserves the name of Salem superstition and sorcery, and it is not fit to be named in a land of such light as New-England is."[56]

Given the high drama of the Salem courtroom, it is easy to forget that witchcraft was a religious crime and in some countries was tried before a religious court. The theological explanations need therefore to be considered. As Boyer and Nissenbaum have suggested, at a another time the behavior of the bewitched could have been taken in a very different way—as an example of religious enthusiasm. They point to how in 1734–35 the youths of Northampton, Massachusetts, suffered fits, terrors, and distempers similar to those seen in Salem. Rather than interpreting these as evidence of witchcraft, young Reverend Jonathan Edwards saw them as the agony of sinners seeing spiritual rebirth. Edwards's contemporaries did likewise, interpreting the behaviors as signs that these young people were religious seers rather than victims of Satan. A generation earlier, Reverend Samuel Parris interpreted much the same evidence as Satan's hand. The response of the ministers and their communities reflects the difference of the times. In Salem and New England more generally, 1692 was a difficult and dangerous time, and Samuel Parris anticipated Satan's attack. Jonathan Edwards and his congregation lived in far more secure times, at the dawn of the religious revival known as the Great Awakening. There have been relatively few efforts over the years to explain the behavior of the "afflicted" during the Great Awakening or the Second Great Awakening a century later. People generally seem content to accept it as religious ecstasy.[57]

Samuel Parris saw Satan in Salem Village because of the divisions that had torn his congregation apart. In *Salem Possessed*, Boyer and Nissenbaum suggest that the pattern of accusation in the early stages of the outbreak as well as the factionalism were rooted in the society, economy, and geography of Salem Village. They noted that the men who had lodged the formal charges of witchcraft on behalf of the afflicted girls were not just supporters of Samuel Parris and covenanted members of his church but tended to come from the poorer western part of Salem Village. The people who were accused tended to be more from the up-and-coming eastern part of town.[58] Recently scholars have raised concerns over specifics of some of these geographic and economic arguments. Still, the basic arguments of *Salem Possessed* remain intact. Witchcraft in Europe and America was tied to the economic uncertainties of the early modern period. It is not a coincidence that the age of witch hunts also saw the birth and development of capitalism.[59]

In the later seventeenth century, capitalism and the beginnings of industrialization in turn led to the start of the consumer revolution; a range of impressive and fashionable manufactured goods quickly became available for those who could afford them. It was a time of economic change and dislocation, with both winners and losers. Samuel Parris described witches as being envious individuals, people who coveted the fine life and superior possessions of their neighbors. In 1692 people confessed that they had been tempted by, or even sold their souls to Satan for, a range of commodities. Satan could not have done better than to entice a poor young girl such as Abigail Hobbs, the orphan Abigail Williams, or the slave Tituba with "fine things" and "fine clothes." Fourteen-year-old Stephen Johnson looked forward to being the height of fashion, wearing the "pair of French fall shoes" promised in return for selling his body and soul to Satan. The seventeenth century was also the time of the Protestant Reformation, the Catholic Counter-Reformation, and associated religious warfare—an age of great spiritual upheaval. In Salem Village the coming together of religious and economic tensions can be seen in such matters as resistance to a disliked minister, to whom some people would refuse ministerial rates or firewood.[60]

Despite the opposition to Parris, in 1692 the members of his church united in support of the embattled minister and the bewitched. Only adult men could swear out a legal complaint, and recent scholarship has demonstrated that the Salem Village church members were very active in filing complaints against those cried out upon for witchcraft. The male and female church members were also vigorous in providing depositions and testimony in support of the bewitched's accusations. In all of these actions, these covenant signers almost invariably aimed their charges and testimony outward, against people who were not members of their church. Nearly three-quarters of the village men (thirteen out of a total of seventeen) who originally signed the village church covenant either initiated complaints or gave evidence against an accused witch. This group was dominated by people from the west of Salem Village and the Putnam family, the leading family of the western part of the village. Ten of the thirteen initial covenant signers who swore out complaints or testified against witches lived west of the meetinghouse, while the three who lived to the east were all Putnams. So the leadership of the church, who filed charges of witchcraft and supported the afflicted, came from the western part of Salem Village and the Putnam family.[61]

In the vanguard was Thomas Putnam Jr., who made complaints against at least thirty-five people and testified against seventeen. His active involvement resulted from the affliction of his wife, Ann senior, his daughter Ann junior, and servant Mercy Lewis. All three would be prominent among the accusers. Thomas also had an official role in the trials, serving as the most productive legal secretary, recording 120 depositions during the proceedings. Some documents were his own testimony, but he also prepared depositions for thirty-eight others involving cases against twenty-nine people. The depositions written by Putnam use remarkably consistent phrasing to describe the actions of the accused and the afflictions they inflicted.

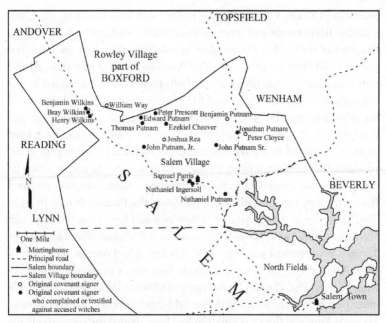

Map of Salem Village with original covenant signers. Drawing by the author.

Furthermore, it is clear from different colors of ink used within an individual deposition that they were written down on two or three separate occasions. Apparently they were mostly recorded when deposing the witness, though details were added when preparing to use them before the grand jury or in a trial. Putnam's depositions had a very high success rate in getting grand juries to return indictments against the accused. Given the bewitchment of Putnam's family, the formulaic nature of his depositions, and the additions to them, one cannot help but wonder if he embellished the documents to strengthen cases. At the very least, one can say that Putnam was far from a disinterested and objective party and that he and his family played a significant role in shaping the course of the trials. Given the prominence of Putnam, his family, and other church leaders from the western part of the village, the proceedings must have seemed to observers of the day to have at least some geographical as well as factional flavor to them.[62]

There were many reasons for Thomas Putnam Jr.'s family to suffer from witchcraft in 1692. As the oldest son of Thomas Putnam Sr., the wealthiest patriarch in Salem Village, Thomas junior must have grown up expecting a similar life of power and privilege. A favorable marriage to Ann Carr, the daughter of the wealthy George Carr of Salisbury, promised economic opportunity and further prosperity. The Putnams engaged in prolonged and bitter legal battles over the estates of both their fathers that ended in disappointment. The Carr estate had to be divided among nine children and the eldest son received a double portion, so Ann and the other siblings each received just 10 percent of their father's wealth. Thomas must have been particularly galled to see the lion's share of his father's estate pass to his youngest half-brother, Joseph Putnam. To add insult to injury, when he was just twenty Joseph had married Elizabeth Porter, daughter of Israel Porter, the very wealthy political opponent of the Putnam family. In addition, Thomas was passed over for offices he might have expected to garner. His father served as a Salem selectman, but the highest office the younger Thomas ever reached was constable. His father had been a lieutenant in the militia, and his uncle Elizur Holyoke had been a prominent captain in King Philip's War. Thomas junior attained only the rank of sergeant, while other members of the family with less field experience served as captain. So Thomas, Ann, and their ten children had been denied the comfortable life and the status they had anticipated. Even worse, Thomas would never have the land or the money to provide farms for all his sons and proper dowries for his daughters, and the war eliminated the possibility of starting farms on the frontier. When Thomas and Ann died—within two weeks of each other in 1699—he left an estate of £437, but it was encumbered with almost £200 of debt. This most atypical man left a very typical estate. It was just the sort of economic uncertainty faced by Putnam and his family that bedeviled Salem Village and all of Essex County in 1692, and created an atmosphere conductive to the spread of witchcraft.[63]

A look at other leading afflicted accusers suggests that many of them faced an uncertain future as well. More than half of Salem's unmarried bewitched girls between the ages of sixteen and twenty-four had lost their fathers, and some were orphans. Mercy Lewis, Mercy Short, Mary Warren, Sarah Churchwell, and Elizabeth Hubbard were all servants. Hubbard, Warren, Lewis, and Short were orphans, and Lewis and Short had lost their parents in Native American raids. Sarah Churchwell's father was alive, but the once prominent refugee family now lived in reduced circumstances. Susannah Sheldon was another war refugee, living with her recently widowed mother.

Orphans, refugees, and servants lacked the dowries that would be necessary for a good marriage. These girls had good reason to believe that Satan might be tormenting them. Even Betty Parris and Abigail Williams lived in a parsonage that lacked firewood, and Reverend Parris, as we've seen, had difficulty collecting his salary, so their future was in question as well.[64]

What caused the afflictions in Salem? It is easier to say what did not happen. Salem was not seized by a mass outbreak of ergot poisoning, encephalitis, or some other physical ailment or disease. Nor was fortune-telling or voodoo to blame. Many preconditions led to the Salem outbreak, and there was more than one explanation for people's torments. In fact, it is possible that one or two people's physical ailments—such as epileptic seizures— could have been interpreted as the work of a witch. Most of the sufferings likely came as the result of some combination of psychological ailments. Some may have suffered a psychological disorder, such as sleep paralysis or post-traumatic stress. Others may have been victims of conversion disorder—a mass hysteria that resulted from the grim circumstances confronted by citizens of Salem Village and New England in 1692. A disastrous and costly war had exacerbated existing economic, political, and spiritual tensions. Meanwhile, in Salem Village, Samuel Parris's combative and unyielding nature would harden factional lines.

Just as there is evidence to support a mass psychosis, there is evidence of deliberate acts of fraud. And the fact that someone was afflicted by a psychological disorder that was beyond his or her control does not rule out the possibility that some of that person's actions were deliberate and willful acts of calumny and deception. Once Bridget Bishop had been executed, a line had been crossed. After this point no one would admit to false accusations, for to do so would be to confess to a murderous conspiracy. As the case of Mary Warren demonstrates, once a young woman had joined the ranks of the accusers, no recanting or changing of sides was possible, even when she recovered from her afflictions and recognized that she had made false accusations.

Most who have studied the witch trials will admit that some fraud took place and that psychological factors were at play as well. However, there is no agreement as to where to place the emphasis. Certainly it is easier to see false testimony when it is clearly laid out in such documents as the recantation by the accused Margaret Jacobs: "The Lord, I hope, in whom I trust, out of the abundance of his mercy, will forgive me my false forswearing myself. What I said, was altogether false against my grandfather, and Mr. Burroughs, which I did to save my life and to have my liberty."[65] We all appreciate the relative certainty of such written records. The evidence of a mass hysteria is much less direct and more problematic for those who are not trained psychiatrists or psychologists. In the end, to explain the symptoms of affliction one has to side with Samuel Parris, who saw bewitchment, or Jonathan Edwards, who saw ecstasy.

Before making that choice, we need to look at the people whom the afflicted accused in 1692, for by learning more about the alleged witches of Salem we can gain insight into what may have been behind the behavior and accusations of the bewitched.

CHAPTER FIVE

The Accused

Others of them denied their guilt, and maintained their innocency for
above eighteen hours, after most violent, distracting, and dragooning
methods had been used with them, to make them confess.

—Thomas Brattle, October 8, 1692[1]

WHY WERE PEOPLE ACCUSED OF witchcraft in 1692? A close examination
of those accused and the patterns of the accusations brought against them
shows a wide range of factors, some predictable and others not. The patterns confirm that people were angry and afraid—about the declining spiritual state of Massachusetts Bay, about religious tensions, about political
and social division, and about the failing war effort on the northern frontier. Those accused of witchcraft were perceived as a threat, directly or indirectly, or as somehow related to a threat to the spiritual, political, or military
stability and well-being of the community or the colony. Furthermore, there
can be no doubt that the accusations involved power and authority, and
in particular their perceived misuse and corruption. The abuse of authority could be at the community level or colony-wide—a politician or military leader who shared responsibility for the disastrous war, a minister who

supported the Halfway Covenant or did not actively promote moral reformation, or someone who had misused his authority over his family.

If any one factor links virtually all of the accused, it has to be religion.
The trials were largely an effort to bolster Puritanism—an orthodoxy under
attack on multiple fronts, for in Massachusetts Bay religion was the fabric
that held the polity and society together. Many of those accused were perceived as posing a threat to the religious order, either because they were true
outsiders, were Puritan saints who stood in the way of moral reformation,
challenged Reverend Parris's effort to build a community of true believers, or were associated somehow with non-Puritan religious practitioners,
including Quakers, Baptists, Catholics, and Native Americans. A number
of them were authority figures—ministers, politicians, militia officers—but
somehow seen as responsible for spiritual decline and the military threat to
the very existence of the Puritan state. The charges were not made against
the heterodox or the heathen themselves. The goal of the Puritan city upon
a hill had once been to convert everyone to the faith. Now, with the failure
of the Puritan experiment seemingly at hand, attention focused more on
those who might switch sides. The enemy was dreaded, but there was even
more fear of and a great deal of anger toward the Puritan who might turn
traitor, becoming a Quaker or joining the Native Americans.

Although witch hunts occurred in all European nations and their colonies, there are strong correlations between Puritanism and witchcraft. The
English colonies that saw the most persecutions were Puritan Massachusetts
and Connecticut, as well as Bermuda, where accusations were led by Puritan
ministers. England's greatest witch hunt was led by Puritans during the
English Civil Wars. The links are not surprising, given the preoccupation
many Puritans had with the evil power of Satan and his efforts to win souls.[2]

According to the surviving court records, which were edited and published by Bernard Rosenthal and his team in *The Records of the Salem
Witch-Hunt*, 156 people were either formally accused of witchcraft or
cried out upon, meaning denounced but never formally charged. Though
the records are quite extensive—this monumental effort includes close to
a thousand documents—a number of them have been lost, so we will never
know the exact number of people who were mentioned, though presumably
the total is less than the 307 sorcerers that William Barker Sr. claimed in
his confession. Thanks to unofficial accounts made by contemporaries, the
names of sixteen more people are known, bringing the total to 172. These

sixteen were cried out upon or implicated during the course of the outbreak but did not face legal action. They make a very interesting group, as most were individuals who the judges were so sure were innocent that they would not consider pressing formal charges.[3]

Looking at those accused, it becomes clear that there were a multitude of factors that might bring someone under suspicion for witchcraft. Indeed, in most cases, several factors had to be at work for someone to be accused, or for an accusation to be taken seriously. All of the victims of 1692 deserve to have their stories told; however, there simply is no room to do so here. Rather, this chapter will look in detail at some of them and focus in particular on the man considered to be the king of hell and leader of the witches' Sabbath, Reverend George Burroughs.[4] His story will help to illuminate those of others, for there appear to be a multitude of reasons he could have been charged. There were many different circles of accused, and Burroughs seemed to fall into nearly all of them. Furthermore, Burroughs's accusation, conviction, and execution signaled a turning point in the proceedings. Men had rarely been charged with witchcraft in the past, and ministers never fell under suspicion. Once a Puritan minister had been charged, in other words, no one was safe. His conviction proved suspicions that Satan was now completely at large, with ministers leading his coven and running his black masses. In the wake of Burroughs's accusation, the evidence against suspected witches took a decided turn as well, as the judges searched increasingly for signs of the satanic rites of communion, baptism, and the devil's book.[5]

Representative though he might be of certain categories of accusation, George Burroughs was anything but typical, though if nothing else the Salem witch trials demonstrate that there was no "typical" witch. Yes, there were the "usual suspects" for the authorities to round up. The first suspects in Salem fit the stereotype of European witches, middle-aged or elderly women who were usually poor, widowed, and often infirm. Roughly three-quarters of those accused of witchcraft were women; most men who fell under suspicion did so because they were related to or associated with female witches. The reason is that women were viewed as the weaker sex, essentially corrupted. Witchcraft was, among other things, a sex crime; a key component of the satanic pact was sex with the devil. Married women also held few legal rights. They could not own property, and they had very limited rights in court, where they had to be represented by a male member of their family. And while unmarried women technically held the same legal rights as men, widows who lacked a husband to defend them were much more vulnerable to charges of witchcraft. Many accused witches were widows, and most had few or no children. Some believed witches were barren.[6]

John Demos and Carol Karlsen, two of the most prominent scholars of the period, have shown in their work that witches in New England prior to 1692 fit a profile similar to that of European witches, though some women who were accused were wealthy and socially prominent. Karlsen has observed that a majority of these wealthy women had inherited substantial estates from relatives because the family lacked a male heir. She suggests that these accusations were therefore related to property and control over resources. Given that the typical accusers were men in their twenties—a group that had limited financial resources, land, and autonomy—this makes a great deal of sense, especially as many of these accusations involved damage to livestock and other property. Nevertheless, accused witches tended to live at the edges of society, often by themselves, due to poverty or other factors that set them apart. They sometimes came from a different culture or religious background, and usually displayed odd and sometimes even deviant behavior. Some may even have suffered from what we would recognize today as a mental illness or dementia. These factors help to explain Demos's findings that many accused witches had a history of conflict with others within their communities. Marginalized, often abrasive, these women sometimes took affront when their occasional requests for help were denied. Their neighbors believed that these witches did more than take affront—they exacted revenge. For example, if she had requested of a neighbor that he give her some milk or cheese and was denied, she might respond with a curse wishing that the cow would dry up and stop producing milk. Should this happen at some point, however far in the future, the neighbor would believe the cow had been harmed by witchcraft.[7]

In looking at the pattern of accusation principally among residents of Salem Village, Boyer and Nissenbaum saw trends similar to those Demos had highlighted, though they were expressed a bit differently. They concluded that the accused generally revealed three characteristics: (1) they were outsiders in some way, (2) they were geographically or socially mobile, having lived in multiple communities or had their social rank rise or fall, and (3) they often refused to show deference to their superiors and to the existing social order. Boyer and Nissenbaum argue that "the witchcraft accusations of 1692 moved in channels which were determined by years of factional strife in Salem Village."[8]

Certainly many of the Salem women, particularly the first ones accused, fit the stereotypical view of a witch. Take the example of Sarah Good. She was raised in a respectable family in Wenham, but the suicide of her father when she was seventeen brought ill fame to the family and left her without a dowry. Unable to attract a wealthy suitor, she married an impoverished former indentured servant. His death at an early age left her deeply in debt. She and her second husband, William Good, were forced to sell his farm to pay off her debts, so William had to work at odd jobs to try to make ends meet. The Goods and their two young children were reduced to renting a room and occasionally had to sleep in a barn or stable. The promising life she had envisioned as a youth now gone, Sarah became sullen and resentful. She sometimes cursed and scolded those who refused to help when she asked for aid. Once, after Samuel Parris gave her charity, she left the parsonage muttering. Not long after this visit the Parris girls were afflicted, and the minister assumed those mutterings had been a curse.[9]

George Burroughs was a Harvard-trained minister and a spiritual and community leader, so on the surface he appears to be an unlikely person to be accused. Yet, upon close inspection, there were a multitude of factors that brought him under suspicion, and many of these surrounded his spirituality and commitment to Puritanism. While most ministers were public figures, open and engaged with their community, Burroughs was an intensely private individual and a man of mystery. Stories circulated about him, including many that described his tremendous strength—so great that some believed it could not be earthly. It was an odd trait indeed for a man in a profession that required many quiet hours dedicated to studying the Bible, preparing and giving sermons, and tending to the spiritual needs of his flock. John Putnam Sr. and his wife, Rebecca, testified that the mysterious minister had required his first wife, Hannah, to "give him a written covenant under her hand and seal that she would never reveal his secrets."[10] This seems to have been a pattern for Burroughs: at his trial he denied that he had not let his second wife, Sarah Ruck Hathorne, write to her father without his first approving the letter. He also denied that his house in Casco Bay was haunted, though he did admit that the house did have toads, commonly believed to be witches' familiars.[11]

Burroughs had also claimed, several times, to have preternatural knowledge, showing familiarity with conversations that took place in his absence. A neighbor testified that when Burroughs returned home "he hath often scolded wife and told her that he knew what they said when he was abroad." Even more damning was the deposition of Burroughs's brother-in-law Thomas Ruck about a strawberry-picking expedition during which he and his sister (Burroughs's late second wife, Sarah) got separated from George. Believing they had left him far behind, they were astonished to see Burroughs waiting for them on the path when they neared home. More amazing, he started "chiding his wife" about the details of her conversation with her brother, "which when they wondered at, he said, he knew their thoughts." This startled Ruck, who replied "that the devil himself did not know so far." Burroughs stunning reply was, "My God makes known your thoughts unto me."[12] Clearly the minister had eavesdropped on his wife and was trying to scare her into not revealing any of his secrets by impressing upon her his ability to hear all. However, this was a dangerous claim; many believed that such power must come from Satan and not from God. Indeed, there were many stories dating from medieval times about travelers encountering a person with preternatural knowledge of their activities—perhaps the devil—on a road near the end of a trip, and being tempted. Geoffrey Chaucer includes such an encounter in *The Canterbury Tales*. In "The Franklin's Tale," Aurelius and his brother are approaching their destination, Orleans, when they meet a "magician" who greets them in Latin. "'He sede a wonder thing' quod he 'I know the cause of your coming.'" The magician then goes on to strike a devilish deal with Aurelius to aid him in his quest for another man's wife. Ruck's story would have sounded very familiar to the courtroom audience, who would have easily associated Burroughs's behavior with that of the demons in such stories.[13]

While no Puritan in his or her right mind would openly brag about having a relationship with Satan, the teenager Abigail Hobbs clearly got a sense of power and freedom from such talk. She warned Lydia Nichols that "she was not afraid of anything for she told me she had sold herself body & soul to the old boy." The next time she saw Lydia, Abigail threatened her, telling her to "hold her tongue" or she would invoke Satan and raise all nearby spirits to torment her.[14] When Priscilla Chubb spoke to Abigail about "her wicked carriages and disobedience to her father and mother," Abigail warned that "she did not care what anybody said to her for she had seen the devil and had made a covenant or bargain with him."[15]

In 1692 magic was quite real, and it is possible some of the accused believed they were practicing it. We do know that at the very least white magic was practiced at Salem Village, as exemplified by the witch cake made under Mary Sibley's supervision. There was also John Hale's account of Dorcas Hoar's palm reading and fortune-telling. White magic could cross the line into black magic, as when the fortune-telling turned to predictions of death. Countermagic was also used to protect homes and their occupants from witches. In 1973, when the Danvers home built by Governor John Endicott's son Zerubabbel was disassembled to make way for a shopping mall, workers found an iron horseshoe and eel spear (shaped like a trident, or devil's pitchfork) nailed to the timber frame near the hearth and outside door, to prevent evil from entering the home. The objects were discovered under the interior sheathing, suggesting they had been placed there when the home was built in 1681. An eel spear was subsequently discovered in the interior of Rebecca Nurse's house, on top of the plate—the beam that supported the roof—in a section of the lean-to built no earlier than 1740. Such countermagic was apparently common, even in the homes of devout Puritans such as the Endicotts and the Nurses, and its use continued well past 1692. Carefully hidden, these objects would be out of view of disapproving eyes of those such as Samuel Parris who considered countermagic—be it horseshoes or witch cakes—to be evil. Still, families could draw comfort from knowing their home was protected.[16]

There also was considerable evidence of image magic—the use of poppets. George Burroughs, John Procter, Ann Pudeator, and Alice Parker allegedly gave poppets to the afflicted for them to use to torment others, and years before, workmen had found poppets in the cellar wall of Bridget Bishop's house. John Procter's son William was seen using a poppet, and Job Tookey allegedly drove a great pin through the heart of a poppet, thus killing a man. Ann Dolliver, the "negro" slave Candy, and Elizabeth Johnson Jr. all confessed to owning poppets. Candy was excused from the court in the middle of her testimony and returned with two poppets she had fashioned by putting knots in rags. Johnson brought her three poppets to court as well, two made "of rags or stripes of cloth," while the third was crafted from birch bark.[17] Dolliver said she had owned one or two poppets made out of wax, though that had been fourteen years earlier. A search of the home of

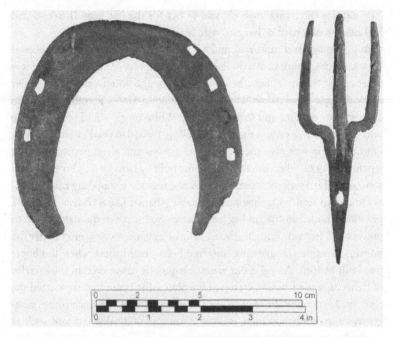

Horseshoe and trident (eel spear) from the Zerubabbel Endicott House. Courtesy of
Richard Trask, photograph by the author.

Mary Lacey Sr. and her daughter produced a suspicious parcel of rags, tape,
and quills tied up—just the sort of supplies used to make poppets.[18]

Clearly there were some who not only believed in the power of poppets
and black magic but also were willing to use it. For marginalized people,
magic was a way to take control of their lives. Bridget Bishop was a poor
woman. Ann Dolliver's husband had abandoned her. Dolliver tried to excuse
her behavior, explaining that "because she thought she was bewitched and
she had read in a book that told her that that was ye way to afflict them that
had afflicted her."[19] As a minister's daughter, Dolliver clearly knew better—
trying to harm someone with magic was the devil's work. Her judgment
may have been tempered by mental illness, though, for in 1698 her father,
Reverend John Higginson, referred to her as "overbearing melancholy,
crazed in her understanding." Several years later she would be declared
mentally incompetent. Simple-minded Elizabeth Johnson Jr. probably did
not fully understand the significance of her actions either. At best there

were only a handful of people practicing magic—especially black magic—in Essex County in 1692. There was no grand conspiracy of hundreds of witches, as some of the deponents described. However, a few poppets and stories of others provided sufficient physical evidence to convince people that Salem was indeed besieged by Satan and his agents.[20]

Witchcraft, black or white, was above all else a very serious religious crime, and spiritual concerns are clearly reflected in the evidence. Salem Village church members felt themselves under attack by Satan and led the accusations, lodging their charges principally against people who were not members of the village church or congregation.[21] Yet the allegations went much further than the bounds of Salem Village church, reaching anyone who might be a threat to orthodoxy, from Quakers and Baptists to even five Puritan ministers and many members of their families.

Many of those accused had ties to Quakers. The Bay Colony's execution of four Quaker missionaries for heresy more than three decades earlier and the resultant outrage from the English crown ensured that no Friends would be harmed in the witch trials. Yet Puritans continued to have grave concerns about Quakers. In his 1684 *Illustrious Providences*, Increase Mather connected the Friends on Long Island to a group of Ranters—an extreme radical Protestant sect known for drinking, blaspheming, and practicing free love—believed to have bewitched their neighbors. He also described the attack of a stone-throwing demon on the debauched tavern owned by a Quaker named George Walton in Portsmouth, New Hampshire.[22] In the late 1680s Increase's son Cotton Mather and three other Puritan ministers (John Allin, Joshua Moody, and Samuel Willard) would engage in a tract war against Quaker George Keith, whose writings attacked the Puritans. Cotton Mather reminded his readers in his account of Goody Glover's bewitchment of the Goodwin children that Martha Goodwin was able to read a "Quakers book" as well as a "popish book" but not the Bible or any orthodox Puritan writing.[23] In 1691 he warned, "I look upon Quakerism, as a snare of the devil." Mather suggested that the "strange Quaking" looked like "diabolical possession." Mather also reminded his readers of the efforts of Quaker women in particular to discredit the Puritan church. In 1663 Lydia Wardwell had walked into the Newbury Sabbath service completely naked to protest against the Puritan faith, which she felt lacked substance.[24] Fourteen years later another Quaker woman walked into Boston's South Church in the middle of Sunday service wearing sackcloth and smeared in ashes. A shocked Samuel Sewall stressed that "it occasioned the most amazing uproar that I ever saw."[25]

Perhaps some had Cotton Mather's admonitions in mind when Samuel Wardwell and others with Quaker ties were accused of witchcraft. Samuel was not himself a Friend, but he and his wife, Sarah, both had Quaker ties. Notably, Samuel's brother Eliakim and sister-in-law (the naked Lydia Wardwell) had adopted the faith. Furthermore, the brothers' parents were Antinomians who followed John Wheelwright to New Hampshire. So there was a streak of religious extremism in the family, and Samuel was well known for his palmistry and fortune telling. It should therefore come as no surprise that both the Wardwells, their daughter Mercy, and Sarah's daughter Sarah Hawkes were accused. There were a number of Quakers in the family of Elizabeth Procter and her sister Mary DeRich, including their father and brother. Furthermore, their grandmother, Ann Burt, had been charged with witchcraft in 1669. Suspicion may even have fallen on respected Puritan saint Rebecca Nurse because of Quaker ties. In 1677 she and her husband, Francis, had become the guardians of the orphaned Quaker Samuel Southwick. Perhaps Sarah Good had had some Quaker leanings, or at least knew their writings well enough to use them against her executioners. Her angry last words on the gallows to Reverend Noyes were drawn from the Bible but they had been used by English Quaker Joseph Nicholson in his 1660 tract to protest Massachusetts' execution of Quaker missionaries. Nicholson warned the magistrates and ministers of the Bay Colony that God would seek vengeance and "you shall have blood to drink who have shed innocent blood."[26]

George Burroughs was not a Quaker, but he was under suspicion of being a Baptist. The Baptists were another Protestant sect that had legal toleration but was considered dangerous by most Massachusetts Puritans because of their belief in adult baptism and adult-only membership in the church. Unfortunately for this mild-mannered sect, their name conjured up images of the Anabaptists of Munster, the radical polygamous extremists who had attempted a violent overthrow of their German state in the 1530s. When the magistrates first questioned Burroughs on May 9, they immediately asked the minister why he had failed to take communion and had not baptized his younger children—both signs that he might have become a Baptist. Burroughs's excuse was that he had never been ordained and hence could not lead the communion service, nor could he baptize children. However, he admitted that since leaving his post in Maine he had visited Boston and Charlestown and had failed to participate in those rites there.[27]

Burroughs's Maine connection certainly placed further suspicions on him and many others. The best place to find non-Christians, apostate Puritans, and other enemies of Massachusetts Bay was of course the frontier. The howling wilderness of northern New England was a dark corner, beyond the pale of Puritan piety, the place where Satan was waiting for his moment to destroy the colony. Furthermore, it was where Puritan merchants could build vast fortunes in furs, fish, lumber, and land speculation that might tempt them away from the path of orthodoxy. Since the time of the first English settlement, Maine had been occupied mainly by Anglicans and radical Protestants. Antinomian John Wheelwright moved north to found first Exeter, New Hampshire, and then Wells, Maine, after he was banished from Massachusetts in 1638. George Burdett, who first settled in Salem in 1636, serving as assistant pastor to Hugh Peter, left, "finding the discipline of the church too strict for his loose conscience," and moved north to Dover, New Hampshire. Here he turned to politics and was elected governor, but was soon forced to leave for "sundry miscarriages" and "foul practices."[28] So he moved on to York, Maine, but shortly after was driven out for his Antinomian leanings and his advocacy for and practice of free love with several married women. Burdett was last seen in Pemaquid, where, according to Maine's deputy governor, Thomas Gorges, "his time he spends drinking, dancing, singing scurrilous songs; for his companions he selects the wretchedest people in the country." Such were the ministers who moved north from the Bay Colony to Maine.[29]

Even when the region came under the control of Massachusetts Bay, there remained a fair degree of religious latitude in Maine. Reverend Robert Jordan, an Anglican, preached on Casco Bay for almost forty years before King Philip's War forced him to abandon the region. Just a few miles south of Casco Bay, Baptist William Milborne became the minister in Saco, Maine, in 1685, having fled Bermuda when the governor there accused him of being a Fifth Monarchist—a member of a revolutionary Protestant sect that believed Jesus would soon return to earth and reform English politics and society. The Baptists also established a congregation in Kittery in 1682, led by William Scriven. By 1692 Milborne had fled from the war zone to the safety of Boston, and authorities were harassing Scriven to the point where he would soon leave for South Carolina, where he would help found the Southern Baptist movement.[30]

Meanwhile, the only remaining minister in Maine with unquestioned Puritan credentials had been killed in a Native American raid. Reverend Shubael Dummer died in York on January 24, 1692, during the Candlemas Raid, in which more than a hundred settlers were killed or taken captive. The destruction of this prosperous shire town shocked residents of Massachusetts; if York could fall, most towns north of Boston were vulnerable. The death of the first Puritan minister at the hands of Native Americans was an ominous sign that Satan was winning the war against Massachusetts. Cotton Mather soon observed that "you have seen a most pious and faithful minister lately assassinated by the brutes of our east." Dummer's death provoked Mather to make an urgent encouragement for moral reformation: "A church of saints is now lately in a manner dissipated by a sudden, furious, treacherous attack.... Doubtless the fall of one golden candlestick in our borders makes noise enough to awaken all our churches unto the doing of some remarkable thing in returning to God."[31] Reverend Dummer came from a prominent Newbury family, one of many York residents with ties to Essex County. Less than a month before the Candlemas Raid he had received money from his cousin Samuel Sewall to aid the victims of the war. Soon after the raid, Salem Town parishioners voted to contribute £32—a considerable sum—to a York relief fund administered by Sewall and Dummer's brother. It is probably not a coincidence that afflictions increased in the Parris household in the wake of the Candlemas Raid, which offered just one more reason to be suspicious of George Burroughs. Burroughs had left Falmouth to live in Wells shortly before the town fell to a combined Native and French force, resulting in the death of most of the defenders. Some wondered why Burroughs had managed to avoid the fate of Shubael Dummer.[32]

Burroughs's accusation solidified the link between witchcraft, the frontier, and attacks on orthodoxy. Burroughs's examination represented the first time in the witch trials that the question of baptism was raised, an issue that subsequently would play an important role, as many of the accused described their baptism by Satan during the proceedings. The connection seems clear. While Salem Village and other communities—particularly those that refused to accept the Halfway Covenant—struggled to maintain membership, Satan had no problem growing his ranks, especially with

George Burroughs and other ministers leading his black masses, assisting with adult baptisms just like the Baptists, and recruiting people to sign the satanic covenant in the devil's book.[33]

Furthermore, once Burroughs was charged, practically anyone could fall under suspicion. Four ministers would subsequently be cried out upon during the witch trials. This did not go without notice in 1692. Writing from Boston on July 11, 1692, Jacob Melyen noted, "They accuse many honest people of being sorcerers and witches, naming three or four ministers and one of them lies in irons, and some 200 have been accused."[34] Historians have given little attention to Samuel Willard, Francis Dane, John Busse, and Jeremiah Shepard, for none was ever formally charged. But they form an important part of an overlooked pattern of accusations against ministers and their families. Twenty of the 172 accused (11 percent) were ministers or their close relatives. In all, five ministers, four minister's wives, three daughters, a son, two brothers, and five grandchildren of ministers were cried out upon. Warrants were issued for only five of the twenty, and only two—Burroughs and Abigail Dane Faulkner (daughter of Andover's Reverend Francis Dane)—would face the Court of Oyer and Terminer. The number grows to fifty if one includes extended kin and in-laws of ministers—fully 30 percent of the people accused in 1692. Admittedly, Francis Dane and his family account for twenty-eight of these fifty, but this is still a remarkable coincidence, one that calls for exploration and explanation.[35]

Virtually all of the ministers who were accused or had family accused preached in New England churches that had accepted the Halfway Covenant. One notable exception was Job Tookey, the son, grandson, and great-grandson of English ministers. Job's former employer had called his father "an Annabaptistical Quaking rogue that for his maintenance went up and down England to delude souls for the devil." Job Tookey defended his father as "a religious Godly man" with solid Puritan credentials, but the slander may have spread and even seemed believable to Samuel Parris and his conservative supporters, given Tookey's lowly status as a transient sailor and fisherman who had spent time on the coast of Maine.[36]

Also accused were people who seemingly were devout Puritans. Given Salem Village's refusal to accept the Halfway Covenant, there may have been concerns about orthodox ministers who supported it. John Higginson, the father of accused Ann Dolliver, had almost threatened to resign his post in Salem Town if the church did not accept the Halfway Covenant. The accusation against Margaret Thacher may have stemmed from her ties to the frontier. In 1692 she still owned frontier lands, including a sawmill in Cocheco (Dover, New Hampshire), inherited from her father and first husband, both very wealthy Boston merchants. Thacher also may have been the mistress of Mercy Short, an afflicted girl with ties to the frontier. However, Thacher's second husband, the late Peter Thacher, had been the founding pastor for Boston's Third Church. This congregation had been established specifically on the principle of the Halfway Covenant. Thacher's successor was Samuel Willard, who, like Margaret, was cried out upon but never brought up on charges.[37]

Perhaps Willard was accused because of his early opposition to the trials, as voiced in the sermons he gave during the summer of 1692. If a later account is to be believed, Willard and Joshua Moody, the assistant pastor of Boston's First Church, were instrumental in helping Philip and Mary English to flee jail in Boston and gain refuge in New York. This story could explain why Moody's wife, Ann, was accused of witchcraft, for those people who opposed the trials or questioned their authority were targeted. Likewise, even witchcraft judge Major Nathaniel Saltonstall was accused after he had left the bench, possibly because he was dissatisfied with the proceedings. It should also be noted that Saltonstall was the son-in-law of Haverhill's Reverend John Ward.[38]

Like Willard, John Busse (or Buss) was cried out upon but escaped formal charges of witchcraft. Busse's case demonstrates that it took multiple factors to trigger an accusation, especially for a minister. Busse's frontier residency and the fact that his mother-in-law, Mary Bradbury, was charged with witchcraft presumably led four people to cry out against him in court. The accusers placed him alongside George Burroughs, assisting with satanic baptisms and black masses. Richard Barker called him a "ring leader" at one gathering where the witches "were all by Mr. Burse and the black man exhorted to pull down the kingdom of Christ and set up the kingdom of the devil."[39] The connection to Burroughs was natural. Busse had even served in Wells, leaving 1677 to become parson and physician in the Oyster River section of Dover, New Hampshire (Oyster River is present-day Durham). Years later he would recount that he had labored in Oyster River "in the time of the late terrible Indian war when many a score fell by the sword both upon ye right hand & the left, and several others forced to flight for want of bread" and still managed to hold services in the garrison "every Lord's Day as God did enable him."[40] His service came at a price. The Joseph and William Buss killed by Natives during the Dover raid in 1689 were probably his sons, and in 1694 his house and valuable library would be destroyed in a Native American raid.

As unordained preachers, besieged by Native Americans on the frontier, and leading the witches' coven, Burroughs and Busse had much in common. Yet, unlike Burroughs, Busse was never formally charged, even though, as noted, his mother-in-law was convicted of witchcraft. Clearly ministers had some protection during the proceedings. Little is known of Busse's religious views, but he did serve in Dover, one of the few towns in the area that had not accepted the Halfway Covenant. This may have alleviated any concerns about his Puritan orthodoxy. Busse's case also speaks to the importance of the multiple factors that came into play with Burroughs.[41]

Thomas Maule said that the "Lynn Priest" was accused of witchcraft, and surely this refers to Jeremiah Shepard, the minister in Lynn.[42] Shepard, the youngest son of Cambridge's beloved Reverend Thomas Shepard, was a member of one of the colony's leading families of divines; his stepfather, his older brother and half-brother were also ministers. Shepard was a political as well as religious leader in Lynn, starting with his active role in the over-throw of Governor Andros. When that revolt began in April 1689, Shepard led a mob "who were like so many wild bears; and the leader, mad with pas-sion, more savage than any of his followers. All the cry was for the governor and Mr. Randolph." Shepard was soon elected as a deputy to the General Court, apparently the first minister in the colony's history to hold this office. The next year he was one of the chaplains for Sir William Phips's failed at-tack on Quebec. This may explain some of the hostility to Shepard. Why would a Puritan clergyman of Shepard's unimpeachable spiritual and po-litical credentials arouse suspicion and even accusation? Presumably it was precisely because of qualifications—particularly his pastorship of a church that supported the Halfway Covenant, as well as his political leadership during the failures of the interim government. He may have also drawn at-tention because of his involvement in past religious controversies in Ipswich and Rowley, controversies that bear some semblance to events in Salem Village. Finally, the substantial number of Quakers in Lynn may have led people to wonder about the state of the Puritan church in that community.[43]

Despite the objections of his parishioners, Beverly's John Hale joined Shepard as one of the chaplains on the unpopular Quebec expedition. This may help explain why his wife, Sarah Noyes Hale, was accused of witchcraft in 1692, though her membership in a family full of divines would have normally protected her from suspicion. Not only was she the wife of a minister, but her father, the late James Noyes, had been the pastor at Newbury, a position he had shared with his cousin Thomas Parker. Sarah's grandfather, great-uncle, uncle, and two brothers were ministers as well. Indeed, her brother James would later be one of the seven ministers who founded Yale University. Nicholas Noyes, the Salem Town minister, was her first cousin. The idea that a woman from such a devout family could be accused of witchcraft shocked not only her husband but many other supporters of the trials, and apparently caused many to change their opinion of the proceedings.[44]

If the Quaker John Whiting is to be believed, the accusations went to the very top of the religious hierarchy. Writing in 1702, he noted that even Cotton Mather's mother was cried out upon.[45] Maria Cotton Mather was the linchpin connecting the two most important families of Puritan divines in Massachusetts. Her father was John Cotton, perhaps the leading Puritan theologian to join the Great Migration. Her husband was Increase Mather, president of Harvard College and son of the prominent minister Richard Mather. In 1692 Increase was the preeminent minister of Massachusetts Bay, as well as a key political figure—the top advisor to Governor Phips. Maria was also the sister of two ministers, sister-in-law of four more, and mother of Reverends Cotton and Samuel Mather. Increase and Cotton were both long-standing advocates of the Halfway Covenant, but their conservative North Church had refused to accept it. During the trials, the Mathers were in the final stages of a campaign to get the North Church to adopt the Halfway Covenant. One of the few stalwart church members who stood in the way was Judge John Richards.[46]

The accusation of George Burroughs and Maria Mather is symbolic of a rebellion against existing authority in Massachusetts in the 1680s and 1690s that helps to explain why so many ministers, politicians, militia officers, and members of their families were cried out on for witchcraft.[47] Members of the political and military elite were equally vulnerable to charges in 1692, and again they started at the top, for no less a figure than Lady Mary Phips, the wife of Governor Sir William Phips, was accused of witchcraft after she overstepped her authority. While her husband was off in Maine building Fort William Henry, Mary responded to a plea to the governor for clemency by ordering the Boston jailer to release a woman accused of witchcraft.[48]

Given the multiple offices held by individuals and the marriage alliances between the ministerial and political elite, one person could have several of the characteristics that worked to bring people under suspicion. Margaret Thacher, as we have seen, had ties to the frontier, to the merchant community through her late father and first husband, to the church through her second husband, and to the leadership of the colony through her son-in-law Judge Jonathan Corwin. Major Saltonstall could have been a target because of his rejection of the trials, his military office, his position as a member of the Governor's Council, or the fact that he was the son-in-law of Haverhill's Reverend John Ward. Perhaps all of these factors combined to bring him under suspicion.

One did not even need a connection to the frontier to be associated with the enemy and fall under suspicion. The merchant Philip English (born Philippe L'Anglais) and his wife may have been accused as a backlash against his wealth and his position as a Salem selectman, but his support of the Anglican Church combined with his birth on the Channel island of Jersey and his French accent certainly raised suspicions as well.[49] While there were several reasons a wealthy person such as Philip English might be accused of witchcraft, it was certainly not to gain that person's property. A popular misconception of the trials is that the individual who accused a witch would gain the witch's property upon his or her conviction. While it was true that under English common law a convicted felon forfeited his personal estate, it went to the king. And when someone was convicted of a crime that carried the death penalty, he or she was automatically placed under attainder and had his or her real estate seized. Technically, being placed under attainder was to be placed "under corruption of blood," by which that person lost all civil rights; that person and any of his or her descendants also lost all right to rank and title. Attainder was very specifically excluded from the 1641 Massachusetts Body of Liberties—one of a number of differences in English and Massachusetts laws.[50]

Yet in 1692, Sheriff George Corwin seized the personal property of seven men and seven women who were convicted of witchcraft or who fled after being charged. He did so because the witch trials took place at the very moment that Massachusetts Bay was attempting to establish a full set of laws "not repugnant" to English law. Until that time, as noted earlier, the colony was in a bit of legal limbo. When Governor Phips created the court on May 27, he instructed it to act "according to the Law and Custom of England," that is, under English common law, as well as under any Massachusetts laws not repugnant to English law. While the English witchcraft statute did allow seizure of a felon's personal property, it protected that person's real estate. Thus Sheriff Corwin acted fully within the law in place when he seized the personal property of the condemned, including the wedding ring of the wife of George Jacobs Sr., because a woman's jewelry—even her wedding ring—was considered her husband's property. However, only the government could profit from this loss, and the people who made the numerous accusations prior to the creation of the court could not have known that any forfeitures would take place. Nor do the forfeitures explain Giles Cory's actions when he was pressed to death. Someone who stood mute could, under common law, have his property seized as well. Corwin acted improperly only when he seized the estates of several of the accused who had fled to avoid arrest, for they had not been convicted or placed under attainder. On October 13, the first act passed in the new session of the General Court included a clause prohibiting forfeitures, perhaps in response to popular complaint over this unusual—and, as it turned out, short-lived—practice in Massachusetts.[51]

Captain Dudley Bradstreet was another well-connected officeholder who came out against the trials. Bradstreet may be best known today as the son of Puritan poet Ann Bradstreet. But in 1692 he would have been recognized as a militia officer who served as Andover's magistrate and deputy to the General Court. He was the son of Governor Simon Bradstreet, grandson of Governor Thomas Dudley, and nephew of future governor Joseph Dudley. He was also the grandson, brother, and nephew of Puritan divines, and had two ministers for brother-in-laws; one of them, Seaborn Cotton, was also the brother-in-law of Increase Mather and uncle of Cotton Mather. Furthermore, his wife, Ann, was the mother-in-law of Andover's Reverend Thomas Barnard. A man of impeccable Puritan credentials of the highest rank, Dudley granted warrants and committed "thirty or forty to prisons, for the supposed witchcrafts," but he "at length saw cause to forbear granting out any more warrants. Soon after which he and his wife were cried out of, himself was (by them) said to have killed nine persons by witchcraft." To avoid arrest, the Bradstreets fled to the Piscataqua, presumably to the home of Dudley's sister Hannah and her husband, Andrew Wiggin, a leading magistrate of New Hampshire. They were joined by Dudley's brother John, whose specter had been seen riding and afflicting a dog in

Salem Village. The hound was subsequently put to death, as was another in Andover whose glance put people into fits—the only two known canine victims of the witch hunt. John held no offices, but his father-in-law was the late Reverend William Perkins of Topsfield.[52]

Perhaps the Bradstreet brothers had been brought under suspicion because many years earlier their kinsman, another John Bradstreet, had openly bragged about his supernatural connections. In 1652 the court had presented John Bradstreet of Rowley for familiarity with the devil. Specifically, Bradstreet had claimed "he read in a book of magic and he heard a voice asking him what work he had for him," the voice clearly being Satan's. Bradstreet supposedly replied, "Go make a bridge of sand over the sea go make a ladder of sand up to heaven and go to God and come down no more." The court found Bradstreet innocent of the charge but did find him guilty of lying about the alleged incident. Still, this episode would have been remembered and may have added to doubts about the Bradstreets in 1692. The accusations against the three Bradstreets, one of the preeminent families of the colony, shows that no opposition to the trials would be tolerated. It also suggests a complete rejection of the political, military, and spiritual establishment of the colony.[53]

Other political and military leaders and members of their families were targeted as well. Daniel Andrew, a Salem selectman and former deputy to the General Court, was accused, as were his sister Rebecca, her husband, George Jacobs Jr., and their daughter Margaret. Rebecca's father-in-law, George Jacobs Sr., was executed. One Andover selectman was accused, as were family of two others. Convicted witch Mary Bradbury was the wife of Captain Thomas Bradbury, the most prominent settler of Salisbury. Captain Bradbury was the grandnephew of both Sir Ferdinando Gorges, the royalist and Anglican proprietor of Maine, and John Whitgift, the archbishop of Canterbury. Bradbury was a militia officer who had performed long service as deputy to the General Court as well as a local magistrate and judge. Mary Bradbury had been accused of witchcraft years before, but her being cried out upon in this instance may also have been influenced by her husband's offices and his ties to prominent Anglicans and royalists. Captain John Floyd (or Flood) was accused presumably as a result of his less-than-successful military efforts on the frontier. Nicholas Frost's father, Charles, was a major in the frontier militia, as was Mary Swayne Marshall's brother. Hezekiah Usher was accused soon after his royalist brother John was named lieutenant governor of New Hampshire. Indeed, John acted as governor, serving for his absentee father-in-law, Governor Samuel Allen, the would-be proprietor who had purchased the Mason family's claim to New Hampshire. Finally, the accused Mary Osgood's husband, John, was Andover's militia captain.[54]

Andover's position near the edge of English settlement made it a likely place for people to see witches. Yet even relatively safe coastal towns considered themselves vulnerable to attack after the raid on York. In the seaport of Gloucester, people began to see Native warriors and French soldiers scurrying about. When no actual soldiers were forthcoming, the town's minister, John Emerson Sr., eventually determined they were "demons in the shape of armed Indians and Frenchmen" produced by the devil and his local agents. In September, Ebenezer Babson, the owner of the Gloucester home that was the focus of the phantom attack, would accuse Margaret Prince and Elizabeth Dicer of witchcraft. Dicer was a war refuge from Saco, Maine. Presumably she was living in Gloucester at the time of her accusation at the home of her daughter and son-in-law, Ann and Richard Tarr, who were also Maine refugees. Soon seven more Gloucester women would be accused.[55]

Many people in Essex County had formerly lived on the frontier or had a close relative with frontier ties, and twenty-four of them were accused, including George Burroughs, who, as we have seen, spent most of his ministerial career in Maine. In Falmouth and Wells, Burroughs certainly would have run across Captain John Alden, whose case exemplifies the perceived spiritual dangers of the frontier and their connections to witchcraft. Alden was a merchant, ship's captain, and militia officer as well as a founding saint of Boston's South Church. An experienced sailor in his mid-sixties, he captained the colony's sloop, *Mary*—the one-ship "navy" of Massachusetts Bay—during King William's War. Between October 1688 and April 1692 Alden made at least sixteen round trips from Boston to the coast of northern New England and Acadia on government business. He was a good man for the job, for he had long been trading with the English, French, and Native Americans of the region. He often worked in concert with fellow Bostonian John Nelson, the leading trader to Acadia. In wartime these connections brought suspicions, particularly against Nelson, who was an Anglican. Unfortunately, the men's behavior did nothing to help their cause, as they repeatedly put profits ahead of the best interests of the colony. On diplomatic missions when he was arranging hostage exchanges Alden had almost certainly been illegally selling the enemy lead shot and gunpowder. Although he was never formally charged, rumors about him had been spreading. By late 1690 Alden had been given specific orders to bring no more gunpowder than necessary on his expeditions—indicating that even officials suspected what he was up to.[56]

People on the waterfronts of Essex County knew Alden all too well. In August 1691, when Alden arrived in Salem with orders for militia men on the ketch *Endeavor* to join his convoy headed to Port Royal, the soldiers refused to serve under him. Alden's old friend and business associate Bartholomew Gedney tried to help, but the men would not go. The captain of the *Endeavor* related that the men "generally said that said Alden was reported to be an old Indian trader and was going to trade with the French and therefore many of them did then reply they would be hanged before they would go with him said Alden." Magistrates Hathorne and Corwin were ordered to arrest the crew for treason. Thus several judges on the Court of Oyer and Terminer would have known of Alden's reputation.[57]

The crew of the *Endeavor* was wise to avoid the trip, for the expedition would prove to be a disaster. Alden, accompanied by his son John junior, John Nelson, and others, was headed to Port Royal to garrison it. They had made a deal with the Massachusetts government to hold the port, in return for a trade monopoly. However, the French sent a force to retake Port Royal, and they captured Alden, his ship, and his associates. They would parole Alden, so that he could return to Boston to arrange a prisoner exchange and raise a ransom for the return of the vessel. Yet Alden would take eight months to return to Port Royal, and when he finally did, in the spring of 1692, he brought only a handful of the soldiers the French expected to be exchanged. In the end, Alden would abscond with the ransom money and even seize a French ship taken while under his letter of safe conduct granted by the French. In the name of profit and greed, Alden would abandon his son, John Nelson, and the others, and it would take years to spring them out of the Bastille, the notorious French prison.[58]

By this time Alden faced even more charges of impropriety from several former captives of the Indians. Pressed into service as a soldier, Mark Emerson had been stationed at Fort Sagadahoc on the Kennebec. He was taken prisoner, and the Wabanaki held him captive for more than two years. Alden had refused to help him negotiate his release from the Natives. When Emerson protested, the captain retorted that "he came to trade and not to redeem captives." Emerson noted that the enemy had been in a bad way, "last winter and spring both French and Indians were forced to eat their dogs and some of their captives, for having no powder and shot could not kill a fowl." But Alden was happy to replenish their munitions and food-stuffs in return for highly profitable fur pelts, for "the Indians have a saying that Mr. Alden is a good man and loves Indians very well for beaver."[59] Only several months later, when Alden returned to the Native village, was Emerson redeemed, his ransom having been paid by John Nelson—himself still a prisoner of the French, thanks in part to Alden. In mid-May 1692 two more English captives escaped. They reported that the leader of the French forces in Maine, the Baron St.-Castin, had been promised goods by Alden that he was still waiting to receive.[60]

These rumors and statements of Alden's conduct in the war would seem to confirm the fears that he was in league with the enemy, a part of Satan's grand coalition bent on destroying Puritan Massachusetts. Alden's behavior would lead to a formal complaint of witchcraft being lodged against him on May 28. Three days later he would appear before the court. He faced the afflicted girls, whom Alden described as "those wenches being present, who played their juggling tricks, falling down, crying out, and staring in peoples' faces." One of the girls said, "There stands Alden, a bold fellow with his hat on before the judges, he sells powder and shot to the Indians and French, and lies with the Indian squaws, and has Indian papooses." Then "Alden committed to the Marshal's custody, and his sword taken from him; for they said he afflicted them with his sword."[61]

Alden's provision of munitions to the enemy was well known, and while there is no evidence of his sexual liaisons with Natives, perhaps this was assumed, given his friendship with Baron St.-Castin, who was married to the daughter of the Penobscot sachem Madockawando. There was a con-stant reminder of that relationship in Boston, where one of the baron's daughters then resided. She had been taken prisoner by Sir William Phips in 1690 when he, aided by Alden and the *Mary*, captured Port Royal. The girl was a servant in the Phips household, waiting for a prisoner exchange to return her to her family. The accusation that Alden afflicted people with his sword—a badge of his military rank—reflected not only fear of the war but also anger and disappointment at the failure of the militia leadership. As a sexually charged object, the sword might also allude to Alden's alleged liaisons with Native women.

The statement that he was "a bold fellow with his hat on before the judges" brought concerns over religious orthodoxy into focus, for it suggested Alden was a Quaker.[62] Normally only a Quaker would refuse to offer hat service, that is, to remove his hat before his superiors, for Quakers believed everyone was equal. Alden was not a Quaker. If he did refuse to remove his hat, presumably it was an angry response to his old friend Bartholomew Gedney. The judge "said he had known Alden many years, and had been at sea with him, and always looked upon him to be an honest man, but now he did see cause to alter his judgment."[63] But there were still legitimate reasons to believe Alden might have sympathies for religious radicals, for his mother-in-law, Bridget Phillips, was not just a Quaker but the daughter of the notorious Antinomian Anne Hutchinson. Bridget and her husband, Major William Phillips, had moved from Boston to the lower Saco River in 1659, presumably because it was a region where Quakers could worship in relative peace. It also was a place of great economic opportunity for a merchant such as Major Phillips. He became a leading magistrate, established a sawmill and trading post at the falls of the Saco in present-day Biddeford, Maine, and also speculatively purchased thousands of acres of land from Native Americans. Phillips turned to his son-in-law Alden to help with these land deals. Alden witnessed two of these deeds, and presumably the seasoned fur trader was responsible for negotiating the sales with the local Wabanaki. Alden's participation in this Native land speculation would have been held against him in 1692 as well. Not only was his family trying to accumulate excessive profits, but they were signing deeds with the Native Americans to do so—effectively signing a covenant with people the Puritans considered heathens and devil worshipers. In short, the case against John Alden stemmed from every possible root of accusation: social, political, religious, sexual, geographical, and military. All, however, shared the common element of the frontier.[64]

John Alden was just one of the many accused who had abused his authority. While Alden took advantage of his offices to achieve personal gain, others abused their patriarchal authority through physical violence. Reading through the hundreds of pages of the surviving witch trial court records, one cannot help but be struck by how many of the afflicted maintained that they had suffered beatings and other physical abuse from specters, a reflection of mistreatment they received in real life. Their accusations may have been made toward those who had inflicted violence, directly or indirectly (such as abetting the Natives in their war, as with Alden), against them or their friends, or who were otherwise known for violent behavior. In early New England, authority figures—particularly men—had considerable latitude in physically disciplining their inferiors: wives, children, and servants. There were relatively few court cases involving domestic abuse, but there were limits to what was acceptable corporal punishment, and those who crossed the line were often brought up on charges. Such behavior was also evidence of a failure to maintain harmonious bonds in the family, which was the most important unit of Puritan society.[65]

Five of the six men put to death by the Court of Oyer and Terminer probably would have been viewed as abusive in this regard, for they were specifically accused of having their specters beat one or more afflicted girls—usually in an effort to force them to sign Satan's book. Three of these men had a history of violence, and there was strong suspicion about two others: John Procter and George Burroughs. Only Samuel Wardwell seems to have escaped claims of having been abusive. Both Giles Cory and George Jacobs Sr. had been convicted in the past for violent crimes. In 1675, in a fit of anger, Giles Cory used a stick to severely beat his hired hand Jacob Goodell (or Goodall), an act that may have led to the man's death. The court fined Cory, though some thought he had gotten away with murder. Four of the afflicted said "Giles Cory or his apparition" beat them, and Mary Warren specified that he did it with his staff. When Giles was pressed to death, Thomas Putnam Jr. wrote to Samuel Sewall to inform him of the well-remembered death of Goodell. Interestingly, Deodat Lawson noted that "an ancient woman, named Goodall," was among the large group of women who claimed to be afflicted by Giles's wife, Martha Cory.[66]

In 1677 the court fined George Jacobs for beating John Tompkins Jr. Jacobs landed just one blow, but a witness testified that he if had not been restrained, Jacobs "would have stuck him more, he being in such a passion." Twelve years later, five of the afflicted girls would testify that Jacobs or his specter had beaten them with his staff or staves—possibly here referring to the walking canes used by the elderly Jacobs.[67] Three of the afflicted girls said they were struck, beaten, or choked by John Willard's specter, and four witnesses testified about the severe beatings he gave his wife. As one put it, "For all his natural affections he abused his wife much and broke sticks about her in beating of her."[68] Another noted Willard's wife's "lamentable complaint" of "how cruelly her husband had beaten her," to the point that she thought she would "never recover of the blows he had given her."[69]

Neither John Procter nor George Burroughs had ever been brought before the court for violence, and only one afflicted girl complained of their specter harming her, but there are still strong suggestions they abused their family authority. When John Indian joined the ranks of the afflicted, Procter told several villagers that if the slave was "in his custody he would soon beat the devil out of him."[70] He seems to have put this philosophy into practice on his own servant, Mary Warren. On the morning of March 25, Procter was on his way to Salem Village when he encountered Samuel Sibley. Procter explained that he was going to the village to fetch the afflicted Mary, whom he described as "his jade," and then he would "thresh the devil out of her." He said that when "when she was first taken with fits he kept her" busy on the spinning wheel and "threatened to thresh her." This seemed to end her fits, at least until Procter left home. Procter believed he could end the whole outbreak quickly if he was given access to the afflicted and the whipping post.[71] Warren denied that John Procter had threatened to run hot fire tongs down her throat if she did not sign the devil's book, but she did say that he "threatened to burn her out of her fit"—presumably with the tongs. Procter clearly believed the afflictions and accusations were nonsense, and he was willing to use force, or at the least the threat of force, to bring it all to an end. Perhaps more disquieting than his suggestion of beatings and whippings was his reference to Warren as "his jade," for the slang term suggests a disreputable or flirtatious woman. It is a rather odd way for a married sixty-year-old father of eleven to refer to his twenty-year-old servant, especially when that servant would later testify that she saw Procter's specter and would pull it down into her lap. Such evidence leads one to speculate if there was more to their master-servant relationship than meets the eye. Little wonder that some have suggested that several of the afflicted girls, including Mary Warren, might have been sexually abused.[72]

The secretive and controlling George Burroughs would never have made violent threats in public, but Cotton Mather noted he "had been infamous for the barbarous usage of his two successive wives, all the country over."[73] John Putnam Sr. and his wife, Rebecca, testified that Burroughs was a "very harsh sharp man" to his dutiful first wife. The minister was a small but rugged man, and known, as we have seen for his great strength, be it the ability to carry barrels of molasses or to pick up a long, heavy musket just by sticking his forefinger in the muzzle. He was comfortable on the frontier amid guns and combat, and acquitted himself well accompanying Colonel Benjamin Church and the troops into battle to defend Falmouth.[74] Presumably his remarkable strength, his rugged frontier character, and the rumors of his mistreatment of his wives were known to the afflicted girls, and this projected a sinister image, for they reported the ghostly visit of Burroughs's two deceased wives. The spirits told Ann Putnam Jr. that he had been "a cruel man to them." Their "blood did cry for vengeance" against Burroughs for his murdering them, and they believed "he should be cast into Hell." Ann was also visited by the ghosts of Deodat Lawson's first wife and daughter, as well as Goodman Fuller's first wife, and they said Burroughs had killed them as well.[75] Mercy Lewis, Mary Walcott, and Susannah Sheldon would make similar claims. There was absolutely no evidence that Burroughs had a hand in anyone's death, but the placing of all this female blood on Burroughs's hands at least suggests that the afflicted believed Burroughs had abused his wives and failed in his matrimonial duties.[76]

Accusations against people of such high rank and social position were uncommon. When it did happen in large-scale European witchcraft outbreaks, it was usually due to condemned or confessed witches implicating community leaders in an effort to bring the trials to an end. This is a sensible explanation, but it does not work for Salem, where the high-ranking people were accused by the afflicted, not by confessed witches. In Trier, Germany, in the 1580s, the usual pattern of accusations against poor, marginalized women broke down. A particularly cold period of the Little Ice Age led to a series of crop failures, which resulted in economic disaster and famine for a good number of farmers. Their plight led many to blame the rich for working with the devil to create their problems. After all, merchants who owned large stores of grain would profit by the price increases and charge usuriously high interest rates to people desperate for money to buy food. The rich were even described as driving to their black Sabbaths in golden coaches. In Trier, witchcraft became a potent weapon used against wealthy and powerful men. Similar forces may have been at work at Salem. Certainly the Little Ice Age's Maunder Minimum and the ongoing war meant that in 1692 a fair number of people were suffering economic distress. Under such circumstances the elite may have become a most useful scapegoat.[77]

In addition to religious controversy, ideological disagreement, and social jealousy, the accusations—as the case of George Burroughs and other community leaders show—grew from local conflict. Indeed, witchcraft was frequently a family or neighborly crime, with accusations stemming from long-standing petty disputes over boundary lines, wandering livestock, or inheritances. In Salem Village, as we have noted, the Putnam family seemed to be involved in many of the disputes in one way or another. Sarah Osburn's first husband, Robert Prince, was a kinsman of the Putnams. Soon after his death and her marriage to Alexander Osburn, the couple entered a protracted legal battle over her first husband's estate with her sons and with Thomas and John Putnam, the executors of the estate. The Putnams had their differences with others in the village, including Rebecca Nurse and her family.[78]

Sarah Holten's accusation against her neighbor Rebecca Nurse reflects this neighborly conflict and shows a side of the elderly Puritan saint rarely noted. Holten testified that three years earlier an angry Rebecca "came to our house and fell a railing" at her husband, Benjamin Holten, "because our pigs got into her field." The Holtens said their pigs were properly yoked and that the fault lay with the Nurses, whose "fence was down in several places." But nothing they said could pacify Rebecca, who "continued railing and scolding" and then called her son to "go and get a gun and kill our pigs and let none of them go out of the field." According to Massachusetts Bay law, the Nurses had the right to kill the swine, and her threat to do so, after first seeking a neighborly solution, suggests her frustration over the situation. Several days after the incident, Benjamin Holten "was struck blind and stricken down two or three times." Then, two weeks before he died, "he was taken with strange and violent fits acting much like to our poor bewitched persons." Sarah's conclusion was that Rebecca had bewitched her "poor husband."[79]

Boundary disputes, broken fences, and trespassing animals were common problems that filled the dockets of early New England courts, and they quickly became part of the accusation pattern. The Holten-Nurse dispute was part of a recurring theme of fences, intruding spectral animals, and harm to livestock in the witch trial depositions. Certainly witchcraft had been used in the past as a way to settle old scores and end long-standing legal disputes. Take, for example, the case of the Portsmouth, New Hampshire, Quaker George Walton. In the summer of 1682 Walton and his tavern, as

Rebecca Nurse House, Danvers, Massachusetts. It is a hall-and-parlor
house, with a lean-to off the back. Today it is a museum, open to the public.
Photograph by the author.

noted earlier, were regularly attacked by unseen stone-throwing assail-
ants. Some neighbors believed that the despised Walton and his debauched
tavern were being attacked by stealthy neighborhood boys. The aged Quaker
probably believed this as well. But he used the attacks as a way to try to end
a thirty-year property dispute, charging his elderly neighbor Hannah Jones
with witchcraft. The widowed Anglican saw through the tactic and leveled
the playing field by accusing Walton of being a wizard.[80]

The Nurses were involved in a similarly enduring grudge. The farm that
Rebecca and Francis Nurse leased from Reverend James Allen was the focus
of a long and complicated boundary dispute between Allen, the Nurses,
and the abutting Endicott and Putnam families. This dispute and another
between the Putnams and several Topsfield landowners likely influenced
the charges against Rebecca and her sisters Mary Esty and Sarah Cloyce,
for their brother, Ensign Jacob Towne, was one of the Topsfield men.
Francis Nurse was also a central figure in the factionalism that gripped
Salem Village and resulted in accusations. Nurse and Daniel Andrew were

members of the anti-Parris village committee elected in 1691. Seventeen people accused of witchcraft were related or in some way connected with them and other leaders of the anti-Parris network, such as Peter Cloyce and Israel Porter. This included the accused members of the Basset, Procter, Jacobs, and Towne families. Others, particularly George Burroughs, were certainly victims of this factional split, even though Burroughs no longer resided in Salem Village.[81]

Along with neighborly and village factionalism, imported English regionalism may have played a part as well. Two-thirds of the men accused of witchcraft in 1692 had surnames that had likely origins in the "Celtic fringe" of Britain: the West Country, Wales, the north, or Scotland. The people from these regions had cultural as well as spiritual differences from the many Massachusetts settlers from the south and east of England, which was the real hotbed of Puritanism.[82]

In Andover, more than half of the accused there and in adjoining Boxford were from families that had migrated from Scotland or the Celtic fringe, though the same population produced a number of accusers as well. Andover had suffered more than a decade of discord, with people in the southern end of town, including many Scots, tending to support the elderly senior minister Francis Dane, while most residents in the north end preferred his young replacement, Thomas Barnard. Now many residents of the southern end of Andover fell under suspicion of witchcraft, and their accusers tended to come from the north. Dane himself would escape formal charges, even though his own specter was seen afflicting people. Doubts may have been cast on Dane for his unwillingness to testify years earlier against John Godfrey, a man habitually under suspicion of witchcraft. When Godfrey had been charged with witchcraft for the second time in 1665, Dane begged off testifying at the trial in Boston, claiming that his "prevailing infirmity" prevented his attendance. Dane's unwillingness to help supervise the touch test when the afflicted came to Andover in 1692 would have added further suspicion. Soon Dane's two daughters and his daughter-in-law were cried out upon, as well as five grandchildren. In all, twenty-eight members of Dane's immediate and extended family would be accused of witchcraft. The turmoil in Andover only really came to an end in mid-October when Dane and Barnard closed ranks and healed any breach by joining twenty other Andover men in petitioning Governor Phips and the General Court in support of the innocence and blameless character of the Andover accused. They went so far as to suggest that some of the people who had confessed to witchcraft were actually innocent, and that there "hath been an inducement to them to own such things, as we cannot since find they are conscious of." The petitioners noted that some of the confessors now said "they have wronged themselves and the truth in their confessions."[83]

Those who confessed to witchcraft in 1692 are a large and important element of the afflicted. Perhaps the most chilling statistic of the trials is that not one of those who confessed to witchcraft was put to death, while all of the nineteen who refused to confess were executed—with the exception of Samuel Wardwell, who first confessed and then retracted his confession at the start of his trial. Wardwell "owned" that the "written confession was taken from his mouth and that he had said it" but now admitted that that he had lied in doing so.[84] Wardwell would soon be found guilty and subsequently executed. His confession highlights a legal strategy he and many other accused took during the trials. Traditionally, a confession had been considered the single most reliable way to gain a conviction and execution on charges of witchcraft. Just four years earlier in Boston, Goody Glover had confessed in court that she had tortured the Goodwin children through image magic. After physicians examined her and determined her to be of sound mind, the court accepted her confession and she was hanged. Yet Tituba had confessed to witchcraft back on March 1, and though she sat in jail in Boston, she had yet even to be indicted.[85]

Meanwhile, throughout most of the summer only those who refused to confess had been tried and executed. So when Wardwell was questioned about witchcraft on September 1, he and others appear to have believed that confessing would at least delay their trial and execution, and might possibly even spare their lives. A plea of not guilty seemed to promise only a quick trial, conviction, and execution, for everyone tried by the court had been found guilty and sentenced to death. Not only did Wardwell confess, but on September 5 he testified against Mary Taylor and Jane Lilly at their examinations. Only when the Court of Oyer and Terminer began its fourth and final session on September 6 were confessors finally being tried and convicted. The first confessed to face the court was Dorcas Hoar. She was convicted and condemned to death. Therefore, on Tuesday, September 13, when Wardwell stood before the grand jury, the court read his confession to him, he recanted it rather than affirmed it. Wardwell decided to clear his conscience by retracting his confession, for he now believed that "he should die for it whether he owned it or no."[86]

Yet others were willing to damn their souls and make a false confession. A total of fifty-five people confessed to being witches in 1692, more than a third of the total accused. When they did so, they had no way of knowing whether their lives would be spared, though by the time Burroughs was executed on August 19 it was clear that straightforward denials would be no use. Anyone who had pled not guilty was quickly convicted and executed—even a minister. Confession and cooperation at least gave the advantage of delay and offered some hope that the individual might ultimately be spared.[87]

Some of the accused yielded to extensive pressure from the court, the community, and even family to plead guilty. In some cases confessions were coerced, and a number of the accused cracked under the strain of their interrogation by officials. From the first examination of the first accused it was clear that the judges accepted the presence of witches and dedicated themselves to rooting them out. When Hathorne and Corwin held the first pretrial hearing on March 1, Hathorne's inquisition of Sarah Good set the tone:

HATHORNE: Sarah Good what evil spirit have you familiarity with?
GOOD: None.
HATHORNE: Have you made no contract with the devil?
GOOD: No.
HATHORNE: Why do you hurt these children?
GOOD: I do not hurt them. I scorn it.
HATHORNE: Who do you employ then to do it?
GOOD: I employ no body.
HATHORNE: What creature do you employ then?
GOOD: No creature but I am falsely accused.

Hathorne was an active and insistent prosecutor, demanding, "Sarah Good do you not see now what you have done why do you not tell us the truth, why do you thus torment these poor children?" Good could only simply reply, "I do not torment them."[88]

Faced with such relentless questioning, along with harsh physical treatment, Tituba would eventually become the first to confess. Robert Calef claimed that Samuel Parris beat Tituba to get her to admit her guilt. As a vigorous critic of Cotton Mather's defense of the trials, Calef was not an unbiased observer. Still, Reverend Hale noted that after her confession Tituba was taken to prison and, being "searched by a woman, she was found to have upon her body the marks of the devils wounding of her." When she confessed, Tituba admitted to being visited by the devil's familiars, who scratched her because she would not serve them. Possibly Tituba wove this detail into her story to explain fresh marks on her body that were the result of a beating. One wonders what would have happened had Parris and the judges not coerced Tituba into confessing. The Salem witchcraft outbreak might conceivably have been limited to three people—a fairly typical case of no particular note, and certainly not a pivotal moment in American history. Instead, Parris, Corwin, and Hathorne's collective fears of witchcraft and their zeal to find it would trigger something they could never have imagined in even their darkest dreams.[89]

Calef was not the only one to describe forced confessions. In October, Increase Mather visited eleven of the confessed witches in prison and recorded their recantations, which included their reasons for initially confessing. Mary Tyler said that her brother and Reverend Emerson put so much pressure on her that she felt she "would be hanged if she does not confess," and the other women spoke to similar pressures.[90] Thomas Brattle complained about "what methods from damnation were taken; with what violence urged: how unseasonably they were kept up; what buzzings and chuckings of the hand were used, and the like; I am sure that you would call them, (as I do), rude and barbarous methods."[91] Nathaniel Cary referred to his wife being "forced to stand with her arms outstretched" and having heavy shackles that gave her convulsions. John Procter wrote from prison to five ministers complaining that three boys, including his son William, had their neck and heels tied together until blood gushed from their noses, to coerce confessions.[92] Endless interrogations, along with sleep deprivation, were punctuated by strip searches that looked for the witch's teat and other preternatural signs of Satan. Samuel Willard pointed to the ministers' abilities to force confessions as well, starting with certain accused who were distracted, melancholy, or otherwise not in their right mind. Brattle complained that some of the fifty-five confessors contradicted themselves in their testimony because they were "crazed, distempered."[93] Reverend Francis Dane described his daughter Elizabeth as "weak, and incapacious, fearful," and his granddaughter Elizabeth Johnson Jr. as "simplish at ye best."[94]

These pressures were combined with others, including women's sense of self-worth. Scholars have quite naturally made a strong link between women's confessions and their place in Puritan society. As the "weaker vessel," women were all too regularly reminded, sometimes forcefully, that they were susceptible to sin and the temptations of the devil, so they tended to believe that they were sinful by their very nature. This is made apparent in their conversion narratives—their public confession made before the congregation when they asked to become a church member. Unlike men, women went to great lengths in these confessions to speak about their sinfulness and despicable condition. It is quite possible that, once accused of witchcraft, a devout woman may have looked inward to search for sins. If she found even ordinary sins such as envy or greed, she may have viewed this as a sign that she was indeed renouncing God and making a pact with Satan. When Rebecca Nurse was told by family and friends that she was under suspicion of witchcraft, she maintained her innocence. Nonetheless, she still believed that the sins she unknowingly committed had led to the charges. "I am innocent as the child unborn but surely she said what sin hath God found out in me unrepented of that he should lay such an affliction upon me in my old age." By confessing, women were acceding to the patriarchal order. If their ministers and authorities were convinced they were witches, then perhaps it was so. Even if they had doubts, it was the New England way for the community to put aside their differences and to come together during a crisis. By admitting guilt, they yielded to the impossible pressure of the community's expectations of female behavior, and set themselves up as models to show how redemption through confession should work to heal differences in the community.[95]

The case of Sarah Keene, of Kittery, Maine, demonstrates how community expectations could combine with women's fears of their sinful nature and concerns over body image to convince themselves they might be a witch. At least ten years after the Salem trials, she asked her neighbor Elizabeth Pettigrew if "a person might not be a witch and not know it." Pettigrew said she thought not, but Keene said "her mistress had often told her she might"; furthermore, Keene was "doubtful of herself" because of a "teat or dug which grew under one of her own breasts." Keene confided in another woman that "she was afraid in the time of the witchcraft she should be taken up for a witch." About four years later, long-standing suspicions about Keene combined with the unexplained death of a neighbor's child led

Sarah to again wonder whether she was indeed a witch. Her sentiments are recorded only because Keene sued a man for slander when she was accused of witchcraft in 1725. At least by this time she had finally recognized that she was not a witch.[96]

In 1692 the confessions began in earnest in early July, when the accusations spread to Andover. In the middle of the month, nine people from Andover and the adjoining towns of Haverhill and Billerica would confess, bringing a total of eighteen confessions out of eighty-two accused. The percentage of confessions would continue to rise over the rest of the summer and into September. A total of forty-five Andover residents would be accused of witchcraft, and all but six would initially confess. A substantial number of the Andover confessions were children and young unmarried adults. Here again one can see the dutiful behavior of youths in a patriarchal order, confessing as they were told to do by their magistrates and other superiors. The Andover confessions were almost formulaic: the judges wrote down only the parts of the confessions that supported the charges. The confessor agreed that the devil had come to them, usually at first in the form of a familiar—perhaps a bird, a dog, or a cat. The devil offered them money, a good life, and even the promise of protection from the Indians in return for signing a contract. Sometimes it was on paper or even on birch bark, but very often it was in the devil's book. Confessors also agreed that they had been baptized by the devil in local bodies of water—Andover's Five Mile Pond, the Shawsheen River, or Newbury Falls. They further attended satanic masses where they ate red bread and drank stolen communion wine.[97]

The July 20 confession of Mary Allen Toothaker is one of the most significant, for it pulls together the fear of the frontier along with other themes. Mary lived in Billerica on the exposed edge of the Essex County frontier, so the threat of war weighed deeply on her mind. In addition to the charge of having her specter torment the afflicted girls, Mary was accused of being among a group of witches who supposedly caused great pain and suffering to Timothy Swan, a thirty-year-old Andover man who suffered from some mysterious illness that would take his life in February 1693. Swan was well known to Mary, for he had been charged with raping her kinswoman Elizabeth Emerson six years earlier. Elizabeth specifically accused Timothy of dragging her upstairs in her home and having sex with her while holding one arm across her throat to ensure her silence. The court found Swan not guilty, though it ordered him to support the child born of that union. Unfortunately, his assistance was irregular—late and often in goods of little or no value. And, Elizabeth's life had gone downhill from that point. In 1691 she was found guilty of murdering her newborn twins, born out of wedlock to another man. Throughout the witch trials Elizabeth remained in the Boston prison under a death sentence, which would finally be carried out on June 8, 1693. Elizabeth's sister Hannah Emerson Dustin would famously redeem the family name several years later when she, aided by a young boy, slew their ten sleeping Native American captors and returned home with their scalps.[98]

Mary Toothaker had not considered herself to be a witch, but events during her examination by the court clearly had an effect on her. After "her striking down of several of the afflicted persons with her looks" and also being confronted her with testimony about the suffering of Timothy Swan, she confessed. "She is convinced she is a witch—she saith now, the devil appeared to her in the shape of a tawny man and promised to keep her from the Indians and she should have happy days with her son," who was a wounded war veteran. She did not sign the devil's book, but she did make a mark on a piece of birch bark. She made a pact with the devil "for he said he was able to deliver her from the Indians and it was the fear of the Indians that put her upon it." The fear of the frontier is palpably clear here, as is the fact that she had convinced herself that she was a witch. The troubled story of Elizabeth Emerson and Timothy Swan was a factor, too, for "she confessed she hurt Timothy Swan… and is afraid that she the said Toothaker squeezed his throat," harming Timothy just as he had done to Elizabeth while he raped her. Clearly Mary Toothaker harbored ill will toward Swan. When he actually did suffer illness, Mary believed that her hard feelings could have been the cause—that she may indeed have invoked Satan's powers just by these feelings, as well as her concern for safety from the war for herself and her family. Yet other factors were at work here, too. Mary was brought under suspicion only after several of her family members were accused of witchcraft. Her husband, Dr. Roger Toothaker, had already died in prison, as we have seen, and her sister Martha Allen Carrier was hanged. The charges against Carrier and her family may have resulted in part from the fact that they were held responsible for spreading smallpox throughout Andover in the fall of 1690, when five members of her extended family died from the disease. In all, nine members of the Allen family would be charged, along with many more kin in the Dane and How families—charges that were closely related to ongoing religious tensions over Andover's ministers Francis Dane and Thomas Bernard.[99]

As with George Burroughs and John Alden, many of the elements of Mary's accusation and confession involve the war. Even the smallpox epidemic of 1690 was associated with the conflict, for many believed the disease had been introduced into the colony by soldiers returning from Phips's failed expedition on Quebec. On August 1, 1692, two days after Mary Toothaker's confession, her Billerica neighborhood was subject to a Native raid. She was fortunate to be in the Salem jail, for two families who lived near her perished. Such attacks brought the war even closer and put Essex County into a panic.[100]

All of these aspects of the confession—owning the devil's covenant by signing his book, being baptized by him, and attending a satanic version of the Lord's Supper at which his covenant was renewed—turned traditional Puritan faith upside down. The inversion of Christianity was a common aspect of witchcraft in Europe at the time, in keeping with the belief that Satan meant to overturn all aspects of European religion and society. But it took a particular twist in 1692 with the emphasis on satanic baptism and signing the devil's book. Signing the paper or the book seems connected to the Puritan emphasis on literacy. Having George Burroughs, a Harvard-educated Puritan minister, leading Satan's church in these dark rites was central to this inversion. These credentials combined with his involvement in Salem Village factionalism, his life on the frontier, his unusual strength, and fears of his orthodoxy and his secretive, controlling ways to make him the perfect witch.[101]

The witch trials would turn Massachusetts itself upside down, and perhaps the most remarkable inversion of all involved the legal system. Traditionally in colonial Massachusetts, people who stood charged before the court could take comfort in the fact that the judges were there to protect the innocent and that justice would usually win out. In Salem all this went horribly wrong. To understand how and why this occurred we must next turn to the judges.

CHAPTER SIX

The Judges

The persons were men eminent for wisdom and virtue, and they went
about their enquiry into the matter, as driven unto it by a conscience
of duty to God and the world.

—Cotton Mather[1]

ON THURSDAY, SEPTEMBER 1, 1692, THE judges of the Court of Oyer and
Terminer took a break from their official duties to celebrate the marriage of
John Richards and Anne Winthrop. It was the first marriage for the bride,
a daughter of the late John Winthrop Jr., and no less a figure than William
Stoughton presided over the ceremony. Though no wedding list survives,
one can guess at some of the likely attendees. As the Winthrop family had
long awaited the marriage of spinster Anne, much of her family was presumably in attendance, including her brother, Wait Winthrop. Her sister,
Margaret, would have made the trip from Salem, with her husband, John
Corwin, and perhaps even her brother-in-law Jonathan Corwin; another of
her brothers-in-law, Peter Sergeant, lived in Boston. Bartholomew Gedney
and John Hathorne may have been there as well. Gedney was an in-law
of the Corwins, and Hathorne's late brother Eleazer had been a business

partner and brother-in-law of the Corwins. Samuel Sewall presumably also attended, for this family friend recorded the ceremony in his diary. The wedding was held at the home of Hezekiah Usher, a kinsman of the Winthrops through several marriages with the Tyng family. This was shortly before Usher was accused of witchcraft himself.[2]

Remarkably, therefore, all eight of the remaining judges of the Essex County witchcraft trials may have been in attendance: John Richards, Wait Winthrop, Samuel Sewall, Jonathan Corwin, John Hathorne, Bartholomew Gedney, Peter Sergeant, and Chief Justice William Stoughton (Nathaniel Saltonstall was not in attendance, but he had quit the court several months earlier). This seeming coincidence is no coincidence at all, for the judges and their families were allied by their offices, by business connections and land speculation, and by kinship. These ties help to explain the behavior of the court.[3]

Historians often dismiss the importance of genealogical research, consigning it to the realm of the antiquarian and octogenarian. However, family ties explain so much human behavior, and they were particularly important to the witchcraft judges, all of whom were merchants. In a time before banks and insurance, trade, credit, and risk operated on a very personal level. The most successful merchants were those with kinship connections in ports throughout the Atlantic world. Family members and business partners would pool resources to share in ownership of ships and overseas ventures, thus preventing a catastrophic loss by any one investor. Strategic marriages strengthened these business partnerships and solidified merchant networks.[4]

Collectively, the witchcraft judges represented the elite of Massachusetts—the political, military, and economic leaders of the colony. Their role in the trials has tended to have been overlooked; historians have been inclined to focus on the conflict in Salem Village and the drama between the afflicted and the people they accused. Though magistrates in seventeenth-century New England played a more active role in court than judges today, they were expected to practice some judicial restraint. In part this was because they were elected politicians who possessed no formal legal training. By and large they had succeeded. In the previous thirty years, fourteen citizens of the Bay Colony had been tried for witchcraft, with only one—Goody Glover—being found guilty and ultimately executed, and she had confessed to the crime. For a generation magistrates had in fact been an important brake on the general public's eagerness to prosecute witches, whom they feared

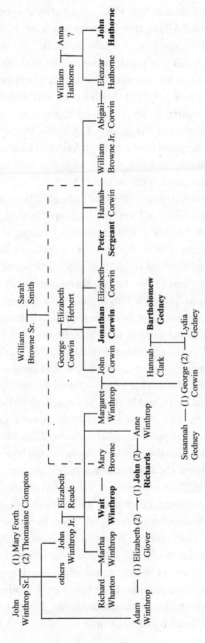

Family connections between the judges of the Court of Oyer and Terminer. Judges are in bold.

and blamed for misfortune. Meanwhile, most judges grew skeptical about previously used ways of establishing that someone was a witch, and some even began to question the existence of witches.[5] Yet in 1692 the Salem judges would reverse course. Their participation in the trials shaped the outcomes—the conviction and execution of nineteen innocent people. No matter how many accusers suffered what they believed were genuine afflictions or, alternatively, conspired to press dubious charges, no one would have died without the sanction of the judges. The judges of the Court of Oyer and Terminer hold the answers to many of Salem's riddles. A closer look at them, both individually and collectively, as well as at their roles in earlier trials, helps to understand their reversal in 1692.

Any study of the judges should begin with Chief Justice William Stoughton. Historian Stephen Foster said Stoughton was "the most cynical, disloyal, worldly, and justifiably infamous graduate Harvard managed to produce in the seventeenth century, with the possible exception of Sir George Downing." He was born in England in 1631 or 1632, just before his parents' immigration from England to Dorchester, Massachusetts. Stoughton's father, Israel, was a community leader who served in the Pequot War and in the General Court before returning home to serve as a lieutenant colonel for Parliament's army in the English Civil War. He died not long after joining the army. After William graduated from Harvard in 1650, he, too, returned to England, where he served as a minister and received a master's degree in divinity from Oxford. He lost his Oxford fellowship in 1660 with the restoration of Charles II, and in 1662 he came back to Dorchester and became a merchant. In 1671 he was elected to the General Court and soon began to be appointed to important offices. During King Philip's War he served as a commissioner for the United Colonies, trying to coordinate the war effort between them. He also became a judge, serving in county courts, and from 1676 to 1679 he served as an agent of Massachusetts Bay in London, working to preserve the charter and the colony's boundaries from encroachment. Soon after he returned home, he was appointed a major in the Suffolk County militia. When the Massachusetts charter was revoked and the Dominion of New England established, Stoughton received a temporary commission as deputy president, serving under his close political ally and business partner, President Joseph Dudley. When Governor Edmund Andros arrived to assume authority, Stoughton served as a member of his council and a judge. Despite his siding with the royal cause against the Puritan old guard, Stoughton managed to maintain some of his reputation thanks to his willingness to quickly switch sides when Andros was overthrown. Yet he would not be elected or appointed to any office again until he was made lieutenant governor under the new charter in May 1692. Unlike his fellow judges, Stoughton had few family connections, as he had only one sister and he himself never married.[6]

Samuel Sewall was in many ways the polar opposite of Stoughton, as one can see from his diary, which he began keeping in 1674 and which is one of the most important historical documents of the period. Among other things, it indicates how central his large family was to his life. His parents were early settlers of Newbury, but they returned to England, where Samuel was born in 1652. They moved back to Newbury in 1661, after the restoration of Charles II signaled an end to the rule of Puritans and Parliament in England. Educated at Harvard, Sewall was destined for a career in the ministry until 1676, when he married Hannah Hull, the only child of John Hull, the silversmith and mint master who was one of the richest merchants in Massachusetts. Sewall soon joined his father-in-law in business, though he maintained a deeply spiritual life. Soon after Hull's death in 1683, Sewall assumed many of his civic responsibilities. He was first elected to the General Court's House of Assistants in 1684 and soon became a Suffolk County judge, as well as a captain in the Boston militia. Samuel declined to serve on the council under the Dominion of New England. Instead, he made an extended trip to England, where he aided Increase Mather in his efforts to restore the Massachusetts Bay charter of 1629. Upon his return in 1690, Sewall joined Bradstreet's interim government in his old office of assistant, and he was formally named to the council (the new body that replaced the House of Assistants in the 1691 charter) when Phips and Mather arrived with the new charter in May 1692.[7]

The Hulls and the Sewalls had been neighbors of Peter Sergeant until Sergeant built his spectacular new home in 1679. The Boston mansion was so opulent that it would later serve as the Province House, the official residence of the governor. Born in London in 1647, Sergeant was a member of a wealthy and influential clan of Puritan merchants. His first cousins, the brothers Sir William and Sir Henry Ashurst, were members of Parliament and aldermen of London. Sir William also served as sheriff and Lord Mayor of London. A close political ally of Increase Mather and Sir William Phips, Sir Henry served as agent for the Massachusetts Bay Company, and

Treasurer of the New England Company. As a part of this kinship network, Sergeant prospered. He migrated to Boston in 1667, where he represented the family business interests and also extended their connections.[8] His first wife apparently was Elizabeth Corwin, whose father and brothers were leading Salem merchants. After her death, in 1682 Sergeant married Elizabeth, daughter of Henry Shrimpton, one of the wealthiest Boston merchants. Like Samuel Sewall, Sergeant was a strong supporter of Boston's Third Church (or South Church) and its minister, Samuel Willard. Sergeant had no political career until he became one of the men who petitioned for Governor Andros's surrender in April 1689. He subsequently served on the Council for Safety, but played only a minor role in the interim government of Governor Bradstreet. He was appointed to the council under the charter of 1692, presumably thanks to his cousin Sir Henry Ashurst, who had helped Mather and Phips secure the charter.[9]

John Richards was one of the leaders of Mather's North Church. Born in the English county of Somerset in 1625, when he was five he migrated to Massachusetts with his parents and siblings. He followed in his father's profession as a merchant, and in 1649 he purchased Arrowsic Island on the Kennebec River from the local Native Americans and established a trading post on it. While he lived there, his neighbors the Phipses gave birth to their son William, the future governor of Massachusetts. In 1654 Richards sold his Maine property and returned to Massachusetts, living first in Dorchester and later in Boston. Perhaps he returned to Massachusetts, because about this time his widowed mother was under suspicion of witchcraft. She was never prosecuted, thanks to her minister, who came to her defense. A successful merchant, Richards also served a number of terms as member of the House of Deputies, including one year as speaker. This office was followed by long service as an assistant. In 1680 he was appointed a trustee for the Society for Propagation of the Gospel in New England, and the next year the Bay Colony sent him to London as a commissioner to defend the Massachusetts charter. A major in the Suffolk militia, Richards was appointed as a judge under Dudley but did not hold office under Andros. He had strong ties to Plymouth colony. One brother-in-law was Thomas Hinckley, the last governor of Plymouth. Under the 1691 charter, Plymouth Colony became a part of Massachusetts Bay, so Hinckley became a member of the council of Massachusetts Bay under the new charter. Another brother-in-law was the son of Governor William Bradford, the great leader of Plymouth. And of course Richards married the sister of Wait Winthrop during the witch trials, thus allying himself to the first family of Massachusetts Bay.[10]

According to biographer Richard Dunn, Wait Winthrop and his brother Fitz-John "were men of ordinary talent, lacking their grandfather's driving moral purpose and their father's breadth and creative intelligence." As Dunn describes them, the brothers "were humorous, easy-going and self-indulgent, half-aware of their many absurd quirks of character."[11] Wait was born in 1642, when his grandfather, John Winthrop, was still governor of Massachusetts Bay. He would spend much of his youth in Connecticut, where his father, John Winthrop Jr., served eighteen years as governor. John junior was a brilliant scientist and physician, and he used his skills as an alchemist as well as his political acumen to counter witchcraft accusations against a number of people. Indeed, the Hartford witchcraft outbreak of 1662–63 did not begin until after John junior had left for England, to gain a charter for Connecticut. Wait entered Harvard in 1658, considering a career in medicine like his father. He left after two years without a degree but would remain an amateur physician for the rest of his life. Wait then turned to the world of business. In 1677 he furthered these ambitions when he married Mary Browne, a member of another wealthy Salem merchant family. Mary's brother, William junior, had married into the Corwin clan. The couple settled in Boston. Wait finally entered politics in 1686, when he was appointed to the council of the Dominion of New England. In 1689 he redeemed himself for what many saw as his defection to the royalist cause, when his name was first on the list of signatures on the letter sent to Governor Andros, demanding his surrender. Subsequently, he would serve as a counselor in the interim government and would be named a counselor in the charter of 1691. In 1692 he was appointed commander in chief of the Bay Colony's military forces. To be put in such a position while Massachusetts faced a dire military threat suggests that Wait Winthrop had at least a bit more talent than his biographer gave him credit for.[12]

Like Wait Winthrop, Bartholomew Gedney was a physician as well as a high-ranking military officer—the colonel of the Essex County militia. Despite his military skill and medical practice, Gedney was above all a merchant. Born in Salem in 1640, he followed his father as a respected civic leader. First elected a deputy to the General Court in 1678, two years later he became an assistant. King James II would appoint him to the Andros council, though, like Stoughton and Wait Winthrop, he would make amends by being one of the men writing to Andros to demand his surrender. Still, voters did not forgive Gedney for his support of Andros, and he did not hold office again until he was appointed to the council in the 1691 charter. In the summer of 1692, when the legislature created a new system of courts, Gedney would be named as the first judge of probate for Essex County.[13]

Bartholomew Gedney's daughter Lydia was married to Sheriff George Corwin, the nephew of witchcraft Judge Jonathan Corwin. This was just one of the many marriages made by the Corwins to cement their business and political partnerships. Born in Salem in 1640, Jonathan Corwin married the daughter of a Boston merchant, and all four of his siblings married into other merchant families. Brother John married Margaret Winthrop, Wait's sister. Sister Elizabeth married Peter Sergeant, while Hannah married William Browne Jr. and Abigail married Eleazer Hathorne. Thus, through the marriages of his siblings and his daughter, Jonathan was related to five other judges of the Court of Oyer and Terminer. No fact better illustrates the common interests of the members of this court. An examination of the debts listed in the probate inventory of Jonathan Corwin's father, George, suggests just how closely these families and other merchants relied on each other, for the extension of credit to trustworthy people made the system work. More than thirty creditors made claims, including future witchcraft judges Peter Sergeant, Wait Winthrop, and Bartholomew Gedney.[14]

Jonathan Corwin first appeared destined to be a minister, for he entered Harvard at age sixteen, but he left after two years and followed the path of his father, a wealthy merchant who held many civic and political offices. Jonathan first served as a deputy to the General Court in 1684. Edward Randolph included Corwin on a list of men suitable to fill vacancies on Andros's council, but he never served. It is unknown if he would have accepted had he been asked, though his brother-in-law William Browne Jr. joined the council in 1688. Corwin took a real leadership role in the colony with the overthrow of Andros, serving first on the Council for Safety and then as an assistant. He too was named a councilor in the 1691 charter.[15] Corwin was the only judge to have a member of his family afflicted in 1692. On the very first day of examinations, when Corwin and John Hathorne examined Tituba, Hathorne asked her why she hurt "Mr. Currins [Corwin's] child." The affliction must have soon passed, for there are no further references to any problems in the Corwin family.[16]

Jonathan Corwin's name will always be linked with John Hathorne's, as they were the local justices of the peace who conducted the initial examinations of suspected witches, though the men had many other things in common. Hathorne was but a year younger, and, like Corwin, was the son of a militia officer and magistrate who was a leading merchant and politician of Salem and Massachusetts Bay. Indeed, Jonathan's father, William Hathorne, had been the first man to serve as speaker of the House of Deputies in the General Court. John was first elected deputy in 1683, a year before Corwin, and became an assistant the next year. Hathorne opposed the Dominion of New England, but interim president Joseph Dudley was a close friend, so Hathorne did choose to serve as an Essex County magistrate under both Dudley and Andros. Like Corwin, Hathorne was on the Council for Safety, and afterward served as assistant under the interim government as well as councilor in the 1691 charter. In 1690 the General Court ordered Corwin and Hathorne to travel north to New Hampshire and Maine to help coordinate the defense of those settlements against Native American attack. Presumably the two were chosen in part for the task because their families jointly owned and operated a sawmill at Kennebunk, on the Maine frontier. John's late brother Eleazer Hathorne had been married to Corwin's sister, and he had managed the mill until his death in 1679.[17]

One member of the Court of Oyer and Terminer stands out from the other eight in several ways, not the least of which was his resignation from the court after just a couple of weeks of service. Nathaniel Saltonstall was not related to the other judges, nor did he live among them in Salem or greater Boston. Rather, he resided on the dangerous edge of the frontier in Haverhill. Despite these differences, his history and his qualifications for the bench were similar to those of his colleagues. Born in Ipswich about 1639, he was the grandson of Sir Richard Saltonstall, one of the original patentees of Massachusetts Bay. Graduating from Harvard in 1659, Nathaniel settled on a large tract of land given him by his father-in-law, John Ward, who was Haverhill's minister. In 1666 he was elected a deputy and appointed as a magistrate. He soon became captain in Haverhill's militia, eventually rising to major, in command of the northern division of the Essex regiment. He first served as an assistant in 1679, a post he held for many years, except during the Andros administration. In 1687 he joined Increase Mather in London to try to restore the charter.[18]

As a group, the judges represented the proverbial 1 percent—the merchant elite who were wealthy, intermarried, and exercised power in social, political, and military circles. In short, they were the superrich of Massachusetts. Simply calling them "merchants" shortchanges them. As a biographer has noted, "Describing Samuel Sewall as a merchant, as he is universally described, is as accurate as calling Thomas Jefferson a farmer."[19] And while Sewall was perhaps the most remarkable of the judges, the others were accomplished men as well. Most had considerable political experience, having served as deputies and assistants in the General Court. Stoughton, Winthrop, and Gedney had even served on Andros's council. Some were skilled diplomats, too. Richards and Stoughton had worked as agents for the colony in London, and Sewall had unofficially aided Increase Mather in this capacity. Stoughton and Gedney had recently served as commissioners sent to Maine to negotiate a treaty with the Wabanaki. Most of them were in early middle age. At forty, Sewall was the youngest, while Richards (sixty-seven) and Stoughton (sixty) were the oldest. The rest were between forty-five and fifty-three. Sergeant migrated to Boston when he was twenty, and Stoughton, Richards, and Sewall all came over from England as children. The others were born in Massachusetts. Except for Sergeant, they were all members of the second generation—the group that required the Halfway Covenant. They were a remarkably well-educated group. Saltonstall, Stoughton, and Sewall had graduated from Harvard, which Winthrop and Corwin had attended. Stoughton also had a master's degree from Oxford. The majority of Puritans who attended Harvard sought a career in the ministry. Therefore, a group that included five Harvard men but not a clergyman among them was exceptional.[20]

Their preparation for and abandonment of the ministry hint at deep tensions felt by the second generation in general and these men in particular. Thanks to his diary and extensive correspondence, the spiritual turmoil is best seen in Sewall. A painfully devout Puritan who easily and regularly recited from the Bible, he turned down a career in the ministry largely in deference to the wishes of his father-in-law, John Hull, who needed Sewall to carry on the family merchant operations. Sewall was riddled with self-doubt over his spiritual worthiness—not just to be a minister but even to become a church member. He wrote in his diary of his "sinfulness and hypocrisy" and believed himself unworthy of sitting at the Lord's table. Only in the spring of 1677, when his wife, Hannah, was nearing the delivery of their firstborn, did he convince himself to make his public confession and state a case for membership before Boston's South Church. Yet even after he was accepted, he worried that he was unworthy and that he might have joined the church just so that his child could be baptized.[21]

William Stoughton struggled with a similar conflict, searching in vain for proof of his worthiness to be a Puritan saint—that select group predestined to go to heaven. Although he had been a clergyman in Sussex, England, in the 1650s, he gave up the ministry when he returned to Massachusetts in 1660. He was repeatedly asked over the next ten years to be minister for his hometown, Dorchester, and also received an invitation from Cambridge, but he always refused, saying "he had some objections within himself against the motion."[22] One wonders what sort of inner turmoil it was that Stoughton faced, given his supposed cynicism and propensity for making money. Bachelors were very unusual in a colony and society where family was all-important. As a Puritan bachelor, Stoughton would have been expected to live a celibate life, and some historians have suggested that his behavior during the trials was evidence that he was a misogynist. His bachelor status at least suggests some ambiguities in his relationships with women and even his sexuality. Perhaps this was an issue with which he struggled as he repeatedly found himself unable to serve in his chosen career of minister.[23]

Trained as they were for the ministry, other Harvard men had tensions in their spiritual worthiness. Church membership was an issue for Bartholomew Gedney. In 1666 he had petitioned the Salem Town church to allow him to become a member through a private interview with the pastor rather than the public confession Sewell and others endured to become a member of a church. Once the church made the exception for Gedney, others took advantage of this looser admissions policy, including Gedney's wife, Hannah, as well as Jonathan Corwin. Both Corwin and Gedney were twenty-six at the time. Two years later, twenty-seven-year-old John Hathorne would own the covenant as well. Had the membership requirements not been eased, perhaps none of the three future judges would have become full church members. John Richards would have denied them membership had he had a say in it, for he was the biggest opponent of the Halfway Covenant and other reforms in the Mathers' North Church. So while all of the judges were

Puritan church members, they did not share uniform religious views—again, collectively reflecting the spiritual tensions felt by a number of members of the second generation. Those tensions had an impact on their decisions in 1692.[24]

In their old charter role of assistants to the governor, the witchcraft judges had considerable experience as county magistrates as well as members of the colony's supreme court. The cases they heard and the decisions they made in these cases must have influenced their behavior in Salem. Notably, in the twelve years leading up to the Salem trials, the Court of Assistants heard five cases of witchcraft. Similar to the meetings of the Court of Oyer and Terminer, these were jury trials, with the governor and assistants sitting as a panel of judges, and also presumably taking some role in questioning witnesses and the accused. As noted, the last execution for witchcraft in Massachusetts had taken place in 1656, so it comes as no surprise that the first four of the accused witches to appear before the court fared well. Mary Hale, Mary Webster, and James Fuller were all acquitted. Unfortunately, there are no transcripts for these proceedings, though the records do note which assistants were present. Mary Hale's 1681 acquittal was attended by fourteen assistants, including Nathaniel Saltonstall, William Stoughton, Bartholomew Gedney, and John Richards. Two years later, Stoughton and Gedney were present for the acquittal of Mary Webster of Hadley. Stoughton was one of only six assistants to hear the 1683 case of James Fuller of Springfield. Fuller admitted that he had bragged to people that he did "call upon or pray to the devil for help" but acknowledged that he had lied in doing so. The disgruntled court found him not guilty of witchcraft. However, they sentenced him "to be severely whipped with thirty stripes severely laid on" and pay a £5 fine for his "wicked and pernicious willful lying" and for wasting the court's time.[25]

In dealing with the case of Elizabeth Morse, the fourth accused witch, the court showed just how reluctant it was to execute anyone for witchcraft, even if that person had been convicted of the crime. Morse's case began in 1679, when a series of strange happenings occurred in the Newbury home she shared with her husband, William, and their grandson John Styles. Furniture moved and objects mysteriously flew about the house, all events that were considered Satan's work, carried out by the agency of a witch. The suspicion of witchcraft seemed to be confirmed when young John Stiles began to have fits. The Morses accused Caleb Powell, a sailor with a reputation for knowledge of the occult, of witchcraft. Powell had actually tried to help the Morses resolve their problems but ended up being implicated in them. When the court refused to convict Powell, suspicion soon turned to Elizabeth Morse herself, and her case was tried before the Court of Assistants in May 1680.[26]

Elizabeth Morse's case sounds quite similar to many heard a dozen years later in Salem. Some neighbors testified that Elizabeth and her specter had caused illness and even the death of two infants, while others said she had killed or sickened livestock. She seemed to have animal familiars and also possessed preternatural knowledge—she mysteriously knew many private things—and had dabbled in fortune-telling. As at Salem, the formal charges of witchcraft brought forward suspicions gathered over many years. Samuel Sewall's mother testified to events "some years since," and another man described the strange death of his cattle sixteen years earlier, soon after a disagreement with Morse.[27]

After the court presented the extensive evidence, Elizabeth Morse was found guilty of witchcraft and sentenced to hang, yet within a few days Governor Simon Bradstreet and the assistants agreed to reprieve Morse's sentence until the court's next session, in October. Remaining in jail, she would be reprieved twice more. Members of the lower house, the deputies, objected to these reprieves, saying they did not understand why the death sentence was not carried out. However, at their June 1681 meeting the assistants issued yet another reprieve to Morse until their next session, this time releasing her from jail and essentially placing her under house arrest. She could not go more than sixteen rods (264 feet) from her home, except to attend worship on Sundays. At this point the case disappeared from the records, and Elizabeth was allowed to stay at home and eventually to die of natural causes. In his 1697 account of the Salem trials, Reverend John Hale (who was among a group of ministers to subsequently meet with Morse) said that she had been reprieved by the governor and assistants because they were concerned about the evidence. In particular, they questioned spectral evidence, and noted that of all the accusations against Morse, none of her alleged acts was observed by two witnesses—the standard called for in English law.[28]

Lacking records, it is impossible to say which assistants called for the reprieve, though Stoughton, Saltonstall, Richards, and Gedney all were assistants in 1681 and 1682, as was John Hull—Samuel Sewall's father-in-law.

John Putnam of Salem Village was a member of the deputies, the body that urged the assistants to carry out the execution, but then so, too, was Thomas Brattle, who later would criticize the Salem trials. Collectively, then, in the early 1680s, the Court of Assistants, which included four of the nine future judges of the Court of Oyer and Terminer, was reluctant to convict anyone of witchcraft, and even with the one conviction they refused to carry out the requisite sentence.[29]

These decisions were very much in keeping with proceedings in England. Witchcraft executions had been on the ebb since the end of the English Civil Wars. By the 1670s, people were still being indicted for sorcery, yet few were executed. The popular belief in witches and the supernatural continued, but it became difficult to meet the burden of proof amid the growing skepticism of judges. The last known executions in England occurred in Bideford, Devon, in 1682. All three victims confessed to being witches. Temperance Lloyd was the first charged. She apparently confessed because she believed that she was still under the protection of the devil. Subsequently Mary Trembles and Susanna Edwards both pled guilty, with Trembles blaming Edwards for initiating her into the dark arts, and Edwards blaming Lloyd. Despite efforts to shift the responsibility, their confessions ensured their execution as well. Witchcraft convictions and executions seemed to be dying out unless someone confessed, as with the Bideford witches or in the case of Goody Glover.[30]

The Massachusetts witchcraft case that immediately preceded Salem was the 1688 trial, conviction, and execution of Goody Glover. That summer the four Goodwin children of Boston, ranging in age from five to thirteen, appeared to become sorely afflicted by witchcraft. They suffered strange fits, contortions, and epileptic-like seizures, and even briefly became deaf, dumb, or blind. They cried out upon their elderly widowed neighbor, Goody Glover. The court records do not survive, so her first name is unknown, leaving historians to refer to her as "Goody"—*Goodman* and *Goodwife* were polite terms of address in the seventeenth century, much as *Mr.* and *Mrs.* are today. Cotton Mather provided almost all of the surviving information about the case, for he worked closely with the Goodwin family to heal the children. Glover was a poor Irish woman, a Roman Catholic who had an imperfect command of English. The judges had to rely on translators at the trial, where she readily confessed, though as Robert Calef complained, when she appeared before the court "her answers were nonsense, and her behavior like that of one distracted."[31] In all likelihood it was the confession of an addled old woman, with confusion growing from her Catholic faith, as well as translation problems. For example, Mather mentions Goody Glover communing with "her spirits, or her saints (for they say, the same word in Irish means both)." Glover may have thought she was simply admitting to veneration of saints, and to a secret Catholic service attended by "her prince and four more" (that is, a lay leader and four other worshipers— not, as Mather believed, the Prince of Darkness leading a black mass).[32] Unfortunately for Glover, there was physical evidence against her that supported her confession. A search of her home turned up poppets made of rags and stuffed with goat hair. These items suggested she used image magic to harm the Goodwin children. Even so, the judges had enough doubts about the validity of her confession that they ordered a panel of physicians to examine her mental well-being. After spending an evening with her, they pronounced Goody Glover to be of sound mind. So the conviction stood, and she was hanged in Boston on November 16, 1688.[33]

Glover was the only person tried for witchcraft that fall, although she named associates who she testified had joined her supposed satanic masses or otherwise practiced witchcraft. She warned from the gallows that the children's afflictions would continue after her death, "for others had a hand in it as well as she," and she even named one. Mather was very careful not to share the names of the others suspected, though there were at least six. And, as Glover predicted, the afflictions of three of the Goodwin children continued and even worsened after the execution, continuing into the spring of 1689.[34]

Goody Glover's conviction and execution after her confession stand in contrast to the events in Salem and raise a series of questions. First, she was the first person executed for witchcraft in Massachusetts in thirty-two years. What made her case different? Like the Bideford witches, and unlike other recent cases in New England, she made a confession—one that was supported by physical evidence. Furthermore, her being a practicing Catholic made it highly unlikely she would be pardoned. Massachusetts Puritans had expressed serious concerns about their Anglican governor Andros and his policy of religious toleration of Protestant sects. Were he to spare the life of a confessing Catholic witch, he risked public outcry and perhaps even rebellion. Plus, with the recent outbreak of what would become King William's War, Andros had enough problems on his hands and needed to avoid more of them. Indeed, six or seven days before Glover's execution, Governor Andros left Boston for the Maine frontier, to deal with the escalating military crisis with the Wabanaki. We cannot say for certain that Andros was in attendance for Glover's trial, though presumably he officiated.[35]

By the time of Goody Glover's execution, most of the lives of the future judges of the Court of Oyer and Terminer had been touched in some way by witches and the supernatural. Saltonstall, Stoughton, Gedney, Richards, and possibly Winthrop had sat as judges for at least one case of witchcraft, albeit in a court that repeatedly proved reluctant to convict and execute. Winthrop surely would have recalled his father's active involvement in adjudicating cases of sorcery in Connecticut, particularly his skill at saving the lives of alleged witches. Richards's mother had been accused of witchcraft, and Corwin's child was briefly afflicted in the Salem outbreak. Stoughton, for one, must have been struck by the Elizabeth Morse case, for it sounded much like the Demon Drummer of Tedworth, a famous case of English witchcraft that had taken place in the home of his cousin. Sewall's mother had testified against Morse, and he surely had heard much about the events of Salem Village from his wife's cousin Samuel Parris.[36]

We have no record of which members of Andros's council attended the Glover trial and served as the panel of judges, but we do know that Stoughton, Winthrop, and Gedney served on the council under Andros. It seems likely that Boston residents Stoughton and Winthrop were in attendance. Clearly the members of this council had no problem executing a confessed witch—after making sure that she was of sound mind. Yet these same men and their colleagues did not do even this much in 1692; there is no evidence that they ever asked doctors to check the mental well-being of the confessors to ensure their sanity. Equally puzzling is that in 1688 Mather and the court strenuously ignored evidence of a witch conspiracy. They had names, given to them by a confessed witch, and after her death the continued suffering of the Goodwin children lent proof to the fact that more witches were at work. Yet, they refused to act. Less than four years later the same men were eagerly rooting out co-conspirators, seeing witches everywhere they turned. The question, of course, is what had turned them into hanging judges, executing only those who did not confess to the heinous crime. The transformation of the judges is one of many unanswered questions surrounding Salem. As with the other questions, it is complicated, defying simple answers. They were influenced by a range of factors, including their lives as Puritans, merchants, kinsmen, military and political leaders, and judges.

One set of trials that occurred between the Glover case and Salem that must have influenced the witch judges' thinking took place in January 1690, when the Court of Assistants, meeting under the interim government of Simon Bradstreet, found ten men guilty of piracy. Thomas Pound and his crew—a group of local sailors turned pirates—had terrorized the coast of New England the previous summer and fall. Not only had they seized several vessels, but they also had sailed north to Casco Bay and encouraged soldiers at Fort Loyal to desert and join them. Several soldiers indeed abandoned their posts, at which they were desperately needed to defend the fort against Native attack, and went off pirating. The buccaneer crew even included two men who had formerly been among Andros's hated redcoats—the British regulars and symbols of royal power that Sir Edmund brought with him from England. Eventually, after a bloody fight, the pirates were captured by the *Mary*, a sloop sent by the governor to chase them down. They were brought to justice—but at a high cost. The *Mary*'s captain, Samuel Pease, was mortally wounded, and four of his crew also received wounds. Pound and his crew had committed not only piracy but murder as well.[37]

The trials took place in several meetings of the Court of Assistants in January 1690. Winthrop, Sewall, Corwin, Hathorne, and Richards all attended at least one of the sessions at which the pirates were convicted and sentenced to hang. Yet Winthrop had reservations, for as soon as the verdicts were in, he, along with assistant Colonel Samuel Shrimpton and clerk of the court Isaac Addington, approached members of the government and other influential people, seeking reprieves for the buccaneers. Winthrop's efforts were spurred by his sister-in-law, the widow of his brother Adam, for the pirate Thomas Hawkins was none other than her brother. After Adam's death, she had married John Richards. Hawkins was fortunate that his other sisters had also married prominent men, including Boston's Reverend James Allen as well as members of the Hutchinson and Foster families, important merchant clans. Colonel Shrimpton helped with the effort. He, too, was related to Hawkins. Governor Bradstreet granted the pardons, and not a moment too soon: Sewall reported that Hawkins was at the scaffold when the reprieve came through. "Which gave great disgust to the people," wrote Sewall in his diary. "I fear it was ill done." Sewall lamented his decision to sign Winthrop's petition: "I rashly signed, hoping so great an inconvenience would not have followed. Let not God impute sin." Indeed, there must have been quite considerable "inconvenience" for Sewall and the others. The citizens of the colony were up in arms. In the end, only one of the pirates, Thomas Johnston, was executed. Hawkins and seven others had their penalty reduced to a substantial fine of 20 marks (approximately £20). Even Pound, the pirate leader himself, had his charge respited and eventually dropped. It was a clear case of the elite of the colony taking care of their own. This decision would leave the public second-guessing the assistants, and it would likewise leave the assistants wanting to prove their willingness to execute justice. Seven of the nine judges of the Court of Oyer and Terminer of 1692 served as assistants under the interim government.[38]

The pirate reprieve was one of a series of controversial decisions made by the assistants in the years leading up to the witch trials. In addition to being named councilors under the new charter, all of the judges had been leaders of the colony since the overthrow of Andros. All served on the interim Council for Safety except for Sewall, who was in England at the time helping to try to restore the charter. All would serve on the council in Bradstreet's interim government except for Sergeant and Gedney, who served the government in other roles. Sergeant was appointed to several committees by the interim government, overseeing levying and paying of soldiers as well as helping to organize and fund Phips's 1690 expedition against Canada. Meanwhile, Stoughton and Sewall were commissioners (that is, appointed representatives of the government) who traveled to New York to help plan an overland invasion of Canada, to be undertaken by New York and Connecticut militia in coordination with Phips's naval attack on Quebec. The attack up the Hudson River, led by Wait Winthrop's brother Fitz-John, would end in total failure, never reaching its intended target, Montreal. As colonel in command of the Essex militia, Gedney was also a key figure in the failing war effort. He had served on the organizing committee for the invasion of Port Royal in the summer of 1690 and even been offered command of it, but he declined it. In the spring of 1691 he was appointed one of seven commissioners to meet with the Natives in Maine to extend the truce.[39]

Gedney was just one of six of the judges who were high-ranking militia officers. Winthrop was a major general with overall command of the Massachusetts militia. Major Saltonstall commanded the northern division of the Essex regiment, while Richards and Stoughton were both majors and Sewall a captain in the Suffolk militia. Hathorne and Corwin were not officers, but their late fathers had been and they were well acquainted with the military world. Collectively, then, in their leadership roles, these men were responsible for the colony's utter military and political failure in the war against the Natives and their French allies and for that had earned the wrath of the electorate.

Divine displeasure must have been as great a concern to the judges as was the popular discontent. As devout Puritans, they interpreted everything as a sign of God's pleasure or displeasure. Ministers had been warning people for several decades that they needed to undergo moral reformation—to turn Massachusetts back to a godly experiment, a city upon a hill. It was time for people to repent. In March 1690 the concern took the form of the campaign for universal moral reformation approved by the General Court, including assistants Richards, Sewall, Corwin, Wait Winthrop, and Hathorne. Two years later it must have been clear to them that the campaign for reformation had failed as miserably as the military campaign. The continued hardships New England faced proved God was still displeased. Now he had set the devil loose to punish New England or at least to try its faith. The first step would have to be rooting out Satan's agents.[40]

The judges must have felt that the destruction of frontier settlements in the war was God's judgment against them personally, for most of them had speculated heavily in frontier land in the 1680s. This exercise in greed had also brought them into contact with the dark world, for these lands were recently purchased or taken from Native Americans. Based on their business ventures, the judges of the Court of Oyer and Terminer were actually better qualified to preside over a land court than cases of witchcraft. Winthrop held title to huge tracts of frontier lands in Connecticut, Rhode Island, and Massachusetts. He inherited much of this land from his father, John Winthrop Jr., and grandfather Governor John Winthrop, though Wait and his brother Fitz-John had supplemented their holdings while both were councilors in Dudley's provisional government of 1686. Their brother-in-law John Richards had an interest in the Winthrop lands through his marriages to two Winthrop brides, but he also had a long history of involvement in the frontier, going back to his 1649 purchase of Arrowsic Island, Maine, from the Androscoggin sachem the English called "Robin Hood." In the 1680s and 1690s Richards was also a major mortgage holder for property in greater

Boston. Although these lands were far from the frontier, his investments would have been sensitive to the declines in value due to the war.[41]

The real estate interests of the Winthrops and Richards were among the most substantial in New England, but those of their late brother-in-law, Richard Wharton, were even greater. As a member of the Atherton Company, Wharton owned lands in Rhode Island. He also was a partner with his kinsman Joseph Dudley in several efforts in the Nipmuc and Merrimac regions, including the so-called Million-Acre Purchase (a speculative land venture in the Merrimac River Valley), and he was an absentee proprietor of Dunstable. In 1683 and 1684 Wharton had purchased the Pejebscot patent from the Purchase and Way families and had the sale of the 500,000-acre parcel confirmed by six Indian sachems of the Androscoggin and Kennebec Rivers. In 1686, Wharton along with Stoughton, Dudley, and several others formed a company to purchase lands from the Mohegans in Connecticut. One of these partners, John Blackwell, had invested in confiscated church lands in England in the 1650s during Oliver Cromwell's tenure. After the Restoration, when these lands reverted to the church, Blackwell and other speculators migrated to New England. Thus some of the frontier investors of the 1680s had ties to Puritan speculation in Cromwell's England. Wharton died in London in 1689, having traveled there to push for the replacement of Governor Edmund Andros after the governor refused to confirm Wharton's title to Pejebscot.[42]

Sewall and Corwin also maintained sizable interests in the frontier. Sewall and his wife, Hannah, inherited tremendous wealth and hundreds of acres of land from her father, John Hull. The family owned shares in the Pettaquamscut Company, on the western side of Rhode Island's Narragansett Bay, and particularly owned a large farm at Point Judith. The Sewalls held numerous properties in the Greater Boston area and also owned sawmills on the Maine frontier. In 1687 Samuel recorded in his diary a visit to his sawmills at Salmon Falls, a few miles upriver from Newichawannock (in present-day Berwick). During the trip he spent the night in York, at the home of his cousin Reverend Shubael Dummer. Sewall also went to Wells, where it is possible he saw the mills belonging to Salem merchant Jonathan Corwin.[43]

Gedney's property interests were not as extensive as those of his kinsmen the Corwins and the Winthrops, but they were still significant. In 1674 Gedney purchased an estimated 100,000 acres of land in Westcustugo from

Thomas Stevens, shortly after the fur trader bought it from the sachem Robin Hood and his followers. Gedney's gristmill and two sawmills burned during King Philip's War. After the war he rebuilt these operations and was granted a house lot in nearby Falmouth, Maine. In 1684 the General Court awarded Gedney an additional five hundred acres in Maine in thanks for his expedition to Casco Bay in 1679 to help reestablish the English settlements that had been abandoned in King Philip's War. In 1686 Gedney, Richard Wharton, and several others (including Shubael Dummer's brother) supported an effort to set up lands in Westcustugo as a home for English refugees forced out of Eleuthera Island in the Bahamas by the Spanish. Bartholomew was not the only member of his family with sizable Maine interests. His brother married Mary Pateshall, whose family consisted of Boston merchants and major investors in Maine lands. Mary's father had been killed on the Kennebec in King Philip's War, and her brother Richard died in the 1689 attack on Pemaquid. Richard Pateshall's great-grandson Paul Revere was one of the many heirs who received a share of his Maine lands when they were finally divided.[44]

Even Nathaniel Saltonstall, who left the witchcraft court early in the proceedings, had extensive property interests. The judge's family owned thousands of acres of land, thanks largely to his grandfather Sir Richard Saltonstall, a Massachusetts Bay Company leader and investor. Most of these tracts were in frontier areas, including Connecticut and the Piscataqua. Nathaniel lived on a substantial estate in Haverhill, one of the most exposed frontier settlements in the colony. He also owned more than a thousand acres of land in Ipswich, where his family's properties included a sizable mill complex. In the early 1680s Saltonstall was granted a house lot in Falmouth, Maine, while there to help reestablish the government. Most of Saltonstall's wealth came from renting his various properties.[45]

The only member of the Court of Oyer and Terminer who was not a substantial holder of frontier lands was Peter Sergeant. However, even this wealthy Boston merchant had at least one such investment. He was a partner with Sewall and Eliakim Hutchinson in the 1684 purchase of 50 percent of the ironworks and sawmill in Braintree. He was also brother-in-law of Samuel Shrimpton, one of the holders of the Million-Acre Purchase. These business ties as well as his kinship ties meant that Sergeant shared the interests and presumably the views of his fellow members of the merchant class.[46]

The judges, their kin, and their fellow merchants suffered the largest financial losses in King William's War, as the frontier settlements were destroyed. Sewall estimated that he and his father-in-law had invested £2,000 in the Kittery sawmills destroyed in raids in 1689 and 1690. Indians also burned the mills owned by Gedney, Corwin, and many others. Without the mills, New England lost one of its most important exports, one that helped to drive the region's economy. The speculative bubble had burst. Frontier lands occupied by the warring Wabanaki had no value and no buyers. They were worthless for the time being. The magnitude of these losses is hard to imagine. Only a little more than 2 percent of all men who died in Boston in this era left an estate worth £2,000, and the richest estate was £3,417. The average Bostonian who died in the 1690s left roughly £200 in personal property and real estate. Sewall and the other merchants had lost enough to bankrupt just about anyone else.[47]

Many of the judges were connected to the Native population not simply through real estate deals and ownership of frontier land but also through their involvement in what was called the Society for Propagation of the Gospel in New England (more commonly known as the New England Company). First established in 1649 by the Puritan-dominated Long Parliament in England, the Protestant missionary society raised and invested funds that were sent to its commissioners in New England to pay the salaries of Puritan missionaries. The company also funded other efforts to see to the education and welfare of Native converts (often known as "Praying Indians"). The New England Company's English benefactors and members were predominantly peers and London merchants. Those merchants worked with their commissioners (or agents) in Massachusetts to invest the funds and to see to their distribution. Their network included many judges of the witchcraft court and their associates. Stoughton, Winthrop, and Richards were all commissioners at the time of the trials, as were Increase Mather and Sir William Phips. Stoughton served as treasurer of the commissioners, and Richards's London business partner, Major Robert Thompson, was governor of the company. Sergeant and Sewall would become commissioners in 1698, though their involvement had started many years earlier. Sergeant's first cousins, the Ashurst brothers, were key members of the company. In 1690 Sewall hosted a meeting attended by Stoughton, Winthrop, and three Native representatives to determine what legislation "might be most expedient for the present settlement of the Friend-Indians."[48]

Surely this was a worthy civic and charitable undertaking for godly Puritan merchants, but their role as protectors and benefactors for these "Friend-Indians" could come into conflict with other needs of the colony, as when John Eliot, one of the missionaries paid by the New England Company, had called for the company to purchase substantial tracts of land to be set aside as reserves for the Praying Indians—a call that later would be echoed by Sewall. Some land speculation by Stoughton and fellow New England Company councilor Joseph Dudley in the Nipmuc country was done at least in part with Native reserves in mind. In 1682 when the two made the huge purchase of lands from the Nipmuc, the deeds specified that five square miles was to be set aside for the tribe. The next year the General Court granted Stoughton, Dudley, and New England Company governor Robert Thompson a township in the Nipmuc country. It would become the town of Oxford. Presumably it was established as an investment for the New England Company, though it may also have been seen as a way to protect the Native reserve, located just a few miles to the south. Such reserves were well-intentioned parts of the Puritan missionary effort, but they interfered with the expansive demands of a growing English population, which coveted all Native lands.[49]

Also, being an advocate for any Native group—even Praying Indians—during a series of devastating wars against a substantial segment of the New England Native community made these men unpopular in some circles, even objects of suspicion. King Philip's War had devastated southern New England and left a deep and long-lasting emotional scar.[50] King William's War brought more destruction. Settlers who had suffered in these conflicts would have taken a dim view of anyone helping any Natives—even Praying Indians, who were Puritans and allies of the English. Furthermore, involvement with Praying Indians was just one more connection between the judges and the frontier, tainting these men with suggestions of ties to the devil and his minions. If John Alden had been charged with witchcraft in large part because of his role as a frontier military officer, trader, and negotiator, imagine how his accusers musts have felt about the judges, whose Native connections ran far deeper. They were military officers who speculated in Native lands and were involved in protecting Native communities and converting their inhabitants. And they were on a losing end of a war against Native Americans.

Collectively, then, there are a number of clues as to why the judges would reverse the legal precedents of the 1680s and convict and execute witches.

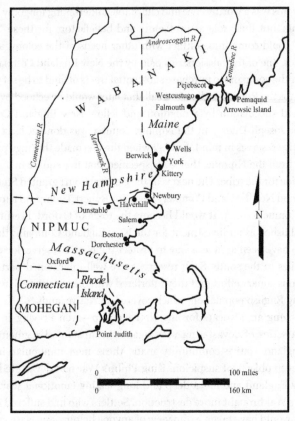

The world of the judges. Drawing by the author.

They must have felt they had a great deal to prove—to God, to their fellow Puritans, and even to themselves, for in one way or another many of these members of the second generation had turned their back on the colony and its mission. A majority of them had attended Harvard, but none now served as ministers. When the Bay Colony had faced its deepest crisis over the loss of the charter, Stoughton, Gedney, Winthrop, and Hathorne had accepted appointments under the Dominion of New England. Indeed, Stoughton had been a member of the panel that had dealt so harshly with the Essex County tax revolt, in which civic leaders had objected to Governor Andros taking away their rights as Englishmen. All the judges held high political offices, and many were military commanders under the provisional government and the new government of William Phips, so they were responsible for the failed political and military policies in a frontier war that threatened the very existence of the colony. Now Providence had given them another chance to prove themselves in defending the colony from Satan's attack.

In addition to the weight of these burdens, the judges must have been mightily out of sorts, for they had suffered major financial losses from their investments in frontier sawmills and speculations in frontier lands. Their losses, and the colony's, would have left them looking for someone to blame. And unless they wanted to accept responsibility themselves, the list of suspects was short. Sad to say, under such circumstances it is often human nature not to look within but to look outward. The judges did exactly that, preferring to hold Satan and his minions accountable for their situation.

Had the trials taken place ten years earlier, therefore, it is quite likely that they would have ended differently—with acquittals or with convictions carrying lesser penalties, as happened in cases heard by many of the same men. The many daunting problems facing the colony in 1692 surely convinced them of the need for an intensified campaign for moral reformation. Gone were the days when witches would be placed under house arrest, or murdering pirates let off with fines. Offenders now "must expect the justice of exemplary punishment." This overriding need to find and convict witches and to mete out severe sentences dominated the legal proceedings. From the start it was clear that the judges accepted the presence of witches and dedicated themselves to rooting them out. Even before the questioning began of Sarah Good, Tituba, and Sarah Osburn, Hathorne and Corwin had assumed their guilt. Rather than weighing the evidence behind the charges, they became interrogators, focusing on determining how the witches operated, identifying their circle of co-conspirators, and finding out why they chose their particular victims.[51]

This assumption of guilt and eagerness to convict helps explain some of the legal irregularities in the proceedings. In the early months of the proceedings the judges failed to enforce the requirement that those lodging the charges had to post a bond. Such financial obligations generally ensured that no spurious charges were made. It became easy to press charges, and accusations grew at a faster rate than they might have otherwise.[52] Given that Corwin's child was believed to be afflicted by the accused, he should have recused himself, for he violated the well-known English common law principle that a person could not be a judge in his own case. Corwin was not the only man who should have recused himself from the proceedings. As the father and uncle of the afflicted witnesses, Samuel Parris should never have served as court secretary. Likewise, Thomas Putnam should not have taken down depositions for the court, given that his wife and daughter were afflicted and that he himself had made formal complaints against at least thirty-five people and testified against seventeen of them. Even more so than the judges, these men believed that Satan was loose in Salem Village. Putnam's depositions seem to have been particularly helpful in convicting witches, perhaps due in part to his embellishing them with a formulaic phrase: "I verily believe in my heart" that the accused was a witch. It is impossible to determine the degree that such enhancements strengthened the prosecution's case, but at any rate, permitting such adversaries of the accused to have an official court capacity certainly did nothing to aid the defendants or to ensure even the appearance of a fair and impartial trial.[53]

When the Court of Oyer and Terminer began its work, it adopted the presumption of guilt first made by Hathorne and Corwin at the early arraignment hearings. Of all the people questioned by the judges in 1692 on charges of witchcraft, only one, Nehemiah Abbot, was found innocent by the court and freed after questioning. The odds were even worse for the accused who were indicted and went to trial. The Court of Oyer and Terminer tried twenty-eight people for witchcraft, and all twenty-eight were found guilty. This is the sort of record one would expect to find only in show trials in an authoritarian state, such as the Soviet Union in the 1930s or North Korea today. It is a prosecutorial success rate unparalleled in American history before or since. Prior to 1692 Massachusetts courts produced only eight guilty verdicts for witchcraft in thirty-one decisions—a 26 percent conviction rate.[54]

An analysis of the magistrate's questions and the responses of the afflicted and the accused demonstrate one way the judges steered the process toward their predetermined verdict of guilty. The judges asked very narrow questions of the afflicted, designed to elicit a short, positive response. Many were designed to lead the afflicted and to show that the judges believed their testimony and were only asking them to confirm the details. In this way, the magistrates' suppositions could be turned into evidence. The judges used a different strategy when questioning the accused. They regularly asked questions that also functioned as accusations, accusations that were difficult to disprove because the judges controlled the interrogations. For example, Hathorne's asking Sarah Good "What evil spirit have you familiarity with?" makes a presumption of guilt.[55] Such questions are designed to elicit a confession, and the interview was merely designed to determine whether there was enough evidence to indict Good and put her on trial—not to acquit her. Their strategy consisted of constructing a "guilty but unwilling to confess" mentality by which they assumed that the defendants who refused to confess were lying. Some tried to fight against this presumption of guilt, but many were eventually browbeaten into accepting the judges' premises. The Salem judges were quite effective at coercing false confessions.[56]

The only body that seemed to act with restraint in 1692 was the grand jury, presumably because they met on their own and without the influence of the judges. Eight suspected witches received at least one finding of "ignoramus," that is, lacking sufficient evidence to be held for trial. Unfortunately, the grand jury found compelling evidence in other charges for seven out of the eight, so they were still held for prosecution. Even on September 17, when the grand jury dismissed both charges against William Procter, the court did not immediately set him free. The son of John and Elizabeth Procter apparently then faced more charges, which would not be dismissed by a grand jury until January 1693. Nonetheless, though lacking education and judicial experience, the grand jury seemed more capable of practicing legal restraint than the judges.[57]

The judges struggled to proceed under English law, and while they consulted many appropriate English legal texts and discussions of witchcraft cases, hard-and-fast rules governing evidence in English courts of the day did not exist for any kind of trial, let alone for witch trials. That is why they pushed hard for confessions and also sought other types of proof, including physical and spectral evidence as well as the evil eye and touch tests. Physical evidence often took the form of poppets. The court also paid close attention to any ointments or oils in the homes of the witches, for these were supposedly used by witches to help them fly on broomsticks. When physical evidence was lacking, the judges turned to more controversial methods, including limited use of judicial torture.

While nobody was tried entirely on spectral evidence, it was what was initially brought against almost everyone at Salem, becoming a litmus test for discovering a witch. Once spectral evidence was deployed, the court began looking for other evidence to corroborate it, given that all authorities urged that it must be used with caution.[58] As early as his May 31, 1692, letter to Richards, Cotton Mather warned, "I must humbly beg you that in the management of the affair in your worthy hands you do not lay more stress upon pure specter testimony than it will bear...it is very certain that the devils have sometimes represented the shapes of persons not only innocent but very virtuous."[59] The "Return of Several Ministers," penned by Cotton and other leading ministers on June 15, not only provided similar caution about spectral evidence but also raised concerns over the efficacy of the evil eye and the touch test: "Nor can we esteem alterations made in the sufferers, by a look or touch of the accused, to be an infallible evidence of guilt, but frequently liable to be abused by the devil's legerdemains."[60]

Unfortunately, however, Mather and his colleagues hedged their advice. While they urged caution, they also knew that Satan was loose and that people were "suffering by molestations from the invisible world," so they exhorted the judges to carry out "the speedy and vigorous prosecution of such as have rendered themselves obnoxious." And the ministers showed deference to the judges, expressing full confidence in their ability to determine who the real witches were and congratulating them for their work so far, including the trial and execution of Bridget Bishop. The ministers thanked God for the success he had provided to the diligent and careful efforts "of our honorable rulers to detect the abominable witchcrafts." In other words, *You need to be careful, but you are doing a great job, so keep it up.* Believing in any case that the accused were very likely guilty, the judges read the "Return of the Ministers" as a confirmation of their procedures and an encouragement to proceed with all deliberate speed. While many believed that it was possible for Satan to produce a specter of the innocent, others suggested that he could only use the form of his willing accomplices. Here again, the judges' presumption of guilt made it far easier to accept this questionable evidence.[61]

Spectral evidence was not just drawn from written depositions made before the trial by the afflicted. It was also used in the courtroom, with high drama and to great effect. The climax of most trials occurred when the afflicted confronted the accused. When this happened, invariably the alleged witch's specter harmed the afflicted, who writhed and shrieked in pain in response to spectral attacks invisible to the jury and rest of the court. This very public demonstration of spectral evidence could not help but have a strong impact on the jury, giving such evidence far more weight than it deserved. Not only did the judges allow this, but they ignored the many suggestions that such afflictions were being faked. Robert Calef provided the most extreme examples of courtroom fraud in his *More Wonders of the Invisible World*. He said that at Sarah Good's trial, one of the afflicted screamed that Sarah had stabbed her with a knife. Upon examination she produced a broken tip of a knife blade. However, a young man showed the court the matching haft and blade of the knife, which he said he had broken the day before in the presence of the afflicted, casting away the useless tip. The afflicted was then "bidden by the court not to tell lies."[62]

Calef also noted the case of John Alden, a complete stranger to the afflicted. In court the judge asked the accusers to pick Alden out of the crowd, but they could not do so until, as one girl admitted to the court, a man behind her identified Alden for her. Rebecca Nurse's daughter-in-law Sarah Nurse testified that she had seen Sarah Bibber stabbing herself with pins. Despite Sarah's testimony, Bibber's accusation that Rebecca Nurse's specter had stabbed her with the pins was entered into evidence, apparently without question. Mary Warren made a statement that the afflicted were dissembling. Clearly there were many suggestions of courtroom fraud that were ignored by the judges in their rush to convict.[63]

Some of the shortcomings of the court were vividly and poignantly evoked by Mary Esty in the petition she wrote to the court in mid-September after she was condemned to die. Her letter was a plea not for her life but for others awaiting trial so "that no more innocent blood may be shed." Given the "wiles and subtlety" of her accusers, Esty urged the judges to keep the afflicted apart and to examine them separately, thus preventing them from conspiring, and bringing to a halt the spectacle of the animated group collectively acting out their afflictions in the courtroom. She also suggested that the confessed witches be put on trial, for she was confident that some of them were lying. Esty did not question the sincerity or earnestness of the judges "in the discovery and detecting of witchcraft and witches," saying that they "would not be guilty of innocent blood for the world," but her own innocence proved that errors had been made.[64]

Esty was very careful to be deferential to the magistrates because the court had made it quite clear it would not stand for anyone questioning its legitimacy or its processes. Those who had done so had been harshly punished. As one legal historian of the trials has pointed out, "No one who behaved defiantly or impudently toward the court escaped with his or her life."[65] The best example of this behavior occurred just days after Esty penned her letter, when Giles Cory was pressed to death for standing mute. Cory had pleaded not guilty, but when asked per custom if he was willing to be tried by the judges and a jury of his peers, he refused to speak, bringing the proceedings to a halt. The court saw this as a direct challenge to its authority, so they literally pressed Cory for an answer. The court did not have to perform this gruesome and ultimately fatal torture to continue with Cory's trial. Just two years before, the Court of Assistants had ignored pirate William Coward when he refused to plea on the grounds that the court did not have jurisdiction on the high seas. Despite the lack of a plea, his trial still took place before the assistants the following day. Coward was convicted of piracy and soon hanged for his crime. Corwin, Hathorne, Richards, and Sewall were among the assistants who had tried Coward, so they certainly knew this precedent and ignored it.[66]

If those who challenged the court fared poorly, those who tacitly approved of the proceedings by confessing to witchcraft did much better. Not only did these results reinforce the authority of the court, but they were in keeping with the spirit of the campaign for moral reformation. The 1690 order had warned "that the jealous God will punish" the unrepentant "seven times more for their iniquities." But if God grants them "the grace to remember whence they are fallen, and repent, and do their first works, it will give a greater prospect of prosperity than can arise from best counsels, and biggest armies." Thus through moral reformation the "back sliding people" can achieve salvation, with "glory dwelling in our land."[67] Yes, witches and other sinners would meet punishment, but it was far preferable for them to admit sin and repent, for this was the only way restore the city upon a hill. The judges therefore eagerly sought confession, as it hastened the process of salvation, especially when the confessors spread the circle of witches—the sinners who needed to confess before glory could dwell in the land. Those who refused to confess faced not only an angry God but also the full and unforgiving wrath of the court for slowing the process of salvation.

One of the biggest puzzles of the trials remains why the court did not execute any witches who confessed. Some have argued that confession was no guarantee of survival and that the court might have convicted and executed all who had confessed once they were no longer useful as witnesses for the prosecution. The court actually began this process in September 1692 when it convicted and condemned to death five confessors. However, only Samuel

Wardwell was executed, and he had recanted his confession. There was no legitimate reason for the other four (Ann Foster, her daughter Mary Lacey Sr., Rebecca Eames, and Abigail Hobbs) not to be executed along with Wardwell and seven others on September 22. It remains unclear whether the court actually ever intended to execute these or other confessed witches. The court's treatment of Dorcas Hoar also shows the special treatment accorded to a confessed witch. Tried and condemned, Hoar confessed on September 21, just a day before she, too, was destined to go to the gallows. With Governor Phips off in Maine, William Stoughton approved a petition for a month's reprieve, submitted by John Hale, Nicholas Noyes, and two other ministers and endorsed by Judge Gedney.[68]

Tituba, the first confessor, also received special treatment. Though she remained in jail for months after she acknowledged her guilt, the Court of Oyer and Terminer never indicted the slave, let alone try her. She finally had her case taken up by the grand jury of the Superior Court of Judicature in May 1693, which returned a verdict of "ignoramus." Surely the court had not kept Tituba around for so long in hopes that she would accuse more witches, for she apparently did not testify or make any depositions for the prosecution after she was sent to the Boston jail on March 7, 1692.[69]

In short, the court treated these confessed witches differently than any other court in English history, though many of these same men helped convict and execute Goody Glover in 1688. And while the judges may have been considering the ultimate trial and execution of the confessors, they clearly did not believe these witches were a threat to the public; otherwise they would have ordered swift trials.[70] Unlike the Goody Glover case, there is no sign that the judges even asked doctors to observe the confessors to examine their mental well-being (another sign that they did not face the death penalty).

The answer to these riddles may lie in Cotton Mather's letter of advice to Richards on May 31, 1692. In it the younger Mather notes, "'Tis worth considering whether there be a necessity always by extirpations by halter or fagot [hanging or burning] every wretched creature that shall be hooked into some degrees of witchcraft. What if some of the lesser criminals be only scourged with lesser punishments, and also put upon some solemn, open, public, and explicit renunciation of the devil? I am apt to think that the devils would then cease afflicting the neighborhood."[71] It is a rarely noted but important and unprecedented suggestion, made by the man often seen as a leading witch hunter: that some convicted witches, having publicly confessed and renounced Satan, might live, and that this might actually bring witchcraft to an end. It is also a suggestion that was entirely in keeping with the campaign for moral reformation.

Evidence of this hope for the defeat of Satan through moral reformation can be seen in the treatment of two confessed witches, Dorcas Hoar and Mary Lacey Jr. Perhaps stern Judge Stoughton approved the temporary reprieve for Hoar in the hope of finding more witches, for the petition noted that "she gives account of some other persons that she hath known to be guilty of the same crime." However, he also may have been taken by the ministers' observation that a reprieve would allow her time to "perfect her repentance for the salvation of her soul." Furthermore, it would "be providential to the encouraging others to confess & give glory to God."[72] Repentance, not execution, could save even the soul of a convicted witch. This was the best way to bring glory to God and ultimately defeat Satan. Similarly, the magistrates offered hope for Mary Lacey Jr. through confession. When she was examined by Corwin, Hathorne, and Gedney, one of the judges let her know, "You are now in the way to obtain mercy if you will confess and repent." Lacey replied, "Lord help me," after which the judge questioned, "Do not you desire to be saved by Christ?" When Lacey answered in the affirmative, the judge counseled, "Then you must confess freely what you know in this matter."[73] Mary Warren had been present during the questioning and had been having fits. However, after Lacey made a detailed confession, "Mary Warren came and took her by the hand and was no way hurt and she viz. Mary Lacey did earnestly ask Mary Warren forgiveness for afflicting of her and both fell a weeping together." Next Mary Lacey Sr. was brought in, and her daughter "earnestly bid her repent and call upon God."[74] Such scenes seem more in keeping with a religious revival than a witch trial. Salem was on the verge of moral reformation and spiritual reawakening in 1692. All that was necessary was for all the afflicted to confess.

Yet all too often the confessions were not forthcoming, and therefore the judges had to act decisively. The more one reads the extensive witch trial court records, the more it is clear that these proceedings were carefully stage-managed by the judges to gain the guilty verdicts they fully expected. Initial examinations were designed to gain confession, with many being forced out of reluctant detainees. Even in his defense of the trials, Cotton Mather noted their formulaic nature. He wrote that "Martha Carrier was indicted for the bewitching of certain persons, according to the form usual in such cases."[75] The proceedings almost seemed to follow a script. The evil eye caused afflictions, which would then be cured by the touch of the accused. Mention of the devil's book could cause afflictions, but a witch's confession could end them. Lacking a confession, the trial that ensued proceeded along a similar path, designed to impress upon the jury the guilt of the accused. The judges regularly asked leading questions that assumed the defendants were guilty but refused to confess. And they were willing to intervene directly when it appeared the guilty might go free. After the jury initially found Rebecca Nurse not guilty, for example, Stoughton sprang into action. He behaved more like a prosecuting attorney than a magistrate, coaxing the jury to reexamine some of the evidence; the jury reconsidered and finally brought back a verdict of guilty.

This unusual behavior of the judges had not gone unnoticed. By late summer of 1692, more than five months after the legal proceedings had commenced, people would finally start to express their growing concern about the proceedings.[76] The judges were being judged.

CHAPTER SEVEN

An Inextinguishable Flame

Being afflicted last night, with discouraging thoughts as if unavoidable marks,
of the divine displeasure must overtake my family, for my not appearing
with vigor enough to stop the proceedings of the judges, when the
inextricable storm from the invisible world assaulted the country.
—Cotton Mather's diary, January 15, 1697[1]

ON OCTOBER 12, 1692, GOVERNOR Sir William Phips wrote to William
Blathwayt, the clerk of the Privy Council, to inform him of the witchcraft
crisis. Phips deflected blame for the affair, misleadingly claiming that he
had missed most of the trials, for he "was almost the whole time of the pro-
ceeding abroad," building forts and trying to win the war in Maine. He had
left the colony and the trials in the hands of Deputy Governor Stoughton
and "depended upon the judgment of the court as to a right method of pro-
ceeding in cases of witchcraft." What he came home to find, however, was
"many persons in a strange ferment of dissatisfaction" and some people in
jail "who were doubtless innocent and to my certain knowledge of good reputation." He was therefore going to stop further arrests and, to calm things
down, ban any publications on the matter. "I have also put a stop to the

printing of any discourses one way or another, that may increase the needless disputes of people upon this occasion, because I saw a likelihood of kindling an inextinguishable flame if I should admit any public and open contests."[2]

On the surface Phips's actions sounded like a sensible short-term plan to allow matters to cool off. Yet it was also a calculated move, designed to redirect blame and squelch the growing opposition to the trials, which threatened to bring down the government. Phips's action ultimately saved his fragile government and preserved the Bay Colony's new royal charter. However, it came at a substantial cost, for the curbing of free speech about the witch trials was a key element of what effectively became the first large-scale government cover-up in American history. In the months and years following the trials, the government would come increasingly under criticism, placing the Puritan covenant with God in jeopardy once again. Collectively the concerns raised about the trials changed people's views of their government and helped bring an end to the Puritan theocracy. In trying to put out a fire by suppressing the truth, Phips actually lit an inextinguishable flame that guaranteed that the Salem injustices would never be forgotten. Furthermore, despite Phips's efforts to preserve the Puritan state and maintain the status quo, the witch trials would trigger political, social, and religious changes that would transform the Bay Colony.

Phips's ban came in response to a growing unease with the seemingly endless proceedings, and a flurry of publications. Reverend Deodat Lawson's *A Brief and True Narrative of Witchcraft at Salem Village* had by then been out for several months, and books by three other ministers would be available to the reading public of Boston by October 28. Word was spreading in other ways, too, notably Thomas Brattle's October 8 manuscript letter. Phips knew about Increase Mather's *Cases of Conscience Concerning Evil Spirits Personating Men* and Samuel Willard's *Some Miscellany Observations on Our Present Debates Respecting Witchcrafts*, as both were circulating in manuscript. Mather's manuscript was specifically shared with Phips, as it reflected the thinking of the elder Mather and many of the senior ministers of the colony.[3]

The elder Mather and Willard made similar arguments, suggesting that extreme care should be used in trying people accused of witchcraft. Even Mather's title reflected this view, for it was an homage to Englishman John Gaule's *Select Cases of Conscience Touching Witches and Witchcrafts* (1646), which urged caution in prosecutions. Both Mather and Willard readily acknowledged the existence of Satan and his ability to harm people, with or without the assistance of witches. However, in a view that was now widely accepted by the Massachusetts clergy, spectral evidence was not to be considered reliable because the devil could use the image of innocent people to harm others. They questioned the authenticity of the touch test and suggested that some of the afflicted were possessed by Satan, making their testimony invalid. Concurrently, neither man criticized the judges or the jury. Willard tactfully ignored their role, while Mather observed that the devil had deluded them.

Nonetheless, Mather seriously questioned the entire proceedings. The trials were doing more harm than good, and the legal system was failing in its duties: "It were better that ten suspected witches should escape, than that one innocent person should be condemned." Because Mather was a close political ally and confidant of Governor Phips, the minister's opinion meant a great deal, especially when it included the endorsements of fourteen other ministers and a supportive preface written by Willard. This book alone must have been enough to convince Sir William that the trials had to end.[4]

An early and relatively outspoken opponent of the trials, Samuel Willard was one of the real heroes of the proceedings. As a young minister in Groton, he had dealt with the possession of Elizabeth Knapp, so he had experience with the sort of thing that was going on in Salem Village. Willard had signed the "Return of Several Ministers," expressing his doubts over spectral evidence, and on June 19 he preached a sermon suggesting it was possible for the devil to create specters of innocent people. Not long after that, apparently during Rebecca Nurse's trial, one of the afflicted girls cried out in court that Reverend Willard was responsible for her torments. Clearly the afflicted had gotten wind of Willard's concerns and felt threatened by him. The judges would not hear of it. Robert Calef reported that "she was sent out of the court, and it was told about she was mistaken in the person." Presumably Judges Sewall, Winthrop, and Sergeant led this effort, as all three were members of Willard's South Church.[5]

Historians have often pointed out that Willard's opposition to the trials was related to his quarrels with the Mathers, but his views were also rooted in his family ties, for he was a relative of the accused witch John Willard. The exact relationship is unclear, as the names of John's parents—like those of many other early New Englanders—are lost to time. Still, the circumstances suggest Samuel was John's uncle or cousin. A number of Willards lived in the Nashaway region (Groton and Lancaster), at the edge of the frontier in central Massachusetts. Willard had started his ministerial career in Groton, where his father, Major Simon Willard, was a leading settler and patriarch of a large clan. John Willard had been living in this area on a thirty-acre grant of land abutting the land of one of Reverend Willard's brothers, Henry, just a year or two before he was accused of witchcraft.[6] One time when John was behaving strangely, his wife, Margaret, went to Henry Willard and Henry's brother Benjamin for help. John fled to Nashaway when a warrant was issued for his arrest in 1692. While John was in prison, Samuel preached sermons against the trials, and particularly condemning the validity of spectral evidence as well as the testimony of the afflicted. His sermons went unheeded. John Willard was among the convicted witches hanged on August 19. Two days later, Samuel Willard may have helped Philip and Mary English to escape from the Boston jail and flee to New York. Willard's son John had already apparently aided the accused witch Elizabeth Cary's escape from the Cambridge jail.[7]

Reverend Willard's book went to press in mid-October, just after Phips's ban; it was published under assumed names to protect him from being prosecuted. The title page announces the authors as "P.E. and J.A."—the initials of Philip English and another accused witch who had taken flight, John Alden. It was listed as published in Philadelphia by William Bradford, a printer there, for Hezekiah Usher. This was another subterfuge to skirt the publication ban, for the book was actually published in Boston. Hezekiah Usher was another accused witch who had fled, and, like John Alden, he was a member of Willard's church. Willard structured the book as a debate between "S" (Salem) and "B" (Boston), with his personal views being expressed by Boston. Both sides readily accepted the existence of witches. Boston even argues that the judges should execute them should sufficient evidence be found, while Salem argues that spectral evidence was sufficient. Boston counters by stressing arguments from Willard's sermons: the devil could take the shape of innocent people, and confessions that named other witches were not to be trusted.[8]

Several manuscript letters survive that suggest there was growing support for the views expressed by Mather and Willard. Major Robert Pike was the Massachusetts Bay councilor and Salisbury magistrate who had collected depositions used to convict and execute Susannah Martin. However, when

Mary Bradbury, one of the most prominent women in Salisbury, was arrested, Pike had a change of heart. On August 8 he wrote a letter to Judge Jonathan Corwin, raising his concerns about spectral evidence. Like all good Puritans steeped in the Old Testament, Pike knew that the Witch of Endor had raised the devil in the likeness of Samuel, the great Hebrew leader and prophet. Furthermore, it made no sense for witches to use their powers against the afflicted in the courtroom and thus to provide such public proof of their guilt: "Self interest teaches every one better." Similarly, why would the devil use his confessing witches to accuse others who had signed his covenant unless "the devil hath changed his nature, and is now become a reformer to purge witches out of the world, out of the country, and out of the churches; and is to be believed, though a liar and a murderer from the beginning"?[9]

Two months later, on October 8, Thomas Brattle wrote his letter—which was addressed to an unnamed "Reverend Sir" but which was intended to be circulated publicly—containing a comprehensive assault on the witch trials, done in the scholarly and scientific manner befitting a Harvard graduate who had worked with Robert Boyle. Like his contemporaries, Brattle believed in the existence of the devil and witches but questioned the use of spectral evidence and the touch test. An observer of some of the trials, he was convinced that evil spirits deluded the confessing witches, and he noted that the confessors often contradicted themselves. Brattle pointed out the special treatment of some of the accused. Why did the court not pursue fugitives such as the Englishes and John Alden? he wondered. Why was Hezekiah Usher allowed to be under house arrest, and then allowed to flee? "If he may be suffered to go away, why may not others? If others may not be suffered to go, how in justice can he be allowed herein?"[10] While noting that there was still some support for the trials, Brattle documented the growing unrest in Massachusetts with the proceedings.

The honorable Simon Bradstreet, Esq. (our late governor); the honorable Thomas Danforth, Esq. (our late Deputy Governor); the Reverend Mr. Increase Mather, and the Reverend Mr. Samuel Willard. Major N. Saltonstall, Esq. who was one of the judges, has left the court, and is very much dissatisfied with the proceedings of it. Excepting Mr. Hale, Mr. Noyes, and Mr. Parris, the reverend elders, almost throughout the whole country, are very much dissatisfied. Several of the late justices, viz. Thomas Graves, Esq. N. Byfield, Esq. Francis Foxcroft, Esq. are much dissatisfied; also several of the present justices; and in particular, some of the Boston justices, were resolved rather to throw up their commissions than be active in disturbing the liberty of their Majesties' subjects, merely on the accusations of these afflicted, possessed children.[11]

Amid this growing clamor for the trials to end and questioning their methods, only Cotton Mather's *The Wonders of the Invisible World* defended the actions of the government. The book was written quickly and rushed into print to try to buttress the government by endorsing the actions of the judges. Though some of the judges' methods might be disputed, the younger Mather insisted, there was clear precedent for their actions. To prove this point, he discussed at length the influential writings of Gaule and other English witchcraft experts. He also cited recent precedent for executions by discussing two relatively recent outbreaks in Europe. In 1662 the Bury St. Edmunds trials resulted in the conviction and execution of two elderly widows from Lowestoft, Suffolk, on thirteen counts of witchcraft. In these trials, spectral evidence had been accepted by no less an authority than the eminent judge and chief justice of the King's Bench, Sir Matthew Hale. Mather also cited the trials in Mora, Sweden, in 1669–70, which bore a strong resemblance to those in Salem.[12]

The younger Mather wrote the book at the request of Governor Phips, so he had the active support of the judges and worked with court clerk Stephen Sewall to get access to all the trial transcripts. Yet his book focuses on just five of the nineteen executed. Officials insisted that he include George Burroughs, to which Cotton added Bridget Bishop, Martha Carrier, Elizabeth How, and Susannah Martin. Mather chose these cases with great care and as part of an effort to defend the use of spectral evidence. All had been accused of *maleficium*, harmful witchcraft, by numerous people, and all but Martin had been accused by confessed witches. Not only were these executions among the least controversial, but they relied far less on spectral evidence than other Salem trials. Thus Mather minimized the impact of spectral evidence. He also was selective even in his discussion of these cases. For example, he failed to mention Elizabeth How's supporters, including Deborah Hadley, who had known Elizabeth for twenty-four years and "found her a neighborly woman conscientious in her dealing faithful to her missus & Christian-like in her conversation." And of course Mather did not mention at all the more controversial cases, such as Rebecca Nurse's.[13]

At the time, the twenty-nine-year-old Cotton Mather was at the peak of his career, one that had started out with incredible promise. He graduated at fifteen from Harvard—the youngest in its history—and was a brilliant intellect who would eventually master seven languages. At eighteen he received his master's and became the assistant pastor at his father's North Church. In 1685, at twenty-two, he was ordained as minister of North Church, sharing duties with his father, who now officially moved to the position of "teacher." As partner and intellectual heir of his father, Cotton had already published widely and was poised to be the next great Puritan theologian. Yet with its selective use of the evidence, *The Wonders of the Invisible World* severely damaged the reputation of one of the last standard-bearers of American Puritanism, and with him the cause itself.[14]

Why, then, did Cotton Mather write his book? And in particular, why did he defend the use of spectral evidence when earlier he had urged caution in its use, such as when writing to John Richards and composing for all the judges the "Return of Several Ministers Consulted"? The answer is that the witchcraft outbreak had blossomed into a political crisis, and Governor Phips as well as Deputy Governor Stoughton and the rest of the witchcraft judges, who were all also members of the governor's council, needed Cotton to carry out spin control. Despite his earlier efforts at moderation, the younger Mather was now willing to compromise his beliefs because he had become convinced that the fate of Puritan colony itself was at stake. Mather's gloss was needed to protect the fragile administration of Phips, a close political ally of the Mathers and a member of their church. Phips and Increase Mather had arrived in Boston from London only the previous May to commence the government under Massachusetts's new Royal Charter of 1691. No one knew what might happen if Phips's government failed. Perhaps Andros or some other military governor might return, again threatening the liberties of the colony and its Puritan church. With Massachusetts beset with internal political division and locked in a desperate military struggle with the French and their Native allies, a public acknowledgment that the judicial system had wrongly executed nineteen people, pressed to death another, and imprisoned well over a hundred more would have brought down the new government and threatened the existence of the city upon a hill. Cotton acknowledged in *Wonders*, "I have indeed set myself to countermine the whole plot of the devil, against New-England, in every branch of it," and he believed that the witchcraft outbreak was part of a process that might bring the Puritan experiment to an end.[15]

Regardless, Governor Phips had what he needed to defend the witch trials and bring the Court of Oyer and Terminer to an end. With *The Wonders of the Invisible World* now published, he could call for a ban on future publications and squelch any further questioning of the judges or the government. A copy of the book traveled to London on the same ship that carried Phips's letter to Blathwayt about the ban. To avoid any confusion about its status in regard to the prohibition, the reverse of the title page of *Wonders* announced that it had been "Published by the Special Command of His Excellency, the Governor of the Province of the Massachusetts-Bay in New-England." It would be reprinted in London, where it would be taken as the official account of the trials.[16]

Once he returned from Maine, Phips brought an end to the court. When questioned during the October 29 session of the legislature as to whether the Court of Oyer and Terminer would stand or fall, Governor Phips said, "It must fall."[17] There would be no more sessions of the court.

Many have praised Phips for his good judgment in the matter. Phips does deserve credit for bringing the trials to an end in the face of opposition from many, including his deputy governor. However, his actions were guided by a series of political, legal, and personal considerations that were sometimes self-serving. Phips had created and ended the Court of Oyer and Terminer

Sir William Phips by Thomas Child,
[1687–1692]. From a private collection,
photograph © Cory Gardiner.

and ultimately had the power to pardon those it had convicted. Phips's circumstances and motives are worth exploring, for they illuminate the politics behind the witch trials.

In 1692, Sir William Phips was perhaps the most famous English colonist living in the Americas. Born and raised on what Cotton Mather referred to as a "despicable plantation" on the coast of Maine, he sought refuge in Boston during King Philip's War. Trained as a shipbuilder, he became a ship's captain, and in 1687 he raised the cargo of a Spanish treasure galleon valued at more than £200,000, winning him instant fame and fortune. It was an immense sum. The more than sixty-eight thousand pounds of silver and twenty-five pounds of gold would be worth in excess of $20 million today. James II was so elated with this huge windfall for the crown and the nation that he knighted Phips—the first man born in America to receive such an honor. Returning to Boston, Phips soon allied himself with the Mathers and became a member of their North Church. His success brought high offices, including command of military expeditions against Acadia and Quebec in 1690. While the attack on Acadia did result in the capture of Port Royal, the much larger Quebec expedition accomplished none of its goals and was deemed a disaster. His reputation compromised, Phips then returned to London, where he worked with Increase Mather to gain a new charter for Massachusetts. His reward was his appointment as the royal governor, under the new charter of 1691.[18]

Despite his high office, Phips was more of a bare-knuckle street politician than a polished diplomat. A man of no formal schooling, he was at best partially literate. His religious credentials were not strong, either, as he became a Puritan saint only in 1690, a move that seemed more politically than spiritually inspired. Phips was a remarkable man. Through savvy and hard work he personified the archetypal rags-to-riches story. Still, his background ill prepared him for the difficult challenge that greeted him and Increase Mather when they arrived in Boston with the new charter in May 1692. Not only was there the witchcraft outbreak and a war that was going badly, but many were upset that Mather and Phips brought an entirely new royal charter, rather than one that restored previous conditions. The new charter was in reality a substantial political accomplishment, giving the colony considerable freedom, but some leading conservative politicians of the colony refused to accept it, believing it did not provide enough freedom. Meanwhile, royalists who had supported Dudley and Andros were at best lukewarm to the changes. So Phips governed a divided General Court, where he had only limited support.[19]

When Phips returned from London it was clear that immediate action was called for to deal with the witchcraft crisis. Hence rather than wait for the General Court to meet the following month, he created the Court of Oyer and Terminer without its consent. Technically, therefore, this was an illegal court, at least until the legislature met and approved it, for the new charter did not allow the governor to form it. Indeed, this restriction had in fact been a victory for Mather and Phips in their negotiations, Andros had held this arbitrary power under the Dominion and used it to great advantage. That Phips would resort to such an extreme measure shows the great concern he and Mather must have about the witchcraft outbreak. The court was always a temporary expedient, one Phips wanted to eliminate as soon as possible, as it lent credence to the fears of his opponents about the wide powers held by the royal governor under the terms of the new charter.[20]

As the head of a new and factionalized government, Phips could not risk alienating the colony's important politicians. More than that, he needed to establish a reputation as a proponent of law and order. Corwin, Hathorne, and Gedney were key Salem politicians who had already been involved in the trials. Phips did not dare snub these men by denying them a place on the Court of Oyer and Terminer, even though they had all demonstrated a willingness to believe in the validity of spectral evidence, about which of course Phips's allies the Mathers had serious reservations. Phips had personal reasons as well for backing an aggressive court. His half-brother Philip White lived in Beverly and had a sick child who Dr. Toothaker said was "under an evil hand."[21]

Despite being the uncle of an afflicted child, Sir William and his wife, Lady Mary, both had good reason to fear that they themselves might come under suspicion of witchcraft. Mary had a relative who had been accused in Maine a few years earlier, and witchcraft was believed to travel in families. Witches were often considered to be barren, and the Phipses had no children. They shared their home with two servants: a black slave, who was Sir William's manservant, and the Catholic daughter of Baron St.-Castin and his Wabanaki princess bride (the girl was a prisoner of war Phips had captured when he seized Port Royal, Acadia, in 1690). It was a most peculiar family, headed by Sir William, the recent convert to Puritanism. Phips had been a successful treasure hunter, an occupation that required divination to find the riches, and also the ability to charm monsters believed to protect them. He had also had his fortune told, as Cotton Mather would later reveal in his biography. While these were all acts of white magic, they were the devil's work nonetheless. Furthermore, Phips would have been perceived to have the same taint of familiarity with Native Americans known to the judges. He had been raised on the coast of Maine, where his playmates included Wabanaki children. He and Mary both had relatives in Falmouth, where they had been parishioners of George Burroughs. Phips had connections to other outsiders, too. Sir William was later accused of associating with pirates, and after taking Port Royal, he had been an outspoken champion of the rights of Acadians as English subjects—including some who would later prove to be French spies.[22]

Phips therefore dared not be seen as soft on witchcraft. Nor did he want to be particularly close to it. He was happy to turn the proceedings over to Deputy Governor Stoughton so that he could focus his efforts on the military crisis and the challenge of passing a new legal code through a legislature that was increasingly divided. Despite spending five or six weeks in Maine leading the war effort in the late summer and fall, Phips was present in Boston during all of meetings of the Court of Oyer and Terminer, except for its September session. He could have played a much more active role in the proceedings had he wanted to, but he even turned over the authority to sign the death warrants to Stoughton. Not only did Phips avoid the proceedings, but when he first reported the witchcraft outbreak to the crown he dissembled about his whereabouts, suggesting that he had been off in Maine and shocked upon his return to find what a poor job Stoughton had done in his absence.[23]

By lying to his superiors in London and by commissioning Cotton Mather's whitewash of the affair and then immediately imposing a publications ban, Phips was following public opinion. While even educated people still believed that witches were real, most were becoming increasingly convinced that some innocent people had died. This was greater than a moral outrage; it was a doctrinal corruption. According to Puritan theology, someone who commits a sin must confess it before God. The state's sin should have been acknowledged publicly. Failure to do so jeopardized the Puritans' special covenant with God and indeed the very foundation of their belief. It was an open invitation to bring down God's wrath on individuals and the entire colony. Yet admitting to the commission of sin would lead to equally dire consequences. If the state acknowledged the wrongful death or imprisonment of more than 150 innocent citizens, the new government would lose all authority. The king would be forced to recall Governor Phips, the charter could be lost, and Massachusetts might wind up with another Andros. It would be the end of Massachusetts as a Puritan colony. Mather and Phips had decided that, at least for this special moment, the government was more important than the covenant, for without the government there would be no covenant. It was a decision that would be long remembered. The suppression of the truth by Phips, Cotton Mather, and others had turned Massachusetts from a city upon a hill, ruled by divine ordination, to an entity governed by political expedient, and for that reason alone the Salem trials became a pivotal moment in American history. The witch crisis was the end of the Puritan covenant, or at least the beginning of the end.

Mather's book was an intellectual and moral sham, one that in many ways discredited this last great Puritan theologian and his cause. Even worse, he unwittingly dragged down his father and most of his esteemed colleagues with him. Increase Mather read *Wonders* when his own book was ready for publication. The gap between the father's thinking and the son's was clear, and Increase's reaction was to close ranks. He added a substantial postscript to his work in which he praised the wisdom of the judges and echoed Cotton's opinion that spectral evidence had not been a deciding factor in any of the court's cases to date. His concerns with it were merely a precautionary warning in the event of future trials. He also said that he knew the controversial decision to convict and execute George Burroughs to be a just one. He ended his postscript by dismissing the notion that Cotton's book contradicted his: "'Tis strange that such imaginations should enter into the minds of men. I perused and approved of that book before it was printed. And nothing but my relation to him hindered me from recommending it to the world." This postscript was added after the fourteen ministers had contributed their own endorsements and Willard had written his preface. Now, without their agreement, the endorsement of all of these other religious leaders of the colony had effectively been extended to Cotton Mather's defense of the government. Collectively the ministry was now implicated in the cover-up.[24]

While Phips's publication ban may have saved his government and the charter, change would come nonetheless. The elections in the spring of 1693 would prove to be a stinging rebuke to Sir William, the Mathers, and their policies—including their handling of the witch trials. More than half of the seventy-two representatives elected to the House had not sat in the previous session. There would be ten new members elected to the twenty-eight-man council, a personal affront to Increase Mather, who had just given an election sermon exhorting the legislature to reelect the standing members of the council, men hand-picked by Increase when the charter was established. These were unheard-of turnovers in bodies known for stability and the longevity of their members. Puritan conservatives and royalists both made gains. The Mathers' role in the witch trials—particularly Cotton's book and Increase's endorsement of it—meant these men were no longer effective political brokers between the governor and these factions.[25]

They had also alienated Samuel Willard and William Stoughton. Willard refused to let go of the trials. Not only did he ignore the ban with his book *Some Miscellany Observations*, he also made the first public call for repentance for the witch trials in his election sermon preached in 1694. *The Character of a Good Ruler* took direct aim at Mather's election sermon of the year before, as well as Phips's political compromises. Willard admonished "that such may be the influence of the maladministration of rulers, though done without malice, and in an heat of misguided zeal for the people of GOD…that the guilt may lie long upon a land, and break out in terrible judgments a great while after, and not be expiated till the sin be openly confessed, and the atonement sought unto." It was a masterly sermon. Willard made no direct mention of Salem, witchcraft, or even Phips, but the implications were nonetheless clear.[26]

Others attacked the Mathers, too. On February 19, 1693, the House of Representatives sent Phips and the council a law requiring the president of Harvard—at the time, Increase Mather—to live in Cambridge, knowing full well that Mather would not leave Boston and his North Church. The bill died, but Mather's opponents would eventually pass such legislation, forcing his resignation. The residency requirement was largely a device to remove Mather, for the General Court had no problem with the appointment of Willard, a fellow Bostonian, to succeed Mather as president of Harvard.[27]

Willard's efforts were aided by his brother in-law Joseph Dudley, the leading royalist in Massachusetts. Dudley returned to England in 1693 to work for Governor Phips's overthrow and to see to his own appointment as successor, yet his political influence and connections in New England remained strong. Dudley's longtime business partner and political ally was Stoughton, who had, as we have seen, been alienated by Phips when he ended the Court of Oyer and Terminer and pardoned the remaining convicted witches. By early 1693 Stoughton and Dudley were scheming with Sir Henry Ashurst for Phips's removal.[28]

The mishandling of the witch trials signaled the decline of the Mathers and provided an opportunity for their opponents to bring down Phips. Many had been leery of the charter of 1691, under which, they felt, Massachusetts became merely another royal colony. The Mathers and Phips tried to calm these fears. After all, Phips was one of them, not an outsider, as had been Andros. And the 1691 charter was the most liberal granted to any English colony, with many elements of self-rule. By trying to deflect blame from the administration and acting to cover up the wrongdoing, Phips and his allies lost support from legislators, who increasingly doubted Phips and his charter. Trust had been broken, and in their eyes he seemed more like a royal official and less like one of their own.[29]

Under the charter of 1691, the governor had limited control over the legislature; increasingly, politicians exercised their prerogatives. Notably, the legislature held the power of the purse. They did not take up the issue of Phips's salary until early 1693, and then they refused to set an annual sum. Instead, they would from time to time grant him payment for past service. The implications were clear: the General Court did not trust Phips and would withhold his salary unless he behaved and passed their legislative agenda. A tradition of distrust of the office of governor had been launched. Eighty years later, Thomas Hutchinson would serve as the last royal governor of Massachusetts, a colony headed toward rebellion. Hutchinson, another Bostonian, faced some of the same problems that had confronted Phips as the first royal governor. It did not have to be this way. Under the 1629 charter, the governor had acted as a trusted partner with the legislature. Sir William's mishandling of the witch trials ended any chance of this happening under the new royal charter. The distrust and antagonism between governor and legislature would become the face of things to come. Phips may have ended the witch trials, but in the process he helped to start America down the long road to revolution and independence.[30] In the immediate aftermath of the trials, factionalism would continue to grow, until Phips was recalled by William and Mary in 1694. He would die in London in February 1695 while awaiting the chance to refute the long list of complaints against him. Except for the brief rule of the Earl of Bellomont, for the next twenty years Massachusetts would be ruled by Deputy Governor Stoughton (1695–1701) and Joseph Dudley (1702–1715). Under Dudley the power of Puritanism would fade, and Massachusetts would evolve into a royal colony.[31]

As the political landscape changed, so, too, would the legal system. Initially the courts favored women, a response to the wrongful conviction and execution of so many accused witches. For several years after the trials not a single Essex County woman was convicted of a crime by a jury. However, women had been the key players and leading witnesses in legal proceedings that had gone horribly wrong. Now men would dominate the courtroom. Scholars have found that by around 1700, for example, a double standard involving sex crimes had set in throughout New England. Men refused to plead guilty to any sex crime other than sex with their wives prior to marriage (this was the crime of "fornication," a charge normally made against both husband and wife when their full-term firstborn child arrived sooner than nine months after marriage). All-male juries almost invariably refused to convict men of any sex crime other than incest. Women now appeared rarely in court. If they did so as a victim of a sex crime, they generally faced humiliation and a disappointing verdict. There had been a slight double standard prior to 1692, with men sometimes getting preferential treatment. Afterward there was a wide gulf in how men and women fared when it came to accusations of rape and incest.[32]

Laws would change as well, and in such a way to prevent another witchcraft outbreak. In December 1692 the General Court passed an act that made practicing magic punishable only by imprisonment and the pillory, unless the magic was used to commit murder. This act reflects the desire for latitude in the punishment for witches expressed by Cotton Mather in his letter to Richards on May 31, 1692. In 1703, the General Court passed a law invalidating spectral evidence. In England, Parliament would finally decriminalize witchcraft in 1736. Other new laws were passed, and while they had nothing to do directly with witchcraft, they alleviated the conditions that had precipitated the Salem outbreak. In 1697 the Massachusetts General Court would pass a law that guaranteed a sure title to any land owned without challenge from 1692 to 1704. In 1698 the General Court passed a law that called for far stricter regulation of land and for enforcement of an owner's responsibility to maintain fences for pastures and fields. Together the two laws would go a long way toward eliminating neighborly disputes over property boundaries and trespassing livestock—key factors in many court cases, including witchcraft accusations.[33]

Most people increasingly questioned the existence of witches, and those magistrates who still believed in sorcerers failed to find sufficient legal evidence to convict them. No American court would ever again execute a witch after 1692, and witchcraft prosecutions came to an abrupt halt in New England. Winifred Benham of Wallingford, Connecticut, was accused of witchcraft in 1697, but with only spectral evidence put forward, the court acquitted her. Interestingly, the last American trial for the capital crime of witchcraft occurred in Virginia in 1706, when Grace Sherwood of Princess Anne County faced charges. The verdict does not survive, but presumably she was acquitted, as her death is recorded as taking place thirty-four years later. In 1730 a Richmond County, Virginia, woman was the last person convicted of practicing white magic, when she was found guilty of "enchantment, charm, witchcraft or conjuration, to tell where treasure is, or where goods left may be found." Under the English Witchcraft Statute of 1604, this lesser crime was punishable by a year in prison and public confession of her sins. Virginia magistrates "reduced" the punishment to thirty-nine lashes at the whipping post.[34]

While the court refused to convict witches, the general population continued to believe in their existence. With no recourse available in the courts, people sought protection in folk magic and countermagic. Most New England homes of the eighteenth and even the nineteenth centuries were given some sort of protection from witches and evil. Shoes that could catch evil spirits as they came down chimneys were buried in walls next to the hearths. Coins placed under door sills, carved daisy wheels—a series of arcs cut within a circle with a compass to resemble a flower—and a range of other talismans continued to be used to ward off evil, as they had before 1692. Many such objects still lie buried in homes, awaiting discovery during renovation or restoration.[35]

Witchcraft accusations would show up from time to time in the court records of New England, usually as cases of slander brought by those accused of being a witch. For example, in 1725 Sarah Keene, after years of innuendo and accusations from her Kittery neighbors, finally sued John Spinney for slander. Perhaps the most interesting testimony came from

Daisy wheel carved in early nineteenth-century door trim of the author's home, in York, Maine. The diameter of the daisy wheel is 1.5 inches. Photograph by the author.

Sarah Keene's son Nathaniel. He said that he asked Spinney "what made him say that my mother had bewitched him and rode him up from the eastward." Spinney retorted that he never claimed he had been transported from the eastern Maine settlements (presumably by broom) by Sarah Keene; rather, a "Nerish [Irish] woman rode me up that lives at the eastward." Several witnesses confirmed that Spinney did indeed claim to have ridden with Sarah Keene and that he told people Keene had been a witch for many years. The deposition shows that as late as the 1720s people still associated witchcraft with the "eastward" or extreme of the frontier—though by that time the frontier was well east of Kittery. Also, outsiders such as the Irish remained likely candidates for witchcraft accusations. Several years earlier, a colony of Scots-Irish immigrants had established small settlements on Casco Bay and on the lower Kennebec River—at the time the very edge of the English frontier in Maine. Perhaps these immigrants had made an impression on Spinney during a voyage to the "eastward." By 1725 many of the Scots-Irish had to abandon this frontier, as another war had erupted between the settlers and the Native Americans. Keene's slander case is one of many that make it clear that traditional beliefs—ranging from the witch's teat and riding on brooms to the fear of foreigners and the dangers of the frontier—were still very much alive in the eighteenth century.[36]

Indeed, belief in witchcraft died very slowly in New England. As late as 1796, four women and a man from Arundel, Maine, were tried for beating and attempting to murder a woman for witchcraft. The victim, an elderly widow named Elizabeth Smith, stood accused by one John Hilton of afflicting him. The four women and Hilton attacked Smith, severely beating her, and threatened to kill her. Smith was obliged to flee to a neighboring town to safety. When brought before the Court of General Sessions of the Peace in nearby Biddeford in November 1796, the judge tried to reason with the group. The newspaper reported that the judge "endeavored to convince them of the gross error into which they had fallen; and the difficulties and dissentions in the neighborhood arose rather from ignorance in themselves than from witchcraft in the poor old woman." The defendants were bound to keep the peace until the following summer, and the incident quietly disappeared. Had the case been tried before the Court of Oyer and Terminer in 1692, the result might have been quite different.[37]

When reprinting the story from the *Eastern Gazette and Herald of Maine*, the editor of the *Polar Star and Boston Daily Advertiser* could not resist adding a rejoinder: "The above law case is a melancholy proof that the monster superstition has not entirely disappeared from this country. In the most bigoted countries, even in the dominions of the Pope, the tales of witchcraft are silenced. How come it that in the bosom of a Democratic Republic founded on reason and information there should exist ignorance so profound, zeal so fanatical, as to be willing to introduce the auto de fe, executions, the burnings of Portugal and the inquisition."[38]

The shifting attitudes about the existence of witchcraft signaled deeper spiritual changes, as Puritan beliefs continued to evolve. Yet while skepticism was on the rise, people did not necessarily become less pious. The witch trials actually reinvigorated the campaign for moral reformation first called for in the Reforming Synod of 1679. Many became increasingly interested in pursuing their individual religious experience instead of communal covenanted devotions. In January 1693 Cotton Mather would for the first time welcome new members to the North Church under the Halfway Covenant, as John Richards had finally yielded. Perhaps this was the elderly judge's personal atonement for the witch trials, though Richards never recorded any statements or expressed any sentiments about the trials before his death on April 2, 1694. Facing declining membership and even the inability to attract a minister, most of the Puritan churches that had resisted the Halfway Covenant now decided to accept it. Dedham, for example, went from 1685 to 1692 without a minister, only managing to land one after the Halfway Covenant was adopted. The witch trials had contributed to a loosening of Puritan church discipline. Before 1692 discipline records are chock-full of censures issued for a variety of offenses. Such censures virtually disappeared from the records of the First Church of Salem following the excommunication of Rebecca Nurse and Giles Cory. Other churches followed suit. Excommunications effectively ceased, and censures were limited to clear-cut cases, mostly involving sexual offenses and drunkenness. Thanks to the witch trials, it became far less clear when one could be considered guilty of a religious offense, and churches much preferred to err on the side of leniency. The conflict in Salem and the trials had served a warning to churches to avoid controversial disciplinary actions that might lead to community divisions.[39]

The witch trials also helped to banish the devil from New England. Ministers stopped talking about Satan the tempter roaming the earth in corporeal form and instead talked about how he waited in the horrible fires of hell for sinners. As a part of a growing focus on the individual, people increasingly took personal responsibility for their sins. And while the devil threatened their salvation, many increasingly came to believe that they could resist his enticements. Only during the Great Awakening in the 1730s would the devil reappear in conversion narratives and ministers' sermons.[40]

Even as Satan was being dispossessed, the Mathers faced a new spiritual threat—the establishment of the Brattle Street church in 1699. Boston's fourth church was built on land donated by Thomas Brattle, and he was joined in the effort by a group of liberal-minded young men, including his brother William and John Leverett, who were the tutors and intellectual leaders of Harvard. Just as Brattle had made a reasoned analysis of the Salem witch trials, so did these men seek a Congregational church founded in reason. In doing so, Brattle Street broke many traditions of New England Puritanism. It had no covenant and no specific church discipline, and was founded not on scripture or the New England way but instead on what it saw as the "law of nature." The Brattle Street church had no particular membership requirements and dispensed with public relation of members' conversion experiences. The minister could offer baptism to any child of any Christian. It had no ruling elders; hence any baptized member had a voice in church affairs, including the election of a pastor. Services consisted of reading scripture, and there was no interpretive sermon.[41]

The manifesto that announced the new church was a formal declaration of rebellion against the Mathers and their colleagues, and indeed against traditional New England Puritan Congregationalism. It would be a church more in tune with the spiritual and intellectual currents of old England than with the New England way. Knowing that their doctrine and their choice of minister—the recent Harvard graduate Benjamin Colman—would not be acceptable in Massachusetts, the Brattle Street group had him ordained in England. Combined with the suspension of the sermon, this smacked of Anglicanism. It also threatened the patriarchal order, for power no longer lay with the male church members but with the entire congregation, which traditionally enjoyed a female majority. Some of the reforms were logical extensions of the Halfway Covenant and other efforts to loosen church membership requirements. In fact, concurrent with the establishment of Brattle Street, Solomon Stoddard, a Northampton minister who was a rival of the Mathers, was pushing for similar reforms, as laid out in 1700 in his *Doctrine of Instituted Churches.* While both Brattle Street and Stoddard posed serious challenges to the Mathers' views, the manifesto went way beyond issues of church membership, threatening the very existence of the New England way.[42]

Given that there was so much change in the air, open criticism of the witch trials, and equally open challenges to the leadership of Phips and the Mathers, it is perhaps surprising that the governor's publication ban lasted three years. In the end, it would be a Quaker and not a Puritan who first dared to break it. Few histories of Salem mention Thomas Maule, but he may be one of the few true heroes of this tragic period, for he was the first to publish an attack on the court's proceedings under his own name. It was a courageous act that cost him dearly, but in the process he struck an important blow for freedom of the press and freedom of religion. Maule and his efforts deserve close attention, for his book, along with his arrest and trial for writing it, would open the floodgates.

Maule was born in Warwickshire, England, in 1645, amid the turmoil of the Civil Wars. His Anglican family supported Charles I in his fight against the Puritan-dominated Parliament. Family tradition suggests that Maule's father was among the hundreds of royalist prisoners of war that Oliver Cromwell sent into exile and forced servitude in the Caribbean. Perhaps this explains Maule's migration to Barbados when he was a teenager. Here he toiled as a tailor and began to work as a merchant. In the late 1660s he moved from the Barbados to Boston, and then relocated to Salem, continuing to work as a merchant. His outspoken nature often got him into trouble. In 1669 Maule was ordered to be whipped for saying that Salem minister John Higginson "preached lies, and that his instruction was 'the doctrine of devils.'" At the time Maule was probably still an Anglican, but he would soon convert to Quakerism and become a leader of the Salem Friends.[43]

This radical Protestant sect was one of many to emerge out of the chaos of the English Civil Wars. Friends came under immediate persecution in Massachusetts, for they were seen as posing a direct threat to Puritan orthodoxy and polity. Puritans, who lived in a hierarchical and deeply patriarchal society, were horrified at Quakers' egalitarian views. Not only did they reject ministers, anyone could speak at Quaker meeting, even women. The Bay Colony felt so threatened by Quakers that in 1658 the General Court invoked the death penalty for any Friend who would dare to enter the colony. Between 1659 and 1661 Massachusetts would execute four Quakers for defying this law. After outcries from the crown, the colony rescinded the act in 1661, only to replace it with the Vagabond Quaker Act, which, while it was supposed to call for leniency for Quaker missionaries, required severe punishment for any Friend who caused trouble, particularly going from town to town proselytizing. The punishment called for the Quaker to be stripped to the waist, tied to the tail of a cart, and whipped. The Quaker then had to follow the cart to the next town, where he would be whipped again, and so on until the cart—or at least the Friend—had left Massachusetts. The Bay Colony's treatment of Quakers would not be forgotten. It would be regularly invoked by opponents of Massachusetts Bay, including Thomas Maule. The Quaker executions would be an important consideration in the crown's decision to revoke the Massachusetts charter in 1684.[44]

Despite punishments for Quaker missionaries who would dare enter the colony, a significant number of residents in Massachusetts adopted the faith. Their numbers were probably the strongest in Salem, long a hotbed for religious passions. Salem minister Roger Williams was thrown out of the colony in 1635 for his religious and political views. He moved south, founding Rhode Island and the Baptist Church in America. Williams was succeeded in his post by Hugh Peter, a Puritan with such staunch views that he returned to England and was a leading and outspoken opponent of Charles I during the Civil Wars. Chaplain to Oliver Cromwell, Peter preached the funeral sermon for the Lord Protector. Upon the restoration of Charles II in 1660, Peter was executed for his treasonous role in the trial and execution of Charles I. The next year, one of Peter's former Salem parishioners, Thomas Venner, led an uprising in London against the king. The leader of the so-called Fifth Monarchists, Venner gathered members of his radical sect, as well as some Quakers and Baptists, to his cause. Venner's Rising was put down by the crown after only four days. Venner was hanged, drawn, and quartered for his efforts.[45]

Though he never faced execution, Maule was often punished for his outspoken beliefs and unconventional behavior, particularly his profaning of the Sabbath. In 1696 he claimed that he had been jailed five times and whipped thrice. His Puritan neighbors also regularly harassed him. Not only was he robbed several times and had his apple trees cut down, but he was also falsely accused of fencing stolen goods. Yet Maule nonetheless grew in wealth and standing in the community and was often asked to serve in local offices. Even this sometimes got him into trouble, particularly since Quakers were pacifists. When the town elected Maule to serve as a constable, he refused and was fined £10—several months' wages for most men. When asked to help the Salem Militia Committee to secure ammunition to safeguard the town in case of invasion, he refused, citing his Quaker beliefs in nonviolence. The more he antagonized local Puritans, the higher his standing in the Quaker community. By the early 1680s, the Quakers were holding their meetings in Maule's home, and in 1688 Maule donated the land and paid for the construction of a Quaker meetinghouse He kept the record book for the Salem Monthly Meeting and was sometimes the Salem delegate to the Quarterly Meeting, the governing body that oversaw Quaker congregations in the region.[46]

It was while attending a Quarterly Meeting in New Hampshire in 1682 that Maule had his first brush with witchcraft. Maule was part of a group of Friends who gathered at George Walton's tavern on Great Island (present-day New Castle) and who observed the tavern and its occupants being subjected to a supernatural barrage of stones—part of a devilish summer-long assault on the Quaker Walton, his family, and his tavern. Maule was one of nine people who signed an affidavit to the effect that they witnessed "at least half a score stones the evening thrown invisibly into the field, and in the entry of the house, hall, and one of the chambers of George Walton's." Walton accused an elderly widowed neighbor of witchcraft.[47]

There is some evidence to suggest that in 1692 Maule initially supported the witchcraft trials. Reverend John Hale wrote that he heard Maule say that he would not pray with Bridget Bishop because she had bewitched to death one of Maule's children. Hale also reported that Maule's wife, Naomi, testified against Bishop. Hale was a direct observer of the trials and generally regarded as a reliable source. However, no surviving documents from Bishop's trial mention the Maules, nor does Maule mention the bewitchment of his child anywhere in his writings. Given his later opposition to the trials, such an omission is not surprising. Maule also makes no mention of Samuel Parris by name in his book, though the two men's lives followed a similar path. Both were born in England, spent part of their youth in Barbados, moved to Boston, and finally settled in Salem. It is unlikely the two had ever met in Barbados, for Maule was eight years older than Parris, and their time on the island overlapped only briefly. Yet Maule would have known Parris's type: a wealthy and privileged Puritan plantation owner. The Quaker must have been predisposed to dislike the minister.[48]

Despite Maule's initial willingness to accuse someone of witchcraft, he quickly became a critic of the witch trials. In the fall of 1695 he published *Truth Held Forth and Maintained According to the Testimony of the Holy Prophets Christ and His Apostles Recorded in the Holy Scriptures*, a description and defense of Quaker theological tenets and practices. It was also a stern denunciation of Massachusetts Puritan practices, particularly the cruel treatment Quakers suffered at their hands. A significant portion of the book attacks the government's handling of the Salem witch trials. Although the criticism is restricted to just one out of the thirty-eight chapters of the book, it is by far the longest—more than 12 percent of the book. Maule saw the witch trials as God's punishment of Massachusetts for its sins and chiefly its harsh treatment of Quakers. A recurring theme of the book is the execution of the four Quaker missionaries by Massachusetts Bay. Not satisfied with particulars, Maule attacked the very nature of Puritanism, blaming the colony's problems on those who consented to the rule of the "priests" and worshipped God the wrong way (that is, as a Puritan and not a Quaker).[49]

It was a truly courageous act for Maule to print this book under his own name and distribute it, for he did it in open opposition to the ban. In the three years since Governor Phips had issued it, no one in Massachusetts had dared publish anything on the trials. Even those who criticized the proceedings before the ban had kept these works in manuscript or published them anonymously. No Massachusetts printer would undertake the printing, so Maule's book was published by William Bradford in New York, for the printer had moved there from Philadelphia in 1693. On December 12, 1695, Lieutenant Governor Stoughton (acting governor since Sir William Phips's death) and his council issued a warrant for Maule's arrest. The complaint against Maule indicates the ban was still in effect, for the first charge noted in the warrant is that he "published without license of authority." Furthermore, he had written "many notorious and wicked lies, and slanders not only upon private persons but upon government, and also divers corrupt, and pernicious doctrines, utterly, subversive of the true Christian, and professed faith." The council also ordered a search for all copies of the book. Two days later, Sheriff George Corwin arrested Maule, and seized and burned thirty-one copies of his book.[50]

On May 3, 1696, at the Superior Court's spring session in Ipswich, Maule had an angry confrontation with the judges who bound him over for trial at the fall session of the court. He would remain in prison until that session, held in Salem five months later, on November 11, 1696. When the proceedings resumed, Maule faced a tribunal consisting of Samuel Sewall, Thomas Danforth, and Elisha Cooke: the prosecuting attorney general was Anthony Checkley, who had replaced Thomas Newton at the witch trials. It must have been a bit unnerving for Maule to stand in the Salem courtroom where the witches had been convicted, in the custody of Sheriff George Corwin, and before three men who had been active participants in the witch trials three years earlier. Sewall had of course served as a judge on the Court of Oyer and Terminer, and Checkley had been the prosecutor at the trials. Danforth, a former deputy governor of Massachusetts Bay, had been a magistrate who attended some of the pretrial hearings for the accused witches, and had later served as a justice on the Superior Court of Judicature, which dealt with the backlog of witchcraft cases after the collapse of the Court of Oyer and Terminer. Still, the Superior Court had cleared all but three accused witches, and Danforth was known to have believed that the trials had gone too far. In his letter of October 1692, Thomas Brattle listed Danforth as one of the men who "utterly condemn the proceedings."[51]

The composition of the jury may have worried Maule as well. The foreman was Captain John Turner, the wealthy merchant who owned the Salem waterfront mansion that would later be called the House of Seven Gables. Turner was a kinsman of Bartholomew Gedney, so he probably did not take kindly to anyone questioning the actions of the witchcraft judges. Thomas Flint Sr. was a prominent member of the pro-Parris faction in

Salem Village and was related to the Putnam family by marriage. His son, Thomas junior, also served on the jury. Samuel Woodwell's sister-in-law had seen Giles Cory's apparition and testified against George Burroughs. Then there was Joseph Eveleth, who had served as a juryman for the Court of Oyer and Terminer. All four of these men would have been predisposed to look unfavorably on Maule and his efforts to denigrate the witch trials.[52]

If the presence of such jurors made Maule nervous, he never showed it. He took the offensive in arguing his case, claiming that *Truth Held Forth* was actually a religious text and thus should be debated in a religious court, not a secular one. Therefore, while he respected the judges, he said, in this case "I do no more value you than I do a jack-straw." Judge Danforth then described Maule in terms that might have been reserved for a witch. He warned the jury that Maule had committed "horrid wickedness" for writing his blasphemous book, and that he had written it intending to "overthrow all good in church and common-wealth, which God hath planted amongst his people in this province." Maule countered that he had broken no laws and not written or caused to be printed "anything contrary to sound doctrine and inconsistent to the holy scriptures of truth." Furthermore, Maule claimed—rather less heroically—that there was not sufficient proof that he was the author of the book. Yes, it had his name on it, but anyone could have put it there. He actually mocked the Court of Oyer and Terminer in his defense, saying that his name on the book was "no more than the specter evidence," for his name had been placed there by the printer, just as the devil might use an innocent man's specter.[53]

The jury deliberated and returned a verdict of not guilty, much to the shock and displeasure of the judges, who immediately quizzed the panel on how they could have reached such a decision. As he listened, Maule must have thought of Rebecca Nurse—first found innocent, only to have the jury change its verdict when Stoughton sent them to deliberate again, and another judge threatened to indict her a second time. Fortunately for Maule, this time the jury stood its ground. The foreman indicated that, as Maule had suggested, while his name was on the title page there was insufficient evidence to prove he was the author of the book. They also agreed with Maule that the book should have been judged by a jury of divines in religious court. Maule's acquittal may have resulted in part from the fact that, despite appearances, he had some jurors in his corner. John Potter was a member of Lynn's Quaker community and the son-in-law of the Quaker (and alleged wizard) Francis Norwood Sr. Samuel Kilham of Wenham was a kinsman of executed witch Sarah Good. Captain Daniel King had tried to have one of George Burroughs's accusers, Eleazer Keyser, meet with the minister prior to his trial to see if they could work out their differences; when Keyser refused, King admonished him that Burroughs was "a choice child of God, and that God would clear up his innocency."[54] John Gowing's sister-in-law was John Procter's daughter, and James Houlton had signed a petition in support of the Procters. Joseph Eveleth had signed a second petition for the Procters. Indeed, Eveleth was one of twelve witchcraft jurors who would sign an apology that was published by Calef in 1697. Clearly Eveleth had had a change of heart, as had others who had supported or at least gone along with the witch trials.[55]

Regardless of the reasons for their verdict, the jury's acquittal of Thomas Maule was a turning point in the history of not only the Salem witch trials but also American jurisprudence. Before 1692, a Massachusetts jury would have undoubtedly convicted a troublemaking Quaker, a habitual offender who impudently challenged authority. Indeed, had the case been tried under the old Puritan-controlled 1629 charter, John Potter could not have served on the jury because he was a Quaker. Maule's not-guilty verdict, announced in the same courtroom and before some of the same magistrates who had sat in judgment of the victims of witchcraft, signals a dramatic change. The case was a landmark victory for freedom of speech, freedom of the press, and freedom of religion. The fact that a jury consisting largely of Puritans would do this in Salem, against the clear wishes of the judges, also shows that the tide of popular opinion had turned against the verdicts in the witch trials.

Officials may not have been happy, but they recognized this sea change for what it was and did not disturb Maule, let alone charge him, when he published his scathing account of his trial, *New-England Pesecutors* [*sic*] *Mauled with their own Weapons*, the following year. Perhaps he avoided persecution because this time he was wise enough to have the book published anonymously. Maule's second book stressed the hypocrisy of Puritan authorities, along with the greed of their ministers. He claimed their avarice was the reason courts fined people for premarital sex or for being a Quaker or other dissenter. Puritans seemed to prefer collecting fines to jailing offenders. He then went on to discuss the cases of 309 people who had suffered persecution by Puritan authorities, concluding his work with an account of his own persecution and trial.[56]

In 1696 there were other signs of regret over the witch trials in Massachusetts, fueled in part by the many difficulties the colony faced. The war with the French and their Native American allies raged on with no end in sight. Throughout the spring and summer, there were constant rumors of invasion, and settlements in Maine and New Hampshire were harassed by a series of small raids. Then in August, Pemaquid's Fort William Henry fell to a French fleet, supported by their Native allies. The stone fortress had been built at great expense by Governor Phips, who bragged that "the fort is sufficient to resist all the Indians in America." Nonetheless, it surrendered after less than a day of fighting.[57] With William Henry reduced to ruins, people feared the French fleet might venture further south, even attacking Boston. Instead, the flotilla turned north to Newfoundland, destroying the English fishing stations and taking possession of the entire island. Newfoundland had been a major commercial partner of Massachusetts, and to lose the trade with these prosperous fishing ports was a major blow to an economy already burdened by a costly war. Massachusetts retaliated by sending an expedition to attack the French stronghold on the St. John River in Acadia. Commanded by former witchcraft judge John Hathorne, the invasion failed miserably. As Samuel Sewall complained in a letter, the news was "nothing but rumors of war and slaughter against us both by sea and land."[58] The symbolism of this must have seemed particularly strong: the destruction of a fort built by the former governor during the witchcraft outbreak, and the failures of one witchcraft judge as acting governor and another as commander of a military expedition. Surely God was punishing Massachusetts for its sinful dealings in 1692 and its failure to admit its guilt.

There were other ominous signs of God's displeasure with Massachusetts. The colony suffered a famine in the spring of 1696; a killing frost had destroyed most of the previous summer's corn crop. Prices of corn doubled, and unseasonably cold weather delayed the planting of crops and threatened the growing season. By December, food shortages were severe, and the winter was considered the worst since the English had arrived in Massachusetts. Political uncertainly continued to cause concern. In May, word reached Boston of foreign plots to assassinate the Protestant William of Orange and restore to the throne the exiled Catholic James II. The plots had been foiled, however, and King William called for a day of Thanksgiving throughout his kingdom. Although the General Court agreed on such a day, the fall legislative session was marked by strife and division. Meanwhile, Massachusetts waited in anticipation of the arrival of a new governor following the death of Sir William Phips in early 1695.[59]

The devout Puritans of Massachusetts saw all of these problems as signs of God's displeasure. Increasingly they sought the source of this disapproval, and increasingly they turned to the witchcraft trials. Samuel Sewall noted that on August 12, 1696, a neighbor "upon a slight occasion, spoke to me very smartly about the Salem witchcraft; in discourse he said, if a man should take Beacon hill on 's back, carry it away; and then bring it and set it in place again, he should not make anything of that." The neighbor was clearly thinking of George Burroughs, who had been executed almost exactly four years before, on August 19, 1692, in part on charges of his supernatural strength. On September 16, Reverend Samuel Willard put a public voice to these concerns. Sewall recorded that Willard preached at a General Court service, "If God be with us who can be against us?" The minister then spoke "smartly at last about the Salem witchcrafts, and that no order had been suffered to come forth by authority to ask God's pardon." Willard criticized authorities for not making a public confession of guilt for the actions of the colony in the trials.[60]

The General Court would soon issue a long-overdue apology for the witch trials, but the process would add to the political tensions. On December 2, 1696, the House of Representatives passed a bill for a day of fasting and reformation, and went so far as to order five hundred copies of the proclamation written by Cotton Mather to be printed. However, the council took offense on several counts. First, the document had been written without their consultation. Second, the focus of the document was not witchcraft. Rather, it was another call for moral reformation, one that described a range of evils, including uncleanness, excessive drinking, vanity of dress, decay of family discipline, fraud, piracy, and even unrighteous discouragement of the magistrates and ministers of the colony. Witchcraft was hidden within this laundry list of concerns: "Wicked sorceries have been practiced in the land; and, in the late inexplicable storms from the *invisible world* thereby brought upon us, we were left, by the just hand of heaven unto those errors, whereby great hardships were brought upon Innocent persons, and (we fear) guilt incurred, which we have all cause to bewail, with much confusion of our face before the Lord."[61] Mather continued to minimize the sin of witchcraft, as he had in *Wonders of the Invisible World.* He could not even admit outright guilt for a miscarriage of justice, but had to qualify it by saying, parenthetically, "(we fear) guilt incurred." Moreover, Mather insisted on blaming the outbreak on the "wicked sorceries"—white magic, such as fortune-telling and even Mary Sibley's witch cake. Finally, the House had added to Mather's draft an exhortation to the magistrates to do a better job in prosecuting all offenders and to dispense justice equitably. As the members of the council were also the justices of the colony, this was an unacceptable slap in the face—another sign of the political tensions in the General Court.

The council passed its own version of a proclamation, authored by Samuel Sewall. Eventually the House and council would agree on Sewall's draft, with some minor edits. While Mather had buried the witch trials amid a list of sins that needed forgiveness, Sewall focused on witchcraft: "And especially, that whatever mistakes, on either hand, have been fallen into; either by the body of this people, or any orders of men, referring to the late tragedy raised amongst us by Satan and his instruments, through the awful judgment of God; he would humble us therefore, and pardon all the errors of his servants and people that desire to love his; and be atoned to his land."[62] Sewall's wife had miscarried that past spring, and on December 23 their infant daughter Sarah died. The next day, as the family mourned, his son recited to him part of Matthew 12. Sewall remarked that "the 7th verse did awfully bring to mind the Salem tragedy": "But if ye had known what this meaneth, I will have mercy, and not sacrifice, ye would not have condemned the guiltless."[63]

Sewall's mind was troubled from the misfortunes that beset his family. Maule's recent trial would have been a very real reminder of the witch trials, and the Quaker's verdict affirmed that he and the other judges had erred in 1692. Sewall was now convinced that God was punishing not only the colony but him personally for the execution of innocent victims. Thanks in part to Maule, he now knew something must be done. During the Fast Day service, Sewall gave Reverend Willard a letter to read to the congregation. Sewall stood before the congregation as the minister read what has come to be known as Sewall's Apology:

Samuel Sewall, sensible of the reiterated strokes of God upon himself and family; and being sensible that as to the guilt contracted, upon the opening of the late Commission of Oyer and Terminer at Salem (to which the order for this day relates) he is, upon many accounts, more concerned than any that he knows of, desires to take the blame and shame of it, asking pardon of men, and especially desiring prayers that God, who has an unlimited authority, would pardon that sin and all other his sins.[64]

It was a breathtaking act of courage, piety, and humility for one of the wealthiest and most powerful men in the colony to take responsibility for his actions and openly admit what some refused to accept and others had only hinted at. Sewall never seems to have fully forgiven himself for his involvement in the trials. According to family tradition, it was about this time that he began to wear a hair shirt. Sewall would wear this undergarment

The Dawn of Tolerance in Massachusetts: Public Repentance of Samuel Sewall for His Action in the Witchcraft Trials, by Albert Herter, 1942. The mural represents one of the five freedoms depicted on the walls of the Chamber of the House of Representatives, Boston, Massachusetts. Courtesy Commonwealth of Massachusetts Art Commission.

for the rest of his life. By making such a public apology, Sewall immediately made a serious enemy of William Stoughton, now of course acting governor of the colony. To the day he died, in 1701, Stoughton remained firm in his belief that the witchcraft court had acted properly—indeed, that it had saved the colony by convicting and executing the witches—and apparently he never forgave Sewall. A year later, Stoughton snubbed Sewall when he invited all the other members of the council to a dinner party at his house. Stoughton's high office and his view of the trials probably kept more people from following Sewall's example. The only others who came forward at this time were twelve men who had served on juries during the witch trials. Their declaration of regret, printed in Calef's *More Wonders*, noted their "deep sense of, and sorrow for our errors, in acting on such evidence to the condemning of any person. And do hereby declare that we justly fear that we were sadly deluded and mistaken, for which we are much disquieted and distressed in our minds; and do therefore humbly beg forgiveness."[65]

The Fast Day and the apologies of Sewall and the jurors must have encouraged John Hale to write his *Modest Inquiry into the Nature of Witchcraft*. He discussed the project with Sewall in November 1697 and completed it in 1698, just two years before he died. Hale had occupied a front-row seat for the trials, having been one of the first men called in to look at the afflictions of Betty Parris and Abigail Williams. Hale quickly became a fervent supporter of the proceedings, a position that would eventually change when on November 14, 1692, seventeen-year-old Mary Herrick would accuse Hale's wife, Sarah Noyes Hale.[66]

In 1695 Sarah died, and this, along with the Fast Day and the apologies and perhaps even Maule's trial, which took place less than two miles from Hale's home, apparently led the elderly minister to reflect upon the trials. His book offers a first-hand account by a person closely involved in the trials who tried to find out what went wrong. Hale never denied the existence of witches. Indeed, no one in Massachusetts in 1697 would have seriously questioned their existence. Rather, Hale suggested, the officials and judges had been so very afraid of the all-too-real threat of witchcraft that they had panicked. Serious errors resulted in the loss of innocent lives. Joining others in comparing the witchcraft to stormy weather, Hale concluded, "Such was the darkness of that day, the tortures and lamentations of the afflicted, and the power of the former precedents that we walked in the clouds, and could not see our way. And we have most cause to be humbled for error on that hand, which cannot be retrieved."[67] Hale did not believe there were any evildoers in Salem. Rather, good and well-intentioned people had made horrible mistakes. To prevent this from happening in the future, Hale rejected the traditional forms of detecting witches. As Salem Town's minister John Higginson said in his preface to the book, the example of Salem would lead "the most learned and pious men to make a further and fuller inquiry" into "how witches may be discovered, that innocent persons may be preserved, and none but the guilty may suffer." Hale's book is an attempt to set the record straight and to make amends. Still, he was not as courageous as Sewall or Maule, for he never had to answer for his work. The manuscript was not published until 1702—a year after Stoughton's death and two years after Hale himself had passed away.[68]

Maule's trial and the Fast Day led Robert Calef, a Boston cloth merchant who had observed some of the witch trial proceedings, to write an account of the trials that would have particularly long-lasting influence. Calef was a friend of Maule's and had posted bond for him when he was arrested for writing *Truth Held Forth* in 1695. An Anglican, Calef had migrated to New England during the Dominion of New England, a time of religious toleration. By August 1697, Calef had completed his manuscript. Its publication was delayed until 1700, however, as his attack on the proceedings in general and Cotton Mather in particular was so scathing that no one in Boston was willing to undertake the printing, which had to be done in London. As the title suggests, *More Wonders of the Invisible World* took direct aim at Mather and his *Wonders of the Invisible World*.[69]

Since at least 1693 Calef had been engaged in an ongoing dispute with the Mathers over witchcraft. In September of that year he had traveled to Salem to observe Cotton Mather's efforts to heal young Margaret Rule, yet another Maine refugee who was exhibiting signs of affliction similar to what had been seen in Salem the year before. Calef wrote down an account of what he observed that night. He suggested that Rule was a fraud and implied that Mather had inappropriately rubbed her breast and naked belly in an effort to heal her affliction by means of laying on of hands. Then Calef circulated his account to friends. Mather became infuriated when he heard this story, accusing Calef of lying and charging him with slander. The men exchanged a series of angry letters, where it became clear that Calef had taken liberties in his account in an effort to bait Mather.[70]

Amazingly, before Calef published his book he first published Cotton Mather's manuscript account of Margaret Rule's affliction, followed by his exchange of letters with Mather. After this inflammatory start, Calef went on to reprint *Wonders of the Invisible World*, along with his own history of the trials, largely a rebuttal of Mather. Calef saw the trials as a conspiracy of the ministers and the government. "A zeal governed by blindness and passion" led by Increase Mather had "precipitated us into far greater wickedness (if not witchcrafts) than any have been yet proved against those that suffered."[71] He believed that the afflicted girls and their families had been frauds who deliberately made their accusations for personal gain and to harm their enemies. Calef's anger shows through in the satirical edge to his writing. The book is far from measured and reasoned. Cotton Mather complained bitterly about this "vile volume," consisting of an "abominable bundle of lies" written "to vilify me and render me incapable to glory the Lord Jesus Christ." One can imagine the Mathers' outrage at the accusation that they had conspired with Governor Phips to manipulate the outbreak, especially considering that Lady Mary Phips and Maria Mather had been cried out upon. Increase showed his disdain by having a copy of the book burned in Harvard Yard.[72]

For all its faults, Calef's book clearly demonstrated the younger Mather's duplicity in defending the government in *Wonders of the Invisible World*. Calef pointed out that when the trials began, Mather was one of the ministers who had urged caution in the use of spectral evidence, yet a year later defended the judges for their actions. Essentially, Calef threw mud at Mather, and by extension the witchcraft judges and the government of Massachusetts, and it contained enough truth to stick. Calef's work helped expose the cover-up.[73]

Cotton Mather and his colleagues unwisely responded to Maule and Calef's confrontational writings, fueling the controversy. In 1699 Mather included a stinging attack on Maule in his 1699 book on the frontier wars, *Decennium Luctuosum*. It would soon be reprinted in *Magnalia Christi Americana*—Mather's crowning accomplishment, a massive two-volume ecclesiastical history of New England published in 1702. Mather was upset that Maule treated the actions of the Indians as justified and had criticized Massachusetts for defending itself against Native attack. Mather also faulted the Quakers for not censuring Maule. Mainstream Quakers actually did disapprove of Maule's bombastic books. In their faith's early days,

Quakers had expressed themselves just as confrontationally, but as time passed, Quakerism adopted pacifism and a quieter and less martyr-like style. Maule fell from his position of leadership among the Salem Quakers, and in 1699 the Rhode Island Yearly Meeting actually condemned Maule's writing. Still, Maule could not resist one last reply. In 1701 he published a response to Cotton Mather in which he claimed Mather stuffed his pamphlets full of lies and peddled them in taverns and alehouses to make a profit. He criticized Mather's view of the witch trials and said that he was destined for hell because of his "friendship with evil, against God's people."[74]

Mather was a bit more cautious about getting caught up in yet another debate with Calef after the publication of *More Wonders of the Invisible World*. Seven of his parishioners are listed as authors of *Some Few Remarks on a Scandalous Book*, though the tract was clearly written under the supervision of the Mathers, and Cotton may have actually authored at least some of the text. The pamphlet pointed out the lies Calef had made about the witchcraft judges and the Mathers. Calef did not respond to *Some Few Remarks*, and this was the last of the published arguments between the Mathers and their detractors. However, this does not mean that people had forgotten about either Salem or the controversy. In 1728, Cotton Mather's son Samuel claimed, "There was a certain disbeliever in witchcraft that wrote against my father's book, but the man is dead, and his book died long before him." That was far from true. Calef's book was reprinted five times between 1796 and 1866. Furthermore, the dispute with Mather was remembered in poetry by John Greenleaf Whittier in his poem "Calef in Boston, 1692."[75] In the 1850 poem Calef tells Mather:

Falsehoods which we spurn to-day
Were the truths of long ago;
Let the dead boughs fall away,
Fresher shall the living grow.[76]

If Samuel Mather was still concerned about the dispute in 1728, the controversy must have also been well remembered by many others, including Calef's numerous descendants. One of Calef's great-grandsons was General Joseph Warren, the patriot hero who died at Bunker Hill. Another great-grandson, George Robert Twelves Hewes, was a cobbler revered in his extreme old age for his participation in the Tea Party and the Boston Massacre, and recently brought to prominence again by historian Alfred Young in his book *The Shoemaker and the Tea Party*. Hewes probably had a low opinion of his wealthy loyalist cousin Dr. John Calef, a grandson of Robert Calef who became a surgeon-general and chaplain in the British army and a leader of the United Empire Loyalists.[77]

Calef's work was in much more demand than the thoughtful and reasoned arguments of Reverend Hale, whose *Modest Inquiry* was reprinted only once before the twentieth century. Calef's arguments were picked up by Daniel Neal, an early historian of the trials. An English clergyman, Neal published his *History of New England* in 1720. Though Neal largely relied on Cotton Mather as his authority, it was Calef's view of the proceedings that dominated his book. Neal was one of many subsequent writers who adopted Calef's version of events, making them the dominant history of the trials for three centuries. As historian Samuel Eliot Morison famously said, "Robert Calef, who had it in for Cotton Mather, tied a tin can to him after the frenzy was over, and it has rattled and banged through the pages of superficial and popular historians."[78]

Faced with a difficult choice, Cotton Mather chose to try to protect the Puritan state by concealing the errors of the trials. It was a decision that would haunt the minister the rest of his life. The day after Fast Day in 1697, Cotton confided in his diary that "being afflicted last night, with discouraging thoughts as if unavoidable marks, of the divine displeasure must overtake my family, for not appearing with vigor enough to stop the proceedings of the judges, when the inextricable storm from the invisible world assaulted the country."[79] The witch trials and their aftermath did not end Puritanism in New England. However, it did seal its fate. By banning all publications except for Cotton Mather's, the Mathers and Phips gave both contemporary and future enemies of the Puritans a club with which to beat them. Calef may have tied a tin can on Cotton Mather, but Mather handed him the can in the first place. Perry Miller summed up the aftermath of the witch trials—the tract wars, the Mathers' fall from power, Increase's removal from Harvard, and the establishment of the Brattle Street church—as "nothing less than the explosion into fragments of the once proudly unified New England society; it could foretend nothing less than that America was about to become hell on earth."[80]

CHAPTER EIGHT

Salem End

I am afraid that ages will not wear off that reproach and those stains
which these things will leave behind them upon our land.

—Thomas Brattle, October 8, 1692[1]

IN 1693, WITH THE STORM RECEDING, residents of Salem Village and others
affected by the crisis still lived under a cloud. Lives had been ruined; neighborly and factional disputes had worsened. The witch trials had been such
an all-consuming crisis, it is easy to forget that daily activities continued
throughout the tempest and its wake. Mothers and daughters had to pre-
pare meals, even if there would be a family member missing from the table.
People still had to milk cows and perform other chores, even as thoughts
turned to the victims. It must have been hard for the Nurse family to repair their fences without remembering the dispute with the Holtens that
contributed to Rebecca Nurse's conviction and death. The Nurses and most
Salem Villagers must have viewed the once-cherished Sabbath day with
apprehension and dread, for with friend and foe gathered together it would
be impossible to avoid the hard looks and awkward moments. Samuel
Parris continued to warn about Satan and to speak to the importance

of church membership in his sermons. Quoting from James 1:21, he urged people to repent, for "sin is the devil's vomit, the soul's excrement, the worst of all evils, the scum."[2] Heavy weather still threatened Salem Village and the entire colony.

Generally the reactions to the witch trials can be divided into two groups—those of the victims and those of the people who had been involved in the prosecution of those victims. The victims of the trials and their families and friends sought to have what they repeatedly referred to as their "innocency" restored. They also asked to be compensated for their losses. Many moved away from Salem. The response from those who accused and prosecuted the witches was more complex. Several apologized and worked to make amends, while others continued to defend their actions. A few families on both sides of the conflict even changed the spelling of their last names. In these actions, whether they intended to or not, people kept alive the memory of the events of 1692 and ensured they would not be forgotten in Salem or across New England.

As Salem Village was at the center of the storm, it is not surprising that it remained in turmoil for many years after 1692. Matters were made worse by the continued presence of Reverend Parris, a lightning rod for controversy. A more politically astute man would have left the village. Then again, such a man would have found a way to avoid the crisis that ripped his community apart in the first place. Unfortunately, the trials only hardened the lines of support and opposition around Parris. The complaints against him grew afterward to include questions about his behavior during the crisis, notably his encouragement of the accusers and his uncritical acceptance of spectral evidence. The anti-Parris faction remained in control of the village committee, and they made life as difficult as possible for him. They still refused to pay his salary and continued to challenge his ownership of the parsonage. They refused to make much-needed repairs to the meeting-house. They repeatedly asked Parris to call a council of outside ministers to resolve their outstanding grievances. Parris rebuffed them on this last point, for he feared, rightly, that such a meeting would result in his being forced to resign his post. So he fought back, accusing them of libel as well as unchristian behavior. In July 1693, fifty villagers signed a petition asking Governor Phips to intervene and appoint a panel of impartial arbitrators. The appeal worked, for the ecclesiastical leadership in Boston, along with Reverends Hale, Higginson, and Noyes, pressured Parris to agree to arbitration, to bring this whole business to an end. Still, Parris stubbornly clung on, managing to delay the meeting of the church council for another year and a half.[3]

By the fall of 1694 Parris knew he was running out of time, so he tried one final ploy to regain control of the village and maintain his post. On November 18, 1694, the minister read aloud to the congregation his "Meditations for Peace," his effort to make amends for the part he had played in the trials. He acknowledged that "God has been righteously spitting in my face." He apologized for his family's involvement in the witch crisis and admitted that he had handled things poorly. He had been deluded by Satan, he confessed, but he now knew that spectral evidence was not reliable, for "God sometimes suffers the devil (as of late) to afflict in the shape not only innocent but pious persons." He asked for God's pardon for his "mistakes and trespasses in so weighty a matter" and begged the forgiveness of his parishioners for anything "you see or conceive I have erred and offended."[4] But it was too long overdue. Moreover, it was an admission of guilt that made everyone complicit. If they did not accept his apology and put their differences aside, Parris warned, their hatred would continue to serve "Satan, the devil, the roaring lion, the old dragon, the enemy of all righteousness." Parris impressed no one by suggesting that his enemies, too, were unwittingly serving Satan by continuing to oppose him.

The anti-Parris faction stuck by their written complaints against the minister, including Parris's acceptance of spectral evidence, his quickness to believe the accusations of the afflicted girls, and "sundry unsafe, if sound, points of doctrine, delivered in his preaching." No specific concerns about doctrine are provided, though it seems likely that his jeremiad sermons, which had triggered the witchcraft outbreak, were one issue. Last and perhaps most egregious was "his persisting in these principles and justifying his practices, not rendering any satisfaction to us when regularly desired, but rather further offending and dissatisfying ourselves." In other words, if he had sincerely wanted to apologize, why did it take him two years?[5]

With things still at an impasse, an ecclesiastical council finally convened in Salem Village on April 3 and 4, 1695. The gathering of seven ministers and ten church elders drawn from communities as far away as Boston was moderated by Increase Mather. In their report, they blamed everyone in the village for the strife and animosity as well as their unwillingness to compromise. They offered Parris a diplomatic exit, suggesting that they would understand if he decided to leave the village. When Parris ignored the hint, more petitions and hard words were exchanged between his supporters and opponents. Worn out by the constant need to defend his job, Parris finally gave up in April 1696, announcing he would step down when his contract expired on July 1. Family considerations may have entered into his decision. The possible onset of his wife's terminal illness in the winter or spring of 1696 (she died in July) may have influenced Parris. Furthermore, his niece, the afflicted girl Abigail Williams, simply disappears from the records at about this time, and some believe that her death may have had an effect.[6]

Parris's departure from the pulpit did not end the dispute. With no other job to move on to, Parris continued to reside in his home. The village sued him for his continued occupation of the parsonage, and he countersued for the years of back pay he felt he was owed. In the summer of 1697 a panel of arbitrators consisting of Wait Winthrop, Samuel Sewall, and Elisha Cook settled the matter. In exchange for £79 in back pay, Parris surrendered the deed to the parsonage.[7]

Gravestone of Elizabeth Parris, died July 14, 1696, with inscription written by her husband, S.P. (Samuel Parris), in Wadsworth Cemetery, Danvers. Photograph by the author.

Shortly thereafter, Parris left for a post as minister in the small frontier community of Stow, the first of a series of moves. He immediately became embroiled in a salary dispute with his new congregation. Now forty-five, Parris left Stow in late 1698, taking with him his new wife, Dorothy Noyes. Over the next decade the Parris family lived in Newton, Watertown, and Concord. He served briefly as a schoolteacher, and also tried his hand as a shopkeeper and running a farm, all without success. He may have even considered migrating back to Barbados. Dorothy had brought a substantial inheritance into the marriage, but Parris did not do a good job of managing the estate. He suffered a series of financial reverses that apparently included a short stint in prison for debt. The birth of four children added to the financial strain.[8]

His situation became so dire that in late 1708 Parris took a post as minister in Dunstable, which at the time was a remote settlement on the Massachusetts frontier and often the target of Native American attack. The small population meant the congregation could not offer much pay, and Parris's predecessor had left after going more than half a year without salary. It was a sign of mutual desperation that Parris ended up in Dunstable. No other minister would take such a dangerous and poorly paid position; on the other hand, no other town would consider Samuel Parris. Three years in Dunstable was enough for Parris. In 1711 he moved to Sudbury, his wife's hometown. Here Parris lived out his last years, briefly teaching school but largely dedicating himself to farming and building up a modest estate for his children to inherit. Son Noyes followed his father's path in attending Harvard.[9]

In declining health, on February 20, 1720, "perceiving the approach of the King of Terrors drawing near," Parris wrote his will.[10] "King of Terrors," a phrase from the Book of Job, was a popular term for death in colonial New England, first noted by the prominent English Puritan William Prynne in 1626: "If once you have the smallest dram of true and saving grace, you need not fear afflictions or temptations, you need not fear the very *king of terrors,* hell and death: you need not fear the most that men or devils can do to you: *they cannot sever you from the love of God, which is in Christ Jesus your Lord,* nor yet disturb you from the state of Grace." At long last, Samuel Parris had overcome his fear of devils. He died a week later at the age of sixty-six or perhaps sixty-seven.[11]

Salem Village had a difficult time trying to attract a new minister to replace Samuel Parris. In November 1696 they kept a Day of Humiliation, to pray over the matter. A little more than a year later, Joseph Green would accept the job as the village's new parson. Though he was fresh from Harvard and only twenty-two, Green turned out to be the right man for the job. Soon after his ordination, he proposed reconciling with the dissenters, who soon agreed to return to taking communion. In 1699, when the meetinghouse was reseated, he put the Putnams and the Nurses—lifelong foes—on the same benches. In 1701 the village agreed to build a new meetinghouse. In 1703 Green asked church members to rescind the 1692 excommunication of Martha Cory. The overwhelming majority voted to do so, with only six votes opposing. In these and other small steps, the villagers gradually began to put 1692 behind them. Green saved the best for last: in 1706 he helped engineer Ann Putnam Jr.'s public apology.[12]

Very little is known about most of the later lives of the afflicted girls. Some disappear from the records entirely after 1692, while most of the others married and, as far as one can tell, appear to have lived unremarkable lives. Betty Parris married in Sudbury in 1710. She bore her husband, a shoemaker, five children, and lived a long life, dying in 1760 in her home on the Lexington Road in Concord. Betty's daughter still lived in the home on April 19, 1775, when the British marched by on the way to the fight at Concord Bridge. Women's subservience in the deeply patriarchal society that was colonial New England makes it difficult to trace young girls or to gain insights into their later lives. Abigail Williams and Mary Warren disappear completely. Susannah Sheldon moved to Rhode Island to live with a cousin, but in 1694 the court identified her as "a person of evil fame." Sheldon was not the only afflicted girl to lead a less than exemplary life. Mercy Lewis bore a bastard in 1695, though she later married. Mercy Short was excommunicated from the Boston church for adultery, and Sarah Churchwell and her husband were fined for premarital fornication.[13]

Ann Putnam Jr.'s parents passed away in 1699, when she was only nineteen, so Ann remained at home to look after her seven younger siblings, whose ages then ranged from seven months to sixteen years. Seven years later Ann wanted to become a member of the Salem Village church. Unlike other churches that had loosened membership requirements, the congregation still required a public statement describing the applicant's conversion experience and confession of past sins. Reverend Green worked with Putnam to compose this. A draft was reviewed by Rebecca Nurse's son Samuel, and he approved of it. So on August 25, 1706, twenty-nine-year-old

Ann Putnam stood before the congregation while Green read it aloud. She said that "it was a great delusion of Satan that deceived me in that sad time" and made her instrumental, "though ignorantly and unwittingly," in the shedding of innocent blood. For causing this "sad calamity to them and their families...I desire to lie in the dust, and earnestly beg forgiveness from God and from all those unto whom I have given just cause of sorrow and offence." Ann Putnam's application was approved by the church. She would die unmarried only nine years later.[14] Some read her apology as an admission that she had deliberately conspired to accuse people of witchcraft. The statement is worded so opaquely and inclusively that it is impossible to say, so people will see in it what they want to see. While Putnam's apology sheds little light on the actions and motives of the afflicted girls, it was another mile marker in Salem's road past 1692.[15]

Salem Village would not achieve its long-sought separation from Salem Town until the 1750s, a process so prolonged that it continued even after the town finally gave its assent in 1751. The petition was sent to the General Court, which voted favorably, but the acting governor, Spencer Phips (nephew and adopted son of Sir William Phips), refused to sign the bill. Beginning in the 1740s the king and the royal governor had frowned upon adding new towns to the colony, for it meant adding an additional representative to the House. Long before the spark of revolution, the independent nature of this body caused trouble for royal governors. Therefore, instead of becoming a township, Salem Village was established as the District of Danvers. A district was essentially an independent town, but one that lacked the ability to elect a member to the House. It is unclear why the new district was named Danvers. During this era many Massachusetts towns were named in honor of prominent Englishmen or their families. Danvers may have been named for Sir Danvers Osborne, the son-in-law of the powerful Earl of Halifax. Massachusetts was without a governor at the time, and Sir Danvers was active in colonial affairs; perhaps officials believed that he might be named as the new governor of the colony. In fact, the next year Osborne would be appointed as governor of New York. Regardless of why it was so named, Danvers historian and town archivist Richard Trask believes that people were quite happy with the new name, for it symbolically cut ties to Salem and Salem Village, whose names remained associated with witchcraft.[16]

In 1757 the General Court voted to make Danvers a true township, over the objections of acting governor Thomas Hutchinson. Two years later, the

Privy Council took up the matter, and King George II disallowed the act. Apparently officials in Massachusetts never received this news, or if they did they ignored it, treating Danvers as a legitimate town and receiving its delegates to the House. From 1768 to 1775 Danvers's representative would be Dr. Samuel Holten, who went on to serve for ten years as a member of the Continental Congress, signing the Articles of Confederation and even officiating as president pro tempore of the Congress for one day in 1785, in the absence of President Richard Henry Lee. Danvers did not formally become a town until July 4, 1776, when the United States declared independence.[17]

Sectional differences and post-trial bitterness would take a long time to resolve in Andover as well. In 1705 the need for a new meetinghouse exacerbated old tensions between people from opposite ends of town that had last been raised during the witch trials. After four years of arguing over the location of the new meetinghouse, townsmen agreed in 1709 to split into two parishes, each with its own meetinghouse and minister. This split seems to have brought a measure of peace to the community. One scholar suggests that the first sign of reconciliation was the 1708 marriage of the eldest son of the most important North Parish family to the eldest daughter of the leading South Parish family. Other symbolically significant marriages would follow in ensuing decades. In 1738 Samuel Phillips Jr. would marry Elizabeth Barnard. He was the son of South Parish minister Samuel Phillips Sr., and she the granddaughter of North Parish minister Thomas Barnard. Their son, yet another Samuel, would bring renown to the community by founding Phillips Academy, one of the nation's preeminent preparatory schools. Salem Street begins in the middle of a campus inhabited by generations of graduates, including both President Bushes, inventor Samuel Morse, Oliver Wendell Holmes Sr., and even Humphrey Bogart (though he was expelled before graduating).[18]

Marriages in early New England were sometimes strategically arranged to cement social, economic, and political relationships between families.[19] A substantial number of marriages within the families of accused and convicted witches after 1692 follow this pattern. Reverend Francis Dane's family suffered the greatest number of witchcraft accusations, and twelve of his twenty grandchildren married into other Andover families who had been involved in the trials. Another married into a non-Andover family deeply touched by the trials. In 1708 Dorothy Faulkner, daughter of convicted witch Abigail Faulkner, married Samuel Nurse of Salem Village, the grandson of Rebecca Nurse. They named their first daughter Abigail and their second Rebecca. Most of these marriages reflect a shared sense of grief and loss. They also may suggest that these families were shunned by suitors from families not involved in the witchcraft trials. Nonetheless, three of Reverend Dane's granddaughters married sons of people who had accused others of witchcraft, and Hannah Dane married the son of one of the accusers of her aunt Abigail Faulkner. Such marriages may have been part of the effort to heal the wounds of the trials.[20]

From a distance of more than three hundred years, armed only with vital statistics, it is admittedly risky to assign too much of a "healing" motive to these weddings. Given how many people in Andover were involved in the witch hunt, directly or indirectly, the odds of marriage between families that had been touched by it were fairly high. Nonetheless, the patterns seem too deliberate to be a coincidence. Normally a substantial percentage of the young people of Andover found spouses in surrounding towns. Yet in the period 1700–1719 they married fellow townspeople in far higher percentages than before or afterward. Furthermore, Andover was not the only town to witness such marriages. In 1694, Topsfield's William Towne (nephew of Rebecca Nurse, Mary Esty, and Sarah Cloyce) married Salem Village's Margaret Wilkins Willard, widow of John Willard. That same year William's sister married Margaret's brother.[21]

Two marriages in the Barker family suggest that the families involved in the trials had long memories; the efforts to repair old rifts that sometimes took many generations to complete. In 1788 Jonathan Barker and his pregnant fiancée, Nancy Swan, made the long and dangerous trek—nearly two hundred miles—from the Maine frontier to central Massachusetts to marry. The couple had grown up in Methuen, Massachusetts, and had been among the first settlers along what is now the Sunday River in Newry, Maine. Even with Nancy in a delicate state, it might have been understandable that they wanted to return to Methuen to marry among family. Instead they extended their trip twenty-five miles beyond Methuen to Acton, there to be married by a justice of the peace, Francis Faulkner. No records survive to suggest that either Jonathan or Nancy had previously been to Acton or had any relatives there. Why did they undertake such a long, difficult trip? The record does not offer an answer, but it is tempting to look to 1692. Jonathan was the great-grandson of William Barker of Andover. When William was arrested for witchcraft, he accused Abigail Faulkner of also being a witch. Abigail was spared from execution only because she was pregnant with a son, born in the spring of 1693. She named her newborn Ammi Ruhammah—Hebrew from the book of Hosea, meaning "my people have obtained mercy." It was Ammi Ruhammah's son Francis who would officiate at the Barker-Swan wedding (Francis was named after his grandfather—Abigail Faulkner's husband). Nancy Swan was the grandniece of Timothy Swan, an Andover resident whose afflictions had been blamed on no fewer than sixteen accused witches. The couple's marriage would seem to have been arranged as a part of a process—one that was completed by a second marriage in 1812, when William and Nancy's niece Dorcas Barker would marry Francis's cousin Lovel Faulkner. This marriage took place back in Andover, though the bride was from Fryeburg in the District of Maine and the groom was from Bolton, Massachusetts. That suggests that it required four generations and 120 years for the breach between these families to be sealed.[22]

Long before the Barkers, Swans, and Faulkners had left Andover, however, many chose to escape Salem Village, part of a diaspora of those victims of the tragedy who decided to start anew elsewhere. A sizable number began again at the appropriately named Salem End. Peter and Sarah Cloyce were the first to seek refuge there in 1693, on part of the sprawling tract owned by Thomas Danforth, known as Danforth's Farm—present-day Framingham, Massachusetts. This former deputy governor of Massachusetts Bay had been given thousands of acres of frontier land by the General Court in the early 1660s as payment for his many services to the colony. In 1684 he purchased the rights from the Natick Indians, to bolster his title. Danforth began to encourage settlers to occupy these lands in the late 1680s, granting them long-term leases but making the first few years rent-free.[23]

In January 1693 the grand jury for the Superior Court of Judicature failed to produce a true bill of indictment against Sarah Cloyce. She was released after almost nine months in prison. Danforth must have had a direct hand in Sarah and Peter's migration. Not only did he own Danforth Farms, but this staunch opponent of the trials was one of the judges of the Superior Court of Judicature that released Sarah. If you were trying to escape Salem Village and its painful memories in 1693, Framingham would have been one of the best places to go. The northern frontier was too dangerous for settlement, given the war still raging with the Wabanaki and the French. Danforth's Farm was in the southern interior of Middlesex County. While there had been some Native unrest in the area, it was still relatively safe compared with settlements such as Haverhill or York.[24]

Little is known about the Cloyces' life at Danforth's Farm. What is certain is that they were soon joined by other members of this family, which had been the hardest hit by the witch trials. For not only had Sarah languished in prison, but her two sisters, Rebecca Towne Nurse and Mary Towne Esty, had been executed for witchcraft. Peter's daughter, Hannah Cloyce, and her husband, Daniel Elliott, moved from Salem Village to Salem End. During the witch trials, Daniel had testified on behalf of his stepmother-in-law, Sarah Cloyce, as well as Elizabeth Procter. Two of Sarah's sons from her first marriage, Benjamin and Caleb Bridges, settled in Salem End as well. Sarah's daughter Hannah Bridges moved to Danforth's Farm with her husband, Samuel Barton. In 1716 after more than twenty years in Salem End, the Bartons moved to another frontier community, becoming original proprietors of nearby Oxford. A little more than a century later, their great-great

Map of New England, showing the Salem diaspora. Drawing by the author.

granddaughter Clara Barton would be born in Oxford. The "Angel of the Battlefield" and founder of the American Red Cross, Barton would win renown for her pioneering nursing service. It is possible Clara was inspired by stories of her great-aunt Martha Moore Ballard, a remarkable Maine woman made famous in Laurel Ulrich's Pulitzer Prize–winning *A Midwife's Tale*.[25]

Sarah's nieces, nephews, and extended kin joined the migration. Nephew Benjamin Nurse arrived in Framingham soon after the Cloyces, settling on Salem Plain. Another nephew, John Towne, moved from Topsfield to Danforth's Farm in 1698. By the time Framingham was incorporated as a town in 1700, there were roughly fifty Salem Village émigrés living in the community. The families made the most of their fresh start. At the first town meeting, on August 5, 1700, Peter Cloyce and John Bridges were elected as two of the selectmen. Benjamin Bridges was named an assessor, and Peter Cloyce Jr. was appointed a surveyor of the highways. The next year, Peter and three relatives were among the eighteen men who signed the covenant to form Framingham's church. Sarah Cloyce died two years later, in 1703, surrounded by her family. Five of the homes built by these Salem Village

Sarah and Peter Cloyce House, Salem End, Framingham. The Cloyce house is now abandoned and vine covered, though there is a local effort to save it. Photograph by the author.

refugees still stand in the Salem End section of Framingham, including the home of Peter and Sarah Cloyce.[26]

Other families made their escape elsewhere. Edward and Sarah Wildes Bishop and her stepmother, Sarah Averill Wildes, were arrested for witchcraft and imprisoned in April 1692. Three months later Wildes would be convicted and executed, and in September Sarah Bishop's sister, Phoebe Wildes Day, was also arrested. The Bishops escaped Boston prison after thirty-seven weeks in jail and went into hiding. Sheriff Corwin responded by seizing their personal property. Their son Samuel paid £10 to recover some of their possessions, but much of their estate was never returned, including six cows, forty-six sheep, and numerous swine. Bishop later estimated their losses (including prison fees) at £100, enough to ruin the couple and leave them with little means to support their large family. Given their considerable suffering, it is understandable that the Bishops no longer felt comfortable in Salem Village, though it is a little surprising that they waited until 1703 to move to Rehoboth, Massachusetts. Rehoboth was an old Plymouth Colony town located on the Rhode Island border. It was a far more liberal community than Salem Village and the location of one of the earliest Baptist churches in New England.[27]

Members of the Raymond family trekked to Plymouth County, settling in Middleborough by 1697. Thomas Haynes and his wife, Sarah, lived in the middle of Salem Village but in 1703 sold their home and moved to Salem County, New Jersey. On October 11, 1696, Samuel Parris made his last entry in the Salem Village church book, noting the dismission of William and Aaron Way, along with their wives and children, from the Salem Village church. William and his wife, Persis, had been among the initial signers of the Salem Village covenant. The Ways were moving to South Carolina with a group led by Reverend John Lord of Dorchester.[28]

People frequently moved away from older established towns in colonial New England, so it is not surprising to see some migration out of Salem Village. Still, the fact that so many victims and their families left in the years immediately following the trials, with many headed to Salem End, suggests something special about this exodus. Furthermore, this migration took place during King William's War and during the subsequent Queen Anne's War, times when fewer people moved because frontier lands were not available. The limited nearby options explain why some families, including the Ways and the Hayneses, sought new homes outside of New England.[29]

In 1713 treaties would end the fighting between the English and French and their Native allies. The peace finally allowed residents of Salem Village and other towns to move into new settlements in the interior. This was particularly important for the children of Thomas and Ann Putnam, as there was very little land to divide among the nine children who reached adulthood. Only the eldest son, Thomas, would marry and raise a family in Salem Village. One brother would take to the sea, and the other two would move inland—one to Tewksbury and another to the settlement known as Fort #4 on the extreme edge of settlement in western New Hampshire (present-day Charlestown). Three of the five Putnam daughters would never marry, and the other two would marry and move away as well.[30]

The families of Salem Village and Essex County produced more children than the land would support. Essex County's largest export crop may have been its youth, who headed off to new settlements in the interior and to the north. This was true even among the better-off families. Thomas Putnam's younger half brother, Joseph, was one of the winners. A firm opponent of the witch trials, he had inherited most of his father's estate and married into the wealthy Porter family. Yet even some of his children would move away, notably his son Israel. Soon after his marriage to Hannah Pope—the granddaughter of Joseph and Bathsheba Pope and hence Ben Franklin's cousin—Israel and his wife would move to Pomfret, Connecticut, where he would embark on a successful military career. In later life he was known as "Old Put," the beloved patriot general famous for issuing the command at Bunker Hill, "Don't fire until you see the whites of their eyes." Putnam is depicted in John Trumbull's epic painting of the Battle of Bunker Hill, *The Death of General Warren*. In one of the most famous paintings in American history, the son of a key participant in the witch trials looks on as the great-grandson of witchcraft critic Robert Calef breathes his last. The year after the battle, the patriot spy Nathan Hale, the great-grandson of Reverend John and Sarah Hale, was executed by the British. The legacy of the witch trials shows up in surprising places.[31]

In the eighteenth century the Putnams and their Salem Village neighbors would spread out to towns throughout New England, including several communities that sprang directly from Salem. In the 1730s the Massachusetts General Court granted "Salem Canada," what would become the towns of Lyndeborough and Wilton, New Hampshire, to the Salem veterans of Phips's 1690 ill-fated expedition against Quebec. In the

The Death of General Warren at the Battle of Bunker's Hill, 17 June, 1775,
by John Trumbull. General Israel Putnam (the white-haired man with dark coat at the
left edge of the painting) looks on as General Warren (on the ground in white) dies from
a mortal wound. The black man whose head appears at the far right edge of the picture
is believed to be the freed slave Peter Salem. He apparently received his last name from a
former owner, Captain Jeremiah Belknap, who had resided in Salem. Photograph © 2014
Museum of Fine Arts, Boston.

1740s, when this territory was claimed by New Hampshire, the Mason
Proprietors (the group of men who then owned the Mason family's claim
to New Hampshire) granted part of the tract to petitioners from Andover,
Massachusetts. Thus did the sons and daughters of Andover and Salem find
themselves neighbors again. The first Wilton settler was Jacob Putnam, the
patriarch of several Putnam families to move there. In 1773 a tragedy struck
the community. During the raising of the new meetinghouse, a support
beam snapped, collapsing the frame, killing five men and severely injuring
more than fifty. The casualty list looks almost like a page of names from
the Salem witch trials: Putnams, Parkers, Holts, Blanchards, a Barker, a
Hutchinson, a Frye, a Chandler, and a Foster.[32]

The township of New Salem in western Massachusetts was first granted
by the General Court to a group of men from Salem in 1729, with settlement beginning in 1736. Here, too, Putnams were among the first settlers,
along with Flints, Feltons, Holtens (who now spelled their name Houlton),

Southwicks, and Trasks. Soon the towns that had sprung from Salem were launching towns of their own. In 1807, New Salem's Aaron Putnam and Joseph Houlton went north in search of a new place to settle. They got about as far from home as they could and still be in New England, founding the town of Houlton, Maine, on the Canadian border. Aaron's wife was Lydia Trask, from yet another old Salem Village family.[33]

Salemites would spread themselves across the country. Twenty-eight states have cities or towns named Salem, many in honor of the Massachusetts community. There is even a television Salem—the setting for the long-running soap opera *The Days of Our Lives*. In many ways, however, there is only one Salem.

✑

Some of the judges' descendants also left the community. Bartholomew Gedney's nephew Eleazar migrated to Mamaroneck, in Westchester County, New York, becoming a very successful merchant. Bartholomew's granddaughter Deborah Clarke would marry William Fairfax Esq., first cousin to Lord Fairfax of Virginia, and live near his estate. Deborah's stepdaughter Anne married Lawrence Washington, and her son, Bryan, was a boyhood friend of Lawrence's half brother, George Washington. Bryan Fairfax— great-grandson of a Salem witch judge—would later rise to become the 8th Lord Fairfax after the death of his cousin.[34]

People who did not leave Salem could always change their name. In the eighteenth century many of the Corwins changed the spelling of their name to Curwen, the Nurses became Nourses, and Hathorne became Hawthorne, as in the writer Nathaniel. First names could be significant, too. Naming a newborn is always an important occasion, with much thought given to the proper choice. Puritans relied overwhelmingly on biblical names, and their choices were often symbolic, as was the case with Ammi Ruhammah Faulkner. In Salem Village, Samuel Parris recorded a total of 182 births from June 1688 until April 1696. During this time, a total of nine boys were named Ebenezer. Five received that name between June 1692 and February 1694—amid or in the immediate wake of the witch trials. Indeed, it was the most popular boy's name in Salem Village in these years. The significance of the name Ebenezer would have been known to villagers. Following a particularly difficult battle with the Philistines, won by the Israelites with the help of a loud thunderclap from God, Samuel ordered a monument built:

"Samuel took a stone and set it up between Mizpah and Shen, and called its name Ebenezer, saying, 'Thus far the Lord has helped us.'" Naming a child Ebenezer signaled thanks to God for his help after a difficult struggle.[35]

On June 7, 1692, a son was born to Ezekiel and Abigail Cheever. At the time, the family was in the thick of the trials. Ezekiel served the court by recording two examinations and several depositions. He did not record the June 4 testimony of Ann Putnam Sr. against John Willard, for she said Willard's apparition told her that he had killed many people, including two of the Cheevers' young children. Three days after they learned that their children might have been victims of witchcraft, Abigail gave birth to a son, whom they named Ebenezer. He would be a monument to the trials and a statement of their faith in God as well as of their desire to start over. Samuel Nurse must have felt similarly in August 1693 when he and his wife, Mary, named their son Ebenezer.[36]

Even as village residents were choosing newborns' names with care, others were working hard to clear their names and the names of loved ones who had died in the tragedy. Many also fought to have seized property restored and to gain reparations from the government for their treatment. For some it was not just a matter of reputation or vindication but a legal necessity. Elizabeth Procter found herself in a dispute with her stepchildren, who refused to honor her share of the estate of her husband, John. They said she was "dead in the law" because she had been condemned for witchcraft (though ultimately reprieved and pardoned). In 1696 she petitioned the General Court "to put her into a capacity to make use of the law to recover that which of right by law I ought to have." Although she did not use the term, essentially Elizabeth was asking the legislature to reverse her attainder—that is, to restore the legal and civil rights that had been lost upon her conviction as well as to remove any stain or corruption associated with it. While some members of the General Court were sympathetic, they were still in the minority, and the legislature ignored the petition.[37]

On June 13, 1700, Abigail Faulkner became the second victim to petition for a reversal of attainder, explaining that she was "accused by ye afflicted who pretended to see me by their spectral sight (not with their bodily eyes)." She appreciated the pardon by Sir William Phips that had saved her life, but she lived "only as a malefactor convict upon record of ye most heinous crimes that mankind can be supposed to be guilty of." Not only was she concerned that this "perpetual brand of infamy" for her and her family, but she worried that her reputation might expose her to future accusations unless the legislature reversed her attainder. The House of Representatives recommended passage of the petition. The council "refused to concur, but addressed His Excellency to grant petitioner His Majesty's gracious pardon, which he expressed his readiness to do."[38] So the council was unwilling to approve the wording of the petition but was comfortable with the governor using his power to grant a pardon. Apparently the governor favored such action, but it never happened. It is possible Governor Bellomont overlooked signing that document before he left for New York on July 17, but it is more likely that Lieutenant Governor Stoughton intervened and convinced the governor to put off the signing. Regardless, Bellomont would never return to Boston, dying in New York City in March 1701. Acting Governor Stoughton had no interest in reversing the attainder, so the effort went nowhere.[39]

In 1703 Abigail and her husband, Francis, headed up another petition on her behalf, as well as for Samuel and Sarah Wardwell, Rebecca Nurse, Mary Esty, Mary Parker, John and Elizabeth Procter, and Elizabeth How. They expressed the innocency of the victims, complained that the "invalidity of the evidence" had led to "errors and mistakes in those trials," and asserted that it now "plainly appeared" that a "great wrong" had occurred. They asked the court "that something may be publicly done to take off infamy from the names and memory of those who have suffered as aforesaid, that none of their surviving relations, nor their posterity may suffer reproach upon that account."[40]

The General Court finally acted in July 1703, reversing the attainder of Abigail Faulkner, Sarah Wardwell, and Elizabeth Procter. The House asked that the bill be drawn up in order that the "infamy, and reproach, cast on the names and posterity of the said accused, and condemned persons may in some measure be rolled away." To prevent a recurrence of the events of 1692, they also ordered that no spectral evidence "may hereafter be accounted valid." Spectral evidence had now been officially discounted.[41]

The question, of course, is why it took a decade. Given the House's approval of Faulkner's previous petition, there was already considerable support in place by 1700. Perhaps members of the council yielded to the pressure of numbers. It was one thing to face a petition from the Faulkners, and quite another to face seven families, five of whom had lost members in 1692. Twelve ministers provided further encouragement, submitting a supporting petition to the governor and the General Court. They observed that innocent persons had suffered and that "God may have a controversy with the land upon that account." So they urged that something "be publicly done to clear the good name and reputation" of those who had suffered." Joseph Green of Salem Village and Thomas Barnard of Andover were among the signatories, as were divines from many surrounding towns. Notably absent on the petition were the names of John Higginson and Nicholas Noyes of Salem Town, as well as Lynn's Jeremiah Shepard. Higginson's absence is a bit puzzling, given his public questioning of the trials in his preface to John Hale's book. Perhaps he felt it would appear self-serving to ask to have the accused's names cleared, given that one of them was his daughter, Ann Dolliver. Such reasoning probably extended as well to Shepard, who had been cried out upon. Noyes's absence from the document is far more open to question, as he had been actively involved in prosecuting witches. Did he still harbor ill will toward the accused, or was he too embarrassed by his behavior to sign the petition? In any event, Noyes never repented, at least not in any surviving written document.[42]

In addition to this collective pressure, legislators probably responded favorably to the 1703 petition because it struck a more diplomatic note. In 1700 Abigail had claimed that people "pretended" to see her with spectral sight.[43] Had the General Court acted on this earlier petition, it would have essentially openly accepted Faulkner's contention of fraud by the afflicted witnesses. The 1703 petition suggested the victims were "accused of witchcraft by certain possessed persons," leaving out any suggestion of fraud or any mention of spectral evidence.[44]

Even with this more modest petition, the legislature would only go so far, however. It exonerated Abigail Faulkner, Sarah Wardwell, and Elizabeth Procter—the only three condemned witches named in the petition who had escaped execution and were still alive. The General Court was willing to clear their names so they could regain their civil rights, but it was not comfortable extending that courtesy to any of the executed witches, given that any such ruling by the legislature could be seen as an official admission that innocent lives had been lost. Nor did the legislature clear the five others who had been convicted and were still alive but who had not been named in the petition.[45]

While the collective weight of these petitioners must have moved the legislature, their efforts probably would have suffered the same fate as earlier attempts had William Stoughton still been alive to oppose it. The unapologetic former chief justice of the Court of Oyer and Terminer and the Superior Court of Judicature had died in 1701. In addition to his judicial offices, Stoughton had been the most powerful man in the colony, due to the death of Governor Phips and the largely absentee administration and death of his successor, the Earl of Bellomont. Stoughton's passing removed the largest obstacle to legislative action.[46]

The 1703 reversal of attainder was a step in the right direction, though some felt it did not go far enough. Writing in the summer of 1704, less than a year before his death, the highly respected Reverend Michael Wigglesworth of Malden confided his concerns in a letter to Increase Mather. The author of the best-selling poem "Day of Doom" (1662), as well as the jeremiad "God's Controversy with New England," Wigglesworth shared the fear that "God hath a controversy with us about what was done in the time of the witchcraft. I fear that innocent blood hath been shed, and that many have had their hands defiled therewith." He believed the judges had acted appropriately at the time but that tragedy had resulted because of the devil's actions. He called for a "public and solemn acknowledgement" of the wrongdoing by everyone involved, plus humiliation. In addition to public repentance, the government needed to provide relief to those families who had had their names ruined and suffered financial hardship. Until these steps were taken, Wigglesworth predicted, New England would remain under God's curse. Proof of this affliction was readily at hand, for war had begun anew against the French and their Native allies—a conflict that would last until 1713 and become known as Queen Anne's War. He asked Mather to lead the Boston ministers in approaching the governor and council during the next legislative session. There is no evidence that Mather made such an effort.[47]

More petitions followed. In 1709 twenty-two people who had either lost family or suffered themselves in the witchcraft crisis petitioned the General Court "to restore ye reputations to ye posterity of ye sufferers and remunerate them as to what they have been damnified in their estates."[48] That fall, the victims gained a somewhat unexpected ally when Cotton Mather urged the legislature to act. In an election sermon presented at the start of its session, he spoke directly to the General Court's members assembled in Boston's Town-House:

In two or three too memorable days of temptation that have been upon us, there have been errors committed. You are always ready to declare unto all the world, that you disapprove those errors. You are willing to inform all mankind with your declarations; that no man may be persecuted, because he is conscientiously not of the same religious opinions, with those that are uppermost. And; that persons are not to be judged confederates with evil spirits, merely because the evil spirits do make possessed people cry out upon them.

Mather indicated that the General Court had already acknowledged errors in their proclamation for the day of public humiliation back in 1697. Any other reparations they could undertake to make up for "the errors of our dark time, some years ago" would be another step in the right direction.[49]

This was as close as Cotton Mather would ever come to a public apology. Samuel Sewall had clearly encouraged Mather to come forward. When the sermon was published, Cotton addressed Sewall directly in a dedication: "My prayers and hopes for America are yours; and I must acknowledge, that you first gave me some of the hints, which my sermon brings for the grounds of them." Sewall not only encouraged the remarks but also paid to have the sermon published. The witchcraft judge, now aging, had never forgotten the Salem trials and would never cease his efforts to make amends.[50]

Prompted by the petitions and the added pressure from Cotton Mather and Sewall, in 1710 the legislature appointed a committee to go to Salem and study what more could be done. That September the panel received a total of forty-five petitions for redress during a six-day visit to Salem. This remarkable outpouring demonstrates the substantial reservoir of pain and suffering still felt by the victims and their families. A total of £796 in claims was submitted, not including a large request made by Philip English. The petitioners also asked for a restoration of innocency. The committee waited more than a year before making its recommendations to the General Court for reversal of attainder and for reparations. The legislature readily approved these measures in the fall of 1711, reversing the attainder of twelve of the executed witches, Giles Cory, and seven more who had been condemned but not executed.[51]

After the acts of 1703 and 1711, all attainders had been reversed and only seven convictions for witchcraft remained in place. Six involved the executed Bridget Bishop, Susannah Martin, Alice Parker, Ann Pudeator, Wilmot Redd, and Margaret Scott. The seventh was Elizabeth Johnson Jr., who had confessed and been convicted by the Supreme Court, then reprieved by Governor Phips. In the case of the six executed witches, no one had come forward to ask for their reversals, so the General Court took no action. Elizabeth Johnson's circumstances are less clear. Her brother had petitioned on her behalf for a reversal of attainder and repayment of the £3 he had paid for her provisions while she was jailed. She apparently was left off the reversal list because she was confused with her mother, also named Elizabeth Johnson, who was accused and tried but found not guilty. In 1712 Elizabeth junior herself petitioned the court for a reversal, reminding officials that she had indeed been convicted but her name had been left out of the reversal act. It seems notable that in 1709 and 1716 Elizabeth junior sold her right to lands that she had inherited from her father. Therefore the court did not consider her legally "dead," as they had Elizabeth Procter. While she probably never did receive a reversal of attainder, the court must have determined that she did not need it, for otherwise she could not have owned land, let alone sell it.[52]

On December 17, 1711, the General Court approved payment of £578 of the £796 claimed. Damages were awarded only to families of executed witches and to those who had been convicted. This largely ended the legislative effort for the families. Presumably inspired by these actions, on March 2, 1712, the Salem Town Church voted to rescind the excommunication of Rebecca Nurse and Giles Cory. In Europe, Great Britain and France had just begun negotiations to end Queen Anne's War. The Treaty of Utrecht was formally signed the next year, as was the Treaty of Portsmouth, which ended hostilities with the Wabanaki. Michael Wigglesworth might have been right about the war being a sign of God's curse, for since 1692 it had dragged on with only short breaks in the fighting, causing great suffering and financial hardship for New England. Providential Puritans must have thought that the peace was a sign that finally God was satisfied with Massachusetts's apology for the witch trials.[53]

Still, the occasional claim came in from aggrieved parties. In 1724 the General Court awarded Thomas Rich £50 in recognition of the personal estate lost by his mother-in-law, Martha Cory, when her husband, Giles, was pressed to death. The government also heard repeatedly from Philip English as well as George Burroughs's heirs. Of all the victims, English had suffered the most substantial financial losses. As one of the richest merchants in New England, he had had the most to lose. English claimed that when he had fled Salem, Sheriff George Corwin had seized a fortune in his possessions. In 1694 English sued Corwin to recover his losses. Seeking to quiet the matter, the Superior Court, composed of Stoughton, Sewall, and Danforth, had ruled in May 1694 that Sheriff Corwin's accounts were true, and held him and his descendants harmless for any efforts to recover debts for property he had seized during the witchcraft crisis. However, English pressed to recover his losses. In January 1696 he sued Corwin for a cow and some swine that had been seized in August 1692. When Corwin did not post bond in the case, he was temporarily jailed. The next year Corwin died, but English still pursued a debt against his widow. It was later rumored that Corwin's family initially had to bury him in the cellar of his home to prevent his body being seized by English for debt.[54]

In 1710 English submitted a long and detailed list of his claims, specifying £1,183 worth of goods, along with "a considerable quantity of household goods and other things which I cannot exactly give a particular account of." In addition, the merchant had forfeited a bond of £4,000 when he and his wife had fled to New York. Yet the General Court did not include any funds for English in its 1711 distribution of funds. In June 1717 English petitioned the General Court directly for his losses. After a committee deliberated the matter for a year, the General Court voted that English be awarded £200 in full satisfaction of his claims. Considering this an insult, English refused the award.[55]

Although English had exhausted his attempts at financial restitution, he continued to quarrel with Reverend Nicholas Noyes, even well beyond the minister's death. English never forgave Noyes for his role in the witchcraft crisis. In the spring of 1722, more than three years after Noyes had died, English denounced the late minister as the murderer of John Procter and Rebecca Nurse, and called Noyes's church "the devil's Church." Brought to court on charges of slander a few months later, the old man used the occasion to affront the church and the judges—including Bartholomew Gedney. After a night in jail he apologized, but he made a similar outburst in 1724. In 1733 English abandoned the Salem Town church when he gave land to build St. Peter's Episcopal Church—Salem's Anglican church. According to family tradition, on his deathbed in 1736 English forgave Noyes and his enemies, though only as a matter of form, adding, "But if I get well, I'll be damned if I forgive them."[56]

The year after Philip English's death, Reverend Israel Loring of Sudbury preached the Election Day sermon to the governor and legislature and raised the specter of Salem. He believed there was "a great duty lying upon us" to restore the innocency of the victims and to make reparations to their children. He cited Reverend Hale's book and the 1696 Fast Day proclamation, noting that while "none dispute the integrity" of the judges, "all orders of persons have since seen reason to condemn the rule of the whole process as fallacious and insufficient to distinguish the guilty from the innocent." He asked that "infamy may be taken from the names and memory of such as were executed, and who it may be did not in the least deserve it; as well as reparations be made to their children for the injuries done them." Loring was concerned that some of the children of the victims continued to live in "mean, low and abject circumstances." This strongly suggests that some of the families were still being shunned and denied economic opportunities because of their heritage. While it had been more than forty years since these events, this was no excuse to not act. "Length of time is no argument that God is not at this day, among other things, contending with us for these," he said, pointing out that during the rule of David, God had brought a three-year famine to Israel as punishment for Saul's slaying of the Gibeonites forty years earlier.[57]

Loring had at least one direct contact with the events of 1692. As the long-tenured minister of Sudbury, Loring would have known Reverend Parris, who spent the last eleven years of his life in Sudbury, and surely he was thinking of Parris as he gave the sermon. Framingham bordered Sudbury to the south, so it is also possible he may have known some of the families of victims who lived at Salem End. Whatever the reason, Loring's sermon resonated with at least some of the audience. On December 8, 1738, Major Samuel Sewall, the son and namesake of the Salem witch judge, who had died eight years before, continued the efforts of his father and introduced an order to create a committee to look into the wrongs of 1692. The House passed the measure unanimously and made Sewall the chair of the committee, which also included Samuel Danforth, grandnephew of Judge Thomas Danforth. On behalf of the committee, Sewall wrote a letter to Salem, to his cousin Mitchell Sewall (son of Stephen) and town clerk John Higginson (great-grandson of Reverend John). He said the committee was "very desirous of making restitution by granting a township or paying money to the families of victims." He asked the men to look over the records and speedily give him an account of who had received funds. He also asked how much Mr. English had received, and whether or not more was due to his heirs. His concern for English probably resulted from the efforts by English's family that year to renew their claims to compensation. Through Major Sewall's efforts, the English heirs received the £200 Philip had rejected.[58]

The legislature never took any action on Sewall's initiative, presumably because of a petition they received just four days after authorizing Sewall's committee. On December 12, Reverend Samuel Mather submitted a request on behalf of the Mather family for the "public and eminent services of his venerable and honored grandfather and father," Increase and Cotton Mather. On December 20, a second petition was submitted from other members of the Mather clan. They asked for funds that would serve as a "perpetual memorial of the good deeds" Increase and Cotton performed for the colony. The Mathers had dedicated much time and money to the colony. A monetary reward would both compensate the family, and serve as a public acknowledgment of the import contributions of the two divines. Like his father and grandfather, Samuel Mather held the post of minister at Boston's North Church, and worked hard to maintain the family name. The Mather petitions were clearly an effort to vindicate their ancestors and to prevent any further actions by the legislature to assign blame for the witchcraft crisis. Samuel wrote "praying this court would please to make him an allowance for the said services, that so he the memorialist may be excited and encouraged to apologize for the liberties of New England, and thereby will arise some standing and perpetual memorial of the good deeds of his worthy ancestors, and the gratitude of their country for them." His petition could be taken two ways, for in the eighteenth century *apologize* had two distinct meanings. Mather here meant *apologize* as a synonym for *vindicate*. Therefore he was asking for a financial award to vindicate his ancestors' role in preserving the "liberties" of Massachusetts—that is, the rights and freedoms confirmed in the 1691 charter. Alternatively, he hinted that if the legislature was planning on asking for forgiveness for the "liberties" taken by New England in 1692 in prosecuting the witches, they would need to compensate his family to avoid their vocal opposition.[59]

The Mather petitions would lead to heated debate in the legislature. A committee was formed to look into the request. Reporting back just nine days later, it showered praise on Increase Mather for his work as minister, as president of Harvard College, and as one of the agents who secured Massachusetts her liberties in the 1691 charter. The committee also noted that Increase's son Cotton Mather and his grandson, the petitioner and his successor in the same church and ministry, "have not behaved themselves unworthy of such an ancestor." Samuel Mather must have been furious at what was at best a backhanded compliment. However, the committee also recommended granting the family a tract of five hundred acres of frontier lands. Perhaps they felt this gesture would be a cheap way to buy off the Mathers and ensure Samuel's silence in the face of further efforts at restitution to the witch families. Yet the request was voted down and the matter tabled. It was taken up again on June 22, 1739, during the next session, and again voted down. Finally, the committee asked if the House of Representatives wished to make any grant at all to the Mathers. The legislators voted even this measure down and ordered that the petitions be dismissed. The Mathers' time had come and gone.[60]

Clearly a majority of the legislature disapproved not only of Samuel Mather's tactics but also of the role Cotton Mather had played in the events of 1692. Robert Calef's tin can continued to rattle. However, the Mathers had their defenders, and enough of them that the report of the reparations committee for witchcraft victims was postponed for several sessions of the legislature. Finally, after several more sessions with no activity, Governor Jonathan Belcher addressed the legislature on November 22, 1740, and urged them to form a committee to examine the sufferings of Quakers and "the descendants of such families as were in a manner ruined in the mistaken management of the terrible affair called witchcraft."[61]

Three days later, Belcher's speech was printed on the front page of a Boston newspaper for all to see and discuss. Again the Sewall family lent their support to the cause. Judge Sewall's other surviving son, Joseph, was the pastor of Boston's South Church. Asked to give the sermon to the governor and the legislature on Fast Day, only a few days after Belcher's impassioned speech, Reverend Sewall made repentance the topic of his sermon. He preached a jeremiad, a form of sermon that had recently regained popularity with the onset of the spiritual revival that would be known as the Great Awakening. With skill that would have made his late father proud, Sewall never once mentioned Salem or witchcraft, or indeed anything that might put him in open opposition to fellow Boston minister Samuel Mather. Yet his message was clear: the legislature should make amends, and if they did not, they would face God's wrath. At the end of the sermon, he directly addressed "our honored rulers," asking them to do the right thing "in this very critical conjuncture... Shake your hands from bribes of every kind, and when called to give your vote, consider seriously what is right in the sight of God."[62] At that moment, the colony faced a currency crisis, and there was a major legislative divide over the issue of a land bank. Reverend Sewall's sermon addressed this issue but at the same time reminded the legislature to make further amends for witchcraft. Amazingly, nearly fifty years after they had taken place, the witch trials were still a very lively topic of debate for the government of Massachusetts and the entire populace.

Thus urged by Governor Belcher and Reverend Sewall, a committee was regularly appointed over the next several years to look at the sufferings of the Quakers and witchcraft families, but it never issued a report. Thanks to the intervention of Samuel Mather, the matter was still too controversial to take up, and the committee disbanded in 1743. The committee was revived briefly in 1749 and 1750, in response to two last petitions from the grand-children of George Burroughs. No report was ever issued, however.

The Massachusetts General Court would not take up the issue of Salem witchcraft trials again for two hundred years, but in some sense there was no need. The earlier legislature had helped keep the trials alive in debates that spanned six decades. Not only did the trials stay in the minds of Salem Villagers, but their memory moved across New England as the victims of the witch trials and the sons and daughters of Essex County moved to new homes in towns spread across the region. Families and communities tried to move on even as they kept the memory alive. Some honored their victim ancestors and sought to restore their innocency. Others sought amends. Still others, like Samuel Mather, sought to defend the actions of their ancestors.[63]

The General Court had made some reparations and restored some inno-cency, but such leaders as Reverend Israel Loring, Major Samuel Sewall, and Governor Belcher made clear that it was not enough. By not confessing to the sin of murder, by neglecting to make full and proper amends, and by not having shown true penitence, the legislature had failed to heed Joseph Sewall's warning: "If we refuse to repent and reform we shall be condemned out of our own mouths, and fall under the threatened judgments of God."[64] Now they would suffer the consequences. Salem would forever remain the Witch City.

CHAPTER NINE

Witch City?

Hegel remarks somewhere that all great world-historic facts and personages appear, so to speak, twice. He forgot to add: the first time as tragedy, the second time as farce...Men make their own history, but they do not make it as they please; they do not make it under self-selected circumstances, but under circumstances existing already, given and transmitted from the past. The tradition of all dead generations weighs like a nightmare on the brains of the living.

—Karl Marx, 1852[1]

IN 2009, ON THE EVE OF HALLOWEEN, the *Boston Globe* reported that "Salem owns Halloween like the North Pole owns Christmas."[2] Anyone who has been to the Haunted Happenings celebration of Halloween in Salem knows that this might be an understatement. Salem has become "Witch City," the Halloween capital of the world. How this happened is part of the continuing story of the witch trials and the two Salems: village and town. Even as the residents of Salem Village, as well as others affected by the crisis, tried to put the past behind them, the wider world would not let them. It has refused to let the story die. The result has been an unbreakable bond between witchcraft and Salem, between Salem Village and "Witch City."

Salem would continue to fall under scrutiny in the years that followed 1692 and, increasingly, become a signifier for violent intolerance, paranoia, and unjust persecution, not just in America but around the world. In the twentieth century, Danvers—formerly Salem Village—would largely manage to dissociate itself from its witch heritage, except among those who know about the change in name. However, the City of Salem, the scene of the trials and executions, would become Witch City despite, or because of, the debate over who or what was responsible for what happened there.

Salem as an example of zealous injustice lies most famously at the core of Arthur Miller's 1953 play *The Crucible*, in which the witch trials serve as an allegory for America's fanatical persecution of supposed Communists in the early 1950s under Joseph McCarthy. However, the term "witch hunt" was in use to describe political attacks by the 1930s, and writers have used Salem as a symbol of extremism for more than three hundred years—long before it became Witch City. Ned Ward, a street-smart London publican and writer, never visited the region but still managed to write a 1699 travelogue called *A Trip to New England*, in which he satirizes the recent witch trials. Ward observes that

> there were formerly among them (as they themselves report) abundance of witches, and indeed I know not but there may be as many now, for the men look still as if they were hag-ridden; and every stranger that comes into the country, shall find they will deal with him, to this day, as if the devil were in 'em. Witchcraft they punish'd with death, till they had hang'd the best people in the country, and convicted the culprit upon single evidence: So that any prejudice person, who bore malice against a neighbor, had an easy method of removing their adversary. But since, upon better consideration, they have mitigated the severity of that unreasonable law, there has not been one accused of witchcraft in the whole country.[3]

Ward managed to hit most of the themes later seized upon by others. The "hag ridden" results of the trial were brought about by a judicial system that convicted and executed people "upon a single evidence," suggesting the use of spectral proof. He saw that the trials were a malicious tool for recrimination and revenge.

Ward wrote in a lighthearted vein, but the Salem trials stirred up a great deal of serious interest in England, which saw a flood of publications on the incident as well as on other cases of the supernatural. The Mathers led the way. *Wonders of the Invisible World* was first published in Boston, but it had gone through four London printings by 1694. *Cases of Conscience* was also published in London, and Deodat Lawson's *A Brief and True Narrative* was reprinted in London in 1693 and 1704. One of the reasons Salem's fame spread is that the outbreak took place as the scholarly debate over the existence of witchcraft was drawing to a close in the English-speaking world. Almost as long as there had been witch trials there had been skeptics, as demonstrated in the writings of Reginald Scot, Montaigne, and Johann Weyer. Scot's *Discoverie of Witchcraft* (1584) was probably the most influential early skeptical argument in England, leading James I (then James VI of Scotland) to write his *Daemonologie* (1597) as a response to Scot and other doubters and asserting "that such assaults of Satan are most certainly practiced, and that the instrument thereof merits most severely to be punished."[4]

Disbelief in witches blossomed in England in the second half of the seventeenth century, however, thanks to a combination of factors: judicial skepticism, a changing religious environment, and the rise of science. The legal system had always had a difficult time accepting the limited proof of witchcraft. Sir Robert Filmer's 1653 *Advertisement to the Jurymen of England Touching Witches* was written in response to the conviction of witches at Maidstone, near his home in Kent, the previous year. In detailed fashion, Filmer rejected all supposed evidence of witchcraft. He even went so far as to argue that if witchcraft did truly exist, logic dictated that witches should only be tried as accomplices, for the devil committed the crime itself. Hence, Sir Robert suggested, unless English justices planned on bringing Satan to court to stand trial, one could not try his accomplices. Despite its force and precision, this view was only gradually adopted by legal minds in England and America over the remainder of the century.[5]

Meanwhile, a debate emerged among religious scholars over the existence of witches. Perhaps the best-known proponent of the latter part of the seventeenth century was Joseph Glanvill, whose *Saducismus Triumphatus* (published posthumously in 1681) recorded numerous cases of witchcraft and related phenomena, including ghosts, spirits, and poltergeists. Glanvill was among those who believed that denying the existence of witches was the first step toward atheism. For if witches did not exist, some would take the next step and say the devil did not exist. And, if the devil did not exist, perhaps neither did God. Glanvill's defense of witchcraft trials was made against a rising tide of religious skepticism and influenced Cotton Mather, who had a copy of *Saducismus Triumphatus* in his library. Other Puritans held to the belief in witches, notably the prominent English minister Richard Baxter. His *Certainty of the World of Spirits* (1691) was one of a handful of books published in England in the 1690s that documented cases of witchcraft and the supernatural.[6]

Many have seen the decline of witchcraft as a logical result of the rise of science. While there is some linkage, Glanvill's career suggests just how unreliable the connection could be. In addition to being an Anglican minister who defended the existence of witches, Satan, and God, Glanvill was a scientist and member of the Royal Society. His complex examination of witchcraft included advanced study on the nature of matter, and he employed scientific approaches to the study of the supernatural. Even Robert Boyle, perhaps the foremost English scientist of the Restoration, was a devout Anglican who was open to the wonder and power of God's providence. Boyle was a leader of the Society for Propagation of the Gospel and known by Increase Mather and other New England Puritan leaders. Mather used Boyle's scientific approaches in gathering examples of providential stories for his *Essay for the Recording of Illustrious Providences* (1684).[7]

In the early eighteenth century, the debate over the existence of witches was nearing its end. The last scholars to do battle made sure to include Salem in their discussions. What is generally regarded as the last defense of witchcraft by a respectable English scholar was Richard Boulton's *A Compleat History of Magick, Sorcery, and Witchcraft*, published in London in two volumes in 1715 and 1716. Boulton's thirty-nine-page account of Salem was essentially a reprint of Cotton Mather's *Wonders*. In 1718 Francis Hutchinson, an Anglican clergyman and future bishop, wrote a response to Boulton, *An Historical Essay Concerning Witchcraft*. Although a generation of English scholars had criticized witch trials, Hutchinson's lengthy and closely argued positions summarized the opposition to witch prosecutions and added an exclamation point to them. Witchcraft could be explained by natural causes, confessions should be ignored, and the use of "spectral evidence was so far from being legal proof, that it is of no weight." Furthermore, "filling people's heads with stories of devils, and spirits, and witches, corrupts the mind and brings them under those frights and afflictions." Most considered Hutchinson to be the last word on the subject, though in 1722 Richard

Boulton wrote a response to Hutchinson, *The Possibility and Reality of Magick, Sorcery, and Witchcraft, Demonstrated*. Few put much faith in Boulton's rebuttal. The debate between Boulton and Hutchinson and their supporters was about politics as well as witchcraft. Hutchinson was a skeptical Whig who attacked not just witches and superstition but traditionalist Tories such as Boulton.[8]

While they seemed to silence the academic debate over witchcraft, these works helped to popularize events at Salem, in part by including them at such length. In the dedication to his expanded edition published in 1720, Hutchinson took aim at Salem and Cotton Mather, noting that while George Burroughs's efforts to defend himself in 1692 had failed, "I humbly offer my book as an argument on the behalf of all such miserable people, who may ever in time to come be drawn into the same danger in our nation."[9] Hutchinson relied on Robert Calef for his narrative, though he also cited Hale. He blamed the Mathers for the witchcraft outbreak, noting that it came on the heels of Cotton's *Memorable Providences*, his 1689 account of the witchcraft in the Goodwin household, and Richard Baxter's 1691 *Certainty of the World of Spirits*. These books, combined with Increase Mather's 1684 *Essay for the Recording of Illustrious Providences*, were the real problem. Their "false principles, and frightful stories... filled the people's minds with great fears and dangerous notions." He then went on to lambaste Boulton for reprinting Cotton Mather's words "without giving any manner of the mischief that follow'd, and the sorrow they had for what they had done." He asked, "Who can be able to give a rational answer to such a case, where the fact is laid before him so partially? How certainly must our people fall into the same follies, if their minds are poisoned with such false history?" It was also an attack on the younger Mather, for he was the one who had written the "partial" and false history.[10]

It was not surprising to see a future Anglican bishop attack the Mathers, but even the English Puritan minister Daniel Neal pointed the finger accusingly at them. Neal was the first historian to mention the witch trials, in his massive two-volume *History of New-England* (1720). Although Neal generally drew upon *Magnalia* and other works by Cotton and Increase Mather for sources, he stated quite plainly that he drew upon their rival, Robert Calef, to describe the witchcraft outbreak. Neal also criticized Cotton for telling only part of the story, and in particular failing to cite the words made by the accused in their defense. Neal complained that "he passes over their defense in such general words as these, *they said nothing worth considering; their discourse was full of tergiversations and contradictions; they were confounded, and their countenances fell,* & c. whereby his reader is left in the dark, and rendered incapable of judging of the merits of the cause." Neal's account was influential, as it was reprinted in 1747, 1755, and 1793. In 1843, when the first American edition was published, its editor believed it was such an important work that he priced it modestly so it could gain wide circulation.[11]

Neal's impact went well beyond these printings, for a number of subsequent writers borrowed heavily from him. In his multivolume work *Modern History: Or the Present State of All Nations* (1739), Thomas Salmon wrote a twenty-four-page account of the Salem crisis, drawing principally upon Neal. John Oldmixon cites Cotton Mather as well as Calef but quotes extensively from Neal in his 1741 *The British Empire in America*. Oldmixon starts the chapter titled "Of the witch-plague, and an account of some that died of it" with his personal view of the affair. Though he notes that it is "the duty of an historian to prefer his readers judgment to his own," he stresses that he did "not believe one word of the evidence" presented against the accused. The evidence was "so trifling and silly, as well as incredible, that they are a disgrace to common sense." Drawing upon Calef, Oldmixon blames Cotton Mather for his zeal and Governor Phips for his inaction. Ultimately, he notes, the majority of New Englanders opposed the trials in 1692, and the witch trials in both England and New England resulted from the Puritan excess.[12] William Burke, in *An Account of the European Settlements in America* (1757), agrees that the trials were "the last paroxysm of puritanic enthusiasm in New England." William's account was written with the help of his kinsman Edmund Burke, who later, as a member of Parliament, would champion the colonists' grievances against George III.[13]

Daniel Defoe also popularized magic and witchcraft in several of his last books, mentioning Salem in his *Political History of the Devil*. Defoe suggested that fakery was at work in the outbreak: "Thus the people of Salem in New-England pretended to be bewitched, and that a black man tormented them by the instigation of such and such, whom they resolved to bring to the gallows." Defoe describes the end of the trials by noting that Satan soon became so weary of such foolishness that when people confessed to be witches who were possessed and "had correspondence with the devil," Satan would not appear "to vouch for them." Thus no jury would convict them, "and they could not get themselves hanged, whatever pains they took to bring it to pass." First published in 1728, Defoe's work went through four editions and many printings in England and America throughout the rest of the eighteenth century.[14]

Thanks in part to all of these works, Salem and the injustices perpetrated there did not disappear. French writer Abbé Raynal wrote about the trials, bringing word of them to France in 1770. Raynal and other Enlightenment authors added their incredulity to the Salem story, looking in vain for the workings of reason in the proceedings. Writing in 1770, John Wynne, bishop of Bath and Wells and a Cambridge scholar, looked for a silver lining in the witch trials. "It is likely this temporary lunacy contributed in a great measure to work off the ill humors of the New England people, and to bring them to a more serious use of their reason."[15] Oldmixon had been more blunt. He said he had always looked at the laws against witchcraft as "absurd, unjust and cruel, contrary to truth, plain reason and credibility." He was pleased that the crime had been outlawed in Britain (in 1735), so "none can thereby make a market of fools" and that the word *witchcraft* would never be heard again.[16]

Many of these English writers' American contemporaries made reference to Salem, usually with similar voices of disapproval and amazement. The subject even came up in Boston in 1721–22 amid a smallpox outbreak. Cotton Mather was an outspoken supporter of the new and controversial smallpox vaccinations. William Douglass's pamphlet accused Mather of wanting to return Massachusetts to the past, comparing the infatuation with smallpox inoculations to the persecution of Quakers and "the hanging of those suspected of witchcraft, about the year 1691."[17] The pamphlet was printed by James Franklin, whose paper, *The New-England Courant*, parodied Mather and other ministers who supported inoculation, asking, "Who have been instruments of mischief and trouble both in church and state, from witchcraft to inoculation?" Even while Mather and other participants were still alive, some in New England had begun to use the tragic events of 1692 as symbols of superstition, injustice, and fanaticism to advance their political arguments. It did not matter that in this case Mather's "infatuation" would save many lives.[18]

Benjamin Franklin, who had worked for his brother James on the *Courant* during the inoculation controversy, would also parody the witch trials. In the October 22, 1730, edition of the *Pennsylvania Gazette*, a supposed news article described the trial of two witches at Mount Holly, New Jersey. The piece is attributed to Franklin, the editor of the paper, who sometimes wrote anonymously or under an assumed name to make it look as if he had a large circle of correspondents. Although the piece does not mention Salem directly, it forms Franklin's frame of reference, poking fun at earlier witch hunts that would no longer stand up to scrutiny in the Age of Reason. Two people "had been charged with making their neighbor's sheep dance in an uncommon manner, and with causing hogs to speak, and sing psalms, &c. to the great terror and amazement of the king's good and peaceable subjects in this province." They agreed to be tested for witchcraft, but only if two of their accusers would undergo testing as well. The challengers believed "that if the accused were weighed in scales against a Bible, the Bible would prove too heavy for them." So all four people were weighed against a huge Bible. When all four passed the test, they moved on to the more traditional practice of swimming a witch. Here all floated—suggesting they were witches—except the accusing man, he "being thin and spare." The accused man was surprised he floated, and began to think he might unknowingly actually be a witch. Meanwhile, the accusing woman quickly claimed that a witch had cast a spell to make her so light she floated. The audience determined, quite sensibly, that anyone who had their hands bound and was thrown into water "would swim till their breath was gone, and their lungs filled with water," so they pulled everyone out of the pond. On reflection they decided that the women's shifts might have made them float, so they agreed to test them all again, naked, when the weather grew warmer. Thus, by 1730 it was acceptable for writers, in this case the nephew of Salem Village accusers, to ridicule such beliefs and legal proceedings. It seems appropriate that on the day he was born, January 14, 1706, Ben Franklin had been baptized in Boston's South Church by none other than Salem witchcraft critic Reverend Samuel Willard.[19]

In 1741, one anonymous Massachusetts writer compared the hysteria and injustice of the witch trials to the slave conspiracy that was consuming New York. Rumors of a plot by slaves to revolt and burn down the city led to the arrest of 160 blacks and twenty-one whites. Thirty blacks were convicted and hanged or burned at the stake, and four whites were convicted and hanged as well. As at Salem, the arrests were fueled by confessions. The first two slaves to be arrested named numerous accomplices, putting the city into a panic. Unlike in Salem, confession did not help their cause, as both men were executed. In the midst of the crisis, a New Englander sent an anonymous letter to Governor Cadwallader Colden, warning the governor of the eerie similarities between the "Imaginary Plot" in New York and the witch trials almost fifty years before. Reading about the events in New York in a Boston paper put the author "in mind of our New-England witchcraft in the year 1692, which, if I don't mistake, New-York justly reproached us for, and mocked at our credulity about." During the witch hunt, New York had served as a safe haven for several accused witches who had fled Massachusetts. And in early October when Governor Phips had sought advice on witchcraft from the New York clergy, their responses largely coincided with those of other critics of the proceedings.[20]

The writer questioned the weak evidence against many of the alleged slave conspirators who would be convicted and executed. "It makes me suspect that your present case, and ours heretofore are much the same, and that negro & specter evidence will turn out alike." The author sent copies of the letter to a Boston and New York paper, and it was published in both places along with a cover letter stressing how "the late terrible combustions at New York revived the remembrance" of the 'tragedy at Salem.'" The anonymous writer was actually Josiah Cotton, a Plymouth magistrate, schoolmaster, and missionary to the Indians. Cotton was also a first cousin of Cotton Mather and a well-known critic of the continued belief in the supernatural. Indeed, his 1733 manuscript "Some Observations Concerning Witches, Spirits and Apparitions" attacked the excesses of the Salem trials as well as the literature of his day on wonders. Though his letter is not overtly an apology for his cousin, presumably he wrote to point out just how easy it was for people anywhere—not just in Massachusetts—to make such mistakes. The slave conspiracy would be the first major incident in American history to draw upon comparisons to Salem as a way of pointing out injustice.[21]

One Massachusetts writer, Thomas Hutchinson, wrote extensively about the witch trials in the second volume of his *History of the Province of Massachusetts* (1767), published just two years before he became the last royal governor of Massachusetts Bay. In 1738, during his first of many terms in the Massachusetts legislature, Hutchinson was part of the unanimous vote to appoint a House committee to examine "the circumstances of the persons and families who suffered in the calamity of the times in and about the year 1692." The issue would come before Hutchinson and his fellow legislators again in 1740, 1749, and 1750, to attempt to make amends for what Governor Belcher labeled "the terrible affair called witchcraft." These debates clearly influenced Hutchinson, who gathered up and studied original documents of the trials, as well as the published contemporary accounts. Some of the documents he studied may have been lost in 1765, when his house was looted and virtually destroyed during the Stamp Act Riot.[22]

Hutchinson, whose account relies heavily on Robert Calef, believed that the afflicted girls had acted fraudulently and that the trials largely resulted from a conspiracy. Hutchinson observes that for many years after the trials, most people assumed that there had been supernatural causes involved, wanting to believe the best of the accusers. Over time, "as the princip[al] actors went off the stage," this opinion gradually lessened. Yet when he was writing many still believed that "bodily disorders" affected their imaginations, leading to the accusations. To Hutchinson, such credence is "kind and charitable, but seems to be winking the truth out of sight." He concludes that "the whole was a scene of fraud and imposture, begun by young girls, who at first perhaps thought of nothing more than being pitied and indulged, and continued by adult persons who were afraid of being accused themselves. The one and the other, rather than confess their fraud, suffered the lives of so many innocents to be taken away, through the credulity of judges and juries." Hutchinson's popular history proved highly influential. His version of the witch trials spread widely and would reverberate for generations; it remains in print today. Textbook writers and historians have drawn heavily on Hutchinson, including George Bancroft, perhaps America's most influential historian of the nineteenth century.[23]

One reason Hutchinson was read by his contemporaries involves the increasing interest in Massachusetts in the 1760s and 1770s, with the lead-up to the American Revolution. Propagandists of both sides drew inspiration from Salem. In 1770, one who used the nom de plume "Patriot King" complained about virtual representation, the concept supported by Prime Minister George Grenville, that while no Americans voted for representatives, members of Parliament still spoke and acted for all British subjects. "This, my countrymen, would, in the days of superstition, be called witchcraft, but, the gentlest of all shepherds, the wisest, virtuousest, discreetest, best of all ministers, Mr. Grenville, calls it a 'virtual representation.' We might have flattered ourselves, that a 'virtual obedience,' would have exactly corresponded with a 'virtual representation'; but no, Mr. Grenville requires real obedience to this virtual power."[24] The most famous exchange was initiated by loyalist Daniel Leonard, writing under the pen name of "Massachusettensis." This Tory muses, "Will not posterity be amazed, when they are told that the present distraction took its rise from a three-penny duty on tea, and call it a more unaccountable frenzy, and more disgraceful to the annals of America than that of the witchcraft?"[25] John Adams—writing as "Novanglus"—refers to witchcraft and earlier crises in Massachusetts in his reply. Adams complains that Massachusetts's "passivity" in accepting the colonial charter of 1691 was considered by some to be "the deepest stain upon its character." It was worse "than the witchcraft or hanging the Quakers." Most residents, argued Adams, disapproved of the charter, with its loss of privileges, and felt betrayed by their agent, Increase Mather. "It has been a warning to their posterity and one principle motive with the people never to trust any agent with power to concede away their privileges again."[26]

Adams was quite familiar with Salem's witch trials. As a young lawyer, he rode the circuit of county courts. When at court in Salem, he stayed with his sister-in-law Mary and her husband, Richard Cranch. Adams's August 14, 1766, entry in his diary notes that after dinner at the Cranches' he "walked to Witchcraft hill, a hill about half a mile from Cranches, where the famous persons formerly executed for witches were buried." He adds, with sardonically grim humor, that somebody had planted some locust trees over the graves, "as a memorial of that memorable victory over the prince of the power of the air."[27] Nine years later, the witch trials would make another appearance in Adams's diary, in the entry for March 5, 1773, when he reflects on the third anniversary of the Boston Massacre. Adams had served as defense attorney for the British soldiers. It had been an unpopular move, but the future president considered it his duty, for a "judgment of death against those soldiers would have been as foul a stain upon this country as the executions of the Quakers or witches, anciently."[28]

The Stamp Act Riot, the Boston Massacre, and the Tea Party: Boston had been the hotbed of the revolution. Yet not all colonists shared this passion. Those who remained loyal to the crown feared the dangerous extremism of Bostonians and their neighbors. Some would draw upon the witch trials as a logical point of comparison, an example of the wrongheaded passions of earlier New Englanders. Reverend Jacob Bailey made this link. A Harvard classmate of John Adams, he became enamored by Anglicanism and was ordained in the Church of England in London in 1760. He returned to New England and became minister at Pownalborough, located on the Maine frontier. Bailey was a vocal opponent of revolution and was treated harshly for his views. In 1779 he was forced to flee Pownalborough and to settle in Nova Scotia, where he became a prolific writer known for his satirical jabs at the rebellious New Englanders. Bailey specifically compared the treatment of the loyalists to that of the Salem witches, claiming that both groups were persecuted by ignorant and zealous Puritans. In one of his fictional pieces, a Ben Franklin–like figure named Faustus draws on dark powers to stir up the Bostonians against the king and the Church of England. Here he makes fun of the patriots for their superstitions about witches as well as what he sees as their equally irrational support of revolution.[29]

After the revolution, when the new republic had been established, Salem crept into the national debate between Federalists and Jeffersonians. Federalists supported a strong national government and believed American foreign policy should favor ties to Great Britain. Meanwhile, the Jeffersonian Democrats called for a limited federal government and endorsed Revolutionary France in her ongoing war against Britain. In late 1800, in the wake of Jefferson's victory over Adams, whose Alien and Sedition Acts were deeply unpopular, an editorial in the *American Mercury*, the staunchly Jeffersonian newspaper in Hartford, Connecticut, noted that it had often been observed "that there can be nothing too absurd to obtain a general belief, if it be extensively propagated, and enforced upon the public mind with zeal and perseverance. A most striking instance of the truth of this observation, we see almost every day, in the clamor about French influence. A more ridiculous absurdity is not to be found in the history of Salem witchcraft."[30] Notably, the editors linked Salem not just with absurdity but also with excessive public zeal. Thus, Salem's witch trials and Puritan extremism were emerging as useful weapons, ones that polemicists would take advantage of in major political debates.

The trials were drawn upon repeatedly in the antebellum era by critics of religion as well as defenders of slavery. Indeed, almost from the moment they were over, they have been used in debates over issues ranging from abolitionism to Prohibition, McCarthyism, abortion, and so forth. Their perceived delusions and excesses proved useful to Protestants who questioned the legitimacy of Mormonism or the Spiritualism movement in the 1830s and 1840s. After the 1834 Charlestown, Massachusetts, riots, in which a

Protestant mob burned down an Ursuline convent, Catholics got their chance to refer to the "narrow minded Puritan of New England...boring with red hot irons the tongues of the inoffensive Quakers, in burning witches, and enacting 'blue laws.'"[31] During this same period, southerners fought back against the oratory of Massachusetts abolitionists by repeatedly drawing upon the image of fanatical and irrational Puritan zealots executing witches, perpetuating the myth that they were burned and not hanged. In December 1849, Virginia congressman Henry Bedinger, angered by Massachusetts representatives who repeatedly referred to the exceptional history of their own state as well as the curse of southern slavery, observed in a speech on the House floor that "Massachusetts is a great state, sir—a very great state, indeed is Massachusetts. She could not well be anything else, sir, for she has Boston, and Bunker Hill, and the Rock of Plymouth! There the Mayflower landed the Pilgrims; and there witches and Indians and Quakers and Catholics, and other such heretics, were in the brave days of old, burned, literally, by the cord!" The speech was included in *The Book of Eloquence*, a declamation book used in schools and colleges, so that young Americans could memorize and recite it. First published in 1851, the book was so popular it went through many editions throughout the rest of the century.[32]

Thus the witch trials were featured prominently in the antebellum era. From 1817 to the publication of the *House of Seven Gables* in 1851, the witch trials would be the topic of two plays, at least a half a dozen novels, some short stories, and several poems. Increasingly in the nineteenth century, New Englanders tended to cast their past as the nation's history, offering a somewhat sanitized view of it, one that featured Plymouth Rock and patriots such as Paul Revere.[33]

Nathaniel Hawthorne reminded readers of the dark side of that past. Indeed, no figure played a larger role in establishing Salem's place in the American imagination than Hawthorne. The Salem native son was a direct descendant of Judge Hathorne (Nathaniel added the *w* to his name soon after graduating from Bowdoin College). He never gave his reasons for the change, though many have suggested it was either to distance himself from his ancestor or to add his own personal scarlet letter to the family name—*w* for *witch*. In fact, the family had spelled their name "Hawthorne" in England in the sixteenth century, and he may have changed the spelling when he made this discovery while researching family history. In any case,

Hawthorne was possessed by his family history and that of his hometown. They were linked, given his ancestors' role in the persecution of witches and Quakers, as well as their treatment of Native Americans.[34]

Many of Hawthorne's stories and novels reflect this concern. In "Young Goodman Brown," one of his first published works, Hawthorne evokes the witch trials and Puritanism, for the title character is surprised to discover a witches' Sabbath that includes everyone from his village, including his new wife as well as his minister. The entire town has been lost to Satan. Like most of Hawthorne's work, the story is historically grounded, for two of the witches celebrating the Sabbath are Sarah Cloyce and Martha Carrier, and he drew upon Cotton Mather's *Wonders of the Invisible World* for some of the details.[35] "Alice Doane's Appeal" was published the same year as "Young Goodman Brown" and explores similar themes. This story within a story is told by the author while on a walk to Gallows Hill. The narrator mourns the lack of appreciation for the past, particularly the "martyrs" buried on the hill: "But we are a people of the present, and have no heartfelt interest in the olden time. Every fifth of November, in commemoration of they know not what, or rather without an idea beyond the momentary blaze, the young men scare the town with bonfires on this haunted height, but never dream of paying funeral honors to those who died so wrongfully, and, without a coffin or a prayer, were buried here."[36]

Though many of Hawthorne's shorter works deal with Puritan Salem and witchcraft, *The House of Seven Gables* brought these themes to national prominence. The book followed closely on the heels of *The Scarlet Letter*, a bestseller that established Hawthorne's reputation as one of America's great authors—and Hester Prynne, who confronts Puritan self-righteousness and hypocrisy, as one of the great fictional heroines. Hawthorne built on these themes in *The House of Seven Gables*. Set in Salem, in an old mansion that was in reality owned by Hawthorne's first cousin Susanna Ingersoll, the novel also looks back to the era when the house was built, during the Salem witch trials. The book explores the role of Hawthorne's ancestors—particularly Judge John Hathorne—in the witch trials. Hathorne's name is changed to Colonel Jaffrey Pyncheon, a man who schemes to have Matthew Maule executed for witchcraft so that Pyncheon can gain Maule's property to build his new mansion—the House of Seven Gables. A subplot of the novel is the thousands of acres of Maine land granted to the colonel by the Indians. The deed was lost so the Pyncheon family was denied this potential source of great wealth. Instead, they had to be content with a wall map of their purchase "grotesquely illuminated with the picture of Indians and wild beasts." Hawthorne clearly knew about the Native land purchases of his ancestor and the other witchcraft judges as well as their fears of the frontier.[37]

Hawthorne also appreciated the story of Thomas Maule, the Salem Quaker and opponent of the witch trials, as Matthew Maule symbolizes not only the persecution of witches but also the mistreatment of Quakers. Prior to his execution, Maule curses the colonel and his family, and by the time of the novel's setting the family does indeed seem cursed. Jaffrey Pyncheon's descendant Clifford Pyncheon has just completed a thirty-year term in prison for murder. His sister Hepzibah helps them scratch out a meager existence by running a modest shop in one room of their decaying mansion. In the preface, Hawthorne speaks to the Pyncheons' plight, as well as the personal burden he bears for his ancestors: "The wrongdoing of one generation lives into the successive ones and... becomes a pure and uncontrollable mischief." Yet, in the end, Hawthorne suggests there is hope. The novel ends with the romance of Hepzibah and Clifford's cousin Phoebe Pyncheon to Holgrave, a young man who has been writing a history of the Pyncheon family. Holgrave turns out to be a descendant of Matthew Maule, and the couple's wedding ends the ancient curse, evoking the actual marriages that took place between families following 1692. The couple will abandon the House of Seven Gables to start a new life.[38]

While *The House of Seven Gables* may represent Hawthorne's attempt to exorcise family demons, its instant success ensured Salem would never be forgotten. Hollywood versions of the story appeared in 1940 and 1967. The 1940 drama included a young Vincent Price, foreshadowing his later career in horror movies. From 1949 to 1960 there would also be four adaptations of the novel on television, drawing up on the talents of such actors as Shirley Temple, Robert Montgomery, June Lockhart, John Carradine, Leslie Nielsen, and Agnes Moorehead. Its continued popularity has drawn hundreds of thousands of visitors to Salem to tour the house, which Caroline Emmerton opened as a museum in 1911. Hawthorne had left Salem in 1849, and the novel was actually written while he was living in Lenox, in western Massachusetts. In his new home, Hawthorne became friends with Herman Melville, who lived in nearby Pittsfield. At the time, Melville was penning *Moby Dick*, which he would dedicate to Hawthorne. Ironically, Hawthorne's departure from Salem resulted largely from the efforts of another student of the witch trials, Reverend Charles Upham, the future Salem mayor and U.S. congressman, who engineered Hawthorne's loss of his political appointment as surveyor of the Port of Salem. The two had once been friends, with Hawthorne praising Upham for his witchcraft lectures, which he had found helpful in rewriting "Alice Doane's Appeal." Upham's 1,100-page history, *Salem Witchcraft* (1867), would usher in the modern age of historical research into the trials. In 1868 Hawthorne's classmate at Bowdoin, Henry Wadsworth Longfellow, added to the notoriety with the publication of his play *Giles Corey of the Salem Farms*. The first transcription of the court documents would also come out in the 1860s.[39]

Hawthorne was not the only descendant of a witch judge to be troubled by his past. Louisa May Alcott, a direct descendant of Judge Samuel Sewall, would begin her most popular and somewhat autobiographical book *Little Women* with the March sisters rehearsing their play, *The Witch's Curse, An Operatic Tragedy*. Louisa certainly was aware of the family heritage. Her uncle Reverend Samuel May spoke defensively in his memoir about the behavior of his ancestor in 1692, trying to minimize Sewall's role in the proceedings.[40]

By 1880 the number of tourists visiting Salem had grown enough to justify the publication of the first *Visitor's Guide to Salem*, which featured information on area museums, attractions, and businesses, including witchcraft sites. It notes that Salem was attracting thirty thousand tourists each year. Some were interested in history, while others came to enjoy the town's new amusement park, called Salem Willows. As Salem neared the bicentennial of the witch trials in 1892, everyone from historians and authors to businessmen looked to capitalize on the event, in the process bringing even more tourism to the city. In 1888 Parker Brothers, the game company, whose factory was located on Bridge Street—not far from the site of the 1692 courthouse and jail—released *Ye Witchcraft Game*. The 1892 edition of the *Visitor's Guide* was the first to make use of the icon of the Salem witch. The guide promoted a Witch Cream skin lotion and souvenir photos of locations associated with the trials. It also advertised a witchcraft souvenir spoon made by jeweler and retailer Daniel Low and believed to be the first souvenir spoon made in America. Low's shop stood at the corner of Essex and Washington streets, the location of Salem's first meetinghouse. One wonders what Reverend John Higginson would have thought of it all.[41]

We do know what the descendants of Rebecca Nurse thought, for they were among the growing number of people who wanted a memorial built to the victims. As early as 1835 in "Alice Doane's Appeal," Hawthorne had commented on the lack of a permanent memorial on Gallows Hill. In *Salem Witchcraft*, Charles Upham had made his plea that one day a suitable memorial might be raised on what he referred to as "Witch Hill." In December 1875 a group of Rebecca Nurse's descendants met in Boston at the New England Historic Genealogical Society and decided to plan a memorial to her. They formed the Nourse Monument Association (using the spelling of the name that had been widely adopted by descendants) and began to raise funds. It was an effort closely controlled by Rebecca's descendants: Worcester architect Walter B. Nourse designed the obelisk, and Charles Upham's son William would be an active participant, for he had married a Nurse descendant. Memorial building was in the air, as virtually every New England town was engaged in a campaign to erect a Civil War monument, yet it would take ten years of donations and fund-raising events to raise the $600 to build the monument and to see to its perpetual care. Given that this was a memorial to Rebecca and not to all the victims, the Nourses chose to put the monument in Danvers, within the cemetery of the old Nurse farm. Family tradition said that her body had been secretly taken from Gallows Hill after her execution and quietly buried in this location. The choice was also politically wise, for it avoided the necessity of a fight with Salemites over putting a memorial at Gallows Hill. Remarkably, there was still opposition to such a memorial in Salem.[42]

Yet the Nurse memorial served as a broader effort to bring the community together and memorialize the victims of 1692. As the story of the witch trials grew, mainly because of textbooks, articles, novels, and histories, Rebecca became the most famous of the victims and so in some way came to represent them all. The conviction and execution of the saintly Puritan matriarch, after the jury had initially found her innocent, was viewed as the most egregious miscarriage of justice. Although the Nourses led the cause, a number of citizens of Danvers and Salem participated in and contributed to the effort to build a memorial. The endeavor also symbolically reconciled the Nurses and the Putnams. Rebecca and Francis Nurse's homestead had remained in their family until 1784, when it was sold to a Putnam, remaining in that family for over a century. The Putnams graciously opened the homestead up to the Nourse Monument Association for a series of picnic fund-raisers that featured addresses "related to the persecution of 1692." The monument was located in the farm's cemetery, amid numerous gravestones belonging to Nurses as well as to Putnams.[43]

More than six hundred people would attend the dedication ceremony in 1885, some of them coming from a great distance. It began with a memorial service at the First Church of Danvers with its minister, Fielder Israel, speaking, as well as Reverend Charles Rice of the First Church of Salem. These were the descendant churches of the Salem Village and Salem Town Churches of 1692. Rice pointedly noted that both of the churches had sinned and that it was time to confess to these errors and make amends. There was still work to be done. This sentiment was reflected in the monument's inscription, written by John Greenleaf Whittier, who was then living in Danvers:

O Christian Martyr! who for Truth could die
When all about thee owned the hideous Lie!
The world, redeemed from Superstition's sway,
Is breathing freer for thy sake to-day.

In the first draft of the monument, Greenleaf's last line had been "Redeemed at last, the world breathes free to-day." The change suggested the work of redeeming "Superstition's sway" was not complete. People were freer than they had been in 1692 but not free. The effort to admit guilt and bring the community together was making progress, but it was also far from over. Indeed, in 1892, on the bicentennial of the trials, the Nourse Monument Association erected a companion monument featuring the names of forty neighbors and friends of Rebecca Nurse who risked their lives to testify on her behalf. The speaker at the dedication ceremony was Reverend Alfred Porter Putnam, reflecting in his ancestry and very name a reconciliation of the two factions of 1692. After 1892, Danvers would increasingly distance itself from the events of 1692, despite the fact that most of the victims were from there. Instead it would be Salem proper, the scene of the trials and executions, that would assume the mantle of Witch City.[44]

In 1892 members of the Essex Institute (Salem's historical, literary, and scientific society and one of the forerunners of the Peabody Essex Museum) initiated an effort to build a memorial to the victims of 1692 in Salem. It was to take the form of a substantial forty-five-foot-high stone lookout tower placed on Gallows Hill. Bronze tablets with the names of the "martyrs" would be attached, Supporters of the proposal believed that a memorial would "help instruct" the thousands of annual visitors as well as local residents in "the lessons to be learned from the history of the delusion of 1692." However, opponents of the monument believed "the whole affair ought to be cast into oblivion as too horrible to contemplate; a shame on Salem and our community." There were also fears it might offend some of the old families in town whose ancestors had participated in the prosecution and execution of the witches. The opponents won—the monument was never built. Even two hundred years later, the trials were a political hot potato.[45]

Though there was no memorial or official commemoration of the bicentennial of the trials in Salem in 1892, some used the anniversary as a reason to bring the national spotlight to Salem and her trials. In its December 1891 issue, *New England Magazine* began a series of "Stories of Salem Witchcraft." Not to be outdone, Harper published Mary Wilkins Freeman's play *Giles Corey, Yeoman* in 1892. The next year, John Musick published his novel *A Witch of Salem*, following close on the heels of the author's popular fourteen-volume series Columbian Historical Novels. In the wake of the bicentennial, Salem's tourism grew exponentially in the early decades of the twentieth century. The city positioned itself to take advantage of the new business. By 1902, for example, the historic house previously known as the Roger Williams House was renamed the Jonathan Corwin House or Witch House, a nod to its former owner, Judge Jonathan Corwin. Even the Nourse Monument Association got involved, placing ads for the Rebecca Nourse souvenir spoon, complete with an engraving of the house on the spoon's bowl. It was around the time of the bicentennial that businesses first embraced the term "Witch City." The first to use the name was Pettengill's Fish Company, which sold fish under a variety of brand names, including Witch City. The 1893–94 city directory includes a boardinghouse and a bottling works sporting the name as well. The use of the term would quickly spread.[46]

Salem had undergone a number of changes over the centuries. At the turn of the nineteenth century it was a great maritime and commercial hub, one of the nation's largest and richest cities, and a leading force in the trade with ports in Asia. It had been home to Nathaniel Bowditch, the father of modern navigation, and Samuel McIntire, the great wood carver and architect, responsible for many of the finer mansions of Salem. Jefferson's

Embargo and the War of 1812 brought an end to Salem's golden age. Decades of economic decline would end with the establishment of the Naumkeag Textile Mill in 1839. By the late nineteenth century, Salem boasted about thirty thousand residents and was known for innovation. Alexander Graham Bell briefly lived in town and made the first public demonstration of the telephone at the Salem Lyceum in 1877.[47]

In the twentieth century, Salem would begin to suffer several shocks that would erode its economy and make it increasingly dependent on its growing tourist industry and the connection to witchcraft. In 1914 a fire destroyed more than thirteen hundred buildings and left 3,500 people homeless, wiping out many blocks of working-class homes as well as thirty-five factories, including the Naumkeag. The fire began on Boston Street, in one of Salem's tanneries, right next to Gallows Hill. Salem's shoe and leather industry, which at one point had thrived, never recovered, and while the Naumkeag quickly rebuilt, it was in decline. It would be rocked by major strikes during the Depression and finally move its operations to South Carolina in 1953.

Amid these downturns, Salem officially still refused to recognize its connection to the witch trials. In 1930 Salem was the center of celebrations of the Massachusetts tercentenary. Pioneer Village was constructed as the setting for a pageant that celebrated the founding of the Bay Colony. It was so popular that it would continue as a living history museum, but it would focus purely on the founding years of Salem and ignore the witch trials. There remained a tension over witchcraft tourism in Salem. While commercial interests hoped to promote it, local historians and preservationists worried that it would put the rest of Salem's history into the shadows. In 1931, the Salem City Council debated but in the end refused to appropriate $1,000 for a suitable witchcraft memorial. Five years later, Thomas Gannon gave the City of Salem a small strip of land on Gallows Hill, still traditionally believed to be site of the executions, as a site for a memorial to the witches and a park. The city accepted the gift but never built the memorial. Popular sentiment still resisted embracing witchcraft, though around 1940 Salem High School adopted a witch as its mascot (which the school still retains). And in 1944 the preservation organization Historic Salem Incorporated was established to save Judge Corwin's "Witch House" and Nathaniel Bowditch's home from demolition when Essex Street was widened.[48]

Salem would be reawakened to its witchcraft heritage in the 1950s. Marion Starkey's *The Devil in Massachusetts* (1949) was the first major history of the witch trials in the twentieth century and became a bestseller when it was featured in *Life* magazine. Although there had been novels and movies about Salem in the 1930s and 1940s, none approached the power and influence of *The Crucible*. Playwright Arthur Miller used the witch trials as an allegory for another zealous witch hunt, the McCarthy hearings and generally the effort to persecute Americans for any connection, however tenuous, to Communism. Soon after the January 1953 premiere of Miller's play at the Martin Beck Theatre in New York, the witch trials first appeared in the new medium of television, featured on Walter Cronkite's popular show *You Are There*. Both *The Crucible* and *You Are There* were turning points in the popularization of the witch trials. The play quickly earned a central spot in the canon of American drama. Some historians lament the influence that it has had over perceptions of Salem. Miller never intended it to be an accurate historical portrayal of the trials, and the liberties he took are sometimes accepted as fact. Furthermore, Miller got wrong a few of the facts he chose to include. Most notably, Miller stated on several occasions that it was a historical fact that Abigail Williams was indeed the servant of the Procter family—a relationship that is critical to his play. However, their servant was actually Mary Warren, not Abigail Williams.[49]

Even before Miller and Starkey had turned their attention to Salem, relatives of one of the victims, Ann Pudeator, pushed for a pardon for her and the five others who had not received a reversal of attainder from the General Court. Through their efforts a bill was first introduced into the legislature in 1945. After twelve years and many failed efforts, in 1957 the General Court and governor finally approved a resolution pardoning "one Ann Pudeator and certain other persons." Massachusetts had seemingly finally made good its formal efforts to restore the innocency of victims of 1692.[50]

Miller's play and its notoriety induced Salem to relent and embrace its past more openly. The daily *Salem Evening News* added a witch on a broomstick to its logo in 1962, and the Salem Chamber of Commerce adopted a similar image. Police Department uniforms and cruisers featured a witch on a broomstick and the phrase "Witch City." The logo is so common in Salem that some people assume it to be the city's official seal, which actually depicts a Salem ship approaching the coast of Sumatra to trade for pepper with a local official. Pepper had been the leading source of Salem's wealth in early days. Salem's official motto is "Divitis Indiae usque ad ultimum Sinum," Latin for "to the farthest port of the rich east." The 1960s saw a nationwide growth in interest in witchcraft and the supernatural, thanks in part to movies such as *Rosemary's Baby* and television sitcoms such as *The Addams Family, The Munsters,* and *Bewitched.* Salem's Parker Brothers bought the rights to make Ouija boards in 1966; sales soon surpassed those of their all-time bestseller, Monopoly. The fact that the boards were made in Salem added a certain cachet. In 1970 Parker Brothers produced Witch Pitch, in which players tossed rings onto the rotating cupola of a haunted house. The game sold poorly, despite the packaging that announced it was "Made in the Witch City, U.S.A."[51]

In the summer of 1970, eight episodes of *Bewitched* were filmed in Salem and Gloucester. The television comedy followed the trials and tribulations of a modern-day spell-casting, nose-twitching suburban witch and house-wife named Samantha Stevens and her hapless mortal husband, Darrin. Robert Montgomery's daughter Elizabeth starred as Samantha, and her mother was played by Agnes Moorehead. In the show's previous six seasons, occasional references had been made to Salem, which took center stage as the Stevens family came to participate in a witches' convention to elect a new Witch in Residence for Salem. Millions saw the episodes, swelling the ranks of Salem tourists. The next year, Laurie Cabot moved to Salem. Cabot practiced Wicca, a modern-day pagan religion with many naturalistic tradi-tions but no hierarchies or central authority. She opened the first shop to

Shoulder patch of the Salem Police De-partment. Photograph by the author.

sell witchcraft-related items such as herbs and tarot cards. Several years later she prevailed successfully on Governor Michael Dukakis to name her the "Official Witch of Salem." She quickly became a celebrity, interviewed by all the major American media outlets. Salem would soon have a substantial Wiccan population, estimated today by some to be as high as 10 percent of the city's 40,000 inhabitants. Most Wiccans belong to small covens or groups that usually meet in private. There may be as many as thirty covens in Salem today. It is a very diverse group of people who are attracted to Salem because they feel generally accepted by the public. Wiccans are involved in all aspects of Salem life, including its government and businesses. Some Wiccans are shop owners, selling items relating to their faith or the tourist trade, but others have more traditional careers, from teaching school and working for the Internal Revenue Service to being a stay-at-home parent.[52]

With the arrival of *Bewitched*, the Salem witchcraft gold rush had officially begun. In 1972, the Salem Witch Museum opened for business. The city's first for-profit witchcraft attraction, designed to accommodate multimedia presentations and displays, the museum was located in the former Second Church—a Gothic-style structure well suited for the purpose. Many visitors assume that the statue standing next to the museum on Washington Square must be a witch; it is a likeness of Roger Conant, the leader of the first English settlers who came in Salem in 1626. In 1974 tourism reached a new high, with more than one million people visiting Salem, and this was due in part to the success of the Salem Witch Museum. The museum would subsequently inspire imitators, starting with the Witch Dungeon in 1979.

In 1982, Biff Michaud, a Salem native and president of the Salem Witch Museum, worked with the Salem Chamber of Commerce to organize the first Haunted Happenings festival around Halloween. Michaud astutely noted that no place had staked a claim to being the "Halloween Capital of the World" and that it represented a golden opportunity for Salem.[53] There are no connections between the events of 1692 and Halloween, though modern-day Wiccans do observe October 31 as Samhain, the most important of the Sabbath days that mark the annual cycle, the Wheel of the Year. Regardless, the festival was an immediate success that now covers the month of October and brings tens of thousands of tourists to Salem. The celebration of Halloween has seen tremendous growth in the past three decades. Americans now spend more money to celebrate it than they do for any holiday other than Christmas. As a part of this growing national obsession, a number of supernatural-themed for-profit attractions sprang up in Salem, including the Salem Wax Museum of Witches and Seafarers, the Salem Witches Village, and the New England Pirate Museum. The revenue and jobs created by the growth of witchcraft tourism made up for some of the losses of factory jobs as Salem became a post-industrial city, and that partly explains why it has been more willing to accept witchcraft tourism. The last two Salem factories, Parker Brothers Games and a Sylvania light bulb production plan, both closed their doors in the early 1990s.[54]

Nonetheless, as witchcraft tourism played an increasingly important role in Salem's economy, so, too, did controversy over it, and particularly over how to memorialize 1692. As we saw, the city had been unwilling to face the bicentennial of the witch trials. There had been repeated efforts again in the early 1960s and in 1970 to build a memorial, but nothing had come of it. Now with the tercentenary looming, Salem finally began to accept the notion that some civic recognition of the trials was needed. In 1986 the city established the Salem Tercentenary Committee and charged it with developing programming that would "lift the shroud of misunderstanding, remorse, and shame that for three centuries has been associated with the trials."[55] Among many other events and programs, the committee sponsored the erection of a memorial to the victims of 1692. Located next to the Charter Street cemetery, it is a low-key memorial, featuring twenty simple granite benches, each inscribed with a name of a victim and the date of his or her death. The Tercentenary Committee also created the Salem Award for Human Rights and Social Justice. Dedicated to honor the memory of the victims of 1692, the award is given annually "to keep alive the lessons of the Salem Witch Trials of 1692 and to recognize those who are speaking out and taking action to alleviate discrimination and promote tolerance." Arthur Miller and Elie Wiesel were the featured speakers at the memorial's dedication. Even Danvers built a memorial to commemorate the tercentennial, placing it across the street from the site of the 1692 Salem Village meetinghouse. The names of the twenty-five people who lost their lives are etched on a twelve-foot-long by eight-foot-high granite panel. Located next to an elementary school and a park, both suburban in their feel, it sees far fewer tourists than the Salem memorial, which is in the middle of a busy city. Danvers seems content to be out of the witchcraft spotlight.[56]

The Salem Witch Memorial, 2006. Each granite bench is inscribed with the name
of one of the victims of 1692. Photograph by the author.

In 1992 Danvers also endorsed another modest act of reconciliation.
There was a tradition in the Jacobs family that George Jacobs's body had
been taken from Gallows Hill after his death and buried on his farm, which
is located within the town's borders. A skeleton exhumed and then reburied on the farm in the mid-nineteenth century was believed to be his, and
this skeleton was rediscovered by a bulldozer when the property was developed in the 1950s. Safeguarded for years by Danvers officials, the skeleton
was quietly reburied on the Rebecca Nurse farm, complete with replica
seventeenth-century coffin and gravestone, in 1992. Although analysis of
the remains established that they were those of an old man and generally
fit Jacobs's description, it will never know whether they really were those of
Jacobs. However, it was still an important and sincere gesture.[57]

The City of Salem remained divided by how to handle its witchcraft heritage. Tensions mounted during and after the tercentenary. Many of the town's
inhabitants considered witch tourism the city's savior; others believed it
was its biggest problem. Everyone—merchants, Wiccans, fundamentalists,
teachers, PTA members, and historians—seemed to have different opinions
as to what was and was not appropriate. The greatest concern was that the

past had become a commodity to be hawked and sold in a theme-park-like atmosphere, and that this detracted from the sober issues—involving sin, tolerance, spirituality, and of course politics—that lay beneath. What had happened in 1692 was too important to be trivialized. And there were those who wished Salem could just ignore its past and go back to the way it used to be, before Haunted Happenings and witchcraft tourism—a pleasantly quaint and historical bedroom community for Boston. There were other reasons for tourists to come to Salem: Nathaniel Bowditch, Nathaniel Hawthorne and the House of Seven Gables, the world-class Peabody Essex Museum, the spectacular architecture of Samuel McIntire, Salem National Maritime Historic Site, and Pioneer Village headed the list of attractions. The focus on 1692, a tragedy mostly involving residents of other towns, seemed to distort the picture.[58]

Others disagree. They see efforts to minimize Salem's role in the witch trials and to emphasize the rest of its history as another episode of the city's collective amnesia. The sites in Salem that were key settings for the witch-craft drama have been all but forgotten. The jail from which the victims were led to their execution was rebuilt in 1763, and then turned into a pri-vate dwelling in 1813. Remarkably, this building—altered and expanded but apparently still containing timbers from the original 1683 jail—managed to survive until 1957, when it was torn down, without complaint, to make way for offices for the New England Telephone Company. The original plaque was removed and now sits several blocks away, attached to the building that houses the Witch Dungeon Museum. Recently another plaque was placed to mark the actual location. There is a marker for the Salem Courthouse, though most visitors miss the weatherworn plaque on a building near its site. The location itself, where the victims were condemned to death, lies paved over in the middle of Washington Street—one of the city's main thor-oughfares. The original structure was torn down 250 years ago and was little mourned. The MBTA commuter rail line runs beneath it, so there's no hope even for peeling back a layer of pavement and looking for what lies beneath.[59]

The execution of the witches was not well recorded in 1692, and the exact place had apparently been lost to time—part of a collective local amnesia that wanted to forget the location. Then excellent detective work by local historian Sidney Perley in the early twentieth century managed to prove, with relatively little doubt, the approximate location on Gallows Hill of the

Site of the Salem courthouse, 2006. Viewed from the south, the courthouse sat
in the middle of Washington Street, at about the location
of the approaching car. Photograph by the author.

executions. Despite this, the amnesia continues. Some people believe that
until the city puts up a memorial on Gallows Hill—Ground Zero, as it were,
of the tragedy—it is denying the significance of the central event of the city's
past, indeed the very essence of it. A memorial in the general location would
be an appropriate way—perhaps the only way—to make amends.[60]

Today, tensions remain. Haunted Happenings is a month-long celebration that pumps an estimated $9 million into the Salem economy, attracting
more than four hundred thousand tourists. Close to a hundred thousand
people celebrate Halloween in Salem. Thousands dress in elaborate cos-
tume and take to the streets, the closest thing New England may have to
Mardi Gras. Fundamentalist Christians, urging modern-day Salem sinners
to repent, join in with street performers, vendors, ghostly tours, and a range
of musical acts to create an eclectic mix. Perhaps Satan, the great trickster,
has indeed had the last laugh.

In all the hoopla, the victims of 1692 seemed all too often to have been forgotten, buried not by neglect but by the spectacle of distractions. Nevertheless,
this is not entirely the case. While taking a graduate course I offer on Salem

The Samantha Stevens statue on Halloween in Salem, 2010. Spider-Man and a shirtless man dance in protest to a speaker who is arguing against gay marriage.
Photograph by the author.

witchcraft, Paula Keene became aware of the fact that five of the executed witches—Susannah Martin, Bridget Bishop, Alice Parker, Margaret Scott, and Wilmot Redd—supposedly exonerated in 1957 had not in fact received a reversal of attainder. Although the intent of the legislation was to pardon them, it did not carry legal weight because none of them had been specifically named. Working with local officials, witch descendants, and Salem's state representative, Michael Ruane, Keene focused on redressing this, an effort that culminated in 2001 when the Massachusetts legislature passed an act to finally exonerate the group. Governor Jane Swift signed the bill officially into law in Salem on Halloween in 2001. Although some historians decried the choice of occasion, everyone approved of the sentiment. Perhaps Salem was at last becoming the city of peace.[61]

While trying to be respectful to the tragedy of 1692, Salem remains reliant on the tourism that misfortune generates. The balance is not an easy one to maintain, as is reflected in the trivializing Chamber of Commerce slogan, "Discover the Magic of Salem," which is of course trying to sanitize "magic."

The 2005 unveiling in Salem of the statue of Samantha Stevens, the fictional housewife-witch from *Bewitched*, echoes this. She is sitting fetchingly on a broomstick in front of a crescent moon. The metal sculpture provoked outrage when it was unveiled. Danvers historian and Salem witchcraft expert Richard Trask said in response to it that "an enlightened society should choose to remember and respect past tragedies rather than purposely or ignorantly make light of them."[62] Yet the statue has become merely more tourist kitsch and is not taken seriously. In the end, Salem—Samantha Stevens notwithstanding—remains a metaphor not for magic but for persecution, paranoia, ignorance, superstition, jealousy, judicial blindness, guilt, shame, and bigotry.

There still is much public debate in Salem about the proper way to acknowledge its heritage. The community seems sometimes reluctant to deal honestly with the associations that saddle it, particularly when it benefits from those associations. "Witch City" brings in tourists, businesses, and income. And one could argue that it is not merely latter-day cynical exploitation but instead is a way of owning up to the past, that it represents Salem's own scarlet letter, which it willingly bears, in remembrance and in repentance.

Salem was the first town of Massachusetts Bay, a cornerstone of the great experiment that was to become the United States of America. It was a part of Winthrop's city upon a hill, a shining example of everything godlike and good, a harmonious place where hatred and persecution were banished. God's justice and mercy would lift the city and prevail. The trials represented a fall from a very great height.

Salem is not alone in its ambivalence about its past. This is perhaps a particularly American phenomenon and generally reflective of the way that the country treats its history, or at least certain aspects of that history. Salem has much in common with Wounded Knee, the site of a massacre of Lakotas; Pequot Hill, where more than four hundred Pequots were murdered; or Gramercy Park and other places in New York City where numbers of African Americans were lynched during the Draft Riots. We struggle to acknowledge our dark moments, so intent are we in moving beyond them in the righteous cause of achieving a more perfect union. Salem's burden is perhaps greater because the city upon a hill set such an impossibly lofty standard. It was not just innocent people who perished in Salem, but innocence itself.

So we do not want to look at the truth of what happened at Salem, and when we do it is with a sense of moral superiority. Americans today gaze back at the people of 1692 as a foolish, superstitious, and intolerant lot. How could they possibly have executed nineteen people as witches? Yet that is to dismiss the figure in the mirror. Imagine for a moment the situation they faced in 1692 and consider their quandary from their perspective. You know in your heart and soul that witches, like Satan, are real, and that they cause death and misery. They threaten to wipe out everything you believe in. If they could, they would overthrow your government, overturn your faith, and destroy your society. Witches are all the more dangerous because they do not have to even be present to strike you or a loved one dead, or to destroy your home. They can be many miles away. And they are constantly recruiting converts among the discontented, with promises of rich rewards. You therefore must take steps to root them out, yet this is nightmarishly difficult. Anyone could be a witch: neighbors, friends, in-laws, wives, husbands, or children. Those who are different arouse your immediate suspicion. Perhaps they dress in an unusual fashion, or speak with an odd accent, or worship God a bit differently. You ask your leaders for help, and while they give reassurances and say that they are taking steps to deal with the danger, you know they have a nearly impossible task, for the devil is a non-state actor.

As I am intimating, change the word *witch* to *terrorist* and we can perhaps better appreciate the complexity of the problem that the people of Salem—not just the judges but the accusers, the afflicted, and even the accused themselves—faced in 1692. By the end of the witch hunt, most Bay Colonists were convinced that Satan had indeed visited their colony and had struck a severe blow. Only now they came to understand that Satan's great work had been to delude them into thinking that many devout Puritans and good people were witches. The devil's victory was in turning steadfast and godly colonists against each other, leading to needless death and prolonged suffering. Even worse, the colony's leaders perceived this phantom threat to be so real and dangerous to the New England way that they temporarily set aside the very rights and liberties that elevated the colony. Wanting to protect what they held most dear, they tore it apart. At the top of the National Security Agency's website is its mission statement: "Defending our nation. Securing the future."[63] It is an important and honorable responsibility, but it could also describe the charge of the Court of Oyer and Terminer in 1692.

During the witch trials bicentennial in 1892, the members of the Essex Institute who sought to build a tower on top of Gallows Hill boiled down to its essence what that memorial would have stood for: "Salem witchcraft, for reasons unnecessary to detail here, has become the most popularly known outbreak of any age or in any land. It will never be forgotten for it never can be."[64]

Yet Salem never built that monument. This was probably just as well, for the top of Gallows Hill turned out to be the wrong site to memorialize. Drawing upon trial documents, contemporary accounts and oral tradition, Sidney Perley had concluded in 1901 that Proctor's Ledge, located near the base of Gallows Hill, was the actual execution site. Based on Perley's work, in 1936 the City of Salem acquired part of Proctor's Ledge, "to be held forever as a public park" and called it "Witch Memorial Land."[65] Again, however, nothing happened. The land gradually became overgrown and largely forgotten. As it was never marked, most people erroneously assumed the executions took place on Gallows Hill's summit, despite occasional newspaper articles and publications to the contrary.[66]

In 2010 a team of researchers that included this author began to review Perley's research and other evidence, and employed more sophisticated technology to help pinpoint the location. Ground-penetrating radar and electronic soil resistivity tests indicated that there are no human remains in the very shallow soils of Proctor's Ledge. (This finding is in keeping with stories that relatives of the victims came under cover of darkness to recover loved ones and rebury them in family cemeteries.) However, what is called "viewshed analysis" determined that only Proctor's Ledge, and not the higher elevations of Gallows Hill would have been visible to observers who witnessed the executions from a distance. In January 2016 the team announced the confirmation of Proctor's Ledge as the execution site.[67]

Fortunately the City of Salem never sold the land at Proctor's Ledge, so it has another chance to acknowledge the past. "Now that the location of this historic injustice has been clearly proven, the city will work to respectfully and tastefully memorialize the site in a manner that is sensitive to its location today in a largely residential neighborhood," announced Salem Mayor Kimberley Driscoll. The response has been overwhelming; local residents as well as people across the country have reached out to express their support for this effort. [68] Generations of descendants, spread far and wide, are preparing to return for the dedication. The target date for the ceremony is June 10, 2017, the 325th anniversary of the execution of Bridget Bishop.

People Accused of Witchcraft in 1692 Who Are Named in the Court Records

The following list has been compiled by Margo Burns, who compiled it through her work as an associate editor and project manager of Bernard Rosenthal et al., eds., *Records of the Salem Witch-Hunt*. The list is from her web site, Seventeenth-Century Colonial New England with Special Emphasis on the Essex County Witch-Hunt of 1692, at www.17thc.us/primarysources/accused.php. The author thanks her for allowing the list to be reproduced here. Note that mnu stands for maiden name unknown.

		Complaint or Arrest	Examination	Imprisonment	Evidence Entered	Grand Jury or Indictment	Jury Trial	Conviction	Execution	Restitution
Arthur Abbott	Topsfield	√								
Nehemiah Abbott, Jr.	Topsfield	√	√							
John Alden	Boston	√	√	√		√				√
Daniel Andrew	Salem Village	√				√				
Abigail (Wheeler) Barker	Andover		√	√			√	√		√
Mary Barker	Andover	√	√	√			√	√		√
William Barker, Jr.	Andover		√	√			√	√		√
William Barker, Sr.	Andover	√	√	√	√	√				
Sarah (Hood) Bassett	Lynn	√		√			√			
Bridget (Playfer) Bishop [also: Wassalbee, Oliver]	Salem	√	√	√	√	√	√	√	√	√
Edward Bishop, Jr.	Salem Village	√		√						√
Sarah (Wilds) Bishop	Salem Village	√		√	√					√
Mary Black	Salem Village	√	√	√	√					
Mary (Perkins) Bradbury	Salisbury			√	√		√	√	√	√
Mary Bridges, Jr.	Andover		√	√			√	√		
Mary (Tyler) Bridges, Sr. [also: Post]	Andover	√	√	√			√	√		
Sarah Bridges	Andover		√	√			√	√		√
Hannah (Farnum) Bromage [also: Tyler]	Haverhill	√	√	√			√			
Sarah (Smith) Buckley	Salem Village	√	√	√	√	√	√			√
George Burroughs	Wells	√	√	√	√	√	√	√	√	√
John Busse	Durham					√				
Candy	Salem	√	√					√	√	
Andrew Carrier	Andover	√	√							√
Martha (Allen) Carrier	Andover	√	√	√	√	√	√	√	√	√
Richard Carrier	Andover	√	√				√			√
Sarah Carrier	Andover		√	√						√
Thomas Carrier, Jr.	Andover		√							√
Hannah (mnu) Carroll	Salem	√								
Bethiah Carter, Jr.	Woburn	√								
Bethiah (Pearson) Carter, Sr.	Woburn	√		√						
Elizabeth (Walker) Cary	Charlestown	√	√	√	√					

Name	Place	Complaint or Arrest	Examination	Imprisonment	Evidence Entered	Grand Jury or Indictment	Jury Trial	Conviction	Execution	Restitution
Sarah Churchill	Salem		√	√	√					
Mary (Johnson) Clark [also: Davis]	Haverhill	√	√	√						
Rachel (Haffield) Clinton	Ipswich	√			√	√	√			
Sarah (Towne) Cloyce [also: Bridges]	Topsfield	√	√	√	√	√				
Sarah (Aslebee) Cole	Lynn	√	√	√	√	√	√			√
Sarah (Davis) Cole	Salem	√		√						
Elizabeth Colson	Reading	√		√	√					
Mary (Dustin) Colson	Reading		√	√						
Giles Cory	Salem Farms	√	√	√	√	√				√
Martha (mnu) Cory [also: Rich]	Salem Farms	√	√	√	√	√	√	√	√	√
Deliverance (Haseltine) Dane	Andover		√	√	√					√
Phoebe (Wilds) Day	Gloucester				√					
Mary (Bassett) DeRich	Salem Village	√		√	√	√				√
Elizabeth (Austin) Dicer	Piscataqua	√		√						
Rebecca (Dolliver) Dike	Gloucester	√			√					
Ann (Higginson) Dolliver	Salem	√	√							
Mehitable (Braybrook) Downing	Ipswich			√						
Joseph Draper	Andover		√							
Lydia (mnu) Dustin	Reading	√		√	√		√			
Sarah Dustin	Reading	√		√		√	√			
Daniel Eames	Boxford		√		√	√				
Rebecca (Blake) Eames	Boxford		√	√	√	√	√	√		√
Esther (Dutch) Elwell	Gloucester	√			√					
Martha (Toothaker) Emerson	Haverhill	√	√	√		√				√
Joseph Emmons	Manchester	√		√						
Mary (Hollingsworth) English	Salem	√		√	√	√				
Philip English	Salem	√		√	√	√				√
Mary (Towne) Esty	Topsfield	√	√	√	√	√	√	√	√	√
Thomas Farrar, Sr.	Lynn	√		√	√	√				
Edward Farrington	Andover					√				
Abigail Faulkner, Jr.	Andover		√	√						√

Name	Residence	Complaint or Arrest	Examination	Imprisonment	Evidence Entered	Grand Jury or Indictment	Jury Trial	Conviction	Execution	Restitution
Abigail (Dane) Faulkner, Sr.	Andover		√			√	√	√	√		√
Dorothy Faulkner	Andover		√	√						√
John Flood	Rumney Marsh	√				√				
Elizabeth (Thomas) Fosdick [also: Lisley, Betts]	Malden	√				√				
Ann (Alcock) Foster	Andover		√			√	√	√	√		√
Nicholas Frost	Piscataqua	√								
Eunice (Potter) Frye	Andover		√	√			√	√		√
Dorothy Good	Salem Village	√	√	√	√					√
Sarah (Solart) Good [also: Poole]	Salem Village	√	√	√	√	√	√	√	√	√
Mary (Green) Green	Haverhill	√		√						√
Thomas Hardy	Piscataqua					√				
Elizabeth (Hawkes) Hart	Lynn	√			√		√			√
Margaret Hawkes	Salem	√								
Sarah Hawkes	Andover	·	√			√	√			√
Dorcas (Galley) Hoar	Beverly	√	√	√	√	√	√	√		√
Abigail Hobbs	Topsfield	√	√	√	√	√	√	√		√
Deliverance (mnu) Hobbs	Topsfield	√	√	√	√					
William Hobbs	Topsfield	√	√	√	√					
Elizabeth (Jackson) How	Ipswich	√	√	√	√	√	√	√	√	√
John Howard	Rowley	√		√						
Frances (mnu) Hutchins	Haverhill			√						
Mary (Leach) Ireson	Lynn	√	√			√				
Elizabeth (Poor) Jackson	Rowley					√				
John Jackson, Jr.	Rowley	√	√	√			√			
John Jackson, Sr.	Rowley	√	√	√			√			
George Jacobs, Jr.	Salem Village	√				√				
George Jacobs, Sr.	Salem	√			√	√	√	√	√	√
Margaret Jacobs	Salem	√			√	√	√	√		
Rebecca (Andrews) Jacobs [also: Frost]	Salem Village	√			√	√	√	√		√
Abigail Johnson	Andover	√		√						√
Elizabeth Johnson, Jr.	Andover		√				√	√	√	√

Name	Location	Complaint or Arrest	Examination	Imprisonment	Evidence Entered	Grand Jury or Indictment	Jury Trial	Conviction	Execution	Restitution
Elizabeth (Dane) Johnson, Sr.	Andover	√	√		√	√	√			√
Rebecca Johnson, Jr.	Andover									√
Rebecca (Aslebee) Johnson, Sr.	Andover		√			√				√
Stephen Johnson	Andover		√	√		√				√
Mary Lacey, Jr.	Andover	√	√	√		√	√			√
Mary (Foster) Lacey, Sr.	Andover	√	√		√	√	√	√		√
Jane (mnu) Lilly [also: Osgood]	Reading		√	√		√				
Mary (Osgood) Marston	Andover		√	√	√		√	√		√
Susannah (North) Martin	Amesbury	√	√	√	√	√	√	√	√	√
Sarah Morey	Beverly	√		√						√
Rebecca (Towne) Nurse	Salem Village	√	√	√	√	√	√	√	√	√
Sarah (Warren) Osburn [also: Prince]	Salem Village	√	√	√						√
Mary (Clements) Osgood	Andover		√	√		√	√			√
Elizabeth (Carrington) Paine	Malden	√			√					
Alice (mnu) Parker	Salem	√	√	√	√	√	√	√	√	√
Mary (Ayer) Parker	Andover		√	√	√	√	√	√	√	√
Sarah Parker	Andover			√	√					√
Sarah (mnu) Pease	Salem	√			√					√
Joan (mnu) Penny [also: White, Braybrook]	Gloucester	√	√	√						
Hannah Post	Boxford		√		√	√	√			
Mary Post	Rowley	√	√		√	√	√	√		√
Susannah Post	Andover		√		√	√	√			
Margaret (mnu) Prince	Gloucester	√	√	√		√				
Benjamin Procter	Salem Farms	√		√	√					√
Elizabeth (Bassett) Procter	Salem Farms	√	√	√	√	√	√	√		√
John Procter	Salem Farms	√		√	√	√	√	√	√	√
Joseph Procter	Salem Farms				√					√
Sarah Procter	Salem Farms	√		√	√					√
William Procter	Salem Farms	√	√	√	√					√
Ann (mnu) Pudeator [also: Greenslit]	Salem	√	√	√	√	√	√	√	√	√
Wilmot (mnu) Redd	Marblehead	√	√		√	√	√	√	√	√

		Complaint or Arrest	Examination	Imprisonment	Evidence Entered	Grand Jury or Indictment	Jury Trial	Conviction	Execution	Restitution
Sarah (Clark) Rice [also: Davis]	Reading	√			√	√				
Susannah (mnu) Roots	Beverly	√			√	√				
Abigail Rowe	Gloucester	√				√				
Mary (Prince) Rowe	Gloucester				√					
Henry Salter	Andover		√	√			√			
John Sawdy	Andover			√						
Margaret (Stevenson) Scott	Rowley					√	√	√	√	√	√
Ann (mnu) Sears [also: Farrar]	Woburn	√			√					
Rachel (Hoar) Slue	Beverly									√
Abigail Soames	Salem	√	√		√	√	√			
Martha (Barrett) Sparks	Chelmsford				√					√
Mary (Harrington) Taylor	Reading			√	√	√	√	√		
Tituba	Salem Village	√	√	√	√	√				
Job Tookey	Beverly		√			√	√	√		
Margaret Toothaker	Billerica	√				√				
Mary (Allen) Toothaker	Billerica	√	√		√	√	√	√	√	
Roger Toothaker	Salem	√		√	√	√				
Hannah Tyler	Andover				√		√	√		
Johannah Tyler	Andover		√	√	√					
Martha Tyler	Andover		√	√						
Mary (Lovett) Tyler	Andover		√	√			√	√		
Rachel (mnu) Vincent [also: Cook, Langton]	Gloucester				√					
Mercy Wardwell	Andover		√				√	√			√
Samuel Wardwell, Sr.	Andover		√	√	√	√	√	√	√	√
Sarah (Hooper) Wardwell [also: Hawkes]	Andover			√	√	√	√	√	√		√
Mary Warren	Salem Farms	√	√	√	√					
Sarah (Averill) Wilds	Topsfield	√	√		√	√	√	√	√	√	√
Ruth (mnu) Wilford	Haverhill	√			√					
John Willard	Salem Village	√	√	√	√	√	√	√	√	√
Sarah Wilson, Jr.	Andover		√	√						√
Sarah (Lord) Wilson, Sr.	Andover		√	√						√
Mary (Buckley) Witheridge	Salem Village	√			√	√	√	√			√

Additional People Accused of Witchcraft in 1692–1693

The following list of names of people accused of witchcraft in 1692 and 1693 is compiled principally from contemporary letters and publications. No formal legal proceedings are known to have taken place against any of the following people. The names of several of them do show up in the records of the Court of Oyer and Terminer, but there is no record of anyone on the list ever being formally charged by the court.

NAME	TOWN	REFERENCE
Ann (Wood) Bradstreet	Andover	Calef, "More Wonders," in Burr, *Narratives*, 372.
Dudley Bradstreet	Andover	Calef, "More Wonders," in Burr, *Narratives*, 372.
John Bradstreet	Andover	Calef, "More Wonders," in Burr, *Narratives*, 372.
Francis Dane	Andover	Rosenthal et al., eds., *Salem Witch-Hunt*, 607–8.
Sarah (Noyes) Hale	Beverly	Calef, "More Wonders," in Burr, *Narratives*, 369.
James How	Ipswich	Rosenthal et al., eds., *Salem Witch-Hunt*, 568.
Maria (Cotton) Mather	Boston	Whiting, *Truth and Innocency Defended*, 140.
Ann (Jacobs) Moody	Boston	Joshua Broadbent to Francis Nicholson.
Mary (mnu) Obinson	Boston	Thomas Brattle Letter," in Burr, *Narratives*, 179.

NAME	TOWN	REFERENCE
Mary (Spencer) Phips	Boston	Whiting, *Truth and Innocency Defended*, 140.
Nathaniel Saltonstall	Haverhill	Sewell, *Diary of Samuel Sewall*, 1:305–6.
Jeremiah Shepard	Lynn*	Maule, *Truth Held Forth*, 182.
Sarah (Clapp) Swift	Boston	Calef, "More Wonders," in Burr, *Narratives*, 383–84.
Margaret (Webb) Thacher	Boston	Thomas Brattle Letter, in Burr, *Narratives*, 177.
Hezekiah Usher	Boston	Thomas Brattle Letter, in Burr, *Narratives*, 178.
Samuel Willard	Boston	Calef, "More Wonders," in Burr, *Narratives*, 360.

* Shepard is not named, but Maule refers to the "Lynn Priest" being accused. This presumably was Reverend Shepard, the minister of Lynn.

Ministers and Their Close Family
Members Accused of Witchcraft in 1692

NAME	TOWN	RELATIONSHIP TO MINISTER
Dudley Bradstreet	Andover	brother of Simon Bradstreet Jr.
John Bradstreet	Andover	brother of Simon Bradstreet Jr.
George Burroughs	Falmouth/Wells	minister
John Busse	Oyster River	minister
Francis Dane	Andover	minister
Ann (Higginson) Doliver	Salem Town	daughter of John Higginson
Abigail (Dane) Faulkner	Andover	daughter of Francis Dane
Abigail Faulkner Jr.	Andover	granddaughter of Francis Dane
Dorothy Faulkner	Andover	granddaughter of Francis Dane
Sarah (Noyes) Hale	Beverly	wife of John Hale
Abigail Johnson	Andover	granddaughter of Francis Dane
Elizabeth (Dane) Johnson	Andover	daughter of Francis Dane
Elizabeth Johnson Jr.	Andover	granddaughter of Francis Dane
Stephen Johnson	Andover	grandson of Francis Dane
Maria (Cotton) Mather	Boston	wife of Increase Mather
Ann (Jacobs) Moody	Boston	wife of Joshua Moody
Jeremiah Shepard*	Lynn	minister
Margaret (Webb) Thacher	Boston	widow of Thomas Thacher
Job Tookey Jr.	Beverly	son of Job Tookey Sr.
Samuel Willard	Boston	minister

* Shepard is not named, but Maule refers to the "Lynn Priest" being accused. This presumably was Reverend Shepard, the minister of Lynn.

Acknowledgments

The road to Salem Village is well traveled and its landscape known to most Americans, even those who have never set foot in Massachusetts. I am fortunate that I get to regularly travel the road to Salem in ways both literal and figurative, for not only am I a scholar of the witch trials, I teach at Salem State University. On my way to Salem from my home in Maine, my preferred route south takes me through Salem Village, present-day Danvers. The first sign of approach is Putnam Hill, with the nearby Putnam Cemetery and the home of Joseph Putnam, younger brother of one of the prosecutors and an early opponent of the witch hunt. Turning off the interstate, I get onto Centre Street and soon pass the training field where the militia gathered and the entire community came together. Then I pass by the site of the Parris parsonage, where thoughts turn to Samuel Parris and Tituba and the family that was at the epicenter of the hysteria. Soon after, on my left, is the Ingersoll Tavern, now a private home but in 1692 where some of the pretrial hearings took place. Beyond it is the site of the 1672 meetinghouse and the Danvers witch memorial. I continue down Centre Street, passing several seventeenth-century houses, including Rebecca Nurse's house and the family cemetery where she is believed to rest. Next come shopping centers that occupy the site of what once was Governor Endicott's farm, with little to mark it except for the ancient Endicott pear tree, planted by the governor himself. Then it is a couple of miles to Salem itself, where I come to the foot of Gallows Hill. Without fail I reflect on the victims of 1692. Salem has changed a great deal in three hundred years, yet the outlines of what happened there are still visible.

As suggested by my itinerary, this book has also been a personal voyage of discovery for me. My love of colonial New England is a gift that my late parents bestowed upon me early in life. My father loved to tell stories of past generations—of ancestors at Lovell's Fight or Bunker Hill—as we sat surrounded by possessions carefully passed down from one generation to the next. Sunday afternoon drives stopped at landmarks such as Redemption Rock or ancient cemeteries where ancestors lay at rest. Yet I never heard much or thought much about the witch trials, for I grew up in Fitchburg, in central Massachusetts, and most of my Massachusetts ancestors were from Middlesex County, not Essex. When I was a child, gravestones of Putnams in the old Lunenburg cemetery near my ancestors meant nothing to me. And the name Dr. Roger Toothaker on a family genealogy chart conscientiously drafted by my great-great-uncle had no significance beyond the thought that it was a pretty funny name—especially if he turned out to be a dentist. In researching this book, I learned that Roger Toothaker died in prison while awaiting trial for witchcraft, having been accused of the crime by Ann Putnam Jr. and others. These connections caused me to realize that I had always been surrounded by links to the witch trials. I now remembered the significance of fishing at Putnam's Pond, buying vegetables at Mr. Procter's Farm, and Thanksgiving dinners with at our family friends the Porters—not to mention my English teacher, Mr. Hawthorne. When I went to prep school at Andover along with students named Putnam and Nourse, I had no idea I was living in a town that played a central role in the events of 1692. I know better now, of course, and realize that my experience is actually typical, as we are all surrounded by the legacy of the witch trials.

While writing a book is a long road, I have been blessed to travel it in good company, and to have received the help of numerous people along the way. It takes a village to make a witch hunt, as well as a book about one. Since much of this book is a synthesis of scholarship, I owe a deep debt to the generations of historians who have studied witchcraft and Salem. I regret that I have had to relegate most of their names to the endnotes, as part of the effort to make this book accessible to a wide audience. Charles Upham, Sidney Perley, James Duncan Phillips, Paul Boyer, Stephen Nissenbaum, John Demos, Carol Karlsen, Larry Gragg, Richard Godbeer, and many more scholars (including those noted below) inform and inspire this book. Several works were indispensable and need to be singled out. Bernard Rosenthal and his team's monumental *Records of the*

Salem Witch-Hunt brings a new level of accessibility and understanding to the primary sources. Marilynne Roach's *The Salem Witch Trials: A Day-by-Day-Chronicle of a Community Under Siege* was invaluable maintaining the complex chronology of events. When questions of fact or interpretation emerged, I knew I could rely on Mary Beth Norton's exemplary *In the Devil's Snare: The Salem Witchcraft Crisis of 1692*.

It is a small and admittedly unusual group who study witchcraft, but I am fortunate to count many of its members as my friends, people who unselfishly shared their time and ideas with me. Four of them—Mary Beth Norton, Margo Burns, Malcolm Gaskill, and James Kences—read the entire manuscript and provided invaluable suggestions. Special thanks to Margo Burns for allowing me to publish her list of accused witches as an appendix. Richard Trask, David Goss, Marilynne Roach, and Benjamin Ray have been very helpful and supportive as well.

The History Department at Salem State is my academic family. It is a warm and collegial atmosphere that has been a great source of strength and encouragement for me. My former department chair, Christopher Mauriello, and current chair, Donna Seger (a fellow scholar of witchcraft), have been particularly supportive. The students in my graduate seminar on the Salem witch trials read the entire manuscript and provided helpful comments. Former graduate student Paula Keene first brought the campaign for innocency to my attention and inspired me with her tireless efforts to pardon the "Salem Five." Jason Peledge's graduate research on the Andover witch hunt was helpful as well. A course release provided by Dean Jude Nixon of the College of Arts and Sciences at Salem State University allowed me the time I needed to complete the manuscript.

I enjoy working with colleagues on projects, and the fruit of two such collaborations contributed to this book. Coauthoring a biography of Sir William Phips with John Reid was critical to my understanding of the royal governor as well as of the imperial and political context of 1692. I have discussed the Salem witch trials with James Kences for close to twenty years. Much of the article we coauthored, "Maine, Indian Land Speculation and the Essex County Witchcraft Outbreak," is incorporated in this book. James is an original thinker. He authored his innovative article on the influence of the frontier on the witch trials when he was just out of college and without the benefit of graduate school, years before most historians had considered this line of inquiry. From the significance of the New England

299

Company and Ebenezers to the impact of the pirate trials, some of the freshest thinking in the book comes from James. I thank him for unselfishly sharing his ideas and encouraging me to include them.

Other friends and colleagues have helped in a variety of ways. Dennis Robinson and Laura Chmielewski read chapters of the manuscript. Matt Harris encouraged me to look closely at events in Le Roy, New York. James F. Cooper directed me to a key resource on Rowley. Peter Follansbee provided photos and information on the Pope cabinet. Richard Candee helped me make sense of the plan of the Salem Village parsonage. Thanks to Howard Kaepplein for allowing me to share his research on the Barker family weddings. I have had many conversations with Peter and Jeanette Sablock about Gallows Hill and other aspects of this book. I have also been fortunate to have many talented and dedicated historians who helped shape my career. James Axtell, James Whittenburg, the late Alaric Faulkner, Anne Yentsch, and the late Robert Bradley all helped me hone my skills as a young historian and archaeologist. I met James Leamon in my first history class in my freshman year at Bates College thirty-six years ago, and he been a mentor, colleague, and good friend ever since.

I have relied on many libraries, archives, and historical societies in researching this book. I would particularly like to acknowledge the assistance of the staff of the Berry Library at Salem State University, the Dimond Library at the University of New Hampshire, the Salem Public Library, the New England Historical and Genealogical Society, the North Andover Historical Society, the Massachusetts Archives, the Danvers Archival Center, the Essex County Courthouse, and the Portsmouth Athenaeum. Special thanks to Thomas Hardiman, keeper of the Portsmouth Athenaeum.

I thank everyone who helped me with illustrations. Christine Bertoni of Peabody Essex Museum went above and beyond to make the image of the Pope cabinet available. Cory Gardiner took the photograph of Sir William Phips's portrait on very short notice. Thanks to Anna Clutterbuck-Cook of the Massachusetts Historical Society, Susan Greendyke Lachevre of the Massachusetts Arts Commission, and Sue Bell of the Museum of Fine Arts, Boston, for providing images from their collections. I deeply appreciate Richard Trask's allowing me to photograph the eel spear and horseshoe he discovered at the Zerubbabel Endicott House.

Several people were instrumental in bringing this manuscript to press. Special thanks to my agent, Matthew Carnicelli, who provided me the opportunity to write this book. I could not have asked for a finer editor than Tim Bent. I thank him and his team at Oxford University Press for their outstanding work. Series editors David Hackett Fischer and James McPherson have been supportive of this project since its inception. David Hackett Fischer also provided some very helpful suggestions. My old friend Mark Mastromarino used his editing talents to craft the index.

Finally, I owe the greatest debt of all to my wife, Peggy, and our daughters, Megan and Sarah. I suspect they consider the dedication to be redundant, for at times they must believe they are the latest victims of the Salem witch trials. Peggy read all of the manuscript at least once, endured endless discussions on arcane aspects of the trials, and in general has served as my sounding board for ideas. She has performed this unasked-for job with grace, tact, and skill, though I know there are a thousand things she would rather be doing. She has been my partner in all things for more than thirty years, and I thank her for putting up with me and the spectral visitors who have intruded into our lives.

Snowshoe Rock, York, Maine
February 2, 2014

Notes

INTRODUCTION

1. Benjamin Harris, "The Bookseller to the Reader," in Deodat Lawson, *A Brief and True Narrative*, in George Lincoln Burr, *Narratives of the Witchcraft Cases, 1648–1706* (New York: Charles Scribner's Sons, 1914), 152. Harris was the publisher of Lawson's work.

2. "The Joseph and Bathsheba Pope Carved and Applied Oak Valuables Cabinet," http://www.christies.com/LotFinder/lot_details.aspx?intObjectID=1729638.

3. For a profile of witch accusers and the nature of their complaints before 1692, see Carol Karlsen, *The Devil in the Shape of a Woman: Witchcraft in Colonial New England* (New York: Vintage Books, 1989), 183–85; John Demos, *Entertaining Satan: Witchcraft and the Culture of Early New England* (New York: Oxford, 1982), 153–66. For other differences in Salem, see Mary Beth Norton, *In the Devil's Snare, The Salem Witchcraft Crisis of 1692* (New York: Alfred A. Knopf, 2002), 7–11.

4. John Demos, "Underlying Themes in the Witchcraft of Seventeenth-Century New England," *American Historical Review* 75 (1970): 1311.

5. Worthington Chauncey Ford, ed., *The Diary of Cotton Mather* (New York: Frederick Ungar, 1957), 1:216 (quote); Cotton Mather's version of the 1696 Fast Day proclamation, from Willam DeLoss Love, *The Fast and Thanksgiving Days of New England* (Boston: Houghton, Mifflin and Co., 1895), 267 (quote). John Demos, *The Enemy Within: 2,000 Years of Witch-Hunting in the Western World* (New York: Viking, 2008), 228.

6. Perry Miller, *The New England Mind: From Colony to Providence* (Cambridge: Belknap Press, 1953), 191 (quote); for East Anglia, see Malcolm Gaskill, *Witchfinders: A Seventeenth-Century English Tragedy* (Cambridge: Harvard University Press, 2005), 128–30, 283–84. For a summary of witchcraft in the British colonies, see Richard Godbeer, "Witchcraft in British America," in Brian Levack, ed., *The Oxford Handbook of Witchcraft in Early Modern Europe and Colonial America* (New York: Oxford University Press, 2013), 393–411.

7. For the geographic and chronological range of witchcraft, see Levack, ed., *Oxford Handbook of Witchcraft*, especially part 2. Wolfgang Behringer, *Witches and Witch-Hunts:*

a Global History (Cambridge: Polity, 2004). Behringer believes the 50,000 figure is a minimum that could grow by as much as 20% depending on future work in regions not yet studied (see 149–51). See also Brian Levack, *The Witch-Hunt in Early Modern Europe* (London: Longman, 1987), 21–26.

8. Behringer, *Witches and Witch-Hunts*, 151, 186–90, 209–28; István Petrovic, "A Witch-Hunt in Szeged in the Early Eighteenth Century," in Blanka Szeghyová, ed., *The Role of Magic in the Past: Learned and Popular Magic, Popular Beliefs and Diversity of Attitudes* (Bratislava: Pro Historia, 2005), 108–16.

9. Miller, *The New England Mind: From Colony to Providence*, 191.

10. Emerson Baker and John Reid, *The New England Knight: Sir William Phips, 1651–1692* (Toronto: University of Toronto Press, 1998), 95–106. The twenty-five victims include nineteen executed, one pressed to death, and five who died in prison (Sarah Osburn, Roger Toothaker, Ann Foster, Lydia Dustin, and Sarah Good's infant. For Sarah's infant, see the 1710 "Petition of William Good for Restitution for Sarah Good, Dorothy Good, and Infant," Rosenthal, ed., *Salem Witch-Hunt*, 871 #907.

11. For Mayflower descendants, see Alicia Crane Williams, "The Society of Mayflower Descendants: Who they are, where to find them, how to apply," *American Ancestors*, http://www.americanancestors.org/the-society-of-mayflower-descendants-pt1/ accessed September 25, 2013.

CHAPTER ONE

1. John Hale, *A Modest Inquiry in the Nature of Witchcraft* (Boston: B. Green and J. Allen, 1702), 167. This section of Hale's book is reprinted in George Lincoln Burr, ed., *Narratives of the New England Witchcraft Cases* (New York: Charles Scribner's Sons, 1914), 427. Note that Hale actually spells it "presidents," but he clearly means the word "precedents."

2. Paul Boyer and Stephen Nissenbaum, eds., *Salem-Village Witchcraft: A Documentary Record of Local Conflict in Colonial New England* (1972; reprint, Boston: Northeastern University Press, 1993), 278. This chapter relies on Marilynne K. Roach, *The Salem Witch Trials: A Day-by-Day Chronicle of a Community Under Siege* (New York: Cooper Square Press, 2002) and Bernard Rosenthal et al., eds., *Records of the Salem Witch-Hunt* (New York: Cambridge University Press, 2009). These important works have made major contributions to the understanding of the witch trials. In neighboring Andover, 22 percent of children born between 1670 and 1699 died before they reached the age of twenty years. See Philip J. Greven Jr., *Four Generations: Population, Land and Family in Colonial Andover, Massachusetts* (Ithaca: Cornell University Press, 1970), 108–9. Betty Parris's first name was Elizabeth. Her nickname will be used here to distinguish her from her mother, Elizabeth.

3. Although she was referred to as a "niece," Abigail's exact relationship to Samuel and Elizabeth Parris cannot be traced. In the seventeenth century the term was more inclusive than today, extending to a wide range of kin relationships. The exact date of the first affliction is unknown but appears to be soon after January 15. See Rosenthal et al., eds., *Salem Witch-Hunt*, 135. The quotes are from Hale, *A Modest Inquiry*, 24, reprinted in Burr, ed., *Narratives*, 413.

4. As Mary Beth Norton has pointed out, Parris's sermons on February 14 gave the impression that he was engaged in a direct confrontation with Satan: God was "sending

forth destroyers," but Jesus "will not suffer any of his sheep to be pluckt out of his hands." See Norton, *In the Devil's Snare: The Salem Witchcraft Crisis of 1692* (New York: W. W. Norton, 2002), 19; Samuel Parris, *The Sermon Notebook of Samuel Parris, 1689–1694*, ed. James Cooper and Kenneth Minkema (Boston: Colonial Society of Massachusetts, 1993), 190–92.

5. In his contemporary account, Reverend Parris mentions only John Indian making the cake, while Tituba is included by John Hale, writing in 1697. See Bernard Rosenthal, *Salem Story: Reading the Witch Trials of 1692* (New York: Cambridge University Press, 1995), 25–27; Hale, *A Modest Inquiry*, 25. For other examples of magical belief as well as countermagic, see Richard Godbeer, *The Devil's Dominion: Magic and Religion in Early New England* (New York: Cambridge University Press, 1992), 24–53.

6. "Records of the Salem-Village Church," in Boyer and Nissenbaum, eds., *Salem-Village Witchcraft*, 278.

7. The tradition that Tituba and the girls were engaged in fortune-telling is investigated and dismissed by Bernard Rosenthal and Mary Beth Norton. The only reference suggests that one of the older girls (not Betty or Abigail) did use fortune-telling to learn about her future husband, but there is no evidence of fortune-telling playing an important role in the outbreak. Rosenthal, *Salem Story*, 13–14; Norton, *In the Devil's Snare*, 23. For white magic, see Keith Thomas, *Religion and the Decline of Magic* (New York: Charles Scribner's Sons, 1971), 212–53, 637–39, and Richard Kieckhefer, *Magic in the Middle Ages* (New York: Cambridge University Press, 1989), 56–94.

8. Roach, *Salem Witch Trials*, 17, 19. Much work has been done by historians to establish the geography and location of homes in Salem Village, starting with a detailed map by Charles W. Upham in his *Salem Witchcraft, with an Account of Salem Village and a History of Opinions on Witchcraft and Kindred Spirits* (Boston: Wiggin and Lunt, 1867). In the 1910s, Sidney Perley published a string of articles in the *Essex Institute Historical Collections* where he exhaustively laid out the property boundaries and location of houses throughout Salem in 1700 (including Salem Village). Marilynne K. Roach's *A Time Traveler's Map of the Salem Witch Trials* (Watertown, MA: Sassafrass Grove Press, 1991) is a very useful source, drawn principally from Perley. For the most recent work on the geography of Salem Village, see Benjamin Ray's "The Geography of Witchcraft Accusations in 1692 Salem Village," *William and Mary Quarterly* 65, no. 3 (2008): 449–78. For the quote, see Hale, *A Modest Inquiry*, reprinted in Burr, ed., *Narratives*, 413.

9. Roach, *Salem Witch Trials*, 19–20; Hale, *A Modest Inquiry*, reprinted in Burr, ed., *Narratives*, 413–14; Paul Boyer and Stephen Nissenbaum, *Salem Possessed: The Social Origins of Witchcraft* (Cambridge, MA: Harvard University Press, 1974), 193–94; "Examination of Sarah Good, Sarah Osburn and Tituba," in Rosenthal et al., eds., *Salem Witch-Hunt*, 32, #5 (quote).

10. Roach, *Salem Witch Trials*, 21–23; "Warrant for the Apprehension of Sarah Osburn and Tituba, and Officer's Return," in Rosenthal et al., eds., *Salem Witch-Hunt*, 125–26 (quote).

11. "Examination of Sarah Good, Sarah Osburn and Tituba as Recorded by Ezekiel Cheever," and "Examination of Sarah Good, Sarah Osburn and Tituba as Recorded by John Hathorn," in Rosenthal et al., eds., *Salem Witch-Hunt*, 126–27 (quotes), 129–30; Roach, *Salem Witch*

Trials, 24–28. For a detailed look at witch hunt events during the pivotal month of March 1692, see Richard Trask, *"The Devil Hath Been Raised": A Documentary History of the Salem Village Witchcraft Outbreak of March 1692* (Danvers, MA: Yeoman Press, 1997).

12. There has been much written about Tituba's origins, though questions remain. All contemporary documents describe her as an "Indian," so she has New World origins. Elaine Breslaw believes she was likely from Guyana. See Breslaw, *Tituba, Reluctant Witch of Salem: Devilish Indians and Puritan Fantasies* (New York: New York University Press, 1996), 3–20. In this era, most English slaves held in New England were "Spanish Indians," captured in the Caribbean or coastal Florida. See Norton, *In the Devil's Snare*, 20–21, 334–35. While traditionally many believed she was African, the only recent scholar who supports this interpretation is Peter Hoffer in *The Devil's Disciples: Makers of the Salem Witch Trials* (Baltimore: Johns Hopkins University Press, 1996), 1–16, 205–10. For Tituba's testimony, see Roach, *Salem Witch Trials*, 28–29, and Rosenthal et al., eds., *Salem Witch-Hunt*, 128–35 (quote). For familiars, see James Sharpe, *Instruments of Darkness: Witchcraft in Early Modern England* (Philadelphia: University of Pennsylvania Press, 1997), 71–74.

13. For a good summary of Tituba's testimony, see Norton, *In the Devil's Snare*, 27–30; Rosenthal et al., eds., *Salem Witch-Hunt*, 128–35 (quotes on 134).

14. Brian Levack, *The Witch-Hunt in Early Modern Europe*, 2nd ed. (New York: Longman, 1995), 27–67; Carol Karlsen, *The Devil in the Shape of a Woman: Witchcraft in Colonial New England* (New York: Random House, 1987), 1–14; Alison Games, *Witchcraft in Early North America* (New York: Rowman and Littlefield, 2010), 7–18. For Parris's gift, see Larry Gragg, *A Quest for Security: The Life of Samuel Parris, 1653–1720* (Westport, CT: Greenwood Press, 1990), 116–17, 128–29.

15. Dorothy Good is erroneously called "Dorcas" in one court document and has subsequently been mistakenly called by that name. See "Warrant for the Arrest of Dorothy Good," in Rosenthal et al., eds., *Salem Witch-Hunt*, 153–54. For the difficulty in stereotyping witches, see Karlsen, *Devil in the Shape of a Woman*, 118–19; John Demos, *Entertaining Satan: Witchcraft and the Culture of Early New England* (New York: Oxford University Press, 1982), 57–94. The quote is from John Higginson, "An Epistle to the Reader," in Hale, *A Modest Inquiry*, reprinted in Burr, ed., *Narratives*, 400.

16. The figures are drawn from Godbeer, *Devil's Dominion*, 235–37.

17. Roach, *Salem Witch Trials*, 33–39. On Dorothy Good, see also Margo Burns and Bernard Rosenthal, "Examination of the Records of the Salem Witch Trials," *William and Mary Quarterly* 65 (2008): 416; "Warrant for the Arrest of Dorothy Good," in Rosenthal et al., eds., *Salem Witch-Hunt*, 153–54. For a detailed biography of Rebecca Nurse, see Marilynne K. Roach, *Six Women of Salem: The Untold Story of the Accused and Their Accusers in the Salem Witch Trials* (New York: Da Capo Press, 2013), 4–15.

18. Roach, *Salem Witch Trials*, 39–73; "George Herrick John Putnam, Jr. v. Mary Esty," in Rosenthal et al., eds., *Salem Witch-Hunt*, 302–3, #192 (quote).

19. "Testimony of Joseph Pope v. John Procter" and "Statement of Samuel Sibley v. John Procter, as Recorded by Samuel Parris," in Rosenthal et al., eds., *Salem Witch-Hunt*, 179, 538 (quotes).

20. Peter Hoffer in particular sees the hearings on April 11 as a turning point; see his *The Devil's Disciples*, 124–25. See also Samuel Sewall, *The Diary of Samuel Sewall, 1674–1729*, ed. M. Halsey Thomas (New York: Farrar, Straus and Giroux, 1973), 1:289 (quote).

21. Some accounts of the Hartford trials indicate that three were executed. However, the most recent account of the trials by Walter Woodward says that a fourth victim, Mary Sanford, was also executed. See Walter W. Woodward, *Prospero's America: John Winthrop, Jr., Alchemy, and the Creation of New England Culture, 1606–1676* (Williamsburg: Omohundro Institute of Early American History and Culture, 2010), 230–35; Karlsen, *Devil in the Shape of a Woman*, 24–28; Demos, *Entertaining Satan*, 340–55, 405.

22. David Green, "Salem Witches I: Bridget Bishop," *American Genealogist* 57, no. 3 (1981): 130–38; Robert Charles Anderson, "Bridget (Playfer) (Wasselbe) (Oliver) Bishop," *American Genealogist* 64 (1989): 207; Rosenthal et al., eds., *Salem Witch-Hunt*, 196–203 (the quote is on 196); Rosenthal, *Salem's Story*, 45–48; Hoffer, *Devil's Disciples*, 127–28; K. David Goss, *The Salem Witch Trials: A Reference Guide* (Westport, CT: Greenwood Press, 2008), 84–90; Roach, *The Salem Witch Trials*, 76–86.

23. "Examination of Abigail Hobbs," in Rosenthal et al., eds., *Salem Witch-Hunt*, 189–93 (the quote is on 189); Norton, *In the Devil's Snare*, 79–81, 118–19; Roach, *Salem Witch Trials*, 79–80, 84.

24. Norton, *In the Devil's Snare*, 118–19. For details on the Wabanaki and their early interaction with Europeans, see Emerson W. Baker et al., eds., *American Beginnings: Exploration, Culture and Cartography in the Land of Norumbega* (Lincoln: University of Nebraska Press, 1995).

25. For the importance of Hobbs's confession, see Norton, *In the Devil's Snare*, 79–81; "Deposition of Ann Putnam, Jr., v. George Burroughs," in Rosenthal et al., eds., *Salem Witch-Hunt*, 245–46, 505–6; Roach, *Salem Witch Trials*, 84–85, 11–15.

26. For the quote, see William H. Whitmore, ed., *John Dunton's Letters from New England* (Boston: Prince Society, 1867), 118–19. See also Roach, *Salem Witch Trials*, 118–19; Rosenthal, *Salem Witch-Hunt*, 631–32.

27. For the quote, see *Records of the Quarterly Courts of Essex County, Massachusetts*, 9 vols. (Salem: Essex Institute, 1911–1975), 8:335; see also Roach, *Salem Witch Trials*, 162. For prison conditions, see Juliet Haines Mofford, *"The Devil Made Me Do It": Crime and Punishment in Early New England* (Guilford, CT: Globe Pequot Press, 2012), 187–91; Larry Gragg, *The Salem Witch Crisis* (New York: Praeger, 1992), 125–40.

28. "Examination of Sarah Osburn," in Rosenthal et al., eds., *Salem Witch-Hunt*, 130 (quote).

29. John Willard and Philip English had fled prior to their arrest. Both would subsequently be taken into custody, but Philip and his wife, Mary (who was also charged), would flee to New York, where they stayed until after the trials came to an end in the spring of 1693. For Willard, see Goss, *Salem Witch Trials*, 105–6, and Boyer and Nissenbaum, *Salem Possessed*, 195–98. For English, see Bryan Le Beau, "Philip English and the Witchcraft Hysteria," *Historical Journal of Massachusetts* 15 (1987): 1–20.

30. Sewall, *Diary*, 1:288; Emerson Baker and John Reid, *The New England Knight: Sir William Phips, 1651-1695* (Toronto: University of Toronto Press, 1998), 144–45, 178–82.

31. Hoffer, *Devil's Disciples*, 135–36; David Konig, *Law and Society in Puritan Massachusetts: Essex County 1629-1692* (Chapel Hill: University of North Carolina Press, 1979), 170; "Order for the Establishment of a Special Commission of Oyer and Terminer," in Rosenthal et al., eds., *Salem Witch-Hunt*, 322 (quote).

32. Richard Dunn, *Puritans and Yankees: The Winthrop Dynasty, 1630-1717* (New York: W. W. Norton, 1971), 264; Norton, *In the Devil's Snare*, 197–99; Goss, *Salem Witch Trials*, 110–11; Gragg, *Salem Witch Crisis*, 86–87.

33. "Order for the Establishment of a Special Commission of Oyer and Terminer," in Rosenthal et al., eds., *Salem Witch-Hunt*, 322; Hoffer, *Devil's Disciples*, 133–35, 138; Norton, *In the Devil's Snare*, 239. For Leisler's Rebellion, see David S. Lovejoy, *The Glorious Revolution in America* (New York: Harper and Row, 1973), 354–58.

34. "Warrant for Jurors for the Court of Oyer and Terminer," in Rosenthal et al., eds., *Salem Witch-Hunt*, 332; Roach, *Salem Witch Trials*, 144; Richard B. Trask, "Legal Procedures Used During the Salem Witch Trials and a Brief History of the Published Versions of the Records," in Rosenthal et al., eds., *Salem Witch-Hunt*, 49–51. Freemen had to own property worth an annual income of forty shillings, or own property worth £50. Cornelius Dalton, John Wirkkala, and Anne Thomas, *Leading the Way: A History of the General Court, 1629-1980* (Boston: General Court, 1984), 37.

35. Norton, *In the Devil's Snare*, 199–201; Konig, *Law and Society in Puritan Massachusetts*, 171–73.

36. Hoffer, *Devil's Disciples*, 146–50, 180, 191; Norton, *In the Devil's Snare*, 166–67, 213–17, 226–27; Konig, *Law and Society in Puritan Massachusetts*, 171–72; Stuart Clark, *Thinking with Demons: The Idea of Witchcraft in Early Modern Europe* (New York: Oxford University Press, 1997), 151–56, 161–72.

37. Cotton Mather to Richards, May 31, 1692, in *Selected Letters of Cotton Mather*, ed. Kenneth Silverman (Baton Rouge: Louisiana State University Press, 1971), 35–40 (quote); Norton, *In the Devil's Snare*, 203.

38. Roach, *Salem Witch Trials*, 139–45. Elizabeth Cary, wife of Captain Nathaniel Cary, a wealthy Charlestown ship captain, was accused on May 23.

39. Roach, *Salem Witch Trials*, 156–57; Boyer and Nissenbaum, eds., *Salem-Village Witchcraft*, 155–62; Goss, *Salem Witch Trials*, 85–86.

40. "Deposition of John Bly Sr., and Rebecca Bly v. Bridget Bishop," in Rosenthal et al., eds., *Salem Witch-Hunt*, 371 (quote); Roach, *Salem Witch Trials*, 156–60; Norton, *In the Devil's Snare*, 205–7, 210.

41. Thomas, *Religion and the Decline of Magic*, 437–38, 513–14; Godbeer, *Devil's Dominion*, 38–40.

42. "Physical Examinations No. 1 and No. 2 of Bridget Bishop, et al.," in Rosenthal et al., eds., *Salem Witch-Hunt*, 362–63 (quote).

43. "Warrant for the Execution of Bridget Bishop, and Officer's Return," in Rosenthal et al., eds., *Salem Witch-Hunt*, 394–95 (quote); Roach, *Salem Witch Trials*, 167–68 (quote). Hanging by the "long drop," which broke the neck and resulted in immediate death, was only developed in the nineteenth century. V. A. C. Gatrell, *The Hanging Tree: Execution and the English People: 1770–1868* (New York: Oxford University Press, 1994), 45–50; Madam van Muyden, ed. and trans., *A Foreign View of England in the Reigns of George I and George II: The Letters of Monsieur César de Saussure to His Family* (London: John Murray, 1902), 125. There is no mention of a gallows anywhere in the court records or contemporary descriptions of the Salem witch trials, and the term "Gallows Hill" was not used until long afterward.

44. Norton, *In the Devil's Snare*, 211; Roach, *Salem Witch Trials*, 166, 172. The exact date of Saltonstall's resignation is unclear, though Roach places it around June 8. It is also unclear exactly how quickly he privately expressed his concerns. Thomas Brattle noted them in his letter, but it was not written until October 8, 1692. See Thomas Brattle, "Letter of Thomas Brattle," in Burr, ed., *Narratives*, 184 (quote). Samuel Sewall mentions "some being afflicted by a person in your shape" in a letter to Saltonstall written before or on March 7, 1693; *Diary*, 1:305–6.

45. Roach, *Salem Witch Trials*, 171–72; Norton, *In the Devil's Snare*, 212–15; "Return of Several Ministers," in Boyer and Nissenbaum, eds., *Salem-Village Witchcraft*, 117–18 (quote).

46. "Petition of William Milborne," in Rosenthal et al., eds., *Salem Witch-Hunt*, 399 (quote).

47. "Order for the Arrest of William Milborne," in Rosenthal et al., eds., *Salem Witch-Hunt*, 399 (quote); Roach, *Salem Witch Trials*, 176; Carla Pestana, *Quakers and Baptists in Colonial Massachusetts* (New York: Cambridge University Press, 2004), 45–65. Phips and Milborne had been on friendlier terms in the past. In 1690 they had led a mob to the Boston prison, where they successfully demanded the release of two men (including Phips's half-brother) who were being held for what many believed to be an unjust debt. See Baker and Reid, *New England Knight*, 79–82.

48. Roach, *Salem Witch Trials*, 177–78; Norton, *Devil's Snare*, 219–21; "Deposition of Sarah Bibber v. Sarah Good," in Rosenthal et al., eds., *Salem Witch-Hunt*, 410 (quote).

49. Roach, *Salem Witch Trials*, 180–83; Norton, *Devil's Snare*, 221–23; Cotton Mather, "Wonders of the Invisible World," in Burr, ed., *Narratives*, 236 (quote); "Summary of Evidence vs. Sarah Good," in Rosenthal et al., eds., *Salem Witch-Hunt*, 416–18.

50. Roach, *Salem Witch Trials*, 183–84, 187. The grand jury indicted John Willard on June 3 as well. See Rosenthal et al., eds., *Salem Witch-Hunt*, 362–63, 364–67, 374–77, 380–85; Norton, *In the Devil's Snare*, 217–19. The reprieve is mentioned by Robert Calef, "More Wonders of the Invisible World," in Burr, ed., *Narratives*, 360. The timing of Phips's reprieve is unclear. It may have come earlier, after Nurse's indictment on June 3, rather than after her conviction. An earlier reprieve might explain the gap in time between her indictment and her trial. Richard D. Pierce, ed., *Records of the First Church in Salem, Massachusetts, 1629–1736* (Salem: Essex Institute, 1974), 172. For excommunication, see David C. Brown, "The Keys to the Kingdom: Excommunication in Colonial Massachusetts," *New England Quarterly* 67 (1994): 531–66.

51. Roach, *Salem Witch Trials*, 184–87, 201–2; Calef, "More Wonders," in Burr, ed., *Narratives*, 358 (quote). The author thanks Malcolm Gaskill for suggesting a search of the Bible for Good's last words.

52. For an excellent treatment of witchcraft in Connecticut in 1692, see Richard Godbeer, *Escaping Salem: The Other Witch Hunt of 1692* (New York: Oxford University Press, 2005). For Gloucester, see Roach, *Salem Witch Trials*, 195–98, 200, 212; Emerson Baker, *The Devil of Great Island: Witchcraft and Conflict in Early New England* (New York: Palgrave Macmillan, 2007), 178–79, 189–91.

53. Roach, *Salem Witch Trials*, 204–10; Larry Gragg, *Salem Witch Crisis*, 141–42. "Petition of John Procter from Prison," in Rosenthal et al., eds., *Salem Witch-Hunt*, 486 (quote); Chadwick Hansen, "Andover Witchcraft and the Causes of the Salem Witchcraft Trials," in Howard Kerr and Charles Crow, eds., *The Occult in America: New Historical Perspectives* (Urbana: University of Illinois Press, 1983), 40–53; Juliet Haines Mofford, *Andover, Massachusetts: Historical Selections from Four Centuries* (Andover, MA: Merrimack Valley Preservation Group, 2004), 20–38. For judicial torture, see Douglas McManus, *Law and Liberty in Early New England: Criminal Justice and Due Process, 1620–1692* (Amherst: University of Massachusetts Press, 2009), 108–9. See also Norton, *In the Devil's Snare*, 260–61. Newbury Falls presumably refers to the falls on the Parker River in the Byfield section of Newbury.

54. Mather, "Wonders," 241–44 (see 244 for the quote); Roach, *Salem Witch Trials*, 195, 220–21. Checkley would have been particularly well known to Richards, for on April 25, 1685, he sold land and buildings near the north meetinghouse in Boston (that is, the Mathers' and Richards' church) to Richards; *Suffolk Deeds* (Boston: Rockwell and Churchill Press), 13: 299. Margo Burns has determined, based on the hand that penned various documents, that in the absence of a crown attorney from June 30 to August 3, Stephen Sewall prepared the documents normally made by the crown attorney (personal communication, Margo Burns to Emerson Baker, November 13, 2013).

55. Roach, *Salem Witch Trials*, 222, 226–27; "Examination of George Jacobs," in Rosenthal et al., eds., *Salem Witch-Hunt*, 252 (quote); Rosenthal et al., eds., *Salem Witch-Hunt*, 524, 533–36. See Norton, *In the Devil's Snare*, 161–62, 244–45, for a discussion of admitting guilt to save one's life. On May 11, George Jacobs said that Margaret was told not to confess.

56. Mather, "Wonders," *Narratives*, 215–22; for the quote, see 216.

57. Mather, "Wonders," 215–22; for the quote, see 221.

58. Mather, "Wonders," 218, 221–22; for the quote, see 222.

59. Roach, *Salem Witch Trials*, 227–30; Increase Mather, *Cases of Conscience Concerning Evil Spirits* (Boston: Benjamin Harris, 1693), postscript (quote). Though it is dated 1693, it was actually printed in the fall of 1692.

60. Calef, "More Wonders," in Burr, ed., *Narratives*, 360–61 (quote); Norton, *In the Devil's Snare*, 256; Roach, *Salem Witch Trials*, 237, 242–43.

61. Calef, "More Wonders," in Burr, ed., *Narratives*, 361; Sewall, *Diary*, 1: 294 (quote).

62. For the quote, see "Will of John Procter, August 2, 1692," Essex County Probate Case #22851. Sidney Perley, "Where the Salem 'Witches' Were Hanged," *Essex Institute Historical Collections* 57 (1921): 14-16; Roach, *Salem Witch Trials*, 245.

63. Gragg, *Salem Witch Trials*, 149-50; Roach, *Salem Witch Trials*, 258; Norton, *In the Devil's Snare*, 305-7, 323-24.

64. Letter from R.P. to Jonathan Corwin, Salisbury, August 9, 1692, in Charles P. Upham, *Salem Witchcraft* (1867; reprint, Mineola, NY: Dover, 2000), 617-21, 697-705; the quote is on 700. Upham makes a very strong case for Robert Pike of Salisbury being the author. See also Norton, *In the Devil's Snare*, 266-69.

65. "Petition in Support of Mary Bradbury" and "Testimony of James Allen, Robert Pike and John Pike for Mary Bradbury," in Rosenthal et al., eds., *Salem Witch-Hunt*, 483-84, 603-4 (quote); Roach, *Salem Witch Trials*, 272-84; Norton, *In the Devil's Snare*, 272-74. For a brief biography of Thomas Bradbury, see Charles Banks, *History of York, Maine* (Boston: Calkins Press, 1931), 1:94-95.

66. Roach, *Salem Witch Trials*, 287-92.

67. Calef, "More Wonders," in Burr, ed., *Narratives*, 367 (quote); David C. Brown, "The Case of Giles Cory," *Essex Institute Historical Collections* 121 (1985): 282-99; Roach, *Salem Witch Trials*, 293, 296-97; McManus, *Law and Liberty*, 109-10; Pierce, ed., *Records of the First Church of Salem*, 173; "Records of the Salem-Village Church," 280.

68. Roach, *Salem Witch Trials*, 285, 295; Norton, *In the Devil's Snare*, 280.

69. Thomas, *Diary of Samuel Sewall*, 1:293 (quote); letter from Jacob Melyen to Dr. Johannes Kerfbij, July 11, 1692, in Evan Haefeli, "Dutch New York and the Salem Witch Trials: Some New Evidence," *Proceedings of the American Antiquarian Society* 110 (2000): 301-4; Larry Gragg, "The Port Royal Earthquake," *History Today* 50, no. 9 (2000): 28-34.

70. Norton, *In the Devil's Snare*, 260-622; Richard Latner, "The Long and Short of Salem Witchcraft: Chronology and Collective Violence in 1692," *Journal of Social History* 42 (2008): 138, 142-46. On October 2, 1692, John Locker of Sudbury posted a £100 bond as recognizance after having falsely accused Coronet William Brown of Sudbury of "the horrid crime of witchcraft." This document was sold at auction on April 7, 2014, just as this book was going to press. The author was only able to view it on line at www.bonhams.com/auctions/21962/lot/28/ though it seems very likely to be authentic. If so, it suggests the accusations may have spread considerably farther than once believed. The author thanks Margo Burns for bringing this document to his attention and for providing a transcript. Interestingly, Locker's wife, Sarah, allegedly slandered William Brown in 1697, supposedly calling him a "red headed devil or red headed rogue," so there was a history of hard words between these families. See "Testimony of Jonathan Rice and Elizabeth Rice, September 8, 1697," Middlesex County Court File Papers 1697-165-I, Massachusetts Archives.

71. Jeremy Belknap, ed., "Recantation of Confessors of Witchcraft," *Massachusetts Historical Society Collections* 13 (1815): 221-25; Roach, *Salem Witch Trials*, 308-9, 313; Stephen Foster, *The Long Argument: English Puritanism and the Shaping of New England Culture, 1570-1700* (Chapel Hill: University of North Carolina Press, 1991), 262-63.

72. Brattle, "Letter," in Burr, ed., *Narratives*, 169-90. Brattle signs his letter "T.B." Burr refers to Brattle as a member of the Royal Society, though his biographer says he never received this honor. See Rick Kennedy, "Thomas Brattle and the Scientific Provincialism of New England, 1680-1713," *New England Quarterly* 63 (1990): 593. See also Roach, *Salem Witch Trials*, 308-9, 313, 320-21. Though the book *Some Miscellany Observations on our Present Debates respecting Witchcrafts, in a Dialogue between S. and B. By P. E. and J. A.* (Philadelphia: William Bradford for Hezekiah Usher, 1692), was published anonymously, it clearly was written by Willard. For example, "P.E. and J.A." were the initials of Philip English and John Alden, who along with Hezekiah Usher were all members of Willard's church. See Burr, ed., *Narratives*, 187-88; Mary Rhinelander McCarl, "Spreading the News of Satan's Malignity," *Essex Institute Historical Collections* 129 (1993): 56-58.

73. See William Phips, "Letters of Governor Phips," in Burr, ed., *Narratives*, 197 (quote); Baker and Reid, *New England Knight*, 147-51, 153-55.

74. Sewall, *Diary*, 1:299 (quote). For Phips's relationship to Increase Mather, see Baker and Reid, *New England Knight*.

75. Norton, *In the Devil's Snare*, 290-91; Hoffer, *Devil's Disciples*, 188-89; David C. Brown, "The Forfeitures at Salem, 1692," *William and Mary Quarterly* 50 (1993): 109-10. The one difference is that the Massachusetts law allowed seizure of property of the hanged. This presumably was to legitimize the seizures already made during the Salem trials by Sheriff George Corwin.

76. Phips, "Letters," in Burr, ed., *Narratives*, 200.

77. Roach, *Salem Witch Trials*, 360; Calef, "More Wonders," in Burr, ed., *Narratives*, 382 (quote); Phips, "Letters," in Burr, ed., *Narratives*, 201.

78. Roach, *Salem Witch Trials*, 361-66; Gragg, *Salem Witch Crisis*, 182-83. On February 21, 1693, Phips wrote in a letter to William Blathwayt, the clerk of the Privy Council, that he had pardoned five people previously convicted by the Court of Oyer and Terminer, though he does not name the individuals. The identity of four of them is clear: Mary Lacey Sr., Abigail Hobbs, Rebecca Eames, and Dorcas Hoar. The fifth was presumably Elizabeth Procter, who gave birth to a son on January 27. After this time she would have been eligible to be executed, if not pardoned. In a letter drafted by the Earl of Nottingham, Queen Mary would confirm Phips's reprieve in early summer. "Phips to Blathwayt," in Burr, ed., *Narratives*, 201.

79. Calef, "More Wonders," in Burr, ed., *Narratives*, 382 (quote).

80. *A further Account of the Tryals* (London, 1693), 10 (quote).

81. Roach, *Salem Witch Trials*, 374-77, 388, 398, 401-3; *A further Account of the Tryals*, 10; Breslaw, *Tituba*, 174-75, 374-77, 388, 398, 401-3.

CHAPTER TWO

1. Cotton Mather, *Wonders of the Invisible World* (Boston: Benjamin Harris, 1693), front matter.

2. John Winthrop, "A Model of Christian Charity," *Collections of the Massachusetts Historical Society*, 3rd ser., no. 7 (1838): 47. A copy of Winthrop's sermon was rediscovered

by scholars and first printed in 1838. For the most recent scholarship on it, see Abram Van Engen, "Origins and Last Farewells: Bible Wars, Textual Form, and the Making of American History," *New England Quarterly* 86 (2013): 543–92.

3. For literacy rates, see Kenneth A. Lockridge, *Literacy in Colonial New England: An Inquiry into the Social Context of Literacy in the Early Modern West* (New York: W. W. Norton, 1974).

4. As Michael Winship has demonstrated, "Antinomian Controversy" is an inaccurate label; however, since it is so widely employed, it will be used here. Winship, *Making Heretics: Militant Protestantism and Free Grace in Massachusetts, 1636–1641* (Princeton, NJ: Princeton University Press, 2002), 1–27; Richard Archer, *Fissures in the Rock: New England in the Seventeenth Century* (Hanover, NH: University Press of New England), 27–52; Louis Breen, *Transgressing the Bounds: Subversive Enterprises Among the Puritan Elite in Massachusetts, 1630–1692* (New York: Oxford University Press, 2001), 10, 17–56.

5. Edward Winslow, *Good Newes from New-England: or a True Relation of Things Very Remarkable at the Plantation of Plimoth in New-England* (London, 1624), 64 (quote); Stephen Innes, *Creating Commonwealth: The Economic Culture of Puritan New England* (New York: W. W. Norton, 1995), 271–307.

6. Innes, *Creating the Commonwealth*, 271–305; John J. McCusker and Russell R. Menard, *The Economy of British America, 1607–1789* (Chapel Hill: University of North Carolina Press, 1985), 91–106; Richard S. Dunn, *Sugar and Slaves: The Rise of the Planter Class in the English West Indies, 1624–1713* (New York: W. W. Norton, 1973), 207, 210–11.

7. Charles F. Carroll, *The Timber Economy of Puritan New England* (Providence, RI: Brown University Press, 1973). The earliest reference to shipping frames from the English colonies to the Caribbean is from New York in 1669; see W. Noel Sainsbury, ed., *Calendar of State Papers, Colonial Series, America and the West Indies* (London: Her Majesty's Stationery Office, 1889), 7:16. The author thanks Thomas Hardiman for this reference.

8. Bernard Bailyn, *New England Merchants in the Seventeenth Century* (Cambridge, MA: Harvard University Press, 1955), 45–111; Charles Clark, *The Eastern Frontier: The Settlement of Northern New England, 1610–1763* (Hanover, NH: University Press of New England, 1970), 36–52; Carroll, *Timber Economy*, 80–84.

9. The key proponent of declension was Perry Miller. See his *The New England Mind: From Colony to Province* (Cambridge, MA: Belknap Press, 1953), 20–146. See also Stephen Foster, *The Long Argument: English Puritanism and the Shaping of New England Culture, 1570–1700* (Chapel Hill: University of North Carolina Press,, 1991), xiii, 213–25; Alan Taylor, *American Colonies: The Settlement of North America* (New York: Viking Penguin, 2001), 179–80.

10. Miller, *New England Mind*, 93–106; Janice Knight, *Orthodoxies in Massachusetts: Rereading American Puritanism* (Cambridge, MA: Harvard University Press, 1994), 184–88; Foster, *Long Argument*, 198–203.

11. Miller, *New England Mind*, 27–39; Foster, *Long Argument*, 214–16; Richard Gildrie, *The Profane, the Civil and the Godly: The Reformation of Manners in Orthodox New England, 1679–1749* (University Park: Pennsylvania State University Press, 1994), 20–22.

12. Foster, *Long Argument*, 216; William Stoughton, *New-Englands True Interest; Not to Lie* (Cambridge: Printed by S.G. and M.J., 1670), 34, 40 (quotes).

13. Foster, *Long Argument*, 219–20; Increase Mather, *The Day of Trouble Is Near* (Cambridge, MA: Marmaduke Johnson, 1674), 24 (quote). Note that italics are used in the original text.

14. The literature on King Philips's War is extensive. Recent works include James Drake, *King Philip's War: Civil War in New England, 1675–1676* (Amherst: University of Massachusetts Press, 1999), 2–6, 168–69; Daniel R. Mandell, *King Philip's War: Colonial Expansion, Native Resistance, and the End of Indian Sovereignty* (Baltimore: Johns Hopkins University Press, 2012); Jill Lepore, *The Name of War: King Philip's War and the Origins of American Identity* (New York: Alfred A. Knopf, 1998); Jenny Hale Pulsipher, *Subjects unto the Same King: Indians, English and the Contest for Authority in Colonial New England* (Philadelphia: University of Pennsylvania Press, 2005), 205, 236–27. Drake sees the conflict in northern New England as a separate war, while Pulsipher views it as a continuation of the southern conflict.

15. Kyle Zelner, *A Rabble in Arms: Massachusetts Towns and Militiamen During King Philip's War* (New York: New York University Press), 17, 201–204; Emerson Baker, "Salem as Frontier Outpost," in Dane Morrison and Nancy Schultz, eds., *Salem: Place, Myth and Memory* (Boston: Northeastern University Press, 2004), 33–34. For connections between King Philip's War and the witch trials, see James E. Kences, "Some Unexplored Relationships of Essex County Witchcraft to the Indian Wars of 1675 and 1689," *Essex Institute Historical Collections* 120 (1984): 179–212.

16. Zelner, *A Rabble in Arms*, 184–86; James Axtell, "The Vengeful Women of Marblehead: Robert Roule's Deposition of 1677," *William and Mary Quarterly* 31, no. 4 (October 1974): 647–52 (quote); Sumner Hunnewell, "'A Doleful Slaughter Near Black Point': The Battle at Moore's Brook, Scarborough, Maine, June 29, 1677," *Maine Genealogist*, May-August 2003 (online version available at www.hampton.lib.nh.us/hampton/history/military/moores-brook.htm); Mary Beth Norton, *In the Devil's Snare: The Salem Witchcraft Crisis of 1692* (New York: W. W. Norton, 2002), 92–93.

17. Cotton Mather, *Magnalia Christi Americana or the Ecclesiastical History of New England* (New York: Russell and Russell, 1967): 2:583 (quote); Emerson Baker, "Trouble to the Eastward: The Failure of Anglo-Indian Relations in Early Maine," PhD dissertation, College of William and Mary, 1986, 221–30; Emerson Baker and John Reid, "Amerindian Power in the Early Northeast: A Reappraisal," *William and Mary Quarterly* 61 (2004): 85–89, 98–104.

18. Gildrie, *The Profane, the Civil and the Godly*, 19–40.

19. Foster, *Long Argument*, 227–30.

20. Emerson Baker, *The Devil of Great Island: Witchcraft and Conflict in Early New England* (New York: Palgrave Macmillan, 2007), 125–48; Charles Levi Woodbury, "Captain John Mason's Patent of Mariana," in John Ward, ed., *Captain John Mason* (Boston: Publications of the Prince Society, 1887), 45–52: Nathaniel Bradstreet Shurtleff, *Records of the Governor and Company of Massachusetts Bay* (Boston: William White, 1854), 5:335–36; See also James Duncan Phillips, *Salem in the Seventeenth Century* (Boston: Houghton and Mifflin, 1933), 31, 102, 271.

21. David Lovejoy, *The Glorious Revolution in America* (New York: Harper and Row, 1972), 122–59; Pulsipher, *Subjects unto the Same King*, 238–52; Cornelius Dalton, John Wirkkala, and Anne Thomas, *Leading the Way: A History of the General Court, 1629-1980* (Boston: General Court, 1984), 9–16.

22. Lovejoy, *Glorious Revolution*, 179–219.

23. Lovejoy, *Glorious Revolution*, 191–95; Gildrie, *The Profane, the Civil and the Godly*, 187–90.

24. Lovejoy, *Glorious Revolution*, 182; Samuel Sewall, *The Diary of Samuel Sewall, 1674-1729*, ed. M. Halsey Thomas (New York: Farrar, Straus and Giroux, 1973), 1:119; Thomas Waters, *Ipswich in the Massachusetts Bay Colony* (Ipswich: Ipswich Historical Society, 1917), 1:236–37.

25. Waters, *Ipswich in Massachusetts Bay*, 1:246, 257 (the quote is on 246); Lovejoy, *Glorious Revolution*, 182–84; J. W. Fortescue, ed., *Calendar of State Papers, Colonial Series, America and the West Indies* (London: Her Majesty's Stationery Office, 1899), 12:473–74. This and the following two paragraphs draw heavily upon Waters, who provides the most detailed description of the tax revolt. It is unclear why Ipswich took the lead in opposition to the policies of the Dominion.

26. Waters, *Ipswich in Massachusetts Bay*, 1:250–54; Lovejoy, *Glorious Revolution*, 184; John L. Sibley, *Biographical Sketches of the Graduates of Harvard University* (Cambridge, MA: Charles William Sever, 1881), 2:1–8; George Bodge, *Soldiers in King Philip's War* (Baltimore: Genealogical Publishing, 1898), 142–58.

27. Lovejoy, *Glorious Revolution*, 188–89; Mather, *Magnalia Christi Americana*, 1:161 (quote); David Konig, *Law and Society in Puritan Massachusetts: Essex County, 1629-1692* (Chapel Hill: University of North Carolina Press, 1979), 162–65, 117–30, 187–91. Konig's is an important book, with key insights on the witch trials. A theme of the book is the importance of the legal system in resolving conflict and maintaining social order.

28. Sidney Perley, *The Indian Land Titles of Essex County, Massachusetts* (Salem: Essex Book and Print Club, 1912), 62–91; Baker, "Salem as Frontier Outpost," 34–35; Lovejoy, *Glorious Revolution*, 186–87, 197; William H. Whitmore, ed., *The Andros Tracts* (Boston: Prince Society, 1868), 1:91–92 (quote).

29. Richard Johnson, *Adjustment to Empire: The New England Colonies, 1675-1715* (New Brunswick, NJ: Rutgers University Press, 1981), 84–85; Whitmore, ed., *Andros Tracts*, 1:90 (quote).

30. John Martin, *Profits in the Wilderness: Entrepreneurship and the Founding of New England Towns in the Seventeenth Century* (Chapel Hill: University of North Carolina Press, 1991), 264–67.

31. Lovejoy, *Glorious Revolution*, 190–91; Michael G. Hall, *Edward Randolph and the American Colonies, 1676-1703* (New York: W. W. Norton, 1960), 100–101, 111; Edward Randolph to the Governor of Barbados, May 16, 1689, in Robert Noxon Toppan, ed., *Edward Randolph* (Boston: Prince Society, 1999), 4:266 (quote).

32. Karen Kupperman, "Climate and Mastery of the Wilderness," in David D. Hall, David G. Allen, and Philip Smith, eds., *Seventeenth-Century New England* (Boston: Colonial

Society of Massachusetts, 1984), 25–35; David Allen, *In English Ways: The Movement of Societies and the Transferal of English Local Law and Custom to Massachusetts Bay in the Seventeenth Century* (Chapel Hill: University of North Carolina Press, 1981), 228–29; Carroll, *Timber Economy*, 93; Thomas L. Purvis, *Colonial America to 1763: Almanacs of American Life* (New York: Facts on File, 1999), 1–3. For the impact of the Little Ice Age and economic conditions, see Wolfgang Behringer, *Witches and Witch-Hunts: A Global History* (Cambridge: Polity, 2004), 56–59, 84–89; Emily Oster, "Witchcraft, Weather and Economic Growth in Renaissance Europe," *Journal of Economic Perspectives* 18 (2004): 215–28.

33. Pulsipher, *Subjects unto the Same King*, 254. This and the following paragraphs rely heavily on Jenny Pulsipher's excellent analysis.

34. Pulsipher, *Subjects unto the Same King*, 254–56; Johnson, *Adjustment to Empire*, 84–85.

35. The French trader Baron St. Castin accompanied the Wabanaki on the raid. For Pemaquid, see Neill De Paoli, "Life on the Edge: Community and Trade on the Anglo-American Periphery, Pemaquid, Maine, 1610–1689," Ph.D. dissertation, University of New Hampshire, 2001, 255–59; Pulsipher, *Subjects unto the Same King*, 256.

36. "By the governour & General Court of the colony of the Massachusetts Bay, in New-England, March 13, 1690," in Robert Moody and Richard Simmons, eds., *The Glorious Revolution in Massachusetts* (Boston: Colonial Society of Massachusetts, 1988), 218–21 (quote).

37. Baker, *Devil of Great Island*, 192–93.

38. Baker and Reid, *New England Knight*, 86–93; the quote is from a letter by Thomas Newton, Public Record Office, London, CO5/1081, no. 138.

39. Baker and Reid, *New England Knight*, 95–109.

40. Baker and Reid, *New England Knight*, 95–96; Konig, *Law and Society in Puritan Massachusetts*, 166; Moody and Simmons, *Glorious Revolution in Massachusetts*, 268 (quote).

41. Emerson Baker and James Kences, "Maine, Indian Land Speculation, and the Essex County Witchcraft Outbreak of 1692," *Maine History* 40 (2001): 170–75; "Falmouth House Lots, March 26, 1688," in James P. Baxter, ed., *Documentary History of the State of Maine* (Portland, ME: Thurston Print, 1897), 6:385.

42. For a list of people with Maine ties, see Norton, *In the Devil's Snare*, 319–20. The literature on ties between Salem witchcraft and the frontier is extensive, beginning with Kences, "Some Unexplored Relationships." The most through treatment is Norton, *In the Devil's Snare*. For a brief historiography, see Baker and Kences, "Maine, Indian Land Speculation," 161, 183 n. 5.

43. David Cressy, *Bonfires and Bells: National Memory and the Protestant Calendar in Elizabethan and Stuart England* (Berkeley: University of California Press, 1989), 141–55; Baker, *Devil of Great Island*, 157–58.

44. Konig, *Law and Society in Puritan Massachusetts*, 167; David Konig, "A New Look at the Essex 'French': Ethnic Friction and Community Tensions in Seventeenth-Century Essex County, Massachusetts," *Essex Institute Historical Collections* 119 (1974): 179–81.

45. Lovejoy, *Glorious Revolution*, 244–45; Baker and Reid, *New England Knight*, 75–78.

46. T. H. Breen, *Puritans and Adventurers: Persistence and Change in Early America* (New York: Oxford University Press, 1980), 87–90; Simon Bradstreet to Edward Randolph, December 8, 1684, *Collections of the Massachusetts Historical Society* 8 (1868): 532–33 (quote).

47. Breen, *Puritans and Adventurers*, 95–102.

48. Baxter, ed., *Documentary History*, 5:108–9, 116, 154–55 (the quote is on 155).

49. Baxter, ed., *Documentary History*, 5:172–73.

50. Moody and Simmons, *Glorious Revolution in Massachusetts*, 303; Baxter, ed., *Documentary History*, 5:232–35.

51. Benjamin Davis to Francis Nicholson, April 17, 1691, quoted in Breen, *Puritans and Adventurers*, 104–105.

52. Cotton Mather, "Preparatory Meditations upon the Day of Judgment," in Samuel Lee, *A Summons or Warning to the Great Day of Judgment* (Boston: Bartholomew Green, 1692), 36.

53. Baker and Reid, *New England Knight*, 110–21; Lovejoy, *Glorious Revolution*, 340–47.

54. Konig, *Law and Society in Puritan Massachusetts*, 162–64, 169–70, 178–80; Baker and Reid, *New England Knight*, 182–83.

55. On the need to rewrite the laws of the colony, see Baker and Reid, *New England Knight*, 182.

CHAPTER THREE

1. Samuel Parris, *The Sermon Notebook of Samuel Parris, 1689–1694*, ed. James F. Cooper Jr. and Kenneth P. Minkema (Boston: Colonial Society of Massachusetts, 1993), 170.

2. The best histories of early Salem are Sidney Perley, *History of Salem, Massachusetts*, 3 vols. (Salem: Published by the author, 1924–28); Richard Gildrie, *Salem, Massachusetts, 1626-1683: A Covenant Community* (Charlottesville: University of Virginia Press, 1975); James Duncan Phillips, *Salem in the Seventeenth Century* (Boston: Houghton and Mifflin, 1933). For the Native American presence in Salem, see Emerson Baker, "Salem as Frontier Outpost," in Dane Morrison and Nancy Schultz, eds., *Salem: Place, Myth and Memory* (Boston: Northeastern University Press, 2004), 21–40.

3. The most comprehensive study of English regionalisms and their transfer to America is David Hackett Fischer, *Albion's Seed: Four British Folkways in America* (New York: Oxford University Press, 1989). For a study of this process in Massachusetts, see David Grayson Allen, *In English Ways: The Movement of Societies and the Transferal of English Local Laws and Custom in Massachusetts Bay in the Seventeenth Century* (Chapel Hill: University of North Carolina Press, 1981). For regional differences in religious belief, see Cedric Cowing, *The Saving Remnant: Religion and the Settling of New England* (Urbana: University of Illinois Press, 1995), 68–90.

4. Perley, *History of Salem*, 1:316–17. Wenham was detached in 1643, Manchester in 1645, Marblehead in 1648, Beverly in 1668, and Danvers in 1752. See Phillips, *Salem in the Seventeenth Century*, 150.

5. Gildrie, *Salem*, 63-67; Perley, *History of Salem*, 1:313-17; Phillips, *Salem in the Seventeenth Century*, 171-87.

6. Edward T. Price, *Dividing the Land: Early American Beginnings of Our Private Property Mosaic* (Chicago: University of Chicago Press, 1995), 29-48; Roger Thompson, *Divided We Stand: Watertown, Massachusetts, 1630-1682* (Amherst: University of Massachusetts Press, 2001), 51-63; Allen, *In English Ways*, 121-31.

7. Gildrie, *Salem*, 65-68. For farming in the West Country, see Joan Thirsk and H. P. R. Finburg, eds., *The Agrarian History of England and Wales*, vol. 4, *1500-1640* (Cambridge: Cambridge University Press, 1967), 64-80.

8. Gildrie, *Salem*, 68-69; Phillips, *Salem in the Seventeenth Century*, 145. For Marblehead, see Christine Leigh Heyrman, *Commerce and Culture: The Maritime Communities of Colonial Massachusetts, 1690-1750* (New York: W. W. Norton, 1984), 209-30; Daniel Vickers, *Farmers and Fishermen: Two Centuries of Work in Essex County, Massachusetts, 1630-1850* (Chapel Hill: University of North Carolina Press, 1994), 129-41.

9. Gildrie, *Salem*, 67; Perley, *History of Salem*, 1:421, 2:18-19, 294-98. Hathorne lived on a large tract at Hathorne's Hill (later known as Asylum Hill or Putnam Hill). Sidney Perley, "Hathorne: Part of Salem in 1700," *Essex Institute Historical Collections* 53 (1917): 338-39.

10. Perley, *History of Salem*, 2:25-27; H. A. MacPherson, *A History of Fowling* (Edinburgh: David Douglas, 1897), 251-55.

11. Perley, *History of Salem*, 2:19-25; Sidney Perley, "Endicott Lands: Part of Salem in 1700," *Essex Institute Historical Collections* 51 (1915): 361-82; Perley, "Hathorne," 332-44. The Nurse farmstead was part of a three-hundred-acre grant given to Townsend Bishop in 1636 and later purchased by Governor Endicott and passed to his son. Thorndike Procter finally purchased the Downing farm from Emmanuel Downing's grandson in 1700.

12. Gildrie, *Salem*, 120-21; Sidney Perley, "Center of Salem Village in 1700," *Essex Institute Historical Collections* 54 (1918): 225-45; Paul Boyer and Stephen Nissenbaum, *Salem Possessed: The Social Origins of Witchcraft* (Cambridge, MA: Harvard University Press, 1974), 110-23. For the evolving economy of Salem and Massachusetts, see Vickers, *Farmers and Fishermen*; Stephen Innes, *Creating Commonwealth: The Economic Culture of Puritan New England* (New York: W. W. Norton, 1995); and Phyllis Whitman Hunter, *Purchasing Identity in the Atlantic World: Massachusetts Merchants, 1670-1780* (Ithaca, NY: Cornell University Press, 2001), 37-44.

13. Gildrie, *Salem*, 119-21; Boyer and Nissenbaum, *Salem Possessed*, 110-30.

14. Jonathan Chu, *Neighbors, Friends or Madmen: The Puritan Adjustment to Quakerism in Seventeenth-Century Massachusetts Bay* (Westport, CT: Greenwood Press, 1985), 125-52; Sidney Perley, "The Woods, Salem in 1700," *Essex Institute Historical Collections* 51 (1915): 177-96; Gildrie, *Salem*, 130-37.

15. Kenneth A. Lockridge, *A New England Town the First Hundred Years: Dedham, Massachusetts, 1636-1736* (New York: W. W. Norton, 1970), 93-103.

16. Perley, *History of Salem*, 2:406-11; Edwin Stone, *History of Beverly* (Boston: James Munroe, 1843), 15; John Langdon Sibley, *Biographical Sketches of Graduates of Harvard University* (Cambridge, MA: Charles Sever, 1881), 2:509.

17. For data on early Massachusetts, see Allen, *In English Ways*, 234.

18. The conflict between Salem Town and Salem Farms/Salem Village is a central argument of Boyer and Nissenbaum, *Salem Possessed*, 39–42; see also Paul Boyer and Stephen Nissenbaum, eds., *Salem-Village Witchcraft: A Documentary Record of Local Conflict in Colonial New England* (1972; reprint, Boston: Northeastern University Press, 1993), 229–34.

19. Boyer and Nissenbaum, *Salem Possessed*, 41–43; Boyer and Nissenbaum, eds., *Salem-Village Witchcraft*, 234. The following pages detailing the growth of factionalism rely heavily on *Salem Possessed*, as well as the primary documents relating to that factionalism that Boyer and Nissenbaum published in *Salem-Village Witchcraft*.

20. Boyer and Nissenbaum, *Salem Possessed*. In 2008, the *William and Mary Quarterly* published the forum "Salem Repossessed," which was dedicated to *Salem Possessed*. Included in the forum was an article by Boyer and Nissenbaum that neatly summarizes the themes of the book, provides details on its development, and also addresses some recent criticisms. See Paul Boyer and Stephen Nissenbaum, *"Salem Possessed* in Retrospect," *William and Mary Quarterly* 65 (2008): 503–34.

21. Boyer and Nissenbaum, *Salem-Village Witchcraft*, 314: Peter Benes, *Meetinghouses of Early New England* (Amherst: University of Massachusetts Press, 2012), 62–74.

22. Boyer and Nissenbaum, *Salem Possessed*, 51–52. Boyer and Nissenbaum cite the example of Newton. They see the key difference between Salem and Newton to be related to economics. Salem Village's factionalism is an outgrowth of the rising commercialism of Salem Town, in contrast to Cambridge and Newton, which were similar agrarian communities. See also Sibley, *Graduates of Harvard*, 2:267–71. Rowley's dispute with Shepard is recorded in Patricia Trainor O'Malley, "Rowley, Massachusetts, 1639–1730: Dissent, Division and Delimitation in a Colonial Town," Ph.D. dissertation, Boston College, 1975, 61–98; the quotes are drawn from O'Malley. Laurel Ulrich has suggested that Shepard's problems may have stemmed from his inability to deal with female members of his congregation. See her *Good Wives: Image and Reality in the Lives of Women in Northern New England, 1650–1750* (New York: Alfred A. Knopf, 1982), 220–21.

23. O'Malley, "Rowley," 92–98; Sibley, *Graduates of Harvard*, 2:268–71, 428–41.

24. Although Philip Greven's classic study, grounded in historical demography, described Andover as a stable and relatively peaceful community, more recently Elinor Abbot has revealed a town with many factions and tensions. Philip Greven, *Four Generations: Land, Population and Family in Andover, Massachusetts* (Ithaca, NY: Cornell University Press, 1970); Elinor Abbot, *Our Company Increases Apace: History, Language, and Social Identity in Early Colonial Andover, Massachusetts* (Dallas: SIL International, 2007), in particular 129–49 for the divisions of the 1680s. Abbot notes that the Dane family may have had Scottish roots as well.

25. Boyer and Nissenbaum, *Salem Possessed*, 42–46; Boyer and Nissenbaum, eds., *Salem-Village Witchcraft*, 315.

26. Boyer and Nissenbaum, *Salem Possessed*, 45–50, 53–54; Sibley, *Biographical Sketches*, 2:293–95.

27. Boyer and Nissenbaum, *Salem Possessed*, 54: Mary Beth Norton, *In the Devil's Snare: The Salem Witchcraft Crisis of 1692* (New York: W. W. Norton, 2002), 123–25; Boyer and Nissenbaum, eds., *Salem-Village Witchcraft*, 319–20.

28. Jeremiah Watts to the Reverend George Burroughs, April 11, 1682, in Boyer and Nissenbaum, eds., *Salem-Village Witchcraft*, 171 (quote); Boyer and Nissenbaum, *Salem Possessed*, 54–56.

29. *Records and Files of the Quarterly Courts of Essex County, Massachusetts*, 9 vols. (Salem: Essex Institute, 1911–1975) 8: 21–22; Boyer and Nissenbaum, *Salem Possessed*, 44–45.

30. *Quarterly Courts of Essex County* (1921) 8: 21–22, 319–23, 9: 168–69, 443; Boyer and Nissenbaum, eds., *Salem-Village Witchcraft*, 235–37.

31. Marilynne K. Roach, *The Salem Witch Trials: A Day-by-Day Chronicle of a Community under Siege* (New York: Cooper Square Press, 2002), xxxi–xxxiii; Charles Banks, *History of Martha's Vineyard, Dukes County, Massachusetts*, 3 vols. (Boston: George H. Dean, 1911), 2: 149–50; Boyer and Nissenbaum, *Salem Possessed*, 57–59.

32. "Letter of Advice to Salem Villagers, February, 1686/7," in Boyer and Nissenbaum, eds., *Salem-Village Witchcraft*, 344 (quote); Boyer and Nissenbaum, *Salem Possessed*, 57.

33. "Pro-Parris Petition (May 20, 1695)," in Boyer and Nissenbaum, eds., *Salem-Village Witchcraft*, 262 (quote); Boyer and Nissenbaum, *Salem Possessed*, 58–60. For the data on ministers from 1680 to 1689, see Larry Gragg, *A Quest for Security: The Life of Samuel Parris, 1653–1720* (New York: Greenwood Press, 1990), 33.

34. Gragg, *A Quest for Security*, 12–13, 30–31. Gragg's outstanding biography is the single most important source of information on Parris.

35. Relatively few documents survive relating to Parris's career in the Barbados in the 1670s. Larry Gragg has pulled the few documents together to give the best view of these admittedly shadowy years. See Gragg, *Quest for Security*, 30–32. See also Elaine Breslaw, *Tituba, Reluctant Witch of Salem: Devilish Indians and Puritan Fantasies* (New York: New York University Press, 1996), 27, 208. Breslaw has noted that the Parris plantation was functioning in 1679.

36. "Samuel Parris 'Mediations for Peace,'" in Boyer and Nissenbaum, eds., *Salem-Village Witchcraft*, 298 (quote); Gragg, *Quest for Security*, 32–35; Emerson Baker and John Reid, *The New England Knight: Sir William Phips, 1651–1695* (Toronto: University of Toronto Press, 1998).

37. Gragg, *Quest for Security*, 46–47.

38. Gragg, *Quest for Security*, 46–49; "Deposition by Samuel Parris (1697?)," in Boyer and Nissenbaum, eds., *Salem-Village Witchcraft*, 184 (quote).

39. Richard D. Pierce, ed., *The Records of the First Church in Salem, 1629–1736* (Salem: Essex Institute, 1974), 138–39; Boyer and Nissenbaum, eds., *Salem-Village Witchcraft*, 314–19; Sibley, *Biographical Sketches*, 2:512–13, 519–20; Roach, *Salem Witch Trials*, xxiii–xxix. These salaries are in "country pay," that is in harvested crops, livestock, and other goods. Silver coinage was in short supply, so it was actually worth more than its face value. For

example, when Joseph Capen was offered £75 in country pay or £20 in silver coin and £40 in country pay, he chose the latter.

40. Gragg. *Quest for Security*, 47–50.

41. Gragg, *Quest for Security*, 47–49.

42. The definitive work on early Massachusetts houses is Abbott Lowell Cummings, *The Framed Houses of Massachusetts Bay, 1625-1725* (Cambridge: Harvard University Press, 1982). For the parsonage, including information from the archaeological dig on the site, see Richard Trask, *The Devil Amongst Us: The Salem Village Parsonage* (Danvers: Danvers Historical Society, 1971). Excavations revealed the remains of a small lean-to, with a cellar measuring about a foot deep. Rooms used for dairying often had such shallow cellars, which helped to keep milk and cream cool. "Reverend Samuel Parris Parsonage: Field Notes by Roland Robbins, December 1 and 2, 1970," plan on file at the Danvers Archival Center; "Examinations of Sarah Good, Sarah Osburn, and Tituba, as Recorded by Joseph Putnam," in Bernard Rosenthal et al., eds., *Records of the Salem Witch-Hunt* (New York: Cambridge University Press, 2009), 132, #5 (quote).

43. Trask, *"The Devil Amongst Us"*; "Reverend Samuel Parris Parsonage: Field Notes." The author thanks Richard Trask for discussing details and sharing plans of excavation of his 1970 excavation of the Salem Village parsonage site.

44. For a discussion of other house forms and less durable housing, see Emerson Baker, "The Framed Houses of Northern New England: An Archaeologist's View," paper presented at the spring meeting of the New England Chapter of the Vernacular Architecture Forum, 2010; James Deetz and Patricia Scott Deetz, *The Times of Their Lives: Life, Love, and Death in Plymouth Colony* (New York: W. H. Freeman, 2000), 171–91, 254–56. Sill-on-grade construction continued well into the eighteenth century in New England; see Ross Harper, "'Their Houses Are Ancient and Ordinary': Archaeology and Connecticut's Eighteenth-Century Domestic Architecture," *Historical Archaeology* 46, no. 4 (2012): 8–47.

45. Archaeology suggests a walkway leading up to the lean-to depicted in Figure 4, so the lean-to could not have initially run the entire length of the building. Samuel Parris's successor in Salem Village, Reverend Joseph Green, noted in his diary on June 17, 1712, that work had been done on the frame of the lean-to, and the next month he "made a chimney in the cellar." This suggests the extension of the lean-to across the north side of the parsonage to create a kitchen—the most typical use of lean-tos. When Green died in 1715, his probate inventory mentions a kitchen in addition to the hall and parlor. "Diary of Reverend Joseph Green of Salem Village," ed. S. P. Fowler, *Essex Institute Historical Collections* 10 (1870): 96–97; "Inventory of the Estate of Joseph Green, July 25, 1715," Essex County Probate Case #11694.

46. K. David Goss, *Daily Life During the Salem Witch Trials* (Denver, CO: Greenwood Press, 2012), 51–74; Jane Nylander, *Our Own Snug Fireside: Images of the New England Home, 1760-1860* (New York: Alfred A. Knopf, 1994). Although it is focused on a later time period, Nylander's book does an excellent job of demonstrating how the reality of early New England domestic life was idealized and obscured by myth in the nineteenth century.

47. For an overview of Puritan society, including sober mirth, see Bruce Daniels, *Puritans at Play: Leisure and Recreation in Colonial New England* (New York: St. Martin's Press, 1995). The most exhaustive study of early Massachusetts material culture can be found in

Jonathan L. Fairbanks and Robert F. Trent, *New England Begins: The Seventeenth Century* (Boston: Museum of Fine Arts, 1982). See also Emerson Baker, "The Archaeology of 1690: Status and Material Life on New England's Northern Frontier," in Georgia Barnhill and Martha McNamera, eds., *New Views of New England: Studies in Material and Visual Culture, 1680–1830* (Boston: Colonial Society of Massachusetts, 2012), 1–16.

48. *The Probate Records of Essex County*, 3 vols. (Salem: Essex Institute, 1916–20), 3:111–15; Roach, *Salem Witch Trials*, xxxvii–xxxviii; Boyer and Nissenbaum, *Salem Possessed*, 110–11. The conflict between the Putnams and the Porters is a key point of *Salem Possessed*.

49. Larry Gragg, *The Salem Witch Crisis* (New York: Praeger, 1992), 33; Boyer and Nissenbaum, *Salem Possessed*, 110–32. Boyer and Nissenbaum stress the long-standing nature of the Putnam-Porter conflict, but the majority of the evidence for it comes from events after Samuel Parris's arrival in the village. See *Salem Possessed*, 110–32.

50. Parris, *Sermon Notebook*, 38–51 (the quotes are on 48 and 49); Gragg, *Quest for Security*, 49–51; Roach, *Salem Witch Trials*, xxxvii–xxxix.

51. Parris, *Sermon Notebook*, 42–51 (quotes).

52. Boyer and Nissenbaum, eds., *Salem-Village Witchcraft*, 268–69. Israel Porter and his wife had become members of the Salem Town Church on March 25, 1686 (a fast day proclaimed by the General Court); see Pierce, ed., *Records of the First Church*, 163.

53. For the list of delinquents, see Boyer and Nissenbaum, eds., *Salem-Village Witchcraft*, 349–51. Marilynne Roach has urged caution in reading too much into the high delinquency rate, for Topsfield and other towns had difficulties raising rates amid the political tumult of the overthrow of Governor Andros and the Glorious Revolution. See Roach, *Salem Witch Trials*, xxxix; T. H. Breen, *Puritans and Adventurers: Persistence and Change in Early America* (New York: Oxford University Press, 1980), 103–5. For the high rates imposed by the colony in 1691, see Robert Moody and Richard Simmons, eds., *The Glorious Revolution in Massachusetts* (Boston: Colonial Society of Massachusetts, 1988), 306–7, 313–14, 335, 337, 339, 343–44, 417.

54. Gragg, *Quest for Security*, 73–74; Gildrie, *Salem*, 143–45; Benjamin Ray, "Satan's War Against the Covenant in Salem Village, 1692," *New England Quarterly* 80 (2007): 143–45; Richard Latner, "'Here Are No Newters': Witchcraft and Religious Discord in Salem Village and Andover," *New England Quarterly* 79 (2006): 95–100. Both Ray and Latner have made important studies of the Salem Village church, its covenant, its membership, and its relationship to the Salem witch trials. This work has helped refocus scholars on the centrality of religion to witchcraft accusations.

55. Gragg, *Quest for Security*, 74–76; Gragg, *Salem Witch Crisis*, 37; Ray, "Satan's War," 76–77; Latner, "Here Are No Newters," 98–101.

56. Boyer and Nissenbaum, eds., *Salem-Village Witchcraft*, 273; Gragg, *Quest for Security*, 88–89. For early communion silver, see Mark A. Peterson, "Puritanism and Refinement in Early New England: Reflections on Communion Silver," *William and Mary Quarterly* 58 (2001): 307–46, especially 320.

57. Stephen Foster has pointed out that the Salem Village ministers had alternating views of the Halfway Covenant. See Stephen Foster, *The Long Argument: English Puritanism and*

the Shaping of New England Culture, 1570–1700 (Chapel Hill: University of North Carolina Press, 1991), 358–59.

58. Latner, "Here Are No Newters," 97.

59. Latner, "Here Are No Newters," 98–101; Parris, *Sermon Notebook*, 147–48 (quote).

60. Roach, *Salem Witch Trials*, xliii; Norton, *In the Devil's Snare*, 107–10; James P. Baxter, ed., *Documentary History of the State of Maine* (Portland, ME: Thurston Print, 1897), 5:188–89, 231–35.

61. Parris, *Sermon Notebook*, 163–64.

62. Parris, *Sermon Notebook*, 168 (quote); Ray, "Satan's War," 80.

63. Roach, *Salem Witch Trials*, xlv; Boyer and Nissenbaum, eds., *Salem-Village Witchcraft*, 350–51, 355–57; Boyer and Nissenbaum, *Salem Possessed*, 66; Gragg, *Quest for Security*, 87–88.

64. Boyer and Nissenbaum, eds., *Salem-Village Witchcraft*, 277–78; Gragg, *Quest for Security*, 95–96; Boyer and Nissenbaum, *Salem Possessed*, 157–59, 163–64.

65. Parris, *Sermon Notebook*, 170–71.

66. Boyer and Nissenbaum, eds., *Salem-Village Witchcraft*, 323, 349, 456; Gragg, *Quest for Security*, 97, 103.

67. Boyer and Nissenbaum, eds., *Salem-Village Witchcraft*, 264–65. Scholars disagree on the date of the meeting referred to in the 1697 deposition. Larry Gragg suggests it was in 1690; Gragg, *Quest for Security*, 94, 96–97. Marilyn Roach suggests it may have been the December 1, 1691, meeting; Roach, *Salem Witch Trials*, xlvi. It is easy to understand why Parris would fail to record such a contentious meeting, regardless of when it took place.

68. Boyer and Nissenbaum, "*Salem Possessed* in Retrospect," 520.

69. Boyer and Nissenbaum, *Salem Possessed*, 110–52; Latner, "Here Are No Newters," 93–94 (quote); Ray, "Satan's War."

70. Sibley, *Biographical Sketches*, 2:293–98.

71. Sibley, *Biographical Sketches*, 2:323–34.

72. Samuel Deane, *History of Scituate, Massachusetts* (Boston: James Loring, 1831), 195–96 (quote); Roach, *Salem Witch Trials*, xxxi.

73. Gragg suggests the figure was "well over 400," while Ray's figures put the number closer to 400. Gragg, *Quest for Security*, 89–90, 102; Ray, "Satan's War," 75.

CHAPTER FOUR

1. This apt quote is used to begin Robert Bartholomew and Simon Wessely, "Canada's 'Toxic Bus': The New Challenge for Law Enforcement in the Post-9/11 World/Mass Psychogenic Illness," *Canadian Journal of Criminology and Criminal Justice*, 2007, 657–58.

2. For the diverse nature of the accused, see Mary Beth Norton, *In the Devil's Snare: The Salem Witchcraft Crisis of 1692* (New York: W. W. Norton, 2002), 8–10.

3. Susan Dominus, "What Happened to the Girls in Le Roy," *New York Times Magazine*, March 7, 2012.

4. Dominus, "What Happened to the Girls in Le Roy" (quote); New York State Health Department, "Investigation of Neurologic Symptoms Among Le Roy Jr/Sr High School Students, October 2011–January 2012 Interim Report," January 31, 2012.

5. Dominus, "What Happened to the Girls in Le Roy"; New York State Health Department, "Investigation of Neurologic Symptoms."

6. Mary's father, Thomas Knowlton, would accuse Rachel Clinton of Ipswich of bewitching his daughter. She would face further accusations in 1692. See Bernard Rosenthal, "General Introduction," in Bernard Rosenthal et al., eds., *Records of the Salem Witch-Hunt* (New York: Cambridge University Press, 2009), 16; John Demos, *Entertaining Satan: Witchcraft and the Culture of Early New England* (New York: Oxford University Press, 1982), 19–35.

7. Paul Boyer and Stephen Nissenbaum, *Salem Possessed: The Social Origins of Witchcraft* (Cambridge, MA: Harvard University Press, 1974), 134–39. For Mary Walcott, see Norton, *In the Devil's Snare*, 54–55.

8. Rosenthal et al., eds., *Salem Witch-Hunt*, 253, 353 (quote on 353); Norton, *In the Devil's Snare*, 22, 48–50, 159; K. David Goss, *The Salem Witch Trials: A Reference Guide* (Westport, CT: Greenwood Press, 2008), 81–82, 84–85; Peter Hoffer, *The Devil's Disciples: Makers of the Salem Witch Trials* (Baltimore: Johns Hopkins University Press, 1996), 92–95.

9. Timothy F. Jones, "Mass Psychogenic Illness: Role of the Individual Physician," *American Family Physician* 62 (2000): 2649–53, available at www.aafp.org/afp/2000/1215/p2649.html.

10. Dominus, "What Happened to the Girls in Le Roy"; Timothy F. Jones et al., "Mass Psychogenic Illness Attributed to Toxic Exposure at a High School," *New England Journal of Medicine* 342 (2000): 96–100.

11. Robert Bartholomew and Simon Wessely, "Canada's 'Toxic Bus': The New Challenge for Law Enforcement in the Post-9/11 World/Mass Psychogenic Illness," *Canadian Journal of Criminology and Criminal Justice*, 2007, 657–58.

12. American Psychiatric Association, *Diagnostic and Statistical Manual of Mental Disorders*, 5th ed. (Arlington, VA: American Psychiatric Association, 2013), 301–9, 318–21. The *DSM-V* includes this under "Somatic Symptom and Related Disorders," with criteria including "evidence of incompatibility between symptom and recognized neurological or medical conditions." Jonathan W. Mink, "Conversion Disorder and Mass Psychogenic Illness in Child Neurology," *Annals of the New York Academy of Science* 1304 (2013): 40–44; Bartholomew and Wessely, "Canada's 'Toxic Bus,'" 657–71.

13. Norton, *In the Devil's Snare*, 305–6, 321–22.

14. For an excellent discussion of causation, see Rosenthal, "General Introduction," 25–32. For the quote, see "Deposition of Margaret Knight v. Abigail Hobbs," in Rosenthal et al. eds., *Salem Witch-Hunt*, 194. A comprehensive summary of the many different possible causes can be found in John Demos, *The Enemy Within: 2,000 Years of Witch-Hunting in the Western World* (New York: Viking, 2008), 189–215. For Abigail Hobbs, see Norton, *In the Devil's Snare*, 79–81.

15. For review of the extensive literature on Salem witchcraft and the frontier, see Emerson Baker and James Kences, "Maine, Indian Land Speculation, and the Essex County Witchcraft Outbreak of 1692," *Maine History* 40 (2001): 161, 183. For Mercy Short, see Cotton Mather, "A Brand Pluck'd out of the Burning," in George Lincoln Burr, ed., *Narratives of the New England Witchcraft Cases* (New York: Charles Scribner's Sons, 1914), 259–87; Norton, *In the Devil's Snare*, 176–81; Baker, *Devil of Great Island*, 189–91. Much has been written on Short relating to both witchcraft and captivity narratives. See, for example, Deborah Kloepfer, "Cotton Mather's 'Dora': The Case History of Mercy Short," *Early American Literature* 44 (2009): 3–38; Janice Knight, "'Telling it Slant': The Testimony of Mercy Short," *Early American Literature* 37 (2002): 39–69.

16. Mather, "A Brand Pluck'd out of the Burning," 261–63 (quote). Norton makes an argument for the connections between Short's afflictions and the frontier war. See Norton, *In the Devil's Snare*, 179–90.

17. This paragraph is drawn from Baker and Kences, "Maine, Indian Land Speculation and Witchcraft," 180–81; "Examination of William Barker, Sr.," Rosenthal et al., eds., *Salem Witch-Hunt*, 561 (quote).

18. Norton, *In the Devil's Snare*, 52, 342; Malcolm Gaskill, *Witchfinders: A Seventeenth-Century English Tragedy* (Cambridge, MA: Harvard University Press, 2005). The author thanks Malcolm Gaskill for his thoughts on the devil's book in relationship to the growing legal and commercial culture, as well as the East Anglia witch hunt.

19. Norton, *In the Devil's Snare*, 180–81; Mather, "A Brand Pluck'd out of the Burning," 282 (quote); Emerson Baker, *The Devil of Great Island: Witchcraft and Conflict in Early New England* (New York: Palgrave Macmillan, 2007), 189–91. John Emerson was the nephew of Reverend John Emerson of Gloucester.

20. Increase Mather, *An Essay for the Recording of Illustrious Providences* (Boston: Samuel Green, 1684), 202–3; Christopher Hill, "Puritans and the 'Dark Corners of the Land,'" in *Change and Continuity in Seventeenth-Century England* (Cambridge, MA: Harvard University Press, 1975), 3–47; Richard Gildrie, *The Profane, the Civil, and the Godly: The Reformation of Manners in Orthodox New England, 1679–1749* (University Park: Pennsylvania State University Press, 1994), 133–56; Henry Burrage, *History of the Baptists in Maine* (Portland: Marks House Printing, 1904), 13–17. For Burroughs, see Christine Heyrman, *Commerce and Culture: The Maritime Communities of Colonial Massachusetts, 1690–1750* (New York: W. W. Norton, 1984), 116–17. This paragraph is drawn in part from Baker and Kences, "Maine, Indian Land Speculation and Witchcraft," 177–78. See also Increase Mather, *An Essay for the Recording of Illustrious Providences* (Boston: Samuel Green, 1684), 202–3 (quote).

21. Cotton Mather, *Decennium Luctuosum* (Boston: B. Green and J. Allen, 1699), 102–3; Baker and Kences, "Maine, Indian Land Speculation and Witchcraft," 160–61.

22. William Simmons, "Cultural Bias in the New England Puritans' Perceptions of Indians," *William and Mary Quarterly* 38 (1981): 67–68; Alfred A. Cave, "Indian Shamans and English Witches in Seventeenth-Century New England," *Essex Institute Historical Collections* 128 (1992): 239–54; Baker and Kences, "Maine, Indian Land Speculation and Witchcraft," 177.

23. Mather is quoted in James Axtell, *The European and the Indian: Essays in the Ethnohistory of Colonial North America* (New York: Oxford University Press, 1981), 276; Baker and Kences, "Maine, Indian Land Speculation and Witchcraft," 179.

24. Baker and Kences, "Maine, Indian Land Speculation and Witchcraft," 171–72, 177–89.

25. Owen Davies, "The Nightmare Experience, Sleep Paralysis, and Witchcraft Accusations," *Folklore* 114 (2003): 181–85; Rosenthal, "General Introduction," 26–27; David J. Hufford, *The Terror That Comes in the Night* (Philadelphia: University of Pennsylvania Press, 1982); "Testimony of Richard Coman v. Bridget Bishop," in Rosenthal et al., eds., *Salem Witch-Hunt*, 372 (quote).

26. "Testimony of John Louder v. Bridget Bishop," in Rosenthal et al., eds., *Salem Witch-Hunt*, 368 (quote); Davies, "The Nightmare Experience," 185.

27. "Testimony of John Louder v. Bridget Bishop," in Rosenthal et al., eds., *Salem Witch-Hunt*, 368 (quote).

28. Increase Mather, *Angelographica* (Boston, 1696), 25.

29. John Hale, *A Modest Inquiry in the Nature of Witchcraft* (Boston: B. Green and J. Allen, 1702), 132 (quote); Norton, *In the Devil's Snare*, 23–24.

30. Norton, *In the Devil's Snare*, 23, 24, 311 (quote). Abigail Williams disappears from the records and presumably had died by 1697. However, fortune-telling for a husband seems a more likely activity for older girls such as Sheldon or Warren than for Abigail, who was eleven or twelve in 1692.

31. Ergotism was first put forward as an idea in Linnda R. Caporael, "Ergotism: The Satan Loosed in Salem?" *Science* 192, no. 4234 (April 2, 1976): 21–26; Mary K. Matossian, "Ergot and the Salem Witchcraft Affair," *American Scientist* 70 (1982): 355–57. For articles that refute the ergot theory, see Nicholas Spanos and Jack Gottlieb, "Ergots and Salem Village Witchcraft: A Critical Appraisal," *Science* 194, no. 4272 (December 24, 1976): 1390–94; Nicholas P. Spanos, "Ergotism and the Salem Witch Panic: A Critical Analysis and an Alternative Conceptualization," *Journal of the History of the Behavioral Sciences* 19 (1983): 358–69.

32. Anne C. Zeller, "Arctic Hysteria in Salem?" *Anthropologica* 32 (1990): 239–64; Laurie Winn Carlson, *Fever in Salem: A New Interpretation of the New England Witch Trials* (New York: Ivan R. Dees, 1999); M.M. Drymon, *Disguised as the Devil: How Lyme Disease Created Witches and Changed History* (n.p.: Wythe Avenue Press, 2008).

33. Deodat Lawson, *Christ's Fidelity, the Only Shield Against Satan's Malignity* (London: R. Tookey, 1704), 110 (quote); Bernard Rosenthal, *Salem Story: Reading the Witch Trials of 1692* (New York: Cambridge University Press, 1995), 38–39. Enders A. Robinson makes the case for a conspiracy by the accusers and the afflicted. See his *The Devil Discovered: Salem Witchcraft 1692* (New York: Hippocrene Books, 1991).

34. For pinching, see Hoffer, *The Devil's Disciples*, 89–90, and Lawrence Stone, *The Family, Sex and Marriage in England, 1500-1800* (New York: Harper and Row, 1977), 167.

35. James Sharpe, *The Bewitching of Anne Gunter: A Horrible and True Story of Deception, Witchcraft, Murder, and the King of England* (New York: Routledge, 2000), 44–45, 103–4, 207.

36. Kenneth Lockridge, *Literacy in Colonial New England: An Inquiry into the Social Context of Literacy in the Early Modern West* (New York: W. W. Norton, 1974), 3–43; Jane Kaminsky, *Governing the Tongue: The Politics of Speech in Early New England* (New York: Oxford University Press, 1997), 3–16. For the spread of news of witchcraft, see Baker, *Devil of Great Island*, 186–88.

37. For the quote, see Deodat Lawson, *A Brief and True Narrative of Some Remarkable Passages Relating to Sundry Persons Afflicted by Witchcraft, in Salem Village* in Burr, ed., *Narratives*,153–4. For an account of the Lowestoft witches and their trial at Bury St. Edmunds, see Gilbert Geis and Ivan Bunn, *A Trial of Witches: A Seventeenth-Century Witchcraft Prosecution* (London: Routledge, 1997). Norton notes the similarities between Lowestoft, the Goodwin case, and Salem. See *In the Devil's Snare*, 36–40, 53–54.

38. For the quote, see *A Tryal of Witches at the Assizes Held at Bury St. Edmonds* (London: 1682), 31–32. See also Geis and Bunn, *A Trial of Witches*, 69–70; Norton, *In the Devil's Snare*, 53–54.

39. Cotton Mather, *Memorable Providences, Relating to Witchcrafts and Possessions* (Boston: 1689), 14–15 (quote), 20–21.

40. Norton, *In the Devil's Snare*, 54 (quote). For Mora and the Swedish trials, see Bengt Ankarloo, "Witch Trials in Northern Europe, 1450–1700," in Bengt Ankarloo and Stuart Clark, eds., *Witchcraft and Magic in Europe: The Period of the Witch Trials* (Philadelphia: University of Pennsylvania Press, 2002), 74, 85–90, 94; E. William Monter, "Scandinavian Witchcraft in Perspective," in Bengt Ankarloo and Gustav Henningsen, eds., *Early Modern European Witchcraft: Centres and Peripheries* (Oxford: Clarendon Press, 1998), 432–34.

41. [Samuel Willard], *Some Miscellany Observations on our Present Debates respecting Witchcrafts, in a Dialogue between S. and B. By P. E. and J. A.* (Philadelphia: William Bradford for Hezekiah Usher, 1692), 7–8 (quote).

42. "Testimony of Daniel Elliott for Elizabeth Procter," in Rosenthal et al., eds., *Salem Witch-Hunt*, 537.

43. Norton discusses the Nurse family's efforts in detail; see *In the Devil's Snare*, 281–89. For the quote, see "Testimony of Thomas Jacobs and Mary Jacobs Regarding Sarah Bibber," in Rosenthal et al., eds., *Salem Witch-Hunt*, 431–32, #265.

44. Hoffer, *The Devil's Disciples*, 97.

45. Marilynne K. Roach speculates that Abigail's accusations may have been an effort to seek attention; see her "That Child, Betty Parris," *Essex Institute Historical Collections* 124 (1988): 1–27. See also Lawson, "A Brief and True Narrative," in Burr, ed., *Witchcraft Narratives*, 161; Norton, *In the Devil's Snare*, 55–57.

46. Lawson, "A Brief and True Narrative," 154 (quotes); Norton, *In the Devil's Snare*, 66–67.

47. John Demos provides a detailed and convincing account of the Knapp case in *Entertaining Satan*, 97–131. For the quotes, see Demos, *The Enemy Within*, 114–15. For Willard's account, see his "A Brief Account of a Strange and Unusual Providence of God Befallen to Elizabeth Knapp of Groton (1671–1672)," in Elaine G. Breslaw, ed., *Witches of*

the Atlantic World: A Historical Reader and Primary Sourcebook (New York: New York University Press, 2000), 235–45.

48. Roach, "The Child Betty Parris," 11–13; Norton, *In the Devil's Snare*, 305–8; Rosenthal et al., eds., *Salem-Witch Hunt*, 790. Samuel Parris's father, Thomas, was the uncle and London agent for Boston merchant John Hull. Hull's daughter, Hannah, married Samuel Sewall. See Bernard Bailyn, *The New England Merchants in the Seventeenth Century* (Cambridge, MA: Harvard University Press, 1955), 87; "The Diaries of John Hull, Mint-Master and Treasurer of the Colony of Massachusetts Bay," *Transactions and Collections of the American Antiquarian Society* 3 (1857): 139. Louis Jordan, *John Hull, the Mint and the Economics of Massachusetts Coinage* (Hanover, NH: University Press of New England, 2002), 129, 132, 238; Hermann Clarke, *John Hull, A Builder of the Bay Colony* (Portland, ME: Southworth-Anthoensen Press, 1940), 102.

49. "Examination of Mary Warren," in Rosenthal et al., eds., *Salem Witch-Hunt*, 196 (quote). For a list of the afflicted accusers and the number of cases they were involved in, see Norton, *In the Devil's Snare*, 321–22; for Mary Warren, see Roach, *Salem Witch Trials*, 38–39, 56–57, 66, 75, 80–86; Rosenthal, *Salem Story*, 46–50.

50. "Testimony of Edward Bishop Jr., Sarah Bishop, & Mary Esty Regarding Mary Warren," in Rosenthal et al., eds., *Salem Witch-Hunt*, 355 (quote).

51. "Examination of Abigail Soames," in Rosenthal et al., eds., *Salem Witch-Hunt*, 268–69 (quote); Norton, *In the Devil's Snare*, 166–67, #150 (quote).

52. "Letter of Thomas Brattle," in Burr, ed., *Narratives*, 171 (quote); Sarah Rivett, *The Science of the Soul in Colonial New England* (Chapel Hill: University of North Carolina Press, 2011), 251–55, 263–66.

53. Rivett, *The Science of the Soul*, 223–27, 254–67.

54. Rivett, *The Science of the Soul*, 227–35, 251–55; Joseph Cope, "The Irish Stroker and the King: Valentine Greatrakes, Protestant Faith Healing, and the Restoration in Ireland," *Éire-Ireland* 46 (2011): 170–200; Michael P. Winship, *Seers of God: Puritan Providentialism in the Restoration and Early Enlightenment* (Baltimore: Johns Hopkins University Press, 1996), 64–65, 117–21, 126–28.

55. Geis and Bunn, *A Trial of Witches*, 85–91; Rosenthal et al., eds., *Salem Witch-Hunt*, 608–9, 737–38; Norton, *In the Devil's Snare*, 37–38, 262–63, "Letter of Thomas Brattle," 171 (quote).

56. "Letter of Thomas Brattle," 171–72.

57. Boyer and Nissenbaum, *Salem Possessed*, 27–30; Laurel Thatcher Ulrich, *Good Wives: Image and Reality in the Lives of Women in Northern New England, 1650-1750* (New York: Alfred A. Knopf, 1982), 21–26. Marion Rust has recently noted the parallels between the behaviors of the youths of Northampton in the 1730s, and Le Roy, New York, today, considering both as examples of conversion disorder. She does not consider the comparison to 1692, but the parallels seem equally clear. See Marion Rust, "An 'Epidemical Distemper': Conversion and Disorder, Then and Now," *Common-Place* 13, no. 3 (2013), accessed at www.common-place.org/vol-13/no-03/rust.

58. Paul Boyer and Stephen Nissenbaum summarize many of their arguments and rebut their critics in "Salem Possessed in Retrospect," *William and Mary Quarterly* 65 (2008): 513–34 (quote, 521).

59. Benjamin Ray's careful research and GIS mapping has demonstrated the limitations in some of the geographic arguments of *Salem Possessed*. Meanwhile, Richard Latner's analysis of tax lists leads him to conclude that there were smaller economic differences between the factions than Boyer and Nissenbaum suggested. Articles by Latner and Ray, along with comments by other historians and a rebuttal by Boyer and Nissenbaum, can be found in a special forum in the *William and Mary Quarterly* 65, no. 3 (2008). In that issue, see Richard Latner, "Salem Witchcraft, Factionalism, and Social Change Reconsidered: Were Salem's Witch-Hunters Modernization's Failures?" 423–48; Benjamin C. Ray, "The Geography of Witchcraft Accusations in 1692 Salem Village," 449–78; John Demos, "What Goes Around Comes Around," 479–82; Mary Beth Norton, "Essex County Witchcraft," 483–88; Carol Karlsen, "Salem Revisited," 489–94; and Boyer and Nissenbaum, "Salem Possessed in Retrospect," 503–34.

60. Rosenthal et al., eds., *Salem Witch-Hunt*, 135, 190 (quote), 198, 343, 552, 574 (quote), 661 (quote); For the consumer revolution, see Richard Bushman, *The Refinement of America: Persons, Houses and Cities* (New York: Vintage, 1993); Emerson Baker, "The Archaeology of 1690: Status and Material Life on New England's Northern Frontier," in Georgia Barnhill and Martha McNamera, eds., *New Views of New England: Studies in Material and Visual Culture, 1680-1830* (Boston: Colonial Society of Massachusetts, 2012), 1–16. For envy and material wealth in Salem witchcraft, see Altin Gavranovic, "Through the Looking Glass Darkly: Episodes from the History of Deviance," Ph.D. dissertation, Harvard University, 2012, 70–83, 90–96. For the influence of the reformation on witchcraft, see Brian Levack, *The Witch-Hunt in Early Modern Europe*, 2nd ed. (New York: Longman, 1995), 100–124.

61. The importance of the Salem Village church membership and their pattern of accusation against non-members is discussed in Benjamin Ray, "Satan's War Against the Covenant in Salem Village, 1692," *New England Quarterly* 80 (2007): 143–45; Richard Latner, "'Here Are No Newters': Witchcraft and Religious Discord in Salem Village and Andover," *New England Quarterly* 79 (2006): 104; and Benjamin Ray's "The Geography of Witchcraft Accusations in 1692 Salem Village," *William and Mary Quarterly* 65, no. 3 (2008). The list of covenant signers can be found in Paul Boyer and Stephen Nissenbaum, eds., *Salem-Village Witchcraft: A Documentary Record of Local Conflict in Colonial New England* (1972; reprint, Boston: Northeastern University Press, 1993), 268–69. Analysis of the covenant signers, their homes, and their role in the trials is drawn from Rosenthal et al., eds., *Salem Witch-Hunt*; W. P. Upham, "Map of Salem Village, 1692," in Charles W. Upham, ed., *Salem Witchcraft* (Boston: Wiggin and Lunt, 1867) and the maps in Ray, "The Geography of Witchcraft."

62. Richard Trask, "Legal Procedures Used During the Salem Witch Trials and a Brief History of the Published Versions of the Records," in Rosenthal et al., eds., *Salem Witch-Hunt*, 46–47; Rosenthal, "General Introduction," 30; Margo Burns and Bernard Rosenthal, "Examination of the Records of the Salem Witch Trials," *William and Mary Quarterly* 65, no. 3 (2008): 413–14). The changing ink colors and the identification of individual samples of handwriting are just two of many important discoveries made by Rosenthal and his team in putting together this invaluable source.

63. This paragraph relies heavily on the detailed discussion of Thomas Putnam Jr. and his family in Boyer and Nissenbaum, *Salem Possessed*, 133–52. Ann's tenth of her father's estate amounted to £168, though her widowed mother retained a third of this until her death in 1691. This amount was determined in the 1683 settlement of the estate and was an increase over the proposed 1682 settlement that is mentioned by Boyer and Nissenbaum. See *Records and Files of the Quarterly Courts of Essex County, Massachusetts*, 9 vols. (Salem: Essex Institute, 1911–1975): 8:348–50, 353–55; 9:36–40. The author thanks Mary Beth Norton for bringing the 1683 settlement to his attention. For office holding, see James Duncan Phillips, *Salem in the Seventeenth Century* (Boston: Houghton and Mifflin, 1933), 361; *Town Records of Salem, Massachusetts*, 3 vols. (Salem: Essex Institute, 1868–1934), 3:206. Thomas Putnam Jr. served in Captain Curwin's cavalry troop during the difficult winter campaign against the Narragansett in 1675. See George Bodge, *Soldiers in King Philip's War* (Boston, 1906), 82–83; for Holyoke, see 245–47, 475.

64. For the afflicted girls who had lost parents, see Carol Karlsen, *The Devil in the Shape of a Woman: Witchcraft in Colonial New England* (New York: Random House, 1987), 222–31; Norton, *In the Devil's Snare*, 22, 47–50, 141–43, 161, 176–81.

65. "Plea of Margaret Jacobs," in Rosenthal et al., eds., *Salem Witch-Hunt*, 742–43, #753 (quote).

CHAPTER FIVE

1. Thomas Brattle, "Letter," in George Lincoln Burr, ed., *Narratives of the New England Witchcraft Cases* (New York: Charles Scribner's Sons, 1914), 190.

2. Richard Godbeer, "Witchcraft in British America," in Brian Levack, ed., *The Oxford Handbook of Witchcraft in Early Modern Europe and Colonial America* (New York: Oxford University Press, 2013), 393–94; Elaine Forman Crane, *Witches, Wife Beaters, and Whores: Common Law and Common Folk in Early America* (Ithaca, NY: Cornell University Press, 2011), 46–84; Virginia Bernhard, "Religion, Politics, and Witchcraft in Bermuda, 1651–1655," *William and Mary Quarterly* 67 (2010): 677–708.

3. There are 980 documents in Bernard Rosenthal et al., eds., *Records of the Salem Witch-Hunt* (New York: Cambridge University Press, 2009). The last three (nos. 978–980), were once thought to relate to the trials but have now been ruled out. These documents were included in an earlier three-volume transcription of the trials, Paul Boyer and Stephen Nissenbaum, eds., *The Salem Witchcraft Papers: Verbatim Transcripts of the Legal Documents of the Salem Witchcraft Outbreak of 1692* (New York: Da Capo Press, 1977).

4. See Appendices 1 and 2 for lists of accused. The most accurate and up-to-date list of the accused has been developed by Margo Burns (one of the editors of *The Records of the Salem Witch-Hunt*), reproduced in this book as Appendix 1. Formal complaints do not survive for all of these accused. In some cases, the only document that survives is a petition for their release from prison for witchcraft, or a petition for a grant of restitution. Burns's list also includes the names of some people accused in evidence that was entered, but who were never formally charged in court. For a list of others who were accused but never faced formal legal proceedings, see Appendix 2. See also "Examination of William Barker, Sr.," in Rosenthal et al., eds., *Salem Witch-Hunt*, 561–62.

5. Bernard Rosenthal and Mary Beth Norton were the first historians to truly establish Burroughs's accusation as a critical turning point in the trials. Rosenthal first noted his possible ties to the Baptist faith and Norton stressed his ties to the frontier. See Bernard Rosenthal, *Salem Story: Reading the Witch Trials of 1692* (New York: Cambridge University Press, 1995), 130–35; Mary Beth Norton, *In the Devil's Snare: The Salem Witchcraft Crisis of 1692* (New York: W. W. Norton, 2002), 149–54, 245–51.

6. Robin Briggs, *Witches and Neighbors: The Social and Cultural Context of European Witchcraft* (New York: Viking, 1996), 20–25, 259–86; Keith Thomas, *Religion and the Decline of Magic* (New York: Charles Scribner's Sons, 1971), 502–34; Brian Levack, *The Witch-Hunt in Early Modern Europe* (London: Longman, 1987), 160–84; James Sharpe, *Instruments of Darkness; Witchcraft in Early Modern England* (Philadelphia: University of Pennsylvania Press, 1997), 169–89; Karlsen, *Devil in the Shape of a Woman*, 80; Alison Games, *Witchcraft in Early North America* (New York: Rowman and Littlefield, 2010), 10.

7. Karlsen, *Devil in the Shape of a Woman*, 117–52; John Demos, *Entertaining Satan: Witchcraft and the Culture of Early New England* (New York: Oxford University Press, 1982), 57–94; Games, *Witchcraft in Early North America*, 40–41. For the power of spoken words and curses for witches and the Salem trials, see Jane Kamensky, *Governing the Tongue: The Politics of Speech in Early New England* (New York: Oxford University Press, 1997), 150–79; Robert St. George, "'Heated Speech' and Literacy in Seventeenth-Century New England," in David D. Hall and David G. Allen, eds., *Seventeenth-Century New England* (Boston: Colonial Society of Massachusetts, 1984), 275–322; Kai T. Erikson, *Wayward Puritans: A Study in the Sociology of Deviance* (New York: John Wiley, 1966), 67–70, 137–59.

8. Paul Boyer and Stephen Nissenbaum, *Salem Possessed: The Social Origins of Witchcraft* (Cambridge, MA: Harvard University Press, 1974), 179–209; see 181 for the quote.

9. Karlsen, *Devil in the Shape of a Woman*, 110–12; Boyer and Nissenbaum, ed., *Salem-Village Witchcraft* 139–47; K. David Goss, *The Salem Witch Trials: A Reference Guide* (Westport, CT: Greenwood Press, 2008), 92–93; Roach, *Salem Witch Trials*, 13–14.

10. "Deposition of John Putnam, Jr. and Rebecca Putnam v. George Burroughs," in Rosenthal et al., eds., *Salem Witch-Hunt*, 246–47 (quote); Roach, *Salem Witch Trials*, 228–29.

11. "Examination of George Burroughs, May 9, 1692," and "Testimony of Mary Weber v. George Burroughs," in Rosenthal et al., eds., *Salem Witch-Hunt*, 240–41, 497.

12. Mather, "Wonders of the Invisible World," in Burr, ed., *Narratives*, 221; "Testimony of Thomas Ruck v. George Burroughs," in Rosenthal et al., eds., *Salem Witch-Hunt*, 531–32, #493 (quote).

13. Jeremy Harte, "Hell on Earth: Encountering Monsters in the Medieval Landscape," in Bettina Bildhauer and Robert Mills, eds., *The Monstrous Middle Ages* (Toronto: University of Toronto Press, 2003), 179 (see n. 3 on that page for references). For the quote, see Geoffrey Chaucer, *The Canterbury Tales* (New York: Bantam Classics, 1982), 316, "The Franklin's Tale," ll. 466–70 (spelling not modernized).

14. "Testimony of Lydia Nichols and Abigail Nichols v. Abigail Hobbs," in Rosenthal et al., eds., *Salem Witch-Hunt*, 194–95.

15. "Deposition of Priscilla Chub v. Abigail Hobbs," in Rosenthal et al., eds., *Salem Witch-Hunt*, 193.

16. Chadwick Hansen makes the strongest argument for the actual practice of black magic in Salem in 1692. See *Witchcraft at Salem* (New York: George Braziller, 1969), 64–77. For the best treatment of magic in early New England, see Richard Godbeer, *The Devil's Dominion: Magic and Religion in Early New England* (New York: Cambridge University Press, 1992); Robert St. George, *Conversing by Signs: Poetics of Implication in Colonial New England Culture* (Chapel Hill, University of North Carolina Press, 1988), 190–92. The author thanks Curtis White for relating to him his discovery of the Nurse eel spear. See also Cynthia K. Riley Augé, "Silent Sentinels: Archaeology, Magic, and the Gendered Control of Domestic Boundaries in New England, 1620–1725," Ph.D. dissertation, Anthropology and Heritage Studies, University of Montana, 2013.

17. Rosenthal et al., eds., *Salem Witch-Hunt*, 198, 261, 371, 390–91, 393, 416, 464, 544, 591 (the quote is on 544). For image magic in Salem, see Godbeer, *The Devil's Dominion*, 213–16. For a good summary of physical evidence, see Margo Burns, "'Other Ways of Undue Force and Fright': The Coercion of False Confessions by the Salem Magistrates," *Studia Neophilologica* 84 (2012): 28.

18. Rosenthal et al., eds., *Salem Witch-Hunt*, 390–91, 470.

19. "Examination of Ann Dolliver," in Rosenthal et al., eds., *Salem Witch-Hunt*, 390–91.

20. "Letter of Reverend John Higginson to his Son Nathaniel Higginson, August 31, 1698," Peabody Essex Museum manuscript collections, available online at Salem Witch Trials Documentary Archive and Transcription Project, http://salem.lib.virginia.edu/letters/higginson_letter.html (quote). See also Burns, "'Other Ways of Undue Force and Fright,'" 27–28. Wendell Craker stresses that some form of nonspectral evidence such as poppets was used for every person put on trial. See Craker, "Spectral Evidence, Non-Spectral Acts of Witchcraft, and Confession at Salem in 1692," *Historical Journal* 40 (1997): 331–58.

21. Latner, "'Here Are No Newters,'" 103–6; Ray, "Satan's War," 90–93.

22. Christine Leigh Heyrman, *Commerce and Culture: The Maritime Communities of Colonial Massachusetts, 1690–1750* (New York: W. W. Norton, 1984), 104–18; Richard Godbeer has noted the connection between magic, witchcraft, and Quakers. See Godbeer, *Devil's Dominion*, particularly 193–203; Increase Mather, *An Essay for the Recording of Illustrious Providences* (Boston, 1684), 188–89, 341–476. For the "lithobolia" attack on the Walton tavern in Portsmouth, see Emerson Baker, *The Devil of Great Island: Witchcraft and Conflict in Early New England* (New York: Palgrave Macmillan, 2007).

23. Heyrman, *Commerce and Culture*, 110–11. For the quote see Cotton Mather, *Memorable Providences, Relating to Witchcrafts and Possessions* (Boston: 1689), 21–23.

24. Heyrman, *Commerce and Culture*, 111–13; Cotton Mather, *Little Flocks Guarded Against Grievous Wolves* (Boston: Benjamin Harris, 1691), quotes on 3 and 9.

25. Samuel Sewall, *The Diary of Samuel Sewall, 1674–1729*, ed. M. Halsey Thomas (New York: Farrar, Straus and Giroux, 1973), 1:44 (quote); Jonathan Chu, *Neighbors, Friends, or Madmen: The Puritan Adjustment to Quakerism in Seventeenth-Century Massachusetts* (Westport, CT: Greenwood Press, 1985), 115, 122.

26. Sybil Noyes, Charles T. Libby, and Walter G. Davis, eds., *Genealogical Dictionary of Maine and New Hampshire* (1928–29; reprint, Baltimore: Genealogical Publishing, 1979), 719–20; for Ann Burt, see David Hall, ed., *Witch-Hunting in Seventeenth-Century New England: A Documentary History, 1638–1692* (Boston: Northeastern University Press, 1991), 185–88; Enders Robinson, *The Devil Discovered: Salem Witchcraft 1692* (Prospect Heights, IL: Waveland Press, 1991), 279–91; Enders Robinson, *Salem Witchcraft and Hawthorne's House of Seven Gables* (Bowie, MD: Heritage Books, 1992), 313–32; Heyrman, *Commerce and Culture*, 104, 112–17; "Examination of Samuel Wardwell," in Rosenthal et al., eds., *Salem Witch-Hunt*, 576–77; *Essex Court Records* 6:294; Joseph Nicholson, *The Standard of the Lord Lifted Up in New-England, in Opposition to the Man of Sin* (London: Robert Wilson, 1660), 20 (quote). The author thanks Malcolm Gaskill for bringing this quote to his attention.

27. "Examination of George Burroughs," in Rosenthal et al., eds., *Salem Witch-Hunt*, 240–41, #120; Roach, *Salem Witch Trials*, 113–15.

28. For Maine as a contested religious frontier, see Laura Chmielewski, *The Spice of Popery: Converging Christianities on an Early American Frontier* (Notre Dame, IN: University of Notre Dame Press, 2012); William Hubbard, *A General History of New England from the Discovery to MDCLXXX* (Boston: Massachusetts Historical Society, 1815), 21, 356 (quotes); Charles Banks, *History of York, Maine* (Boston: Calkins Press, 1931), 2:113–18.

29. Banks, *History of York*, 2:118–19; "Thomas Gorges to John Winthrop, February 23, 1641," *Massachusetts Historical Society Collections*, 4th ser., 7 (1865):335 (quote).

30. Noyes et al., *Genealogical Dictionary*, 390–91, 478–79, 615; Baker, *Devil of Great Island*, 121–23; Emerson Baker and James Kences, "Maine, Indian Land Speculation, and the Essex County Witchcraft Outbreak of 1692," *Maine History* 40 (2001): 171–72.

31. This paragraph is largely drawn from Baker and Kences, "Maine, Indian Land Speculation, and the Witchcraft," 166–67. See also "Proposals by the Committee of Militia of Salem, October 31, 1691," in James P. Baxter, ed., *Documentary History of the State of Maine* (Portland: Maine Historical Society, 1897), 5:302–3; Banks, *History of York*, 1:287–307; Cotton Mather, *A Midnight Cry: An Essay for our Awakening Out of that Sinful Sleep, to which We are at this Time too Much Disposed* (Boston: John Allen, 1692), 48; Francis Hooke to the Governor and Council, January 28, 1692, in Baxter, ed., *Documentary History*, 5:317–18; Cotton Mather, *Fair Weather: Or Considerations to Dispel the Clouds, & Allay the Storms of Discontent* (Boston: Bartholomew Green and John Allen, 1692), 85.

32. Baker and Kences, "Maine, Indian Land Speculation, and the Witchcraft," 167; Noyes et al., *Genealogical Dictionary*, 210–11; Samuel Sewall to Shubael Dummer, Joshua Moody, and Benjamin Woodbridge, Jan. 9, 1692, in *Samuel Sewall's Letterbook*, *Massachusetts Historical Society Collections*, 6th Ser., 1 (1886), 125; Richard D. Pierce, ed., *The Records of the First Church in Salem, Massachusetts, 1629–1736* (Salem: Essex Institute, 1974), 171.

33. For the importance of Burroughs's accusation, see Rosenthal, *Salem Story*, 130–35.

34. Letter from Jacob Melyen to Dr. Johannes Kerfbij, July 11, 1692, in Evan Haefeli, "Dutch New York and the Salem Witch Trials: Some New Evidence," *Proceedings of the American Antiquarian Society* 110 (2000): 303 (quote).

35. See Appendix 3 for ministers and close family members accused of witchcraft. Francis Dane and twenty-seven members of his family and extended kin network were accused. This includes the Allen, Toothaker, Carrier, Jackson, and How families. See Robinson, *Salem Witchcraft and Hawthorne's House of Seven Gables*, 273–99. Enders Robinson does note the accusation of four ministers (he leaves out Busse), and he sees the Court of Oyer and Terminer acting in part as a "mock ecclesiastical court," punishing ministers "who might show glimmerings of religious tolerance." See Robinson, *The Devil Discovered*, 203.

36. "Deposition of Job Tookey, June 23, 1682," *Records and Files of the Quarterly Courts of Essex County, Massachusetts*, 9 vols. (Salem: Essex Institute, 1911–1975), 8:336 (quote); Boyer and Nissenbaum, *Salem Possessed*, 206–208. Noyes et al., *Genealogical Dictionary*, 688. Tookey witnessed a deed sale on the Hariseeket River (present-day Freeport) in 1679 and another one in Saco in 1680. He may have been living there at the time, or visited the region as a sailor or fisherman. The coast of Maine was a popular fishing ground for the Essex County fleet, and there was considerable coastal trade in the region as well. *York Deeds*, 18 vols. (Portland: John T. Hull, 1887–1911) 3:53, 82.

37. For the accusation against Thacher, see Norton, *In the Devil's Snare*, 176–81, 201; Stephen Foster, *The Long Argument: English Puritanism and the Shaping of New England Culture, 1570–1700* (Chapel Hill: University of North Carolina Press, 1991), 200–205; Richard Gildrie, *Salem, Massachusetts, 1626–1683: A Covenant Community* (Charlottesville: University of Virginia Press, 1975), 143–44; Richard Simmons, "The Founding of the Third Church of Boston," *William and Mary Quarterly* 26 (1969): 241–52. Margaret Thacher was not formally charged with witchcraft, but Brattle notes that she had been "much complained of by the afflicted persons"; see Brattle, "Letter," in Burr, ed., *Narratives*, 177–80. Margaret Thacher's father was Henry Webb and her first husband was Jacob Sheafe. She was presumably protected from prosecution because her daughter Elizabeth was the wife of Judge Jonathan Corwin. For Samuel Willard's accusal and opposition, see Calef, "More Wonders" in Burr, ed., *Narratives*, 360, and Brattle, "Letter," 184.

38. John Langdon Sibley, *Biographical Sketches of Graduates of Harvard University* (Cambridge, MA: Charles Sever, 1881),1:376–77; Brattle, "Letter," October 8, 1692, in Burr, ed., *Narratives*, 184. Willard had already been cried out upon, by July 11. See Letter from Jacob Melyen to Dr. Johannes Kerfbij, July 11, 1692, 301–4. Samuel Sewall notes the accusation against Saltonstall; see Sewall, *Diary*, 1:305–6.

39. Rosenthal et al., eds., *Salem Witch-Hunt*, 393–94, 481–82, 562–63, 568; the quote is on 562. Mary Warren (June 8), Mary Lacey Jr. (July 22), William Barker (August 29), and Elizabeth Johnson Sr. (August 30) all mentioned Buss in their descriptions of Satanic gatherings.

40. "Petition from Reverend John Buss, Durham, 1718," *New Hampshire Provincial and State Papers*, 40 vols. (Concord: State of New Hampshire: 1867–1943), 17:736; "The Rev. John Buss of Durham (Oyster River), New Hampshire," *New Hampshire Genealogical Record* 26 (2009): 57–64. Some historians of the witch trials place Buss in both Wells and Oyster River, but there is no record of him in Wells after his departure in 1677, and his 1718 petition notes he had served regularly in Oyster River for forty years.

41. Robert Lawrence, *The New Hampshire Churches* (Author, 1856), 321.

42. Thomas Maule, *Truth Held Forth and Maintained* (New York: William Bradford, 1695), 182.

43. Sibley, *Graduates of Harvard*, 2:267, 273(quote); Robert Moody and Richard Simmons, eds., *The Glorious Revolution in Massachusetts* (Boston: Colonial Society of Massachusetts, 1988), 70, 81, 264, 387. See Chapter Three above for details on Shepard's career in Rowley and Chebacco Parish, Ipswich. It is unfortunate that no details are known about the accusation against Shepard, as the identity of the accuser might explain a great deal.

44. Sibley, *Graduates of Harvard*, 1:514–18.

45. John Whiting, *Truth and Innocency Defended Against Falsehood and Envy* (Boston, 1702), 140.

46. Robert Charles Anderson, George F. Sanborn, and Melinde Lutz Sanborn, *The Great Migration: Immigrants to New England, 1634–1635* (Boston: New England Historical and Genealogical Society, 1999–2011), 5:87–89, 484–87; Robert Charles Anderson, ed., *The Great Migration Begins: Immigrants to New England 1629–1633* (Boston: New England Historical and Genealogical Society, 1995), 1:484–87; Sibley, *Harvard Graduates* 1:286–93, 496–508. Robert G. Pope, *The Half-Way Covenant: Church Membership in Puritan New England* (Princeton, NJ: Princeton University Press, 1969), 193–97; Foster, *The Long Argument*, 222–23.

47. This rebellion against authority is described in T. H. Breen, *Puritans and Adventurers: Persistence and Change in Early America* (New York: Oxford University Press, 1980), 82–84.

48. Whiting, *Truth and Innocency Defended*, 140; Emerson Baker and John Reid, *The New England Knight: Sir William Phips, 1651–1695* (Toronto: University of Toronto Press, 1998), 147–51, 53–54. Whiting mentions the accusation of Maria Cotton and Mary Phips in the same passage. It is the only place the accusation against Cotton is mentioned, but Calef also mentions the accusation against Phips, so it is likely both were indeed cried out upon. Calef says, "In answer to the commendations of Sir William, for his stopping the proceedings about witchcraft, viz. That it was high time for to stop it, his own Lady being accused; if that assertion were a truth." See Robert Calef, *More Wonders of the Invisible World* (London: Nathaniel Hillar, 1700), 165.

49. Norton, *In the Devil's Snare*, 143–46; David Konig, "A New Look at the Essex 'French': Ethnic Friction and Community Tensions in Seventeenth-Century Essex County, Massachusetts," *Essex Institute Historical Collections* 119 (1974): 167–80.

50. The authoritative source on these forfeitures is David Brown, "The Forfeitures at Salem, 1692," *William and Mary Quarterly* 50 (1993): 85–111.

51. Brown, "The Forfeitures at Salem, 1692," 85–111; "Order for the Commission of a Court of Oyer and Terminer for Suffolk, Essex and Middlesex Counties," in Rosenthal et al., eds., *Salem Witch-Hunt*, 322 (quote).

52. John A. Shutz, *Legislators of the Massachusetts General Court, 1691–1780* (Boston: Northeastern University Press, 1997), 71–72. Dudley's brother Simon junior was the minister of New Haven, his sisters were married to Rev. Seaborn Cotton and the late Rev. Richard Hubbard, and his late uncle Samuel Dudley had been the minister of Exeter. Calef, "More

Wonders," 372 (quote); Anderson, *The Great Migration Begins*, 1:209–15, 484–87; Moody and Simmons, eds., *Glorious Revolution in Massachusetts*, 174.

53. Hall, *Witch-Hunting in Seventeenth-Century New England*, 87–88; *Essex County Quarterly Court* 1:265 (quote). John Bradstreet of Rowley was apparently a second cousin once removed of the Bradstreet brothers. Their common ancestors were John and Joan Bradstreet of Gilsingham, Surrey. John's will, proved October 20, 1559, includes his sons Simon and Thomas. Simon was the great-grandfather of the Bradstreet brothers, and Thomas was the grandfather of John Bradstreet of Rowley. See Gary Boyd Roberts, *English Origins of New England Families* (Baltimore: Genealogical Publishing, 1984), 1:106–11; Anderson, *The Great Migration Begins*, 1: 209–15; Anderson et al., *The Great Migration*, 1:384–88.

54. Robinson, *Devil Discovered*, 274, 333–43; Noyes et al., *Genealogical Dictionary*, 104; Norton, *In the Devil's Snare*, 184–85, 261. Andover selectman John Aslebee's two sisters, Rebecca Johnson and Sarah Cole, were accused, as was John Abbot Jr.'s brother-in-law William Barker Sr. Sarah Loring Bailey, *Historical Sketches of Andover* (Boston: Houghton, Mifflin and Co., 1880), 140.

55. "A Faithful and Wonderful Account of the Surprising Things which happened in the Town of Glocester, in the Year, 1692" by J.E. (John Emerson), May 19, 1693, in Cotton Mather, *Decennium Luctuosum* (Boston, 1699), 104–12 (quote); Baker, *Devil of Great Island*, 178–79; Heyrman, *Commerce and Culture*, 105–106; Norton, *In the Devil's Snare*, 232–33, 261–62; Noyes et al., *Genealogical Dictionary*, 196, 672.

56. The most detailed studies of Alden in relation to the witch trials can be found in Louise Breen, *Transgressing the Bounds: Subversive Enterprises and the Puritan Elite in Massachusetts, 1630–1692* (New York: Oxford University Press, 2001), 197–208, and Norton, *In the Devil's Snare*, 185–93. For Nelson, see Richard R. Johnson, *John Nelson, Merchant and Adventurer: A Life Between Empires* (New York: Oxford University Press, 1991). Norton provides a list of twenty-three accused (including some who confessed and accused others) with frontier ties, though the list does not include Job Tookey, who had previously spent time on the coast of Maine.

57. Baker and Reid, *The New England Knight*, 95–96; Norton, *In the Devil's Snare*, 187–88; for the quote, see "Benjamin Allen to Massachusetts Governor and Council, August 12, 1691," Massachusetts Archives Manuscript Collection 37:120.

58. Breen, *Transgressing the Bounds*, 203–6; Norton, *In the Devil's Snare*, 188; Johnson, *John Nelson*, 77–86.

59. "Samuel Ravenscroft to Francis Nicholson, November 5, 1691," Calendar of State Papers Colonial Series, Gay Transcripts III, Massachusetts Historical Society; Breen, *Transgressing the Bounds*, 203; Norton, *In the Devil's Snare*, 188–89.

60. Elisha Hutchinson to Isaac Addington, May 19, 1692, in Baxter, ed., *Documentary History of the State of Maine*, 5:341; Norton, *In the Devil's Snare*, 190.

61. Calef, "More Wonders," 353.

62. Calef, "More Wonders," 353 (quote); Baker and Reid, *The New England Knight*, 92, 149.

63. Calef, "More Wonders," 354.

64. Fluellin to William Phillips, March 30, 1661, *York Deeds*, 8:220; Hombinowitt to William Phillips, August 29, 1660, *York Deeds*, 8:220; Baker and Reid, *The New England Knight*, 143–44. John Spencer, the brother-in-law of Sir William Phips, witnessed one of Phillips's deeds as well; see Baker and Kences, "Maine, Indian Land Speculation and the Essex County Witchcraft Outbreak," 172–73; Breen, *Transgressing the Bounds*, 197–212.

65. David Konig, *Law and Society in Puritan Massachusetts: Essex County 1629–1692* (Chapel Hill: University of North Carolina Press, 1979), 178–79; Laurel Thatcher Ulrich, *Good Wives: Image and Reality in the Lives of Women in Northern New England, 1650–1750* (New York: Alfred A. Knopf, 1982), 186–89; Mary Beth Norton, *Founding Mothers and Fathers: Gendered Power and the Forming of American Society* (New York: Alfred A. Knopf, 1996), 77–80, 114–37.

66. *Essex County Quarterly Court*, 6:190–91; Mather, "Wonders," 250; Lawson, "A Brief and True Narrative," in Burr, ed., *Narratives*, 155 (quote); Roach, *Salem Witch Trials*, 296.

67. *Essex County Quarterly Court*, 6:292–93 (quote). Mary Warren, Sarah Bibber, Mary Walcott, Mercy Lewis, and Sarah Churchwell all testified to spectral beatings by Jacobs. See Rosenthal et al., eds., *Salem Witch-Hunt*, 251–54, 522–23.

68. "Examination of John Willard, Second Version, May 18, 1692," in Rosenthal et al., eds., *Salem Witch-Hunt*, 289–90 (quote). See also depositions by Elizabeth Hubbard, Mercy Lewis, and Ann Putnam Jr., 291, 296–97.

69. "Deposition of Lydia Nichols and Margaret Knight v. John Willard, August 4, 1682," in Rosenthal et al., eds., *Salem Witch-Hunt*, 526–27. Bernard Rosenthal goes so far as to suggest that Sarah Putnam had been beaten to death by her mother, Ann Putnam, Sr., and that this explains Ann Jr.'s call for justice for John Willard, claiming he whipped the six-week-old Sarah to death. See Rosenthal, *Salem Story*, 40.

70. "Statement of Samuel Parris, April 12, 1692," in Rosenthal et al., eds., *Salem Witch-Hunt*, 181–82.

71. "Statement of Samuel Sibley v. John Procter, as Recorded by Samuel Parris," in Rosenthal et al., eds., *Salem Witch-Hunt*, 538 (quotes).

72. "Examination of Mary Warren, April 21, 1692," and "Examination of Mary Warren, May 12, 1692," in Rosenthal et al., eds., *Salem Witch-Hunt*, 201 (quote), 263. Hoffer is cautious in this interesting suggestion, noting the evidence is only hinted at in testimony. See Peter Hoffer, *The Devil's Disciples: Makers of the Salem Witch Trials* (Baltimore: Johns Hopkins University Press, 1996), 91–95.

73. Mather, "Wonders," 218.

74. "Deposition of John Putnam, Jr. and Rebecca Putnam v. George Burroughs," in Rosenthal et al., eds., *Salem Witch-Hunt*, 246–47 (quote); Norton, *In the Devil's Snare*, 100, 123–32, 249; Roach, *Salem Witch Hunt*, 228–29.

75. "Deposition of Ann Putnam, Jr. vs. George Burroughs," in Rosenthal et al., eds., *Salem Witch-Hunt*, 245–46.

76. For the testimony of Sheldon, Walcott, and Lewis against Burroughs, see Rosenthal et al., eds., *Salem Witch-Hunt*, 244–45, 247–48.

77. Behringer sees many of the outbreaks of European witchcraft being linked to extremes of the Little Ice Age, and the Salem witch hunt certainly fits into this pattern. See Wolfgang Behringer, *Witches and Witch-Hunts: A Global History* (Cambridge: Polity, 2004), 97, 159.

78. Roach, *The Salem Witch Trials*, 20; Paul Boyer and Stephen Nissenbaum, *Salem Possessed: The Social Origins of Witchcraft* (Cambridge, MA: Harvard University Press, 1974), 193–94.

79. Konig, *Law and Society*, 181; "Deposition of Sarah Holten v. Rebecca Nurse," in Rosenthal et al., eds., *Salem Witch-Hunt*, 427–28 (quote). For legislation on pigs, see William Cronon, *Changes in the Land: Indians, Colonists and the Ecology of New England* (New York: Hill and Wang, 1983), 135–37. The author thanks Margo Burns for bringing this reference to his attention.

80. Examples of witchcraft and neighborly disputes before Salem are numerous. See, for example, Demos, *Entertaining Satan*; Briggs, *Witches and Neighbors*; Baker, *Devil of Great Island*. The Walton tavern stood on Great Island. At the time it was part of Portsmouth, but today it is New Castle, New Hampshire.

81. Charles W. Upham, ed., *Salem Witchcraft* (Boston: Wiggin and Lunt, 1867), 47–64; Boyer and Nissenbaum, *Salem Possessed*, 149, 181–86; *Essex County Quarterly Court*, 7:116–21 9:52–55, 247, 258; Walter G. Davis, *The Ancestry of Lieutenant Amos Towne 1737–1793 of Arundel (Kennebunkport), Maine* (Portland, ME: Southworth Press, 1927), 499–500, 505; see Chapter 3 for the dispute between the Putnams, Jacob Towne, and others over lands on the Salem-Topsfield border.

82. Cedric Cowing, *The Saving Remnant: Religion and the Settling of New England* (Chicago: University of Illinois Press, 1995), 68–90.

83. Elinor Abbot, *Our Company Increases Apace: History, Language, and Social Identity in Early Colonial Andover, Massachusetts* (Dallas: SIL International, 2007), 149–52; Robinson, *Salem Witchcraft and the House of Seven Gables*, 273–300; "Petition of Twenty-Six Andover Men Concerning Townspeople Accused of Witchcraft," in Rosenthal et al., eds., *Salem Witch-Hunt*, 690–91 (quote). In her confession Mary Osgood helped to protect Reverend Dane. Apparently in response to people saying that Dane's specter had been seen, Osgood acknowledged this fact, but "she and Goody Dean carried the shape of Mr. Dean, the minister, between them, to make persons believe that Mr. Dean afflicted." See "Examination of Mary Osgood," in Rosenthal et al., eds., *Salem Witch-Hunt*, 608–609; Hall, *Witch-Hunting in the Seventeenth-Century*, 124; Latner, "Here Are No Newters," 110–11; Demos, *Entertaining Satan*, 36–56.

84. "Examination of Samuel Wardwell," in Rosenthal et al., eds., *Salem Witch-Hunt*, 576–77.

85. Rosenthal, *Salem Story*, 152–59. For Goody Glover's affliction of the Goodwin children, see Karlsen, *The Devil in the Shape of a Woman*, 33–35.

86. "Examination of Samuel Wardwell," in Rosenthal et al., eds., *Salem Witch-Hunt*, 576–77. It is possible that the trial, conviction, and condemnation of confessed witch Ann Foster

might have taken place before Wardwell's, but the order of these trials is unclear from the surviving record. For the sequence of events from Wardwell's confession to trial and retraction, see Roach, *Salem Witch Trials*, 260-88. Although Roach puts Hoar's confession prior to her conviction, the surviving documents are unclear on this, and it is possible she confessed after her conviction.

87. For the number of accused and confessed, see Burns, "The Coercion of False Confessions," 45; John Demos, *The Enemy Within: 2,000 Years of Witch-Hunting in the Western World* (New York: Viking, 2008), 176-77.

88. "Examination of Sarah Good," in Rosenthal et al., eds., *Salem Witch-Hunt*, 127-28 (quotes). For the importance of forced confessions, see Burns, "The Coercion of False Confessions"; Demos, *Enemy Within*, 177.

89. Calef, "More Wonders," 343; Rosenthal, *Salem Story*, 23-24; Hale, "Modest Inquiry," in Burr, ed., *Narratives*, 415 (quote).

90. "Recantations of Mary Osgood, Eunice Fry, et al.," in Rosenthal et al., eds., *Salem Witch-Hunt*, 693-94, #699. Rosenthal notes that the attribution of this document to Increase Mather is likely but cannot be proved.

91. Burns, "The Coercion of False Confessions," 29; Rosenthal et al., eds., *Salem Witch-Hunt*, 134; for the quote, see "Letter of Thomas Brattle," 189 (quote).

92. Calef, "More Wonders," 351 (quote), 362-63.

93. Burns, "The Coercion of False Confessions," 29-30; Samuel Willard, *Some Miscellany Observations on our Present Debates respecting Witchcrafts, in a Dialogue between S. and B. By P. E. and J. A.* (Philadelphia: William Bradford for Hezekiah Usher, 1692), 11; "Letter of Thomas Brattle," 173 (quote),

94. Burns, "The Coercion of False Confessions," 30; "Statement of Francis Dane, Sr., Regarding Some of the Accused of Andover," in Rosenthal et al., eds., *Salem Witch-Hunt*, 734-35 (quote).

95. Elizabeth Reis, *Damned Women: Sinners and Witches in Puritan New England* (Ithaca, NY: Cornell University Press, 1997), 121-63; Games, *Witchcraft in Early North America*, 63-64; "Statement of Israel Porter, Elizabeth Procter, Daniel Andrew and Peter Cloyce for Rebecca Nurse," in Rosenthal et al., eds., *Salem Witch-Hunt*, 162 (quote); Norton, *In the Devil's Snare*, 263-64.

96. Neal Allen, ed., *Maine Province and Court Records* (Portland: Maine Historical Society, 1975), 6:211-13 (quotes); Baker, *Devil of Great Island*, 196-97.

97. Norton, *In the Devil's Snare*, 264. For the similarity of the Andover confessions, see Burns, "The Coercion of False Confessions," 26-28.

98. Ulrich, *Good Wives*, 167-70; 184-88, 196-201; Roach, *Salem Witch Trials*, 142, 145, 174-75, 216.

99. "Confession of Mary Toothaker," in Rosenthal et al., eds., *Salem Witch-Hunt*, 491-92, #441 (quotes); Norton, *In the Devil's Snare*, 239-40; Robinson, *Salem Witchcraft and Hawthorne's House of Seven Gables*, 99-104.

100. Norton, *In the Devil's Snare*, 108, 240–41; Baker and Reid, *New England Knight*, 99.

101. Stuart Clark, "Inversion, Misrule and the Meaning of Witchcraft," in Darren Oldridge, ed., *The Witchcraft Reader* (New York: Routledge, 2002), 149–60. See also Stuart Clark, *Thinking with Demons: The Idea of Witchcraft in Early Modern Europe* (New York: Oxford University Press, 1997), 11–21, 80–93, 346–53, and passim.

CHAPTER SIX

1. Cotton Mather, *Magnalia Christi Americana, or the Ecclesiastical History of New England* (Hartford: Silas Andrus, 1820), 1:188.

2. This paragraph and the next are borrowed with minor changes from Emerson Baker and James Kences, "Maine, Indian Land Speculation, and the Essex County Witchcraft Outbreak of 1692," *Maine History* 40 (2001): 159–60. See also Mather, *Magnalia Christi America*, 1:188. It was the second marriage for Richards, whose deceased first wife was the widow of Anne's uncle Adam Winthrop. Her exact date of birth is unknown, but Anne Winthrop would have been roughly forty in 1692. Sewall, *The Diary of Samuel Sewall, 1674–1729*, ed. M. Halsey Thomas (New York: Farrar, Straus, and Giroux, 1973), 1:295; James Savage, *A Genealogical Dictionary of the First Settlers of New England* (Baltimore: Genealogical Publishing, 1981), 4:611–13; Sybil Noyes, Charles T. Libby, and Walter G. Davis, *Genealogical Dictionary of Maine and New Hampshire* (1928–29; reprint, Baltimore: Genealogical Publishing, 1979), 585. For the Usher-Tyng family and their connections, see Bernard Bailyn, *The New England Merchants in the Seventeenth Century* (Cambridge, MA: Harvard University Press, 1955), 134–38; Thomas Brattle, "Letter of Thomas Brattle, October 8, 1692," in George L. Burr, ed., *Narratives of the Witchcraft Cases* (New York: Charles Scribner's Sons, 1914), 178.

3. "Letter of Thomas Brattle," Burr, ed., *Narratives*, 178.

4. For the importance of merchant family connections, see Bailyn, *New England Merchants*.

5. Edgar J. McManus, *Law and Liberty in Early New England: Criminal Justice and Due Process, 1620–1692* (Amherst: University of Massachusetts Press, 1993), 140–41, 147–48, 211–12; Peter Hoffer, *The Devil's Disciples: Makers of the Salem Witch Trials* (Baltimore: Johns Hopkins University Press, 1996), 159–61; David Konig, *Law and Society in Puritan Massachusetts: Essex County 1629–1692* (Chapel Hill: University of North Carolina Press, 1979), 176; Richard Weisman, *Witchcraft, Magic and Religion* (Amherst: University of Massachusetts Press, 1984), 105–12; Mary Beth Norton, *In the Devil's Snare: The Salem Witchcraft Crisis of 1692* (New York: W. W. Norton, 2002), 197–99. Hoffer and Norton pay close attention to the background and role of the judges. See also Norton, *In the Devil's Snare*, 405–8; John Demos, *The Enemy Within: 2,000 Years of Witch-Hunting in the Western World* (New York: Viking, 2008), 111–17; John Murrin, "Coming to Terms with the Salem Witch Trials," *Proceedings of the American Antiquarian Society* 110 (2000). A second person, Elizabeth Morse, was convicted of witchcraft, but the governor and assistants issued a reprieve.

6. Stephen Foster, *The Long Argument: English Puritanism and the Shaping of New England Culture, 1570–1700* (Chapel Hill: University of North Carolina Press, 1991), 214–16

(quote on 214); Robert Charles Anderson, *The Great Migration Begins: Immigrants to New England, 1620–1633* (Boston: New England Historic Genealogical Society, 1995), 3:1773–7; John L. Sibley, *Biographical Sketches of Graduates of Harvard University* (Cambridge, MA: Charles William Sever, 1873), 1:194; K. David Goss, *The Salem Witch Trials: A Reference Guide* (Westport, CT: Greenwood Press, 2008), 112–13; Enders Robinson, *The Devil Discovered: Salem Witchcraft 1692* (Prospect Heights, IL: Waveland Press, 1991), 22–32; Hoffer, *The Devil's Disciples*, 136–37.

7. Sibley, *Biographical Sketches*, 2:345–60; Richard Francis, *Judge Sewall's Apology: The Salem Witch Trials and the Forming of an American Conscience* (New York: HarperCollins, 2005), 4–75; Sewall, *Diary*, 1:xxiii–xxv.

8. F. R. Raines, ed., *The Visitation of the County Palatine of Lancashire, 1664–5, by Sir William Dugdale* (Manchester: Chetham Society, 1872), 1:9; James Savage, *Genealogical Dictionary of the First Settlers of New England* (Boston: Little, Brown, 1860–62), 4:18; John Palfrey, *History of New England* (Boston: Little, Brown, 1875), 4:291. For Sergeant's inventory, see Suffolk County, Massachusetts Probate Records, 18:79. Robert Thompson called himself a cousin of Peter Sergeant. Thompson was governor of the Society for Propagation of the Gospel from 1691 to 1694. Thompson's daughter was married to Sir William Ashurst, See *New England Historical and Genealogical Register* 39 (1885): 301.

9. Although many genealogists consider Elizabeth Shrimpton to be Sergeant's first wife, Henry Waters believed he was first married to Elizabeth Corwin until she died. Just before his marriage to Shrimpton, Sergeant wrote a letter addressed to "Bro. Corwin, Bro. Jonathan and Bro. Browne," inviting them to his wedding reception, signing the letter "yr. affectionate brother." The "Bro." referred to are John Corwin, Jonathan Corwin, and their sister Hannah's husband, William Browne. Sergeant had to are married to a sister of the Corwins to refer to the three as "brother." Waters presumed this sister would have been Elizabeth. She was born July 2, 1648, but no record survives for her marriage. *New England Historical and Genealogical Register* 28 (1874): 20. In December 1681, Samuel Sewall does record in his diary the deaths of "Mrs. Mary Davis and Mrs. Eliza. Sargent," and calls them "Two of the chief Gentlewomen in Town." The date, the name, and the description all fit with the theory that this was Elizabeth Corwin. See Sewall, *Diary*, 1:52. In 1701 Sergeant would marry his third wife, Lady Mary Phips, the widow of Sir William Phips.

10. Noyes et al., *Genealogical Dictionary*, 585; Savage, *Genealogical Dictionary*, 3:533–34; Anderson, *The Great Migration Begins* 3:1575–79; Emerson Baker, *The Clarke and Lake Company: The Historical Archaeology of a Seventeenth-Century Maine Settlement* (Augusta: Maine Historic Preservation Commission, 1985), 10; *Winthrop Papers, 1650–1654*, ed. Malcolm Freiberg (Charlottesville: University of Virginia Press, 2005), 6:336; Oliver Ayer Roberts, *History of the Military Company of Massachusetts, Now Called the Ancient and Honorable Militia Company of Massachusetts: 1637–1888* (Boston: A. Mudge and Son, 1895), 1:143.

11. Richard Dunn, *Puritans and Yankees: The Winthrop Dynasty of New England, 1630–1717* (New York: W. W. Norton, 1971), 191 (quote).

12. Dunn, *Puritans and Yankees*, 191–264; Roberts, *History of the Military Company of Massachusetts*, 1:296–97. For an impressive biography of John Winthrop Jr. and his alchemy, see Walter W. Woodward, *Prospero's America: John Winthrop Jr., Alchemy, and the Creation*

of New England Culture (Chapel Hill, NC: Omohundro Institute of Early American History and Culture, 2010).

13. Henry Waters, *The Gedney and Clarke Families of Salem, Massachusetts* (Salem: Salem Press, 1880), 4–13; A. C. Goodell, "A Biographical Notice of the Officers of Probate for Essex County," *Essex Institute Historical Collections* 2 (1860): 223–25.

14. Marilynne Roach, "The Corpse in the Cellar," *New England Ancestors* 8, no. 4 (2007), 42–43. Sheriff Corwin's first wife was the late Susannah Gedney, the daughter of Bartholomew's brother John; *Records and Files of the Quarterly Courts of Essex County, Massachusetts*, 9 vols. (Salem: Essex Institute, 1911–1975), 9:563–64. Jonathan's son Reverend George changed the spelling to Curwin; see *Essex Institute Historical Collections* 2 (1860): 229.

15. *Colonial Collegians: Biographies of Those Who Attended American Colleges Before the War for Independence* (Boston: Massachusetts Historical Society, 2005), 413; Emory Washburn, *Sketches of the Judicial History of Massachusetts* (Boston: Little, Brown, 1840), 274; Albert Matthews, *Notes on the Massachusetts Royal Commissions, 1681–1775* (Cambridge, MA: John Wilson, 1913), 32–35; Robert E. Wall Jr., "The Membership of the Massachusetts General Court," Ph.D. dissertation, Yale University, 1965, 510.

16. "Examinations of Sarah Good, Sarah Osburn and Tituba," in Bernard Rosenthal et al., eds., *Records of the Salem Witch-Hunt* (New York: Cambridge University Press, 2009), 16; John Demos, *Entertaining Satan: Witchcraft and the Culture of Early New England* (New York: Oxford University Press, 1982), 127–28 #3 (quote); it is possible but unlikely that "Mr. Currins child" refers to one of the children of Jonathan's brother John Corwin. John's youngest child was eighteen in 1692, and there were not yet any grandchildren with the Corwin surname. Furthermore, John Corwin had died in 1683, so it seems unlikely Hathorne would have been referring to him, especially when Jonathan was sitting next to him. Edward Corwin, *The Corwin Genealogy in the United States* (New York: S. W. Green, 1872). Savage notes that "often this name is written Corwin, sometimes Currin, to conform to sound." Savage, *Genealogical Dictionary*, 1:488–89.

17. George Bodge, *Soldiers in King Philip's War* (Boston, 1906), 318–19. Like his father and brother, John Hathorne would have a distinguished military career. He served as a colonel and commanded an expedition against Nova Scotia. However, this service was in the years following the witch trials. James P. Baxter, ed., *Documentary History of the State of Maine* (Portland: Maine Historical Society, 1897), 5:87; Washburn, *Sketches of the Judicial History*, 272.

18. Sibley, *Biographical Sketches*, 2:1–9.

19. For the quote, see Eve LaPlante, *Salem Witch Judge: The Life and Repentance of Samuel Sewall* (New York: HarperCollins, 2007), 20.

20. Fifty-two percent of Harvard's graduates in the seventeenth century became ministers, and presumably more entered the college with that as their goal. See Samuel Eliot Morrison, *The Founding of Harvard College* (Cambridge, MA: Harvard University Press, 1935), 247.

21. Richard Francis, *Judge Sewall's Apology: The Salem Witch Trials and the Forming of an American Conscience* (New York: HarperCollins, 2005), 31–33. The literature on Sewall is extensive. For an excellent overview of his mental world, see David D. Hall, *Worlds of*

Wonder, Days of Judgment: Popular Religious Belief in Early America (Cambridge, MA: Harvard University Press, 1989), 213–38.

22. Sibley, *Biographical Sketches*, 1:196 (quote); Hoffer, *The Devils' Disciples*, 136.

23. Despite the fact that William Stoughton was one of the most important figures of the era, he remains a shadowy figure with little written on him. A biography of Stoughton is long overdue.

24. Sibley, *Biographical Sketches*, 1:195–96; Richard D. Pierce, ed., *Records of the First Church in Salem, Massachusetts, 1629–1736* (Salem: Essex Institute, 1974), 107, 111, 118; Foster, *The Long Argument*, 208, 222–23.

25. Konig, *Law and Society*, 53–54; John Noble, ed., *Records of the Court of Assistants of the Colony of Massachusetts Bay*, 3 vols. (Boston: Suffolk County, 1901–28), 1:179, 188–89, 228–33, see 228–29 for the quotes; David Hall, ed., *Witch-Hunting in Seventeenth-Century New England: A Documentary History, 1638–1692* (Boston: Northeastern University Press, 1991), 260–64.

26. The most complete discussions of the Morse case can be found in the following: Demos, *Entertaining Satan*, 132–52; Wendy West, "Enchanted Newbury: A Prelude to Salem's Witch Hysteria," M.A. thesis, Salem State University, 2010; Emerson Baker, *The Devil of Great Island: Witchcraft and Conflict in Early New England* (New York: Palgrave Macmillan, 2007), 24–30.

27. Hall, *Witch Hunting*, 230–59 (quote on 249).

28. Demos, *Entertaining Satan*, 136–37; Hale, "Modest Inquiry," in Burr, *Narratives*, 412; Hall, *Witch Hunting*, 253–55.

29. Nathaniel Shurtleff, *Records of the Governor and Company of Massachusetts Bay* (Boston: William White, 1854), 5:265–66, 308–309.

30. Alice Molland, also of Devon, was sentenced to death for witchcraft in 1685, but no evidence survives to confirm that the execution was carried out. James Sharpe, *Instruments of Darkness: Witchcraft in Early Modern England* (Philadelphia: University of Pennsylvania Press, 1997), 213–29; Malcolm Gaskill, "Witch Trials in England," in Brian Levack, ed., *The Oxford Handbook of Witchcraft in Early Modern Europe and Colonial America* (New York: Oxford University Press, 2013).

31. Mather, "Memorable Providences," in Burr, *Narratives*, 124 (quote).

32. Mather, "Memorable Providences," 106 (quote).

33. Mather, "Memorable Providences," 104–5; Sewall, *Diary*, 1:183.

34. Mather, "Memorable Providences," 106–7 (quote); Glover may have named her own daughter as a witch, for while Mather does not give a name, he notes "it might have been thought natural affection would have advised the concealing of." It is unclear if Glover's warning from the gallows was given in her limited English or translated from Gaelic.

35. For the departure of Andros, see Sewall, *Diary*, 1:182; John Murrin, "Coming to Terms with the Salem Witch Trials," *Proceedings of the American Antiquarian Society* 110 (2000): 322.

36. John Mompesson, who owned the house assaulted by the Demon Drummer, was a third cousin once removed of Stoughton through his mother, Katherine Mompesson. See George W. Marshall, ed., *Visitation of Wiltshire, 1623* (London: George Bell and Sons, 1882), 96–97; Anderson, *The Great Migration Begins*, 3:1773-1777. For the Demon Drummer, see Baker, *Devil of Great Island*, 22–24; Joseph Glanvill, *Saducismus Triumphatus: Or Full and Plain Evidence Concerning Witches and Apparitions* (London, 1688), 313-30. For the Hull-Parris kinship, see chapter 1.

37. George Francis Dow and John Henry Edmonds, *The Pirates of the New England Coast, 1630-1730* (Salem: Marine Research Society, 1923), 54–65. The author is deeply indebted to James Kences for bringing the pirate trials and their impact on the thinking of the witch judges to his attention.

38. Dow and Edmonds, *Pirates of the New England Coast*, 66–72; Sewall, *Diary*, 1:248-50 (the quotes are on 250).

39. Robert Moody and Richard Simmons, eds., *The Glorious Revolution in Massachusetts: Selected Documents, 1689-1692* (Boston: Colonial Society of Massachusetts, 1988), 182–85, 192–96, 226–27, 235, 244, 249, 251, 284, 303, 340; Baxter, *Documentary History*, 5:108–9, 116, 154–55, 172–73; Emerson Baker and John Reid, *The New England Knight: Sir William Phips, 1651-1695* (Toronto: University of Toronto Press, 1998), 96, 101–3.

40. Moody and Simmons, *The Glorious Revolution in Massachusetts*, 218–21.

41. This and the following six paragraphs are drawn from Baker and Kences, "Maine, Indian Land Speculation," 167–70; Richard S. Dunn, *Puritans and Yankees: The Winthrop Dynasty of New England, 1630-1717* (New York: W. W. Norton, 1971), 234–38, 243–46; John Martin, *Profits in the Wilderness: Entrepreneurship and the Founding of New England Towns in the Seventeenth Century* (Chapel Hill: University of North Carolina Press, 1991), 100–110; Baker, *The Clarke and Lake Company*, 10; *Suffolk Deeds*, 14 vols. (Boston: Rockwell and Churchill, 1880-1906) 2:44, 88.

42. Wharton's first wife, Bethia Tyng, was a first cousin of Joseph Dudley's wife, Rebecca. Bailyn, *New England Merchants*, 135–37; George A. Wheeler and Henry W. Wheeler, *History of Brunswick, Topsham, and Harpswell, Maine* (Boston: Alfred Mudge and Son, 1878), 11–16; Savage, *Genealogical Dictionary*, 4:439–41, 494–95. For a brief summary of Wharton's land ventures, see Martin, *Profits in the Wilderness*, 69–70, 90, 108–9, 261. For Richards's mortgage business, see *Suffolk Deeds*, 12:248-51; 13:128-31; 14:62-63, 126-27. A branch of the Way family lived in Salem Village, where they were supporters of Reverend Samuel Parris. Members of the Stoughton, Winthrop, and Leverett families had all fought in the same parliamentary regiment in the English Civil War. This experience may have helped bring them together as speculators. Ian Gentles, "The Sale of Bishops' Lands in the English Revolution, 1646-1660," *English Historical Review* 95 (1980): 586–87; Martin, *Profits in the Wilderness*, 90–93.

43. Vernon Loggins, *The Hawthornes* (New York: Columbia University Press, 1951), 68, 76, 84–85; Martin, *Profits in the Wilderness*, 73–77; Sewall, *Diary*, 1:148-50; Noyes et al., *Genealogical Dictionary*, 255, 318, 534; Savage, *Genealogical Dictionary*, 1:488–89; 2:240–41, 376; John F. Curwen, *A History of the Ancient House of Curwen* (Kendal, UK: Titus Wilson and Son, 1928), 210-14. The Corwin mills were located in the northeastern part of Wells, in present-day Kennebunk.

44. *York Deeds*, 2:190–91, 428, 433; Wilbur Spencer, *Pioneers on Maine Rivers* (Baltimore: Genealogical Publishing, 1973), 235; Noyes et al., *Genealogical Dictionary*, 534; Baxter, ed., *Documentary History of Maine*, 6:210, 222–25, 238–39; Shurtleff, *Massachusetts Bay Records*, 5:286–89; Savage, *Genealogical Dictionary*, 3:369; Moxes to Richard Pateshall, August 3, 1685, *York Deeds* 8:229; 9:230; 10:261–62.

45. Robert E. Moody, "The Saltonstall Papers," *Massachusetts Historical Society Collections* 80 (1972): 13–21, 38–49; "Letter of Thomas Brattle, October 8, 1692," in Burr, ed., *Narratives*, 184; William Willis, *The History of Portland, from 1632 to 1864* (Portland: Bailey and Noyes, 1865), 229; Sewall, *Diary*, 1:305–306; Wall, "Membership of the Massachusetts General Court," 665.

46. "John Hubbard to Samuel Sewall, Eliakim Hutchinson and Peter Sergeant, November 19, 1684," *Suffolk Deeds*, 14:5–6; Bailyn, *New England Merchants*, 173, 192–94. Sergeant's wife was Mary Shrimpton. She was almost certainly a relative of Samuel Shrimpton, most likely his cousin. Savage, *Genealogical Dictionary* 3:90–91; Clarence Torrey, *New England Marriages Prior to 1700* (Baltimore: Genealogical Publishing, 1985), 651.

47. "Samuel Sewall to Ichabod Plaisted, March 1, 1701," *Samuel Sewall's Letterbook*, *Massachusetts Historical Society Collections*, 6th Ser., 1 (1886): 252–53. For wealth in Boston, see Gary Nash, *The Urban Crucible: Social Change, Political Consciousness, and the Origins of the American Revolution* (Cambridge, MA: Harvard University Press, 1979), 19–20, 400.

48. The author would like to thank James Kences for bringing the connection between the witchcraft judges and the New England Company to his attention. William Kellaway, *The New England Company, 1649–1776: Missionary Society to the American Indians* (Westport, CT: Greenwood Press, 1975), 67, 77–79, 156, 166–67, 200–202; Sewall, *Diary*, 1:254 (quote).

49. Kellaway, *New England Company*, 85–87, 261–67. George F. Daniels, *History of the Town of Oxford, Massachusetts* (Oxford, MA: Author, 1892), 3–8; Shurtleff, *Massachusetts Bay Records*, 5:342–43, 361–71, 408–409.

50. For the long-lasting impact of King Philip's War and how it strengthened the enmity between colonists and Native Americans, see Jill Lepore, *The Name of War: King Philip's War and the Origins of American Identity* (New York: Alfred A. Knopf, 1998).

51. Moody and Simmons, eds., *Glorious Revolution*, 220 (quote); "Examination of Sarah Good, Sarah Osburn and Tituba," in Rosenthal et al., ed., *Salem Witch-Hunt*, 126–29.

52. This principle of recusal was set forward by English chief justice Edward Coke in 1610. See Sir Edward Coke, *The reports of Sir Edward Coke, Kt., Late Lord Chief Justice of England* (London: Printed for H Twyford, 1680), 588–91. For posting bond, see Rosenthal, "General Introduction," in Rosenthal et al., eds., *Salem Witch-Hunt*, 18.

53. The importance of Thomas Putnam in taking depositions was discovered by Bernard Rosenthal. See his "General Introduction," in Rosenthal et al., eds., *Salem Witch-Hunt*, 30 (quote). See also Richard B. Trask, "Legal Procedures Used During the Salem Witch Trials and a Brief History of the Published Versions of the Records," in Rosenthal et al., eds., *Salem Witch-Hunt*, 46–49.

54. "The Examination of Nehemiah Abbott, Jr.," in Rosenthal et al., eds., *Salem Witch-Hunt*, 205–6; Hoffer, *The Devil's Disciples*, 154–55, 258. For a list of cases prior to 1692, see Weisman, *Witchcraft, Magic and Religion*, 191–203.

55. Dawn Archer, "'Can Innocent People Be Guilty?': A Sociopragmatic Analysis of Examination Transcripts from the Salem Witch Trials," *Journal of Historical Pragmatics* 3 (2002), 1–30; Margo Burns, "'Other Ways of Undue Force and Fright': The Coercion of False Confessions by the Salem Magistrates," *Studia Neophilologica* 84 (2012): 23–38; "Examination of Sarah Good, Sarah Osburn and Tituba as Recorded by John Hathorn," in Rosenthal et al., eds., *Salem Witch-Hunt*, 126–27 (quote).

56. Archer, "'Can Innocent People Be Guilty?'" 1 (quote); Burns, "'Other Ways of Undue Force and Fright,'" 23–38.

57. Trask, "Legal Procedures," 50–51; "Examination of William Procter," in Rosenthal et al., eds., *Salem Witch-Hunt*, 664–65; Hoffer, *The Devil's Disciples*, 169–71, 762; Patricio Martínez Llompart, "Reinstating Rationality Within the Salem Witch Hunt: A Look into the Ignoramus Indictments of 1692," Cornell University History Department, 2010, available at http://ecommons.library.cornell.edu/retrieve/111856/Mart%C3%ADnez%20Llompart-Reinstating%20Rationality%20within%20the%20Salem%20Witch%20Hunt.pdf.

58. Konig, *Law and Society*, 172–73; Hoffer, *The Devil's Disciples*, 133–34; Rosenthal, "General Introduction," *Salem Witch-Hunt*, 23–24; Wendel D. Craker, "Spectral Evidence, Non-Spectral Acts of Witchcraft and Confession at Salem in 1692," *Historical Journal* 40 (1997): 331–58; Burns, "Coercion of False Confessions," 27–28. For the judges' use of English authorities, see Norton, *In the Devil's Snare*, 36–38, 199–201; Hale, "A Modest Inquiry," in Burr, ed., *Narratives*, 414–15.

59. "Cotton Mather to John Richards, May 31, 1692," *Selected Letters of Cotton Mather*, ed. Kenneth Silverman (Baton Rouge: Louisiana State University Press, 1971), 36 (quote).

60. "The Return of Several Ministers Consulted, June 15, 1692," in Boyer and Nissenbaum, eds., *Salem-Village Witchcraft*, 118 (quote).

61. "The Return of Several Ministers," 117–18 (quote); Hoffer, *The Devil's Disciples*, 149–50; Norton, *In the Devil's Snare*, 213–16.

62. Calef, "More Wonders," in Burr, *Narratives*, 357–58 (quote).

63. Calef, "More Wonders," 353; "Testimony of Sarah Nurse," in Rosenthal et al., eds., *Salem Witch-Hunt*, 432. For a brief summary of fraud in the trials, see Rosenthal, "General Introduction," 30. For a more comprehensive view, see Bernard Rosenthal, *Salem Story: Reading the Witch Trials of 1692* (New York: Cambridge University Press, 1995), Hoffer, *The Devil's Disciples*, 97–101, 163–68; Burns, "Coercion of False Confessions," 33; Murrin, "Coming to Terms," 34–35.

64. "Petition of Mary Esty," in Rosenthal et al., eds., *Salem Witch-Hunt*, 657–58 (quote).

65. Konig, *Law and Society*, 173 (quote).

66. Noble, ed., *Records of the Court of Assistants*, 1:305, 319–20. Jacob Leisler and Jacob Milborne had refused to plea, as they did not accept the jurisdiction of Joseph Dudley's court, but the trial proceeded with their conviction and execution just a year earlier in New

York with Thomas Newton as crown attorney. See David Lovejoy, *The Glorious Revolution in America* (New York: Harper and Row, 1972), 354–56.

67. Moody and Simmons, *The Glorious Revolution in Massachusetts*, 221 (quote).

68. Burns, "Coercion of False Confessions," 25–26; Norton, *In the Devil's Snare*, 275–78; Roach, *Salem Witch Trials*, 287–94; "Petition of John Hale, Nicholas Noyes, Daniel Epps Jr., and John Emerson Jr., for Dorcas Hoar," in Rosenthal et al., eds., *Salem Witch-Hunt*, 673.

69. Roach, *Salem Witch Hunt*, 35–36; Rosenthal et al., eds., *Salem Witch-Hunt*, 752, 820. Tituba's name was included on a summons on June 27, 1692, to appear as a witness against Sarah Good. See "Summons for Witnesses v. Sarah Good, and Officer's Return," in Rosenthal et al., eds., *Salem Witch-Hunt*, 402–3, #323. However, there is no evidence that Tituba did in fact testify. The author thanks Margo Burns for her help in interpreting this document.

70. Evidence from England suggests a belief that detaining a witch could neutralize her powers. See Malcolm Gaskill, *Crime and Mentalities in Early Modern England* (New York: Cambridge University Press, 2000), 44–46.

71. "Cotton Mather to John Richards, May 3, 1692," in *Selected Letters of Cotton Mather*, 39–40; Murrin, "Coming to Terms with the Salem Witch Trials," 337 (quote).

72. "Petition of John Hale, Nicholas Noyes, Daniel Epps Jr., and John Emerson Jr., for Dorcas Hoar," 673 (quote).

73. "Examination of Mary Lacey, Jr., Mary Lacey, Sr., Ann Foster, Richard Carrier and Andrew Carrier, July 21, 1692," in Rosenthal et al., eds., *Salem Witch-Hunt*, 472 (quote). There are two extant records of this examination and confession. The one quoted here is the version first published by Thomas Hutchinson.

74. "Examination of Mary Lacey, Jr., Mary Lacey, Sr., Ann Foster, Richard Carrier and Andrew Carrier, July 21, 1692," 476 (quote). This version of the examination survives in manuscript, in the hand of John Higginson Jr.

75. Mather, "Wonders," in Burr, ed., *Narratives*, 242 (quote).

76. Hoffer, *The Devil's Disciples*, 161–62.

CHAPTER SEVEN

1. Cotton Mather, *The Diary of Cotton Mather*, ed. Worthington Chauncey Ford (New York: Frederick Ungar, 1957), 1: 216.

2. "Phips to Blathwayt, October 12, 1692," in George Lincoln Burr, ed., *Narratives of the New England Witchcraft Cases* (New York: Charles Scribner's Sons, 1914), 197 (quotes).

3. Jacob Melyen wrote that the Mathers' books were in press by October 12, and their books as well as Samuel Willard's were in print by October 28. Letter from Jacob Melyen to Dr. Johannes Kerfbij, October 12, 1692, and letter from Jacob Melyen to Dr. Johannes Kerfbij, October 28, 1692, in Evan Haefeli, "Dutch New York and the Salem Witch Trials: Some New Evidence," *Proceedings of the American Antiquarian Society* 110 (2000): 306–7.

4. Increase Mather, *Cases of Conscience Concerning Evil Spirits Personating Men* (Boston: Benjamin Harris, 1693), 66 (quote); P.E. and J.A., *Some Miscellany Observations on Our*

Present Debates Respecting Witchcrafts (Philadelphia: Printed by William Bradford for Hezekiah Usher, 1692). While Mather's book is dated 1693, there is no doubt it was in press by 1692. Mary McCarl Rheinlander, "Spreading the News of Satan's Malignity in Salem: Benjamin Harris, Printer and Publisher of the Witchcraft Narratives," *Essex Institute Historical Collections* 129 (1993): 57–58; Mary Beth Norton, *In the Devil's Snare: The Salem Witchcraft Crisis of 1692* (New York: W. W. Norton, 2002), 280–82; Larry Gragg, *The Salem Witch Crisis* (New York: Praeger, 1992), 172–76; Stephen Foster, *The Long Argument: English Puritanism and the Shaping of New England Culture, 1570–1700* (Chapel Hill: University of North Carolina Press, 1991), 262–64.

5. Robert Calef, "More Wonders," in Burr, *Narratives*, 360 (quote); Norton, *In the Devil's Snare*, 224–25; Stephen L. Robbins, "Samuel Willard and the Spectres of God's Wrathful Lion," *New England Quarterly* 69 (1987), 599. Willard had been accused by July 11, when Jacob Melyen wrote of it. See Melyen to Kerfbij, July 11, 1692, 302.

6. Henry S. Nourse, *History of the Town of Harvard, Massachusetts, 1732–1893* (Harvard, MA: Printed for Warren Hapgood, 1894), 28–29. Foster, *The Long Argument*, 265–67; Robbins, "Samuel Willard and the Spectres of God's Wrathful Lion," 596–603.

7. "Deposition of Lydia Nichols and Margaret Knight v. John Willard," in Bernard Rosenthal et al., eds., *Records of the Salem Witch-Hunt* (New York: Cambridge University Press, 2009), 526–27; Calef, "More Wonders," 361; Mark Peterson, "'Ordinary Preaching' and the Interpretation of the Salem Witchcraft Crisis by the Boston Clergy," *Essex Institute Historical Collections* 129 (1993): 94–102; "Letter of Thomas Brattle," in Burr, ed., *Narratives,* 186–88; Marilynne K. Roach, *The Salem Witch Trials: A Day-by-Day Chronicle of a Community under Siege* (New York: Cooper Square Press, 2002), 246–47.

8. The book was noted as early as October 20. A contemporary letter confirms that the book was in print by October 28 and was authored by Willard. See Melyen to Kerfbij, October 28, 1692, 307; "The Salem Witchcraft Trials: Samuel Willard's *Some Miscellany Observations*," *Essex Institute Historical Collections* 122 (1986): 215. Scholars generally believe the work to have been actually published in Boston. See Norton, *In the Devil's Snare*, 280–81, 403; Perry Miller, *The New England Mind: From Colony to Province* (Cambridge, MA: Belknap Press, 1953), 205–6; Rheinlander, "Spreading the News of Satan's Malignity," 57–58. Analysis of the typeface indicates Willard's book was published in Boston, not Philadelphia.

9. Letter from R.P. to Jonathan Corwin, Salisbury, August 9, 1692, in Charles W. Upham, ed., *Salem Witchcraft* (Boston: Wiggin and Lunt, 1867), 697–705; for quotes, see 704.

10. Brattle, "Letter," 178 (quote); Norton, *In the Devil's Snare*, 282–83; Sarah Rivett, *The Science of the Soul in Colonial New England* (Chapel Hill: University of North Carolina Press, 2011), 261, 264–65; Rick Kennedy, "Thomas Brattle and the Scientific Provincialism of New England, 1680–1713," *New England Quarterly* 63 (1990): 590–94.

11. Brattle, "Letter," 184 (quote).

12. Cotton Mather, "Wonders of the Invisible World," in Burr, ed., *Narratives*, 205–51; Norton, *In The Devil's Snare*, 284–85. For the Bury St. Edmunds trials, see Gilbert Geis and Ivan Bunn, *A Trial of Witches: A Seventeenth-Century Witchcraft Prosecution* (New York: Routledge, 1997), 66, 88, 135. Hale would become chief justice in 1671. For Mora and the context of Swedish trials, see Bengt Ankarloo, "Sweden: The Mass Burnings, 1668–1676,"

in Bengt Ankarloo and Gustav Hennigsen, eds., *Early Modern Witchcraft: Centres and Peripheries* (New York: Oxford University Press, 1993), 285–317.

13. "Deposition of Deborah Hadley for Elizabeth How," in Rosenthal et al., eds., *Salem Witch-Hunt*, 397, #316 (quote); Norton, *In the Devil's Snare*, 284–85.

14. John L. Sibley, *Biographical Sketches of Graduates of Harvard University* (Cambridge, MA: Charles William Sever, 1873), 3: 6–8; John Demos, *The Enemy Within: 2,000 Years of Witch-Hunting in the Western World* (New York: Viking, 2008), 216–21.

15. Emerson Baker and John Reid, *The New England Knight: Sir William Phips, 1651–1695* (Toronto: University of Toronto Press, 1998), 153–55; Cotton Mather, "Wonders of the Invisible World," 211 (quote). Mather authored the "Return" for the group of ministers who made up the Cambridge Association. Foster, *The Long Argument*, 256–57, 264; Richard Weisman, *Witchcraft, Magic and Religion in Seventeenth Century Massachusetts* (Amherst: University of Massachusetts Press, 1984), 170–71; "The Return of Several Ministers (June 15, 1692)," in Boyer and Nissenbaum, eds., *Salem-Village Witchcraft*, 117–18; Cotton Mather, *Selected Letters of Cotton Mather*, ed. Kenneth Silverman (Baton Rouge: Louisiana State University Press, 1971), 30–44.

16. Mather, "Wonders," 209 (quote); Rheinlander, "Spreading the News of Satan's Malignity," 56–58.

17. Samuel Sewall, *The Diary of Samuel Sewall, 1674–1729*, ed. M. Halsey Thomas (New York: Farrar, Straus and Giroux, 1973), 1: 299 (quote); Roach, *Salem Witch Trials*, 325–26; Gragg, *Salem Witch Crisis*, 170–72.

18. The most recent biography of Phips is Baker and Reid, *The New England Knight*. This and the following paragraphs follow closely on its arguments. For the treasure, see 54–55 in particular. The crown received a tenth of the treasure. Phips's personal share was £11,000.

19. Baker and Reid, *The New England Knight*, 144–45, 178–83.

20. Baker and Reid, *The New England Knight*, 144; Peter Hoffer, *The Devil's Disciples: Makers of the Salem Witch Trials* (Baltimore: Johns Hopkins University Press, 1996), 135–36; David Konig, *Law and Society in Puritan Massachusetts: Essex County 1629–1692* (Chapel Hill: University of North Carolina Press, 1979), 170; John Murrin, "Coming to Terms with the Salem Witch Trials," *Proceedings of the American Antiquarian Society* 110 (2000), 336–37.

21. Baker and Reid, *The New England Knight*, 143–47; "Deposition of Thomas Gages v. Roger Toothaker," in Rosenthal et al., eds., *Salem Witch-Hunt*, 318, #215 (quote).

22. Baker and Reid, *The New England Knight*, 147–51, 233–34; Baker and Reid, "Sir William Phips and the Decentring of Empire in Northeastern North America, 1690–1694," in Germaine Warkentin and Carolyn Podruchny, eds., *Decentring the Renaissance: Canada and Europe in Multidisciplinary Perspective, 1500–1700* (Toronto: University of Toronto Press, 2001), 87–300; George Francis Dow and John Henry Edmonds, *The Pirates of the New England Coast, 1630–1730* (Salem: Marine Research Society, 1923), 72. Phips's connection to piracy may have sprung in part from the fact that one of Thomas Pound's pirates captured in 1690 was Richard Phips, who either died in prison or disappeared. Richard had been one of the members of the Fort Loyal garrison who abandoned their post to turn

pirate. Sir William was said by Mather to have been one of twenty-six children, including twenty-one sons. While this may have been an exaggeration, he clearly came from a large family and only the names of thirteen siblings and half-siblings are known for this, the only Phips family in Maine. So it is possible that Richard, a militiaman stationed in Maine, was a brother.

23. Baker and Reid, *The New England Knight*, 155; Norton, *In the Devil's Snare*, 390 n. 11; "Warrant for Execution of Sarah Good, et al.," in Rosenthal et al., eds., *Salem Witch-Hunt*, 466, #418. There is no formal document to suggest Phips gave this power to the deputy governor, but Stoughton did sign the death warrant for the July executions, even though Phips was present in Boston.

24. Mather, *Cases of Conscience*, postscript (quote); Foster, *The Long Argument*, 263–64.

25. Baker and Reid, *The New England Knight*, 180, 185–86; Foster, *The Long Argument*, 264–66.

26. Samuel Willard, *The Character of a Good Ruler* (Boston: Benjamin Harris, 1694), 17–18 (quote); Foster, *The Long Argument*, 264–68; Baker and Reid, *The New England Knight*, 198.

27. Sibley, *Biographical Sketches*, 1:425–29. Though technically he held the office of vice president, Willard exercised all powers and duties of the president of Harvard from 1701 until his death in 1707.

28. Baker and Reid, *The New England Knight*, 188–89.

29. Baker and Reid, *The New England Knight*, 178–81, 188–90, 221–22; Foster, *The Long Argument*, 264–65.

30. Baker and Reid, *The New England Knight*, 180–86. The General Court also failed to set a salary for Anthony Checkley for his work as crown attorney. On June 13, 1693, he petitioned to receive payment and to have a salary set. "See Petition of Anthony Checkley," in Rosenthal et al., eds., *Salem Witch-Hunt*, 828–29, #852.

31. Baker and Reid, *The New England Knight*, 221–48.

32. Murrin, "Coming to Terms with the Salem Witch Trials," 347; Cornelia N. Dayton, *Women Before the Bar: Gender, Law and Society in Connecticut, 1639–1785* (Chapel Hill: University of North Carolina Press, 1995), 59–60, 187–89.

33. Konig, *Law and Society in Puritan Massachusetts*, 186–87; "An Act Against Conjuration, Witchcraft, and Dealing with Evil and Wicked Spirits," *The Acts and Resolves, Public and Private, of the Province of the Massachusetts Bay*, 21 vols. (Boston: Printed by the State, 1869–1922), 1:90–91; the Privy Council disallowed this law, but the sentiment in Massachusetts was clear. "Cotton Mather to John Richards, May 31,1692," in Mather, *Selected Letters*, 36; Weisman, *Witchcraft, Magic and Religion*, 175; Owen Davies, *Witchcraft, Magic and Culture, 1736–1951* (Manchester: Manchester University Press, 1999), 1–11.

34. Calef, "More Wonders," 385; Gragg, *Salem Witch Crisis*, 199; John Demos, *Entertaining Satan: Witchcraft and the Culture of Early New England* (New York: Oxford University Press, 1982), 387–94; Carson O. Hudson Jr., *These Detestable Slaves of the Devill: A Concise Guide to Witchcraft in Colonial Virginia* (Haverford, PA: Infinity, 2001), 48–55; "The

Virginia Case of Grace Sherwood," in Burr, ed., *Narratives*, 433–42. Sherwood was first charged with witchcraft in 1697.

35. Robert St. George, *Conversing by Signs: Poetics of Implication in Colonial New England Culture* (Chapel Hill: University of North Carolina Press, 1988), 190–92; M. Chris Manning, "Homemade Magic: Concealed Deposits in Architectural Contexts in the Eastern United States," M.A. thesis, Ball State University, 2012; Cynthia K. Riley Augé, "Silent Sentinels: Archaeology, Magic, and the Gendered Control of Domestic Boundaries in New England, 1620–1725," Ph.D. dissertation, Anthropology and Heritage Studies, University of Montana, 2013. For the continued belief in witchcraft and magic and England, see Davies, *Witchcraft, Magic and Culture*.

36. Deposition of Nathaniel Keene Jr., December 31, 1725, in Neal Allen, ed., *Maine Province and Court Records* (Portland: Maine Historical Society, 1975), 6: 214 (quote); R. Stuart Wallace, "The Scotch-Irish of Provincial Maine: Purpooduck, Merrymeeting Bay, and Georgia," in Michael C. Connolly, ed., *They Changed Their Sky: The Irish in Maine* (Orono: University of Maine Press, 2004), 41–49.

37. *The Eastern Herald and Gazette of Maine*, November 17, 1796, 2 (quote); Dane Yorke, *A History and Stories of Biddeford* (Biddeford, ME: McArthur Library, 1994), 144–46. For other accusations in the eighteenth and nineteenth centuries, see Demos, *Entertaining Satan*, 387–94. A comprehensive treatment of witchcraft belief after 1692 can be found in Owen Davies, *America Bewitched: The Story of Witchcraft After Salem* (New York: Oxford University Press, 2013).

38. *Polar Star and Boston Daily Advertiser*, December 9, 1796, 3 (quote).

39. Richard Gildrie, *The Profane, the Civil, and the Godly: The Reformation of Manners in Orthodox New England, 1679–1749* (University Park: Pennsylvania State University Press, 1994), 181–209; James F. Cooper Jr., *Tenacious in the Liberties: The Congregationalists in Colonial Massachusetts* (New York: Oxford University Press, 1999), 134–36, 155–57; Miller, *The New England Mind*, 209–25; Kenneth Lockridge, *A New England Town, the First Hundred Years: Dedham, Massachusetts, 1636–1736* (New York: W.W. Norton, 1970), 34–36.

40. See Elizabeth Reis, *Damned Women: Sinners and Witches in Puritan New England* (Ithaca, NY: Cornell University Press, 1997), 164–93, for a detailed discussion of "Satan Dispossessed."

41. Foster, *The Long Argument*, 281–82; Miller, *The New England Mind*, 240–42; Benjamin Colman, *A manifesto or declaration, set forth by the undertakers of the new church now erected in Boston in New-England, November 17. 1699* (Boston, 1699), 3 (quote).

42. Foster, *The Long Argument*, 279–84 (quote is on 282); Miller, *The New England Mind*, 225–47. Stoddard's eventual successor as Northampton minister would be his grandson Jonathan Edwards, a leader of the Great Awakening.

43. James Edward Maule, *Better That 100 Witches Should Live* (Villanova, PA: JEM, 1995), 20–39; Don Jordan and Michael Walsh, *White Cargo: The Forgotten History of Britain's White Slaves in America* (New York: New York University Press, 2007), 161, 181–91. In the 1669 incident his name is written in the court record as "Thomas Male," *Records and*

Files of the Quarterly Courts of Essex County, Massachusetts, 9 vols. (Salem: Essex Institute, 1911–1975), 4:174 (quote).

44. Carla Gardina Pestana, *Quakers and Baptists in Colonial Massachusetts* (New York: Cambridge University Press: 1991), 25–43; Jonathan Chu, *Neighbors, Friends or Madmen: The Puritan Adjustment to Quakerism in Seventeenth-Century Massachusetts* (Westport, CT: Greenwood Press, 1985), 3–58. For the law, see Thomas Maule, "New-England Pesecutors [*sic*] Mauled with their own Weapons," in James Edward Maule, *Better That 100 Witches Should Live,* 518–19.

45. Chu, *Neighbors, Friends or Madmen,* 125–52; A. L. Rowse, *Four Caroline Portraits: Thomas Hobbes, Henry Marten, Hugh Peters, John Selden* (London: Gerald Duckworth, 1993), 97–123; Sidney Perley, *History of Salem, Massachusetts,* 3 vols. (Salem: Author, 1924–28), 1:298–301, 424–25.

46. Maule, *Better That 100 Witches Should Live,* 36–44; *Essex Court Records,* 5:63, 103, 8:222–26, 341–42.

47. Emerson Baker, *The Devil of Great Island: Witchcraft and Conflict in Early New England* (New York: Palgrave Macmillan, 2007), 7–14; Richard Chamberlain, "Lithobolia: Or the Stone-Throwing Devil," in Burr, ed., *Narratives,* 69.

48. Maule, *Better That 100 Witches Should Live,* 103–4.

49. Maule, *Better That 100 Witches Should Live,* 89; Maule, "New-England Pesecutors Mauled."

50. Maule, *Better That 100 Witches Should Live,* 111. The warrant can be found in Maule, "New-England Pesecutors Mauled" (quote).

51. Maule, *Better That 100 Witches Should Live,* 117–22; Brattle, "Letter," 184 (quote). Sewall noted in his diary that on October 15, 1692, he had met with Danforth, who made clear his concerns about the trials. Sewall, *Diary,* 1:298.

52. Maule, *Better That 100 Witches Should Live,* 123; James Savage, *A Genealogical Dictionary of the First Settlers of New England,* 4 vols. (Baltimore: Genealogical Publishing, 1981), 2:174–75, 240. John Turner's daughter Elizabeth was sister-in-law of Bartholomew Gedney. See also Perley, *History of Salem,* 2:276–77, 279; Paul Boyer and Stephen Nissenbaum, *Salem Possessed: The Social Origins of Witchcraft* (Cambridge, MA: Harvard University Press, 1974), 62; Marilynne K. Roach, "Biographical Notes," in Rosenthal et al., eds., *Salem Witch-Hunt,* 964; "Statement of Elizer Keyser v. George Burroughs," and "Statement of Elizabeth Woodwell v. Giles Cory," in Rosenthal et al., eds., *Salem Witch-Hunt,* 244, 619; Calef, "More Wonders," 387–88.

53. Maule, "New-England Pesecutors Mauled," 560–62 (quotes); Maule, *Better that 100 Witches Should Live,* 122–27.

54. Potter later moved to Leicester and is buried in the Quaker Cemetery there. Samuel Kilham's first cousin, Thomas, was married to Sarah Solart Good's sister. And like her sister Sarah Good, Martha Kilham was left out of her father's estate. Maule, *Better that 100 Witches Should Live,* 127; Maule, "New-England Pesecutors Mauled," 60–62; Emory Washburn, *Historical Sketches of the Town of Leicester, Massachusetts, During the First Century from*

Its Settlement (Boston: John Wilson and Son, 1860), 116, 388; Heyrman, *Commerce and Culture*, 103–4, 107–8; William S. Mills, "The Early Kilhams," *New England Historical and Genealogical Register* 56 (1902), 344–46; "The Estate of John Solart of Wenham," 283–85;*The Probate Records of Essex County, Massachusetts*, 3 vols. (Salem: Essex Institute, 1916-1920), 2:283–85; Boyer and Nissenbaum, *Salem Possessed*, 203–4; "Statement of Elizer Keyser v. George Burroughs," in Rosenthal et al., eds., *Salem Witch-Hunt*, 243–44 (quote); Calef, "More Wonders," 358.

55. Eleanor Tucker, "The Gowing Family of Lynn," *Essex Genealogist* 8 (1988): 39–41, 144; "Petition in Support of John and Elizabeth Procter," in Rosenthal et al., eds., *Salem Witch-Hunt*, 533–36; Calef, "More Wonders," 387–88.

56. Maule, *Better That 100 Witches Should Live*, 129–33; Maule, "New-England Pesecutors Mauled."

57. Phips to Nottingham, September 11, 1693, Public Record Office, London, CO5/751, No. 37; Robert L. Bradley and Helen Camp, *The Forts of Pemaquid, Maine: An Archaeological and Historical Study* (Augusta: Maine Historic Preservation Commission, 1994), 10–12.

58. Sewall, *Diary*, 1:352–55; Samuel Sewall to John Storke, July 31, 1696, in "Letter-Book of Samuel Sewall," *Collections of the Massachusetts Historical Society*, 6th ser., vol. 1 (1886): 165–66 (quote); Roach, *Salem Witch Trials*, 534–35; *Acts and Resolves of Massachusetts Bay*, 7:512–14; John C. Webster, *Acadia at the End of the Seventeenth Century* (St. John: New Brunswick Museum, 1934), 89–97, 178.

59. Roach, *Salem Witch-Hunt*, 530, 536–41; Karen Kupperman, "Climate and Mastery of the Wilderness," in David D. Hall, David G. Allen, and Philip Smith, eds., *Seventeenth-Century New England* (Boston: Colonial Society of Massachusetts, 1984), 31; Jane Garrett, *The Triumphs of Providence: The Assassination Plot, 1696* (Cambridge: Cambridge University Press, 2008); Richard Johnson, *Adjustment to Empire: The New England Colonies, 1675-1715* (New Brunswick, NJ: Rutgers University Press, 1981), 285–88.

60. Sewall, *Diary*, 1:354, 6 (quotes); William DeLoss Love, *The Fast and Thanksgiving Days of New England* (Boston: Houghton, Mifflin, 1895), 265; *Acts and Resolves of Massachusetts Bay*, 7:531.

61. *Acts and Resolves of Massachusetts Bay*, 7:532–33 (quote); Richard Francis, *Judge Sewall's Apology: The Salem Witch Trials and the Forming of an American Conscience* (New York: HarperCollins, 2005), 176–77; Mather, *Diary*, 1:211–12.

62. Sewall, *Diary*, 1:362 (quote).

63. Sewall notes that Sam recited the verses in Latin, so the actual quote was "Si autem sciretis quid est misericordiam volo et non sacrificium numquam condemnassetis innocents." Sewall, *Diary*, 1:364.

64. Sewall, *Diary*, 1:366–67.

65. For Sewall's hair shirt, see Eve LaPlante, *Salem Witch Judge: The Life and Repentance of Samuel Sewall* (New York: HarperCollins, 2007), 201–3; Sewall, *Diary*, 1:403, 450–51. They appear to have reconciled only when Sewall visited Stoughton on his deathbed in 1701. Sewall took Stoughton's hand and kissed it, and the lieutenant governor asked Sewall to

pray for him. Three days later Stoughton died. The juror's apology is undated. Most likely it was made around the time of the Fast Day in 1697. Francis, *Judge Sewall's Apology*, 186–87; Calef, *More Wonders*, 387–88 (quote).

66. John Hale, "A Modest Inquiry," in Burr, ed., *Narratives*, 397–432; Sibley, *Biographical Sketches*, 1:514–18.

67. Hale, "A Modest Inquiry," 427 (quote). See Hansen, *Witchcraft at Salem*, 200–202; K. David Goss, *The Salem Witch Trials: A Reference Guide* (Westport, CT: Greenwood Press, 2008), 106–7.

68. John Higginson, "An Epistle to the Reader," in Burr, ed., *Narratives*, 402 (quote); Gragg, *Salem Witch Crisis*, 200–202.

69. Calef is first noted in Boston when his son was born in 1688. Copies of the book were first in Boston in November 1700. Burr, *Narratives*, 291–95; Maule, *Better That 100 Witches Should Live*, 115.

70. Sybil Noyes, Charles T. Libby, and Walter G. Davis, *Genealogical Dictionary of Maine and New Hampshire* (1928–29; reprint, Baltimore: Genealogical Publishing, 1979), 600; Gragg, *Salem Witch Crisis*, 194–95; Hoffer, *The Devil's Disciples*, 191–92.

71. Calef, "More Wonders," 299–300 (quote); Gragg, *Salem Witch Crisis*, 194.

72. Burr, *Narratives*, 293. See Mather's diary entry for November 15, 1700, in Mather, *Diary*, 1:371 (quotes). Mather notes the book had arrived that week in Boston from London. Gragg, *Salem Witch Crisis*, 194–95; Hoffer, *The Devil's Disciples*, 192–94.

73. Kenneth Silverman, *The Life and Times of Cotton Mather* (New York: Harper and Row, 1984), 130–34; Gragg, *Salem Witch Crisis*, 194–95.

74. T.M., *An Abstract of a Letter to Cotton Mather, in New-England* (1701), 6–9, 11. Thomas Maule is undoubtedly the author of the letter. Carla Gardina Pestana, "The Quaker Executions as Myth and History," *Journal of American History* 80 (1993): 452–54; James Maule, *Better That 100 Witches Should Live*, 134–36.

75. Obediah Gill, John Barnard, John Goodwin, William Robie, Timothy Wadsworth, Robert Cumbey, and George Robinson, *Some Few Remarks on a Scandalous Book, against the Government and the Ministry of New England, written by Robert Calef* (Boston: T. Green, 1701). For a discussion of the authorship of *Some Few Remarks*, see Perry Miller, *The New England Mind: From Colony to Providence* (Cambridge, MA: Belknap Press, 1953), 249; Burr, *Narratives of the Witchcraft Cases*, 295. Specifically, the book was reprinted in 1796, 1823, 1828, 1861, and 1866; see William S. Harris, "Robert Calef, Merchant of Boston in New England," *Granite Monthly: A New Hampshire Magazine Devoted to History* 39 (1907), 157–63, and Samuel Mather, *The Life of the Very Reverend and Learned Cotton Mather* (Boston: Samuel Gerrish, 1729), 46 (quote).

76. John Greenleaf Whittier, "Calef in Boston, 1692," in John Greenleaf Whittier, Horace Scudder, and Elizabeth Whittier, eds., *The Poetical Works of John Greenleaf Whittier, in Four Volumes* (Boston: Houghton and Mifflin, 1982), 3:357–58.

77. Harris, "Robert Calef," 162–63; Alfred F. Young, *The Shoe Maker and The Tea Party: Memory and the American Revolution* (Boston: Beacon Press, 1999); W. W. Everts, "Robert Calef and Cotton Mather," *Review and Expositor* 13 (1916): 232.

78. Burr, *Narratives of the Witchcraft Cases*, 398. In addition to a complete reprinting in 1771, part of Hale's narrative of events in Salem was included by Cotton Mather in *Magnalia Christi Americana*, at the end of Book VI, so his work was not altogether lost. Gretchen Adams, *The Specter of Salem: Remembering the Witch Trials in Nineteenth-Century America* (Chicago: University of Chicago Press, 2008), 33; Daniel Neal, *The History of New England* (London: J. Clark, R. Ford, and R. Cruttenden, 1720), 2:495–532; Samuel Eliot Morison, *The Puritan Pronaos: Studies in the Intellectual Life of New England in the Seventeenth Century* (New York: New York University Press, 1936), 251 (quote).

79. Weisman, *Witchcraft, Magic and Religion*, 175. Mather, *Diary*, 1:216 (quote).

80. Miller, *The New England Mind*, 241 (quote).

CHAPTER EIGHT

1. Thomas Brattle, "Letter of Thomas Brattle," in George Lincoln Burr, ed., *Narratives of the Witchcraft Cases, 1648–1706* (New York: Charles Scribner's Sons, 1914), 190.

2. Samuel Parris, *The Sermon Notebook of Samuel Parris, 1689–1694*, ed. James F. Cooper Jr. and Kenneth P. Minkema (Boston: Colonial Society of Massachusetts, 1993), 215–323 (quote on 295); Marilynne K. Roach, *The Salem Witch Trials: A Day-by-Day Chronicle of a Community Under Siege* (New York: Cooper Square Press, 2002), 397, 400, 405–6, 410–11, 416, 419, 426, 431, 435, 441.

3. Paul Boyer and Stephen Nissenbaum, *Salem Possessed: The Social Origins of Witchcraft* (Cambridge, MA: Harvard University Press, 1974), 69–71; Larry Gragg, *A Quest for Security: The Life of Samuel Parris, 1653–1720* (New York: Greenwood Press, 1990), 153–62; Paul Boyer and Stephen Nissenbaum, eds., *Salem-Village Witchcraft: A Documentary Record of Local Conflict in Colonial New England* (1972; reprint, Boston: Northeastern University Press, 1993), 255–64.

4. "Samuel Parris's Meditations for Peace," in Richard Godbeer, *The Salem Witch Hunt: A Brief History with Documents* (New York: Bedford St. Martin's, 2011), 168–71 (quote).

5. "Summary of Grievances Against Samuel Parris," in Godbeer, *The Salem Witch Hunt*, 171–72 (quote); Gragg, *Quest for Security*, 163–66.

6. Boyer and Nissenbaum, *Salem Possessed*, 74–78; Gragg, *Quest for Security*, 166–68.

7. Boyer and Nissenbaum, *Salem Possessed*, 77–78; Gragg, *Quest for Security*, 168–70.

8. K. David Goss, *The Salem Witch Trials: A Reference Guide* (Westport, CT: Greenwood Press, 2008), 68; Sidney Perley, *History of Salem, Massachusetts*, 3 vols. (Salem: Author, 1924–28), 3: 360; Gragg, *A Quest for Security*, 177–82; "Reverend Samuel Parris," *New England Historical and Genealogical Register* 12 (1858): 63–64.

9. Gragg, *A Quest for Security*, 182–85.

10. "The Will of Samuel Parris (1720)," in Boyer and Nissenbaum, eds., *Salem-Village Witchcraft*, 194 (quote).

11. William Prynne, *The Perpetuitie of a Regenerate Man's Estate* (London: William Jones, 1626), 409 (quote); "Death: King of Terrors," *Vast Public Indifference*, June 8, 2008, accessed

at www.vastpublicindifference.com/2008/06/death-king-of-terrors.html (the phrase is from Job 18:14). The exact day Parris was born in 1653 is unknown, so he could have been either sixty-six or sixty-seven when he died.

12. Roach, *Salem Witch Trials*, 544; Boyer and Nissenbaum, *Salem Possessed*, 217–21.

13. Marilynne K. Roach, "That Child Betty Parris," *Essex Institute Historical Collections* 124 (1988): 20–27; Mary Beth Norton, *In the Devil's Snare: The Salem Witchcraft Crisis of 1692* (New York: W. W. Norton, 2002), 310–11; *The Early Records of the Town of Providence* (Providence, RI: Snow and Farnham, 1896), 10:13–14 (quote); Goss, *Salem Witch Trials*, 80–85.

14. "The Public Confession of Ann Putnam," in Godbeer, *The Salem Witch Hunt*, 176 (quotes); Goss, *Salem Witch Trials*, 68–69; Roach, *Salem Witch Trials*, 568–69.

15. For example, Bernard Rosenthal sees Ann's confession as being as far as she could go to confessing the fraud she had perpetrated. Others, including Chadwick Hansen, view the sincerity of her apology and its acceptance by the congregation as a true sign that her actions had not been deliberate. Bernard Rosenthal, *Salem Story: Reading the Witch Trials of 1692* (New York: Cambridge University Press, 1995), 36–38, 40–41; Chadwick Hansen, *Witchcraft at Salem* (New York: George Braziller, 1969), 215.

16. Richard Trask has done an excellent job of researching Danvers's long and complicated path to town status. See Richard Trask, "The Creation of Danvers," Danvers Archival Center at the Peabody Institute Library, www.danverslibrary.org/archive/?page_id=211, accessed September 8, 2013. Osborne would have the shortest tenure of any colonial governor, for two days after assuming office he hanged himself. Sir Danvers had apparently been melancholy for many years, grieving the death of his wife.

17. Trask, "The Creation of Danvers."

18. Elinor Abbot, *Our Company Increases Apace: History, Language, and Social Identity in Early Colonial Andover, Massachusetts* (Dallas: SIL International, 2007), 152–75; John L. Taylor, *A Memoir of His Honor Samuel Phillips, LL.D.* (Boston: Congregational Board of Education, 1856), 1–16, 191–210. The two parishes would eventually become the separate townships of North Andover and Andover, but this would not happen until 1855.

19. For parental involvement in marriage and its contractual nature in the colonial and early national era, see Mary Beth Norton, *Founding Mothers and Fathers: Gendered Power and the Forming of American Society* (New York: Alfred A. Knopf, 1996), 108–11; Mary Beth Norton, *Liberty's Daughters: The Revolutionary Experience of American Women, 1750–1800* (Boston: Little, Brown, 1980), 58–60, 229–31; Laurel Ulrich, *A Midwife's Tale: The Life of Martha Ballard, Based on Her Diary, 1785–1812* (New York, Alfred A. Knopf, 1990), 138–46.

20. Abbot, *Our Company Increases Apace*, 167–68; Perley, *History of Salem*, 2:143.

21. Abbot, *Our Company Increases Apace*, 162–66, 173–75; Philip Greven, *Four Generations: Land, Population and Family in Andover, Massachusetts* (Ithaca, NY: Cornell University Press, 1970), 210–11; William Richard Cutter, *Genealogical and Personal Memoirs Relating to the Families of Boston and Eastern Massachusetts* (New York: Lewis Historical Publishing, 1908), 3: 1194–95; Enders Robinson, *The Devil Discovered: Salem Witchcraft 1692* (Prospect Heights, IL: Waveland Press, 1991), 278, 316.

22. The author would like to thank Howard Kaepplein for sharing his discovery of the Barker weddings and their significance. See his unpublished manuscript "The Andover Connection: The Life and Times of Jonathan Barker, Jr. (1728–1794)"; see also *Vital Records of Acton, Massachusetts, to the Year 1850* (Boston: New England Historical and Genealogical Society, 1923), 131, and *Vital Records of Andover, Massachusetts, to the End of the Year 1849* (Topsfield: Topsfield Historical Society, 1912), 40. There is no surviving evidence to suggest that Timothy Swan accused Abigail Faulkner or William Barker of afflicting him, though such an accusation may have been made. His afflictions were blamed on Mary Toothaker and Richard Carrier, both members of Abigail Dane Faulkner's extended kin network. See Enders Robinson, *Salem Witchcraft and Hawthorne's House of Seven Gables* (Bowie, MD: Heritage Books, 1992), 273–79, 288–96; "Indictment of Richard Carrier for Afflicting Timothy Swan," and "Examination of Mary Toothaker," in Bernard Rosenthal et al., eds., *Records of the Salem Witch-Hunt* (New York: Cambridge University Press, 2009), 491, 788.

23. Josiah H. Temple, *History of Framingham, Massachusetts, Early Known as Danforth's Farms 1640-1680* (Framingham: Town of Framingham, 1887), 91–94, 108, 111–25.

24. "Indictment of Sarah Cloyce, for Afflicting Mary Walcott (Returned Ignoramus)" and "Indictment of Sarah Cloyce, for Afflicting Abigail Williams (Returned Ignoramus)" in Rosenthal et al., eds., *Salem Witch-Hunt*, 789–90.

25. Temple, *History of Framingham*, 467, 483–84, 506–10, 541; Ulrich, *A Midwife's Tale*, 11, 348–49; William E. Barton, "The Barton Family of Oxford, Massachusetts," *New England Historical Genealogical Register* 84 (1930): 416–17.

26. William Barry, *A History of Framingham* (Boston: James Munroe, 1847), 43; Temple, *History of Framingham*, 653–55, 723–25; William Ballard, *A Sketch of the History of Framingham* (Boston, 1827), 20–21; Barton, "The Barton Family of Oxford," 404–5.

27. "Receipt of Sheriff George Corwin to Samuel Bishop" and "Petition of Edward Bishop Jr. for Restitution," in Rosenthal et al., eds., *Salem Witch-Hunt*, 686, 856; Roach, *Salem Witch Trials*, 311, 569–70; Robinson, *Devil Discovered*, 297–99; Leonard Bliss, *The History of Rehoboth, Bristol County, Massachusetts* (Boston: Otis, Broaders, 1836).

28. Charles W. Upham, ed., *Salem Witchcraft* (Boston: Wiggin and Lunt, 1867), 633; Thomas Weston, *History of the Town of Middleboro, Massachusetts* (Boston: Houghton, Mifflin, 1906), 80, 335; "John Rayment to Nathaniel Rayment, August 11, 1697," Essex Deeds 12:32a; "Samuel Sibley to Joseph Hutchinson, May 30, 1696," Essex Deeds 11:115; Boyer and Nissenbaum, eds., *Salem-Village Witchcraft*, 269, 312.

29. Jack P. Greene, "Recent Developments in the Historiography of Colonial New England," *Acadiensis* 17 (1988): 150–52; John W. Adams and Alice Bee Kasakoff, "Migration and the Family in Colonial New England: The View from Genealogies," *Journal of Family History* 9 (1984): 24–43.

30. Boyer and Nissenbaum, *Salem Possessed*, 142–43; Eben Putnam, *History of the Putnam Family in England and America* (Salem: Salem Press, 1891), 74–79.

31. Putnam, *History of the Putnam Family*, 49–55, 87–126; Henry Phelps Johnston, *Nathan Hale 1776: Biography and Memorials* (New Haven: Yale University Press, 1914), 3–7.

32. Charles E. Clark, *The Meetinghouse Tragedy* (Hanover, NH: University of New England Press, 1998), 5–10, 55–58, 107–108.

33. Florence C. Cox, comp., *History of New Salem, Massachusetts* (Amherst, MA: Hamilton I. Newell, 1953), 5–8; A. V. House, "Salem and New Salem," *Historical Collections of the Danvers Historical Society* 5 (1917): 90–109; George H. Gilman, *History of the Town of Houlton, Maine, from 1804 to 1883* (Haverhill, MA: C. C. Morse and Son, 1884), 3–12.

34. Henry F. Waters, comp., *The Gedney and Clarke Families of Salem, Massachusetts* (Salem: Salem Press, 1880), 15–16, 32–36.

35. The author wishes to thank James Kences for bringing the naming pattern of Ebenezer and its significance to his attention. See also Marilynne K. Roach, "Records of the Reverend Samuel Parris, Salem Village, Massachusetts, 1688–1696," *New England Historical and Genealogical Register* 157 (2003), 11–18. For naming, see Daniel Scott Smith, "Child-Naming Practices, Kinship Ties, and Change in Family Attitudes in Hingham, Massachusetts, 1641 to 1880," *Journal of Social History* 18, no. 4 (Summer 1985): 541–66; Gloria L. Main, "Naming Children in Early New England," *Journal of Interdisciplinary History* 27 (1996): 1–27; David Hackett Fischer, "Forenames and the Family in New England: An Exercise in Historical Onomastics," in Robert M. Taylor Jr. and Ralph J. Crandall, eds., *Generations and Change: Genealogical Perspectives in Social History* (Macon, GA: Mercer University Press, 1986), 215–41. The quote is from 1 Samuel 7:12.

36. Roach, "Records of the Reverend Samuel Parris," 14, 16. For the documents recorded by Cheever, see Rosenthal et al., eds., *Salem Witch-Hunt*, 126–29, 149–51, 183–84, 386 (documents #3, 18, 63, 302, 333, and 334). The author thanks Margo Burns for the details on Cheever's involvement. "Testimony of Ann Putnam, Sr., v. John Willard, William Hobbs and Martha Cory," in Rosenthal et al., eds., *Salem Witch-Hunt*, 360.

37. "Petition of Elizabeth Procter, May 27, 1696," in Rosenthal et al., eds., *Salem Witch-Hunt*, 844–45 (quote).

38. "Petition of Abigail Faulkner, June 13, 1700," in Rosenthal et al., eds., *Salem Witch-Hunt*, 847–48 (quote); Gragg, *The Salem Witch Crisis*, 189.

39. The copy of the petition in the Massachusetts Archives does not mention the legislative action (see Rosenthal et al., eds., *Salem Witch-Hunt*, 847–48), but it is found on the copy sent to the Privy Council. See "Petition of Abigail Faulkner," Cecil Headlam et al eds., *Calendar of State Papers, Colonial Series, America and the West Indies*, 45 vols. (London: 1860–1994), 18:393 (quote). Upham, in *Salem Witchcraft*, 643, makes note of the Privy Council version, but his discovery has been largely overlooked. The document and the pivotal role of Stoughton was brought to the author's attention by his former graduate student Paula Alyce Keene in her "William Stoughton's Governance Manners: Suppressing the Politics of 'Innocency' and the Salem Witchcraft Trials of 1692," History 990 paper, Salem State College, February 22, 2006. For Bellomont's departure, see Sewall, *The Diary of Samuel Sewall, 1674–1729*, ed. M. Halsey Thomas (New York: Farrar, Straus and Giroux, 1973), 1:433.

40. "Petition of Francis Faulkner et al., March 2, 1703," in Rosenthal et al., eds., *Salem Witch-Hunt*, 848–49 (quote).

41. "Order of the General Court Concerning a Bill of Attainder of Abigail Faulkner Sr., et al., July 20, 1703," in Rosenthal et al., eds., *Salem Witch-Hunt*, 852 (quote).

42. "Petition of Ministers of Essex County, July 8, 1703," in Rosenthal et al., eds., *Salem Witch-Hunt*, 851 (quote). William Bentley (1759–1819), the Salem minister, scholar, and diarist, claimed that Noyes later publicly confessed his error and begged for forgiveness. Bentley may have heard oral traditions of Noyes, but as Charles Upham—a later Salem minister and witchcraft historian—pointed out, no written evidence survives to suggest Noyes ever repented. See John L. Sibley, *Biographical Sketches of Graduates of Harvard University* (Cambridge, MA: Charles William Sever, 1873), 2: 242.

43. "Petition of Abigail Faulkner, June 13, 1700," in Rosenthal et al., eds., *Salem Witch-Hunt*, 847–48 (quote).

44. "Petition of Francis Faulkner et al, March 2, 1703," in Rosenthal et al., eds., *Salem Witch-Hunt*, 848–49 (quote).

45. "An Act Reversing the Attainder of Abigail Faulkner Sr., et al.," in Rosenthal et al., eds., *Salem Witch-Hunt*, 850. The five convicted witches who were not covered by the act were Mary Lacey Sr., Rebecca Eames, Dorcas Hoar, Elizabeth Johnson Jr., and Mary Post.

46. Surprisingly little has been written on William Stoughton's career. Keene, "William Stoughton's Governance Manners" examines the quest for innocency by the victims, including the importance of Stoughton's death in facilitating that process.

47. "Michael Wigglesworth to Increase Mather, July 22, 1704," *Massachusetts Historical Society Collections*, 4th ser., 8:646 (quotes); Hansen, *Witchcraft at Salem*, 216–17; Gragg, *The Salem Witch Crisis*, 189.

48. "Petition of Philip English et al.," in Rosenthal et al., eds., *Salem Witch-Hunt*, 853 (quote).

49. Cotton Mather, *Theopolis Americana* (Boston: Samuel Gerrish, 1710), 29–30 (quote); Hansen, *Witchcraft at Salem*, 217.

50. Mather, *Theopolis Americana*, unnumbered front matter (quote); Sewall, *Sewall*, 2:628–29; Richard Francis, *Judge Sewall's Apology: The Salem Witch Trials and the Forming of an American Conscience* (New York: HarperCollins, 2005), 228–30, 332–33; Eve LaPlante, *Salem Witch Judge: The Life and Repentance of Samuel Sewall* (New York: HarperCollins, 2007), 260.

51. Roach, *Salem Witch Trials*, 569–70; "Petition of Francis Johnson for Restitution for Elizabeth Johnson Jr.," "An Act to Reverse the Attainders of George Burroughs et al.," and "Petition of Elizabeth Johnson Jr. for Reversing Attainder and for Restitution," in Rosenthal et al., eds., *Salem Witch-Hunt*, 875–76, 888–89, 901.

52. For information on Elizabeth Johnson and her family, see Robinson, *Salem Witchcraft*, 294–96; "Stephen Johnson et al. to Francis Johnson, June 15, 1709," Essex Deeds 33:43; "Stephen Johnson and Elizabeth Johnson to James Black, May 10, 1716," Essex Deeds 28:236. Elizabeth was presumably the unmarried Elizabeth Johnson who died in Andover, January 3, 1747; see *Vital Records of Andover, Massachusetts to the End of the Year 1849* (Topsfield: Topsfield Historical Society, 1912), 2:479.

53. "Order for Payment of Damages by Governor Joseph Dudley," in Rosenthal et al., eds., *Salem Witch-Hunt*, 892; Richard D. Pierce, ed., *Records of the First Church in Salem, Massachusetts, 1629-1736* (Salem: Essex Institute, 1974), 218-19.

54. "Resolve allowing £50 to Thomas Rich," in Rosenthal et al., eds., *Salem Witch-Hunt*, 917; Bryan LeBeau, "Philip English and the Witchcraft Hysteria," *Historical Journal of Massachusetts* 15 (1987): 6-8, 17; Roach, *Salem Witch Trials*, 453, 520; Upham, *Salem Witchcraft*, 639-40; Hansen, *Witchcraft at Salem*, 212, Gragg, *Salem Witch Crisis*, 190.

55. "Petition of Philip English for Restitution," in Rosenthal et al., eds., *Salem Witch-Hunt*, 866-68, 915-17 (quote on 868); William Bentley, "A Description and History of Salem," *Collections of the Massachusetts Historical Society* 1st ser., 6 (1799), 270; Gragg, *Salem Witch Crisis*, 190; LeBeau, "Philip English and the Witchcraft Hysteria," 7-8.

56. Roach, *Salem Witch Trials*, 572; LeBeau, "Philip English and the Witchcraft Hysteria," 8; Bentley, "A Description and History of Salem," 270; Claude Simpson, ed., *Nathaniel Hawthorne, The American Notebooks* (Columbus: Ohio State University Press, 1972), 75 (quote).

57. George H. Moore, *Notes on the History of Witchcraft in Massachusetts* (Worcester: Charles Hamilton, 1883), 27-28; Israel Loring, *The Duty of an Apostatizing People* (Boston, 1737), 23, 45, 51-53, 67 (quotes on 51-53); Foster, *The Long Argument*, 296-97.

58. Alfred Hudson, *The History of Sudbury, Massachusetts, 1638-1889* (Sudbury: Town of Sudbury, 1889), 274-75; Moore, *Notes on the History of Witchcraft*, 27 (quote); "Deposition of Susannah Touzel, Regarding Philip English," and "Deposition of Margaret Casnoe Regarding Philip English," in Rosenthal et al., eds., *Salem Witch-Hunt*, 918-19; Upham, *Salem Witchcraft*, 646-47; Bentley, "A Description and History of Salem," 270. For Samuel Danforth, see John A. Schutz, *Legislators of the Massachusetts General Court, 1691-1780: A Biographical Dictionary* (Boston: Northeastern University Press, 1997), 201; Sibley, *Biographical Sketches*, 6:80-86; John J. May, comp., *Danforth Genealogy* (Boston: Charles H. Pope, 1902), 18-26, 30-33, 40-41. For John Higginson, see Thomas W. Higginson, *Descendants of the Reverend Francis Higginson* (n.p.: Privately printed, 1910), 15-16.

59. Moore, *Notes on the History of Witchcraft*, 29 (quote).

60. Moore, *Notes on the History of Witchcraft*, 29 (quote).

61. Upham, *Salem Witchcraft*, 647 (quote); Moore, *Notes on the History of Witchcraft*, 29-31; "Memorial and Petition by Thomas Newman et al. for George Burroughs," Rosenthal, ed., *Salem Witch-Hunt*, 919-20.

62. *New England Weekly Journal*, Nov. 25, 1740, p. 1; Joseph Sewall, *Ninevah's Repentance and Deliverance* (Boston: J. Draper, 1740), 32 (quote).

63. *Journal of the Honourable House of Representatives, of His Majesty's Province of the Massachusetts-Bay in New England* (Boston: Printed by Samuel Kneeland, 1740), 151; Moore, *Notes on the History of Witchcraft*, 30-32.

64. Sewall, *Ninevah's Repentance and Deliverance*, 17 (quote).

CHAPTER NINE

1. Karl Marx, "The Eighteenth Brumaire of Louis Napoleon," Marx and Engels Internet Archive, accessed at www.marxists.org/archive/marx/works/1852/18th-brumaire/ch01.htm. The first sentence of this quote is actually drawn from an 1851 letter from Engels to Marx. The author thanks David Hackett Fischer for reminding him of this quote.

2. Patricia Harris and David Lyon, "13 Frights," *Boston Globe*, October 25, 2009 (quote); Robert E. Weir, "Bewitched and Bewildered: Salem Witches, Empty Factories, and Tourist Dollars," *Historical Journal of Massachusetts* 40 (2012): 181.

3. Edward Ward, *A Trip to New England* (London: 1699), 12; Edward Ward, *The London-Spy Compleat* (London: 1709), 185 (quote). For use of the term "witch hunt," see the *Oxford English Dictionary*.

4. James Sharpe, *Instruments of Darkness: Witchcraft in Early Modern England* (Philadelphia: University of Pennsylvania Press, 1997), 47–57; Michael Winship, *Seers of God: Puritan Providentialism in the Restoration and the Early Enlightenment* (Baltimore: Johns Hopkins University Press, 1996), 119–22; Emerson Baker, *The Devil of Great Island: Witchcraft and Conflict in Early New England* (New York: Palgrave Macmillan, 2007), 197–98; George Lincoln Burr, ed., *Narratives of the New England Witchcraft Cases* (New York: Charles Scribner's Sons, 1914), 147–49; James VI, "Preface to the Reader," in *Daemonologie in forme of a Dialogue, diuided into Three Books* (Edinburgh: Robert Walde-grave, 1597), 2 (quote).

5. Sharpe, *Instruments of Darkness*, 220–34.

6. Winship, *Seers of God*, 119–22; William E. Monter, "Scandinavian Witchcraft in Anglo-American Perspective," in Bengt Ankarloo and Gustav Henningsen, eds., *Early Modern European Witchcraft: Centres and Peripheries* (Oxford: Oxford University Press, 1990), 431–33; Sharpe, *Instruments of Darkness*, 244–47.

7. Sharpe, *Instruments of Darkness*, 244–48; Winship, *Seers of God*, 64–68.

8. Richard Boulton, *A Compleat History of Magick, Sorcery, and Witchcraft* (London, 1715–16); Francis Hutchinson, *An Historical Essay Concerning Witchcraft* (London: R. Knaplock, 1720), 287 (quotes). This quote is also in the 1718 edition, on page 229. Sharpe, *Instruments of Darkness*, 284–86; Ian Bostridge, *Witchcraft and Its Transformations, c. 1650–c. 1750* (Oxford: Oxford University Press, 1997), 108–54; Malcolm Gaskill, *Crime and Mentalities in Early Modern Europe* (Cambridge: Cambridge University Press, 2003), 95–99.

9. Boulton, *A Compleat History*, 4–43; Francis Hutchinson, *An Historical Essay*, dedication (quote).

10. Francis Hutchinson, *An Historical Essay Concerning Witchcraft* (London: 1718), 101, 122 (quotes).

11. Daniel Neal, *The history of New-England containing an impartial account of the civil and ecclesiastical affairs of the country to the year of Our Lord, 1700* (London: 1720), 2:495–541 (quote on 512); John Choules, ed., *The History of the Puritans, or Protestant Non-Conformists* (New York: Harper and Brothers, 1843), vi–vii.

12. Thomas Salmon, *Modern History: or The Present State of All Nations* (Dublin: George Grierson, 1739), 25: 256–80; John Oldmixon, *The British Empire in America* (London: J. Brotherton et al., 1741), 1:148–57 (quote on 148–49).

13. William Burke, *An Account of the European Settlements in America* (London: R. and J. Dodsley, 1757), 2:155.

14. Daniel Defoe, *The Political History of the Devil: As Well Ancient as Modern* (London: T. Warner, 1726), 388.

15. Raynal published his *L'Histoire philosophique et politique des établissements et du commerce des Européens dans les deux Indes* in Amsterdam in 1770. It would be translated into English in 1779. See Abbé Raynal, *A Philosophical and Political History of the British Settlements and Trade in North America* (Aberdeen: J. Boyle, 1779), 1:75–77; John Wynne, *A General History of the British Empire in America* (London: W. Richardson and L. Urquhart, 1770), 1:89.

16. Oldmixon, *The British Empire in America*, 1:148 (quote).

17. William Douglass, *Inoculation of the Small Pox as practised in Boston, consider'd in a Letter to A— S— M.D. & F.R.S. in London* (Boston: James Franklin, 1722), A2 (quote); Gretchen Adams, *The Specter of Salem: Remembering the Witch Trials in Nineteenth-Century America* (Chicago: University of Chicago Press, 2008), 32–33.

18. Mr. [Nathaniel] Gardiner, "Another Dialogue Between the Clergyman and the Layman," *New-England Courant*, January 22, 1722, 3; Adams, *Specter of Salem*, 32–33, 169–70; Joseph Fireoved, "Nathaniel Gardner and the New-England Courant," *Early American Literature* 20 (1985–86): 219; Perry Miller, *The New England Mind: From Colony to Province* (Cambridge, MA: Belknap Press, 1953), 345–66.

19. "A Witch Trial at Mount Holly," *Pennsylvania Gazette*, October 22, 1730, 3–4 (quotes); Marc Mappen, "The Trial of Witches in Mt. Holly," *New York Times*, October 28, 1984, 32; Carla Mulford, "Franklin, Modernity, and Themes of Dissent in the Early Modern Era," *Modern Language Studies* 28 (1998): 21–22. For Franklin's baptism, see John L. Sibley, *Biographical Sketches of Graduates of Harvard University.* (Cambridge, MA: Charles William Sever, 1873), 2:22–23.

20. Jill Lepore discusses the letter at length in *New York Burning: Liberty, Slavery, and Conspiracy in Eighteenth-Century Manhattan*, reprint ed. (New York: Vintage Books, 2006), 203–10, 304–5; see also *New England Weekly Journal*, September 29, 1741, issue no. 754 (quote on 1). For New York and the trials, see Mary Beth Norton, *In the Devil's Snare: The Salem Witchcraft Crisis of 1692* (New York: W. W. Norton, 2002), 286–87; Evan Haefeli, "Dutch New York and the Salem Witch Trials: Some New Evidence," *Proceedings of the American Antiquarian Society* 110 (2000): 293–300.

21. *New England Weekly Journal*, September 29, 1741, issue no. 754 (quote on 1). For Salem as a metaphor and subject of debate, see Adams, *The Specter of Salem* and Marion Gibson, *Witchcraft Myths in American Culture* (New York: Routledge, 2007). For Josiah Cotton, see Douglas Winiarkski, "'Pale Blewish Lights' and a Dead Man's Groan: Tales of the Supernatural from Eighteenth-Century Plymouth, Massachusetts," *William and Mary Quarterly* 55 (1998): 487–530; John Demos, *Entertaining Satan: Witchcraft and the Culture*

of Early New England (New York: Oxford University Press, 1982), 286. Cotton's manuscript was never published.

22. George H. Moore, *Notes on the History of Witchcraft in Massachusetts* (Worcester: Charles Hamilton, 1883), 28 (quote); Thomas Hutchinson, *History of the Province of Massachusetts* (Boston: Thomas and John Fleet, 1767), 2:12–62; Adams, *Specter of Salem*, 34–35.

23. Hutchinson, *History of the Province of Massachusetts* 2:62 (quotes); Adams, *Specter of Salem*, 59–61.

24. *The American Gazette* (London, 1770), 200 (quote).

25. Daniel Leonard, *Massachusettensis* (Boston: 1775), 9 (quote).

26. *Novanglus and Massachusettensis, or Political Essays Published in the Years 1774 and 1775* (Boston: Hews and Goss, 1819), 99 (quotes); Adams, *Specter of Salem*, 35–36, 171. For details on Adams's use of Massachusetts history in the revolution, see Larzer Ziff, "Revolutionary Rhetoric and Puritanism," *Early American Literature* 13 (1978): 45–49.

27. L. H. Butterfield, ed., *Diary and Autobiography of John Adams* (Cambridge, MA: Belknap Press, 1961), 1: 319 (quote); Adams diary, quoted in Sidney Perley, "Where the Salem Witches Were Hanged," *Historical Collections of the Essex Institute* 62 (1921); 11.

28. Butterfield, ed., *Diary and Autobiography*, 2:79; Adams, *Specter of Salem*, 35–36, 171.

29. James Leamon, *The Reverend Jacob Bailey, Maine Loyalist: For God, King, Country, and for Self* (Amherst: University of Massachusetts Press, 2012), 178–94.

30. "French and British Influence," *American Mercury* 18, issue 859 (December 18, 1800): 2 (quote).

31. The use of Salem as a metaphor in the nineteenth century and on into more recent times has been well established by Gretchen Adams; see her *Specter of Salem*. M.J.S., "Retrospect of the Past Year," *United States Catholic Magazine and Monthly Review* 4 (January 1845), 6 (quote); Adams, *Specter of Salem*, 64–93, 149–58. See Nancy L. Schultz, *Fire and Roses: The Burning of the Charlestown Convent* (New York: Free Press, 2000) for the convent riots.

32. Adams, *Specter of Salem*, especially 94–118; Charles W. Warner, comp., *The Book of Eloquence: A Collection of Extracts in Prose and Verse, from the Most Famous Orators and Poets; Intended as Exercises for Declamation Colleges and Schools* (Boston: Lee and Shepard, 1887), 45 (quote). New Englanders fought back, reminding Virginians that they had tried Grace Sherwood for witchcraft more than a decade after the Salem trials, though also getting history wrong by suggesting Sherwood was black or mulatto. Gibson, *Witchcraft Myths*, 49–51.

33. Adams, *Specter of Salem*, 43–62.

34. Nancy Schultz, "Salem as Hawthorne's Creation," in Dane A. Morrison and Nancy L. Schultz, eds., *Salem: Place, Myth and Memory* (Boston: Northeastern University Press, 2004), 163–83; Edward C. Sampson, "The 'W' in Hawthorne's Name," *Essex Institute Historical Collections* 100 (1964): 297–99.

35. "Young Goodman Brown" was first published in *New England Magazine* in April 1835. Hawthorne also included it in his collection *Mosses from an Old Manse* (1846). For

Hawthorne's use of Mather as well as early historians of the trials, see John Ronan, "'Young Goodman Brown' and the Mathers," *New England Quarterly* 85 (2012): 253-80.

36. "Alice Doane's Appeal," in Nathaniel Hawthorne, *Hawthorne's Short Stories* (New York: Vintage Books, 2011), 411 (quotes).

37. Nathaniel Hawthorne, *The House of Seven Gables* (New York: Dover, 1999), 21 (quote). This paragraph draws from Emerson Baker and James Kences, "Maine, Indian Land Speculation, and the Essex County Witchcraft Outbreak of 1692," *Maine History* 40 (2001): 181-82.

38. Hawthorne, *House of Seven Gables*, x (quote); Robin DeRosa, *The Making of Salem: The Witch Trials in History, Fiction and Tourism* (London: McFarland, 2009), 100-108.

39. Bryan LeBeau, "Foreword," in Charles W. Upham, ed., *Salem Witchcraft* (Boston: Wiggin and Lunt, 1867), vii-xxvii; Lorinda Goodwin, "Salem's House of Seven Gables as Historic Site," in Morrison and Schultz, eds., *Salem: Place, Myth and Memory*, 299-313; Stephen Gencarella, "Touring History: Guidebooks and the Commodification of the Salem Witch Trials," *Journal of American Culture* 30 (2007): 273-74; W. Elliot Woodward, *Records of the Salem Witchcraft, Copied from Original Documents* (Roxbury, MA: Author, 1864), 2 vols. Information on the movie and television productions of *The House of Seven Gables* is drawn from the Internet Movie Database (IMDb).

40. Eve LaPlante, *Salem Witch Judge: The Life and Repentance of Samuel Sewall* (New York: HarperCollins, 2007), 272-73; Karen Halttunen, "The Domestic Drama of Louisa May Alcott," *Feminist Studies* 10 (1984): 233-54.

41. Gencarella, "Touring History," 273-75; Pamela E. Apkarian-Russell, *A Collector's Guide to Salem Witchcraft and Souvenirs* (Atglen, PA: Schiffer, 1998), 8-11, 22.

42. Upham, *Salem Witchcraft*, 572-73; William P. Upham, "Account of the Rebecca Nurse Monument," *Essex Institute Historical Collections* 23 (1886): 151-60; Gibson, *Witchcraft Myths in American Culture*, 57-62; Bernard Rosenthal, *Salem Story: Reading the Witch Trials of 1692* (New York: Cambridge University Press, 1995), 90-91.

43. Upham, "Account of the Rebecca Nurse Monument," 151-52 (quote); Gibson, *Witchcraft Myths in American Culture*, 59-63.

44. Abby J. Woodman, *Reminiscences of John Greenleaf Whittier's Life at Oak Knoll, Danvers, Massachusetts* (Salem: Essex Institute, 1908); Gibson, *Witchcraft Myths in American Culture*, 62-63 (quotes); Rosenthal, *Salem Story*, 91.

45. "The Proposed Memorial 'Lookout' on Gallows Hill, Salem," *Putnam's Historical Magazine* 1 (1892-93): 294-96 (quotes).

46. Gencarella, "Touring History," 274-76. Roger Williams actually had no association with the house, which was constructed after he left Salem, so the renaming was appropriate. John Goff, *Salem Witch House: A Touchstone to Antiquity* (Charleston: History Press, 2009) 29-30; *Essex Antiquarian* 2, no. 12 (1898): 4; Jim McAllister, *Salem: From Naumkeag to Witch City* (Beverly, MA: Commonwealth Editions, 2000), 125-26.

47. Aviva Chomsky, "Salem as a Global City, 1850-2004," in Morrison and Schultz, eds., *Salem: Place, Myth and Memory*, 221-22; McAllister, *Salem*, 79-83; Weir, "Bewitched and Bewildered," 187-88, 193.

48. Chomsky, "Salem as a Global City," 222–28; Weir, "Bewitched and Bewildered," 190–94; Rosenthal, *Salem Story*, 207; Gencarella, "Touring History," 277–78. McAllister, *Salem*, 126; Marilynne K. Roach, *Gallows and Graves: The Search to Locate the Death and Burial Sites of the People Executed for Witchcraft in 1692* (Watertown, MA: Sassafras Grove Press, 1997), 14–15.

49. Gencarella, "Touring History," 279; Adams, *Specter of Salem*, 151–54; DeRosa, *The Making of Salem*, 108–12, 132–40. For Miller's historical errors, see Margo Burns, "Arthur Miller's *The Crucible*: Fact and Fiction," accessed at www.17thc.us/docs/fact-fiction.shtml.

50. Daniel Lang, "Poor Ann," *New Yorker*, September 11, 1954, 89; The 187th General Court of the Commonwealth of Massachusetts: Session Laws, www.malegislature.gov/Laws/SessionLaws/Acts/2001/Chapter122 (quote); Rosenthal, Salem Story, 85.

51. For the City of Salem logo, see "The City Seal" at www.salemweb.com/community/city.shtml; McAllister, *Salem*, 127; Gencarella, "Touring History," 279; Owen Davies, *America Bewitched: The Story of Witchcraft After Salem* (New York: Oxford University Press, 2013), 224 (quote).

52. Gibson, *Witchcraft Myths in American Culture*, 202–16; Rosenthal, *Salem Story*, 209; Christopher White, "Salem as Religious Proving Ground," in Morrison and Schultz, eds., *Salem: Place, Myth and Memory*, 55–59; Tom Dalton, "A Dummies Guide to Salem Witches: From Witchcraft School to Vampire Balls and Everything in Between," *Salem Evening News*, October 10, 2007.

53. Weir, "Bewitched and Bewildered," 195; Frances Hill, "Salem as Witch City," in Morrison and Schultz, eds., *Salem: Place, Myth and Memory*, 286–89.

54. Weir, "Bewitched and Bewildered," 195–96; Gencarella, "Touring History," 279. For the history of Halloween and the growth of its celebration in recent decades, see Lesley Bannatyne, *Halloween: An American Holiday, an American History* (New York: Pelican, 1998) and Lesley Bannatyne, *Halloween Nation: Behind the Scenes of America's Fright Nation* (New York: Pelican, 2011).

55. *Final Report of the 1692–1992 Salem Witch Trials Tercentenary Committee*, prepared by Alison D'Amario and Linda McConchie (Salem: n.p., 1993), 3 (quote); Paul E. Chevedden, "Ushering in the Millennium, or How an American City Reversed the Past, and Single-Handedly Inaugurated the End-Time," *Prospects* 22 (1997): 35–38; Hill, "Salem as Witch City," 287–91; Rosenthal, *Salem Story*, 207–8.

56. The Salem Award for Human Rights and Social Justice, www.salemaward.org (quote); McAllister, *Salem*, 126 (quote); Chevedden, "Ushering in the Millennium," 35–49.

57. The identification of the bones as Jacobs is debated by scholars. See Marilynne K. Roach, *The Salem Witch Trials: A Day-by-Day Chronicle of a Community Under Siege* (New York: Cooper Square Press, 2002), 587; Rosenthal, *Salem Story*, 123, 242; Diane E. Foulds, *Death in Salem: The Private Lives Behind the 1692 Witch Hunt* (Guilford, CT: Globe Pequot Press, 2010), 263–64.

58. Kenneth Foote, "To Remember and Forget: Archives, Memory and Culture," *American Archivist* 53 (1990): 385–87; DeRosa, *The Making of Salem*, 152–86.

59. Sidney Perley, "Salem in 1700, Part 14," *Essex Antiquarian* 8 (1904): 30, 36–37; DeRosa, *The Making of Salem*, 165–67.

60. For a discussion of the location of the execution and burial sites, see Sidney Perley, "Where the Salem 'Witches' Were Hanged," *Essex Institute Historical Collections* 57 (1921), 1–18 and Roach, *Gallows and Graves*.

61. Paula Keene, "Removing the Taint of Witchcraft," *Past and Present: The Newsletter of the Salem State College History Department* 5, no. 1 (2001): 1; The 187th General Court of the Commonwealth of Massachusetts: Session Laws, www.malegislature.gov/Laws/SessionLaws/Acts/2001/Chapter122. Keene came across this fact while reading Rosenthal, *Salem Story*, 55. See also "Massachusetts Clears Five from Salem Witch Trials," *New York Times*, November 2, 2001.

62. Richard Trask, "Statue of TV Witch Makes Light of Past Tragedies," *Boston Globe*, June 26, 2005 (quote); Weir, "Bewitched and Bewildered," 180.

63. National Security Agency website, www.nsa.gov (quote).

64. "The Proposed Memorial 'Lookout,'" 296 (quote).

65. Sidney Perley first suggested Proctor's Ledge as the location in "Salem in 1700, Part 14," 144–49. He fully developed his argument in "Where the Salem 'Witches' Were Hanged," 1–18; Roach, *Gallows and Graves*, 14–15. For the quote see "Report of the Park Department," *City of Salem Annual Reports for the Year Ending December 31, 1936* (Cambridge: Hampshire Press, Inc., 1937), 146 (quote); "Thomas Gannon to City of Salem, June 29, 1936," Essex County Registry of Deeds (South District), 3080: 469–70. Remarkably, in 1914 the Great Salem Fire began only a few feet from Proctor's Ledge, at the Korn Leather Factory at 57 Boston Street. The fire burned 253 acres, leaving 20,000 people homeless and 10,000 unemployed.

66. Roach's *Gallows and Graves* (1997); Joe Harrington, "Where did Salem Hang her 'Witches?'" *Boston Globe* November 3, 1963, A5. In 1976 Robert Booth went so far as to carry out a brief archaeological excavation at Proctor's Ledge. See David W. Johnson, "Witch Execution Site Believed Found," *Salem Evening News*, October 20, 1976, 1; David W. Johnson, "Witch Hanging Site May have Survived Intact," *Salem Evening News*, October 29, 1976, 14. The author thanks Marilynne Roach for these newspaper stories.

67. The project team consists of Elizabeth Peterson, Tom Phillips, Marilynne Roach, Benjamin Ray, Peter Sablock and Emerson Baker. Arianna McNeill, "Ground Zero: Proctor's Ledge Confirmed as Witch Execution Site," *Salem News*, January 12, 2016, 1; Benjamin Ray, *Satan and Salem: The Witch-Hunt Crisis of 1692* (Charlottesville: University of Virginia, 2015), 192–96; "The Gallows Hill Project," http://www.salemstate.edu/~ebaker/Gallows_Hill; Peter Sablock, "An ElectroMagnetic Geophysical Survey of the Execution Site of the Victims of the 1692 Salem Witch Trials, Salem, Massachusetts, USA" Geology Department, Salem State University.

68. McNeill, "Ground Zero" (quote); Arianna MacNeill, "Salem Witch Trials Descendants Share Thoughts on Proctor's Ledge," *Salem News*, January 15, 2016, 1.

Index

Page numbers in *italics* refer to illustrations.

Brattle, Thomas, 217, 309n44
  Brattle Street Church and, 212
  on coerced confessions, 156
  criticizes Salem witchcraft trials, 39–40, 117–18, 174, 195, 198
  as member of Royal Society, 312n72
Brattle, William, 212
Bridges, Benjamin, 239, 240
Bridges, Caleb, 239
Bridges, John, 240
Bridges, Mary, Jr., accused of witchcraft, 288
Bridges, Mary Tyler, Sr., accused of witchcraft, 288
Bridges, Sarah, accused of witchcraft, 288
broomsticks, 19, 20, 31, 187, 210, 276, 284
Brown, Coro. William, accused of witchcraft, 311n70
Browne, Hannah Corwin (Mrs. William Browne Jr.), 168, 341n9
Browne, William, Jr., 167, 168
Burdett, George, 135
Burke, Edmund, 261
Burke, William, 261
Burns, Margo, 287, 310n54, 311n70, 330n4, 338n79, 347n69, 358n36
Burroughs, Rev. George, 82, 219, 255, 260
  as abusive husband, 149–50
  accused of murder, 23, 35
  accused of witchcraft, 23, 34, 124, 136–37, 140, 144, 288, 295, 331n5
  arrested, charged, and tried, 23, 34–35, 139, 199, 218
  assists Wheelwright, 81, 82
  executed and buried, 35–36, 97, 155
  in Falmouth, 81, 97, 204
  at Harvard, 160
  heirs of, 250
  Increase Mather on trial of, 205
  opposes Halfway Covenant, 93
  as perfect witch, 160
  physical strength of, 129, 149–50, 160
  poppets and, 131
  preternatural knowledge of, 130
  as putative ringleader of witches, 34, 127, 138, 160
  recites Lord's Prayer, 35
  in Salisbury, 81, 82
  survives Wells raid, 136
  as victim of factionalism, 153
  violence of, 148
Burroughs, Hannah (Mrs. George Burroughs), 129
Burroughs, Sarah Ruck Hathorne (Mrs. George Burroughs), 129, 130
Burt, Ann, charged with witchcraft (1669), 134
Bush, George H. W., 236
Bush, George W., 12, 236
Buss, Joseph, 139
Buss, William, 139

Busse (Buss), Rev. John, 139, 334n39, 334n40
  accused of witchcraft, 137, 138, 288, 295, 334n35

Cabot, Laurie, 277, 278
Calef, Dr. John, 228
Calef, Robert, 156, 196, 219, 242, 254
  on Burroughs, 35, 260
  on Cory's death, 38
  descendants of, 227–28
  on Goody Glover's case, 174
  Hutchinson uses as source, 265
  Cotton Mather vs., 225–28
  as Maule's friend, 225
  More Wonders of the Invisible World, 189, 224, 225–28, 354n69, 354n71
  provides examples of courtroom fraud, 189
  Neal uses as source, 260
  Oldmixon uses as source, 261
  on Tituba, 155–56
Calvin, John, 44
Calvinism, Calvinists, 46
Cambridge, Mass., 78, 139, 171, 197, 206, 319n22
Cambridge Association, 349n15
Canada, 62, 178
  border of, 244
  See also Acadia; France, French; and names of provinces
Candlemas Raid (York, Maine, 1692), 136
Candy (slave)
  accused of witchcraft, 288
  poppets and, 131
Cape Ann, 70
Capen, Rev. Joseph, 86, 321n39
capital crimes, 40, 209
capitalism, witch hunts and, 119–20
Caribbean, 213, 306n12
  Bahamas, 181
  Barbados, 18, 213, 216, 233, 320n35
  Bermuda, 126, 135
  exports to, 47, 75
  Jamaica, 39, 54
  Tituba from, 18
  West Indies, 47–48, 58
Carr, George, 122
Carradine, John, 270
Carrier, Andrew
  accused of witchcraft, 33, 288
  tortured, 33
Carrier, Martha Allen, 192
  accused of witchcraft, 28, 33, 289
  tried, convicted, and executed, 34, 35, 159, 199
  in "Young Goodman Brown," 269
Carrier, Richard
  accused of witchcraft, 33, 288, 357n22
  tortured, 33
Carrier, Sarah, accused of witchcraft, 288
Carrier, Thomas, Jr., accused of witchcraft, 288

Griggs, Dr. William, 16
Groton, Mass., 114, 196, 197
Gunter, Anne, witchcraft fraud of, 111–12
Guyana, as Tituba's homeland, 306n12

Hadley, Deborah, 199
Hale, Rev. John, 90, 109, 131, 173, 191, 230, 242
  in Beverly, 86
  as chaplain on Quebec expedition, 139
  death of, 225
  examines afflicted Parris girls, 14–15
  Modest Inquiry into the Nature of Witchcraft,
    109, 224–25, 228, 247, 252, 355n78
  supports Salem witch trials, 198
  on Tituba, 156, 305n5
Hale, Mary, acquitted of witchcraft, 172
Hale, Sir Matthew, 118, 199
Hale, Nathan, 242
Hale, Sarah Noyes (Mrs. John Hale), 224, 242
  accused of witchcraft, 140, 224, 293, 295
Halfway Covenant, 48–49, 126, 136
  in Boston's Third Church, 138
  logical extensions of, 213
  Mathers and, 140, 211
  Salem Village ministers and, 92–93, 137, 322n57
  as threat to orthodoxy, 139
  witchcraft accusations and, 137, 139, 170
Halifax, George Montagu, 1st Earl of, 235
Halloween in Salem, 11, 256, 278–279, 282, 283
hanging, hangings, 29, 32, 262, 309n43. *See also*
  executions for witchcraft
Hansen, Chadwick, 332n16, 356n15
Hardy, Thomas, accused of witchcraft, 290
Harris, Richard, 84
Hart, Elizabeth Hawkes, accused of
  witchcraft, 290
Hartford, Conn., 46–47, 267
Harvard College, 160, 198, 200, 212, 228, 233
  Calef's book burned at, 226
  ministers educated at, 81, 84, 96, 213, 234,
    342n20
  president and vice president of, 206, 253,
    350n27
  witchcraft trial judges and, 164, 165, 167,
    169, 184
Hathorne, Abigail Corwin, 168
Hathorne, Eleazer, 161, 168, 169
Hathorne, John, 22, 74, 156, 161, 162, 169, 179,
  185, 186
  Acadia expedition and, 220
  accepts spectral evidence, 203
  choices of, 12
  church membership and, 171
  on Court of Oyer and Terminer, 25, 61, 145
  interrogates witches, 17, 21, 23, 155, 168,
    169, 187
  military career of, 342n17

piracy trial and, 177
  touch test and, 116–17
Hathorne, William, 74, 75, 169, 318n9
Hathorne Hill, Salem Farms, 318n9
Hathorne family, changes spelling to
  Hawthorne, 244
Haunted Happenings, 11, 256, 278, 281, 282
Haverhill, Mass., 138, 158, 239
Hawkes, Margaret, accused of witchcraft, 290
Hawkes, Sarah, accused of witchcraft, 134, 290
Hawkins, Thomas, piracy and, 177–78
Hawthorne, Nathaniel, 6, 244, 268–71, 281
  "Alice Doane's Appeal," 269, 272
  House of Seven Gables, 12, 268–70
  Mosses from an Old Manse, 363n35
  The Scarlet Letter, 269
  "Young Goodman Brown," 269, 363n35
Haynes, Sarah (Mrs. Thomas Haynes), 241
Haynes, Thomas, 241
Henry VIII, King of England, 44
heritage, Salem's witchcraft, 11, 272
Herrick, Mary, accuses Sarah Hale of
  witchcraft, 224
Herter, Albert, *223*
Hewes, George Robert Twelves, 227–28
Higginson, Rev. John, 20, 58, 132, 214, 230, 252,
  271, 359n42
  Halfway Covenant and, 137
  Salem Town church and, 86, 92
  sermons of, 49
  writes preface to Hale's book, 225, 247
Higginson, John, Jr., 66, 347n74
Higginson, John (Salem town clerk), 252
Hilton, John, 210–11
Hinckley, Gov. Thomas, 166
Historic Salem Incorporated, 275
Hoar, Dorcas Galley
  accused of witchcraft, 290
  confession, trial, and conviction of, 37, 154, 191,
    339n86, 359n45
  fortune telling of, 131
  reprieved and pardoned, 191, 192, 312n78
Hobbs, Abigail
  accused of witchcraft, 119–20, 290
  avoids execution, 38, 191
  confession of, 23, 103
  examined as suspected witch, 22
  mental illness and, 104
  pardoned, 312n78
  pleads guilty, 37
  as refugee from Maine, 23, 104
  relation with Satan, 130–31
Hobbs, Deliverance, accused of witchcraft, 290
Hobbs, William, accused of witchcraft, 290
Hoffer, Peter, 111, 113
Holmes, Oliver Wendell, Sr., 236
Holten, Benjamin, 151